DUKE · UNIVERSITY · PUBLICATIONS

The FRANK C. BROWN COLLECTION *of*
NORTH CAROLINA
FOLKLORE

ALL DAY SINGING

The FRANK C. BROWN COLLECTION *of*

NORTH CAROLINA FOLKLORE

The Folklore of North Carolina Collected by Dr. Frank C. Brown during the Years 1912 to 1943 in Collaboration with the North Carolina Folklore Society of which he was Secretary-Treasurer 1913-1943

IN SEVEN VOLUMES

General Editor
NEWMAN IVEY WHITE

Associate Editors

HENRY M. BELDEN   PAUL G. BREWSTER
WAYLAND D. HAND   ARTHUR PALMER HUDSON
JAN PHILIP SCHINHAN   ARCHER TAYLOR
STITH THOMPSON   BARTLETT JERE WHITING
GEORGE P. WILSON

PAULL F. BAUM

Wood Engravings by
CLARE LEIGHTON

DURHAM, NORTH CAROLINA
DUKE UNIVERSITY PRESS

The FRANK C. BROWN COLLECTION *of*

NORTH CAROLINA FOLKLORE

VOLUME FOUR

THE
MUSIC
OF THE
BALLADS

Edited by

JAN PHILIP SCHINHAN

DURHAM, NORTH CAROLINA
DUKE UNIVERSITY PRESS
1957

© 1957 by the Duke University Press

L.C.C. card no. 57–8818

I.S.B.N. 0–8223–0256–x

Second printing, 1974

PRINTED IN THE UNITED STATES OF AMERICA

CONTENTS

III. NORTH CAROLINA BALLADS

IV. ADDITIONAL BALLADS

xii CONTENTS

FOREWORD

EPPUR se muove.
In the Foreword to volume II I said that the Ballads and Songs were expected to occupy one volume and they required two; it is now the same with their tunes. What was planned as volume IV becomes the present IV, complementing the texts of II, and the forthcoming volume V, complementing the texts of III. This expansion, moreover, has had its effect on the distribution of our illustrations, and the frontispiece of volume II is here repeated as most appropriate to the subject.

So far as possible the plan of this volume follows that of volume II. In the table of Contents the Ballads are numbered as before; but where no tune was available both number and title are silently omitted. Nos. 315-340, ADDITIONAL BALLADS, are new, that is, from materials not received by the editors of II.

In his Preface Professor Schinhan has explained some of the reasons for the long delay, his handicaps and hardships. Although certainly the course was arduous, the haven is what matters and it is hoped that those who have expressed interest in the music to accompany the bare texts and have waited five years for it will now be gratified. This and its following volume should serve two ends: they will provide for those who enjoy folk music in and for itself a large gathering of melodies drawn directly from North Carolina singers, and they will afford the specialist an opportunity to study the forms, some genuine and some no doubt corrupt, which this localized folk music has taken.

The collecting, comparing, and editing of folk ballads and songs has had a long history, dating back to the eighteenth century, and the methods are now established as a special discipline. With folk tunes it is different. Even the name is new: is it *folk-song* or *folk song* or *folksong?* (It did not get into the O.E.D. until the 1933 Supplement.) Child had, of course, included a number of airs—actually fifty-five, more or less equivalent to fifteen in our Collection—from manuscript sources; but only after Edison's phonograph came into use was it possible to take down words and music together just as the ballad was sung and so have a record of folk music as it is now and presumably was in the long past. For many of the tunes are traditional like the words. Still there are difficulties. To transfer the sounds that come from the recording instrument into standard musical notation is not simple. The untrained singer does not always sing true; he may flat or sharp or unconsciously transpose downwards for convenience; he seldom sings the second stanza quite like the first; he may even forget and extemporize a little. Or, aware of a 'learned' audience and eager to please, he will sometimes embellish and so falsify the melody. Or, on the other hand, the trained singer will invent, improve;

he is an artist in his way. So, as one writer has put it: folk song is "begotten of a long succession of singers, altering, extending, elaborating, and corrupting."

What in German is called *Dorfkunst*, the natural ways of the unsophisticated singer, may suffer a sea change by musicological analysis and transcription. The traditional singer knows nothing of plagal cadences, of the Mixolydian mode or the pentatonic mode or the well-tempered scale, or of quarter tones and neutral tones, or of the disturbing influence of the familiar major and minor. The tonal center is a matter of indifference to him. He may alter the tune almost beyond recognition by unpremeditated formulaic borrowing or by the necessity of contracting and expanding to fit a different or an imperfectly remembered text. Thus the scholar faces a bewildering range of possibilities. How far shall he go in normalizing, correcting the inevitable shortcomings of the record? He must have not only a sensitive ear but also a delicate judgment to distinguish bad singing from the subtle mysteries of folk memory, to tell a legitimate variation from a careless mixture of different melodies; and so on. "The study of tunes," wrote Professor Entwistle in 1939, "encounters a number of difficulties which have not been adequately surmounted." This about says it all.

It also enables us to recognize Professor Schinhan's skill in meeting those difficulties. His painstaking annotations have some of the immitigable minuteness of our preceding volumes. They may be caviar to the reader, who will not understand them or perhaps need them, but they have their place. (Anyone who thinks them a bit excessive should glance through the 450 pages of *Serbo-Croatian Folk Songs* edited by Béla Bartok and Albert B. Lord, New York, 1951.) They have their place if only to remind us again of the abiding strength of tradition, which preserves in the musical habits of our untutored contemporaries so much that is not only 'primitive' but also classical (Greece and Rome) and mediæval (the Church) and so being both classical and mediæval is also modern. Even some of the language and methods of analysis are ancient; and those of us who have a "leaven of malice" in our make-up will note, without distress, that just as many of the tunes have lost part of their modal correctness, just so many of their previous commentators have been led astray by their harmonic prepossessions.

P.F.B.

PREFACE

WILLIAM A. Neilson, writing in the first edition of *Encyclopedia Americana* (1918) says: "Thus, the life of a modern poem begins when it is committed to paper; a ballad then begins to die." Having this in mind, it was reluctantly and with serious concern that this editor, after two weeks of consideration, finally accepted the invitation extended to him by the late Dr. Newman I. White, the general editor of this Collection, to join his editorial staff. This meant to take over the transcription of the recordings of more than one thousand ballads and songs, and the editing of volumes IV and V which contain the music of the ballads and songs.

It was only the hope that these transcriptions of the tunes recorded by Dr. Brown might serve someone who loved this precious heritage to refresh his mind, recall impressions of earlier days and thus relive them in happy reminiscence, which assuaged the troubled mind of this editor. Perchance, they might also serve to introduce some persons to tunes they never heard before, or at least not in the versions given here. They might thus add to the store of treasures which have come down to us from the early settlers on this continent. And so, it was the hope such persons might sing the airs for themselves and others, and, in the course of time, the old process of 'collective composition' would take up where it left off, and our ballad tradition, oral as usual, would again come to life.

When Dr. White approached this editor some years ago, he said there were more than a thousand songs recorded by Dr. Brown, but that all of them, not counting the ones destroyed in transit to the Library of Congress, had been transferred by technicians of the Library using the best of recording discs and the most modern means available today. On the strength of this and this writer's familiarity with the excellence of work done by the Music Division of the Library of Congress, he accepted the task. Only later did Dr. White inform him that Dr. Brown, in his enthusiasm over his recordings, had played these records (wax cylinders) numerous times for his students, without so much as changing needles. The result was that the 'dubbing' reproduced the resultant scratch of the needle with a disconcerting degree of fidelity. Add to this the fact that too many of the cylinders, while not totally destroyed in transit, were cracked enough so that the needle used in playing them produced, in passing over the cracks, a sound pattern similar to that of a railroad car passing over the joints of the tracks. This is mentioned only to explain to some degree why it has taken so very long before even the part containing the ballads could appear.

Several additional factors added to the general difficulties. First, for the longest time, only very few of the texts to the ballads and songs were available to this editor before the galley proofs had been printed. None but one experienced in these matters will be able to understand how, when listening to such a recording, one might be convinced of hearing certain words, only afterwards to find out that he was mistaken. Another psychologically interesting factor is that, because of the singing as well as recording, at first the words could not be understood at all; but with the text available for reference, the words, after several hearings, became perfectly clear. Thus, it once happened that this editor, complying with the request of the co-editors of volumes II and III, supplied them with the words as they had been taken down from a very poor recording. Only much later, upon visiting the singer of this song, fortunately still alive, was he able to find out what some of the words really were.

The second factor has to do with the process of transferring the recordings from the wax cylinders to the discs. The work supposedly was done by experts in this field but the product delivered made it quite evident that, at that time, all the personnel suitable for painstaking and very exacting work was drained off for war purposes. There are several reasons for this opinion. First, the technician doing that work evidently never gave it a thought that anyone would expect to have the whole song reproduced as it was originally recorded. But time and time again it happens that the song as given on the disc starts three to four measures after the beginning. Fortunately, in such cases more than one stanza was recorded. Being familiar with the great care which Dr. Brown used in his recording procedures—always signaling his informant when he was ready to record—the editor is certain that the fault lies with the technician entrusted with that work.

The third factor has to do with the needle scratch and the noise produced by the cracked cylinders. This editor, during 1931-32, while engaged in similar work at the Anthropological Institute at the University of California at Berkeley, also had to work with many wax cylinders containing some very valuable Indian songs. Similar scratching sounds caused him to try, but in vain, to get the co-operation of the Physics Department, in order to have someone construct an electric device incorporating scratch filters which would greatly mitigate the difficulty. He finally explained his idea to Dr. Alfred Kroeber, who transmitted it to the department at Yale University, of which Miss Helen Roberts was a member. She was more fortunate in receiving the necessary co-operation, a fact that can readily be verified from her article dealing with this matter. (ZVMW III (1935) 75-83). Why these means were not used in 'dubbing' the wax recordings of this Collection this editor has never learned.

The fourth and last factor proved the most exasperating and time-consuming of all. The easiest explanation would be, of course, to suspect some subversive influence with the intent to destroy the value of the work. While this editor does not subscribe to such ideas, he finds it nevertheless difficult to understand how such things ordinarily could happen.

All of the original records were carefully labeled and catalogued, using various means like I, II, III; 1a, 1b, 1c,; A, B, C, etc. How it was possible to mix up the labels on the new discs for recordings which are as widely separated as cylinders C and X, to name but one instance, is still an open question. When each cylinder contains between 15 and 20 songs, and one tries to make out songs of cylinder X (according to the catalogue), which finally are found to represent the songs on cylinder C, the resulting confusion and difficulty should be evident. It was only through the good fortune that this editor happened to know some related versions and was sure about the relationship, that he, through laborious research, finally uncovered all the mistakes resulting from labeling more than a half dozen discs incorrectly.

Now that all of the more than 1250 songs have been transcribed, these troubles fortunately belong to the past and seem mere bad dreams. If it has taken an inordinate amount of time until at least volume IV is ready for publication, perhaps the editor can plead for mercy under extenuating circumstances. He wishes to state, though, that many times during all these many months he thoroughly sympathized with Thomas Morley, who, after finishing his *A Plain and Easy Introduction to Practical Music,* said: ". . . if I had before I began it, imagined half the pains and labour which it cost me, I would sooner have been persuaded to anything than to have taken in hand such a tedious piece of work. . . ."

In this connection, however, it is a pleasant duty to express my sincere appreciation of the kind consideration and superhuman patience shown me by Professor Paull F. Baum of Duke University and the director of its Press, Mr. Ashbel Brice.

Last but not least I wish to acknowledge my indebtedness and express my unbounded gratitude to my wife, Mrs. Elizabeth Logan Schinhan, who, throughout these years, has stood by me not only uncomplainingly, but always encouragingly. And it is no exaggeration to say, that without her invaluable assistance in many ways, this volume would have never reached completion.

J.P.S.

Chapel Hill
February, 1957

INTRODUCTION

THERE are a number of songs in the following pages of which volume II gives only one version, but in many cases the transcription of the recordings made by Dr. Brown has increased the number of versions considerably. All these additional versions have been specially marked, thus: if the number of the song is 20, then any additional versions are 20(1), 20(2), etc. On the other hand, if volume II contains a number of versions marked 20A, 20B, 20C, etc., then the new versions are marked with letters, beginning where the others had left off: 20D, 20E, etc.

Preceding each musical score will be found the name of the singer and the place and date of recording, whenever available. Following this are appropriate references concerning melodic relationships with any other version of this Collection, according to the number of the ballad or song as found in volumes II and III. The very few exceptions to this method are explicitly noted. Text references are usually to such versions as are found in the various other published collections available.

The numbers above the music score at the right coincide with those affixed to each scale as found in Appendix B. The scale picture given there will enable anyone to acquaint himself at a glance with the tonal material basic to the particular melody. In the music score itself, the sign ' merely indicates a perceptible break in the tonal flow without, however, suggesting a measurable amount of lapsed time. The same is true of the sign ⌃ . In general, this symbol indicates the traditional extension of duration by half the value of the note above which it occurs. Sometimes, however, whether because the singer was trying to reassure himself of what was to follow, or because he merely enjoyed holding the tone, the limits indicated above are ignored. It was not felt necessary to indicate these few instances by a special sign. Another sign frequently used in the notation of primitive music, the double slur ⌢ , merely serves to indicate a *portamento*, which, at times, really approaches the primitive. The two barlines (lighter than those at the end), serve to separate the chorus or refrain from the stanza. They are always placed before the first full measure of the former, thus ignoring any up-beat with which this part might begin. Anyone with even a slight musical knowledge will have no difficulty ascertaining the beginning of the chorus.

Immediately below the score will be found all the melodic variations which the singer made while rendering the several stanzas of a song, if more than one were recorded. The numbers above the various measures representing the variations refer to the measures thus affected, number 1 always indicating the first full measure. If several consecutive measures are involved, this is indicated accordingly: 3-5, 7-9, etc. Only in rare cases, when it seemed important to give the continuity of the line rather than disjunct parts, is the complete varied stanza given.

The melodic variations are followed by a comparison of the respective melody with other versions found in the leading collections available. This section carries the designation: *For melodic relationship cf.* Thus, three asterisks indicate the highest percentage of relationship: identical to very close; two asterisks indicate very close relationship to considerable similarity; and for anything less than that, one asterisk is used.

Next follows an analysis of each individual song: the scale or mode, the tonal center, and the structure of the melody. For the scales, the reader is referred to the detailed discussion under *Scales* below, explaining the procedures followed as well as the pitfalls and mistakes to be avoided. It need only be added here that in tetra-, penta-, and hexatonic scales, the missing tone is always indicated thus: (3), (6), etc.

The term *tonal center* for the fundamental tone of a scale or mode, has been chosen in order to get away from the concept of tonic and dominant, which nowadays always involves harmonic connotations.

To indicate the structure of each song, the familiar aa, ab, abc, etc., are used. Only in the case of the barform and inverted barform are the symbols adopted which Alfred Lorenz used:[1] e.g. m, m^1, n, or n, m, m^1. The number of measures represented by each letter is always given.[2]

The sign + when occurring above any note merely serves to indicate that this tone was sung a fraction higher than normally expected.

Whenever the song ends on a degree other than the fundamental, this is indicated by the term "Circular tune."

Any text variant not found in volumes II or III, e.g., a text of a song available only through transcription from the recording, will be found following all the above-mentioned remarks in connection with the individual song.

Methods of Analysis

In any approach to folk music, even if not quite to the same extent as in the study of so-called primitive music, one must leave behind many a cherished concept of what certain things are, or what they should be. Since the music to which we are daily exposed is completely based on harmonic relationships, it is not easy for us to dissociate ourselves from this kind of thinking; and this fact is readily seen in many of the publications dealing with folk songs. From the key signatures imposed on the various melodies it is easily seen how this traditional way of thinking dominates the field. More of this, however, later.

One thing is absolutely certain. In all attempts at analysis it is essential not only to find means and methods which are adequate for the task, but also to agree upon terms which are understandable and acceptable to others. Definitions should be as clear and concise as it is humanly possible to make them. That all such terms and all such definitions will be accept-

---

[1] Cf. Alfred O. L. Lorenz, *Das Geheimnis der Form bei Richard Wagner*, Berlin, 1926, II, 191-2. Also *Harvard Dictionary*, pp. 74-5, and *Journal of American Musicological Society*, VIII (Spring, 1955), No. 1, 77-8.

[2] In dealing with the various structures, any variation in the restatement of a phrase is always indicated by a^1, a^2, a^3, or b^1 b^2, b^3, etc., the different numerals merely suggesting the progressive status of the variation technic.

able to all scholars is, perhaps, too Utopian a hope to indulge in, but it would be ideal if all scholars would say what they mean, and mean what they say.

The analysis of music has a long history and it is therefore proper that the established technical vocabulary, familiar to trained musicians, should be adopted in the discussion of what has become a rather specialized field, folk music. This conviction has been the point of departure in the following analyses; for only when the standard, accepted terms and methods prove inadequate should others be tried, and then only after careful definition and explanation.

The present method has been developed over a period of more than twenty-five years in the discussion of ballads and folk songs. It is based on six comprehensive features which, though they sometimes overlap, must be treated separately:

1. Scales and modes
2. Range
3. Melodic line, or interval succession in pitch
4. Meter, or interval succession in time
5. Structure, or *Gesalt:* over-all rhythm
6. Rendition

In all attempts at analysis one cannot afford to omit or neglect anything, or to take anything for granted. In the case of music, if one omits the very tonal material which is the basis of all musical expression, namely the scales used in the songs, why concern oneself with what one author has termed 'tonal sequence,' in the sense that one tone follows another in all melodies—although of course mostly with varying intervals? This expression has a definite and different meaning, well established. 'Tonal' denotes two distinct factors in music, both of which have the same basic idea, that of pertaining to the same key or tonality. The first application of this term is found in discussions of the fugue, when dealing with several possible answers to the original theme, and then refers specifically to one particular type of answer, which is so constructed that it preserves completely the tonality in which the theme was announced. This then is called a 'tonal answer.' The second application serves simply to state the fact of staying within the key. The term 'sequence,' aside from its use in early liturgical music, is now universally accepted to indicate "the repetition in one and the same part of a short musical phrase at another pitch. . . ." If the repetitions are made without accidentals (no change of key), the sequence is called tonal, or diatonic.[3]

1. Scales. From the preceding discussion of the term 'tonal sequence,' even if the intended meaning of 'one tone following another' should be accepted, it would not be surprising if someone asked what tones. A house can be built of brick, brick-veneer, rocks, cement blocks, or just lumber, and in each case, it will differ considerably in looks as well as cost. The same is true of a piece of jewelry. It might be made of plati-

[3] Willi Apel, *Harvard Dictionary of Music,* Cambridge, Mass., 1944, p. 672.

num, gold, silver, or any kind of composition metal and have either precious stones or just imitations. In each case, not only the looks and cost,
but also the quality and therefore the aesthetic value will differ. All this
is not less true of a melody. It is only too frequent that the latter is of a
very trite quality and conveys nothing but the cheapest kind of musical
expression.

In language the different kinds of material, as vowels, consonants,
diphthongs, etc., take the form of alphabets; and each different language
has its own alphabet providing the symbols which, arranged in various
combinations, convey ideas, feelings, or moods. Music also has its alphabet. From the limited material offered by scales, consisting at first of
two or three tones, through the mediaeval modes and up to our twelve-
tone scales, the creative musician selects, mostly intuitively, the necessary
items which will serve him for the expression of an idea, a feeling, or a
mood. As a spoken language is simply a means of thinking in words, so
the language of music is a mode of thinking in tones. As the alphabetic
symbols, or letters, however, do not by themselves convey any meaning,
so likewise single tones—arbitrary selections of all possible tones—have
no real meaning by themselves. As with words, so in music, there must
be a selection of single parts and a varied combination of them. For
example, the same five letters in different arrangement yield six different
English words, some of which are familiar, others rare: *tones, notes,
stone, sonet, seton, tosen.* So in music one may instance the beginning
of Wagner's Bridal Chorus in *Lohengrin* and that of the overture to
his *Meistersinger.* There is, however, an important difference. Whatever
has been achieved in program music based on the power of suggestion
(something like the echoic words *buzz, snip,* etc.), no combination of
musical tones has the absolute concrete signification of words like *hard,
soft, house, tree,* and so on.

For years the present writer has stressed in his teaching the necessity
of considering the quantitative value of each individual tone in relation to
all others which occur in any given melody. It may, perhaps, be surprising to many people to find out what a great difference a varying emphasis
on certain tones can make in two melodies which otherwise share exactly
the same tonal material. What makes the difference? The choice of
material? Yes, but mostly the judicious use of this material, the decision
about when and how much of this and how much of that. The choice
made as well as the use of and emphasis on some of the selected ingre-
dients of the available tonal material is known as mode.[4]

All modes consist of the identical tonal material; they differ only in
their use of it. This may be likened to the different behavior of individual
persons when confronted with an identical situation. The situation, like
the tonal material, is the same; only the handling of it, the behavior, differs. Our C major, for example, is tonally identical with the Church
mode known as Ionian, but the latter 'behaves' in a considerably different
manner from the former; and the same is true of our minor scale and the
Church mode called Aeolian. Although both our major and minor scales,

[4] Knud Jeppesen, *Counterpoint,* New York, 1939, p. 62.

on the basis of their characteristic behavior, could be classified among the modes traditionally accepted as such, they have never been officially so classified. There is, however, one group of tonal rows, the various members of which *have* been taken into the family of modes. This tonal row is known as pentatonic scale or mode.

At this point some technical matters must be frankly discussed. The first is the various ways in which the five possible versions of a pentatonic mode are derived. Of the infinite variety of such scales theoretically possible, only two are given in *The Harvard Dictionary* (pp. 563-64), the 'tonal' and 'semitonal penta-scale.' Of the former, the author says: "Properly speaking, there exists only one such scale (transpositions apart), namely: c d f g a c'." In this statement there is only one thing wrong. The different modes which can be derived from this basic scale are not the result of transposition but of inversion. Dr. Jackson[5] uses this same approach, calling each new mode derived by inversion, progressively I, II, III, IV, V. Helmholtz[6] begins the same way, up to the second mode, which constitutes the first inversion of the original scale. Then, for reasons only known to him, he seems to abandon all logic and calls the second inversion (based on the third tone of the original scale) IV, the following inversions III and V. Rieman[7] recognizes only three possibilities: c'd'f'g'a'(c"d"); g'a'c'd'e'(g"a"); and d'e'g'a'b'(d"e"). It will readily be seen, however, that in this case, these so-called three possibilities are really nothing but the same pattern, only this time actually transposed. H. K. Andrews, in *Grove's Dictionary*,[8] begins the series with what in Dr. Jackson's series and that given in *Harvard Dictionary* would be V, or the fourth inversion.

In view of these divergences a choice must be made. Since the Greeks in the pre-Terpander period had a tuning which corresponds to the first mode, transposed (which is mentioned in the *Harvard Dictionary*), and a new mode is readily to be had by inverting the mode at hand, the system adopted by Dr. Jackson should satisfy anyone by the sheer logic of its procedure. Therefore, in the analyses which follow all songs, this order (I, II, III, IV, V) has been adhered to. The first mode is taken to be that given by Dr. Jackson and the *Harvard Dictionary:* c'd' f'g'a' (c"d").

Let us now look at the method used in determining the mode or scale[9] which a folk song is based on. First of all, one should realize that originally no harmonic connotations were involved. The present editor is in complete agreement with Dr. Jackson, quoting Hilton Rufty: "For purposes of harmonic treatment it is quite necessary to decide upon which particular mode a gapped tune suggests, but in studying the purely melodic aspects, it is reasonable to accept the tune as an entity, considering it in its actual tonal structure and not with regard to its possible modal permutations."[10]

[5] SFSEA, p. 15, quoting Hilton Rufty. The chart is at the end of the volume.
[6] Herman L. F. Helmholtz, *On the Sensations of Tone*, London, 1875, pp. 400-3; 5th ed., revised by Alexander J. Ellis, London, 1930, p. 273.
[7] Hugo Riemann, *Folkloristische Tonalitätsstudien*, Leipzig, 1916, p. 2.
[8] *Grove's Dictionary of Music*, 5th ed., ed. Eric Blom, London, 1954, v, 799.
[9] Jeppesen, p. 62.
[10] SFSEA, p. 15.

In determining a scale then, an editor or arranger must not succumb to the years of exposure to this major or minor infection and, *nolens volens,* hear every melody under this hypnotic influence.[11] To be sure, sometimes a more careful editor will discover that a particular sharp or flat does not occur in the melody and put this sharp or flat in parentheses, probably in order to indicate that it really is not present, but that the reader might *feel* it in that key. (See Lomax, OSC, p. 129: 'Jennie Jenkins,' to cite but one.) Then comes the dilemma. If there is a tune which does not use the complete major scale, but does use the leading tone, —f-sharp for example—the editor puts the signature of f-sharp in parentheses.[12] This would indicate the song might be felt to be in G major. Since the leading tone actually appears, however, it should be in the signature; or else it should be treated as an accidental in a tone row which is not actually G major, but discounting the 'corrupting' changes to a-sharp and f-sharp, is the first mode of the pentatonic scale.

To repeat, if the tone actually occurs, one should not put the particular signature in parentheses. On the other hand, if a specific tone, possible in any given mode or tonality, does not actually occur in the melody, it should never be indicated in the signature. Arrangements for popular use may be an exception, but we are here dealing with traditional folk tunes *as* they were sung by real folk singers. And, as we hear them, we should note them down.

It is regrettable that, beginning with the Child ballads and through Cecil Sharp's splendid collection up to the very latest publications in the field, editors are open to criticism for this biased and illogical use of signs which actually have no meaning whatsoever. (You might as well put up a sign "No Smoking" in a place where tobacco is unknown, if there is such a place.) The apex of a ludicrous situation is reached when the editor puts one or more sharps or flats in the signature and then, every time this tone occurs, finds it necessary to place a natural sign before it, indicating that the directions implied by the signature should be ignored.[13]

No better example of this confusion and wishful thinking could be found than Dr. Jackson's note on the tune of 'Villulia or Bartimeus' (*Original Sacred Harp,* 331). Although he correctly classifies the scale as the fourth mode of the pentatonic scale based on f-sharp, he adds: "The *Sacred Harp* editor evidently looked upon this tune as one in a-minor, whereas it is probably a dorian melody with *f*-sharp as its tonic, and should have also a *d*-sharp in its key signature."[14] Now if there were a third, supposedly 'a,' we might well speak of the lower Dorian tetrachord, but not, as yet, of a Dorian mode. When Dr. Jackson, however, continues: "and should have also a *d*-sharp in its key signature," one must justly wonder. This "*d*-sharp" indeed turns out to be *the* crucial point.

[11] As to hearing harmony everywhere in folk song, cf. James F. Mursell, *The Psychology of Music,* New York, 1937, p. 102.
[12] Cf. Lomax, OSC, p. 128: 'Where Have You Been, My Good Old Man?'
[13] Cf. EFSSC and SharpK. In all examples specifically marked Dorian, Mixolydian, or Aeolian, there is always either one sharp or flat in the signature which, however, is invariably canceled whenever that specific tone occurs in the melody.
[14] SFSEA, p. 50, No. 21.

As can easily be seen, there is no sixth degree in the scale as extracted
from the melody, and therefore it is anybody's guess what this sixth degree might be, *if* it occurred. This is equally true, of course, when we
consider the imaginary 'a.' But somebody, following Dr. Jackson's example, might prefer an a-sharp. If, in addition to this imaginary member,
we added the sixth degree as d-sharp, the Mixolydian mode would result.
If someone else expressed his preference for 'a' and 'd' respectively, we
would have the Aeolian mode. The creator of the melody seems to have
made his own choice. He used a pure pentatonic scale in his own individual way, and the result is the fourth mode of the pentatonic scale. This
should be sufficient.

Of many possible examples only one need be submitted. In *A Song
Catcher in Southern Mountains* we find not only the same generous distribution of sharps and flats, but also some new and unfortunate terms.[15]
On page 381 the writer after classifying 'Fair Ellen' (p. 393E) as Pentatonic I, speaks of it as having a "false Mixolydian ending"—a term bor-
rowed from Cecil Sharp. On page 401 we meet a frustrated "septatonic"
scale; and on page 404 a "Variable Aeolian mode" for what is only a
chromatically altered (corrupted) pentatonic mode. Now what is a false
Mixolydian ending? 'False' is an old term for what is generally known
as 'deceptive.' Thus, a false Mixolydian ending should be a deceptive
cadence which, although usually associated with the progression from the
fifth to the sixth degree, is also applicable to any other progression from
the fifth degree excepting that to the first. But in all deceptive cadences,
the fifth degree is the point of departure, not the resting point. According
to the writer, however, a major song apparently has a false Mixolydian
ending if it *ends* on the fifth degree, which, judging from the examples,
is approached from above. The difficulty is that there are quite a number
of songs in the same collection which are circular tunes and which have
identically the same ending. The question then arises: When is a tune
circular, and when does it have a false Mixolydian ending? It seems
somewhat arbitrary to deny a major melody (*no harmonic thinking*) to
come to rest by way of a descending motion, actually implied by the term
cadence. The major mode, according to our present knowledge, was
already established in secular music by the thirteenth century; and its
'subversive' influence can be traced throughout the succeeding centuries.
Folk music in these periods being inevitably influenced by the music of the
Church, just as the reverse was true, it should not be so surprising that
the modal tradition, although accepted by the people, gradually, under the
influence of secular music, experienced numerous modifications.

In the method adopted here to determine the type of scale or mode
underlying each tune, the scalic material is always counted from the tonal
center up, regardless of the fact that in the majority of cases the fundamental tone of the scale or mode is *not* the lowest tone in the scale picture.[16] Many times the scale goes four tones or more below this tonal
center, while at other times it is less, even only one tone below. In all

[15] SCSM. The section on "Modal Aspects" is the work of Elna Sherman.
[16] Out of 512 versions of ballad tunes, 384 are plagal.

these instances, the term plagal is affixed to indicate that the tonal material extends below the fundamental tone of the particular scale. As in the terminology pertaining to the Church modes, plagal indicates a mode beginning a fourth below the fundamental; any extension or lack of the norm might be indicated by plus or minus signs, but for the sake of simplicity these are omitted here. Tones which duplicate those that are part of the designated scale, either below or above the terminal points, do not affect the character of the scale or mode (beyond the plagal quality) and are not considered; they appear, however, in the scale picture (see Appendix B), where also the relative frequency of their occurrence can be seen. On the other hand, sometimes the complete scale picture can be shown only by transferring some of the tones one octave higher or lower.

While classifying the varying tonal material, no consistent effort has been made to indicate the modal character of the many tunes which are based on tetratonic, pentatonic, hexatonic, or, as the case may be, on tetrachordal, pentachordal, hexachordal, or heptachordal material. There is no gainsaying the fact that many of the tunes so based could be taken as incomplete Mixolydian, Dorian, or even Aeolian modes, but likewise, that such classifications would remain mere assumptions. In the case of the tetratonic scales the question whether they are incomplete pentachordal or pentatonic would be left open. It was felt that those who really know modal characteristics do not need to be told, and those who do not, would not be any wiser if they were told, for example, that Nos. 422, 474, and 478 showed strong Dorian qualities. A more difficult problem is presented by other tunes like No. 401, which, while definitely modal, cannot without some challenge be classified as Dorian. In this particular case, the normally major sixth degree is consistently flattened.

We have seen that when it comes to deciding what scale a particular song is based on, some additional things besides the signature must be considered. One of these concerns the terms used to designate and classify the tonal material of which the melody is built. How careful one needs to be in applying sometimes well-known terminology to this task can be shown by another example again drawn from one of Dr. Jackson's works. It is a pity that his otherwise outstanding contributions are marred by such lapses, merely because he failed at times to ask for advice from a musically more informed consultant. The following passages are taken from *White and Negro Spirituals*.[17] Very appropriately, the author names "a tetrachordal structure one, whose tones, up to four of them, range only between 1 and 4 of the diatonic scale" and a "pentachordal structure one whose tones, up to five of them, range only between 1 and 5 of the diatonic scale." Then, proceeding further, he calls "tetratonic structure" one whose four tones form an incomplete example of one of the pentatonic scales. Being aware, however, that some formations have certain different characteristics, he names pentachordal forms (from 1 to 5) with one tone missing and "therefore also tetratonic," "tetratonic-pentachordal" tunes. In all logic then, a tetratonic structure, "whose four tones form an incomplete example of one of the pentatonic scales," would

[17]WNS, p. 233.

have to be called tetratonic-pentatonic. Who is willing to usurp dictatorial powers to declare categorically which of two possible tones in the series c-d-f-g is missing, the e or the a?[18] The decision is vital, for in the first case we would have a tetratonic-pentachordal, in the second, a tetratonic-pentatonic scale.

Now, let us take the case of mode I of the pentatonic series, which goes from 1 to 6. According to a strict and logical application of the procedure described above, this scale could not be called pentatonic, which is the generally accepted term; it would have to be called pentatonic-hexachordal; therefore, a gapped scale with six tones, hexatonic-heptachordal, etc. Confusion worse confounded.

Then, in the next chapter, Dr. Jackson uses terms like "augmented and diminished seventh," and (p. 240) "the *perfect* sixth in minor environment." But actually, he is not talking about any seventh which, in musically accepted terminology, could ever be called augmented or diminished. And what a *perfect* sixth is, is unknown to musical science.

To follow logically a manner of naming the scales which, partially, has been in use for a long time, the present editor decided to name all scales showing a consecutive series of tones, *chordal,* and those with one or more skips, *tonic.* Thus we have tetrachordal, pentachordal, hexachordal, and heptachordal as well as tetratonic, pentatonic, and hexatonic scales. Naturally, according to the previous definition, there can be no such thing as a heptatonic scale.[19] Another slip of Dr. Jackson's is his use of the terms "heptatonic dorian" and "heptatonic ionian."[20] As he himself recognized, when we deal with genuine Dorian or Ionian, they are without exception *hepta-.* Otherwise, they would be *hexa-* or *penta-,* and certainly not Dorian or Ionian. Here should be added, however, that if either of them were *hepta-,* it would be heptachordal and not heptatonic.

There is a diversity of scales to be found in the ballads as well as the folk songs and games. All of these have been classified according to their content—from those containing only a few tones, up to those representing the full scale as we know it, including those that have some chromatic alterations of the diatonic tones as well.[21] It should be noted that the latter, although given in the scale picture as they occur (see Appendix B), are not taken into account with regard to the underlying tonal structure of the scale. Scales that do not conform, so to speak, to any of those familiar to all of us, are, following Helmholtz,[22] called irrational. And Helmholtz says that the Greeks already used this term (ἄλογα) for such formations.

[18] Ann G. Gilchrist, "Note on the Modal System of Gaelic Tunes," in JFSS, IV, 1910-1913, 150-3.
[19] Cf. SharpK. In volume I alone, there are 115 scales thus classified.
[20] SFSEA, pp. 29, 214 and *passim.*
[21] Of all possible modes, the majority of tunes are based on one of the different forms of the pentatonic scale. The next in frequency is the heptachordal; the third, one of the forms of the hexatonic scale, differing only in the omitted scale degree.
[22] Helmholtz, p. 406; 5th ed., p. 264. For other deficient scales cf. Quintilian, in Marcus Meibom, *Antiqvæ Mvsicæ Avctores Septem,* Amsterdam, 1652, p. 21.

It remains to explain the methods used in Appendix B, which records not only the scales of all the songs, but also the relative frequencies in which the individual tones occur in each particular song. This plan was evolved while the present editor was working on the music of the American Indians on the Pacific coast.[23] It aims to show the relative importance of each scale tone in any given melody, as well as the seemingly endless variety which could be achieved with the same tonal material. Such basic information might serve well for a later comparative study of the songs of various nations, thereby showing their respective preferences and tastes as well, perhaps, as relationships. This could also be extended to the use of the various intervals.

The method of arriving at a means of measurement for determining the frequency of the individual tones is simply this. Each tone, as often as it occurs in the melody, is counted in values of sixteenths. The total aggregate will then give the numerical frequency or weight of the tone in relation to others.

Let one song taken at random from this Collection (No. 173) serve as example to show the method used in ascertaining the 'weight' of the individual tones occurring in a melody and therefore a scale. The number

1   1   11   8   24   8   13   7   6   6

below each note gives the total numerical value of its frequency. There are a number of other songs which have the very same or almost the same tonal content, but what a difference in the resultant melody—as may be seen in a comparison of No. 173 with Nos. 229, 241, 256, 323, 409, and 512. A scale is merely the raw building material; a mode is the architectural design using that material. And as each mode has its characteristic melodic progressions and idioms, a valuable study, space permitting, could be made by examining the frequency as well as occurrences of the different possible progressions.

[23]Cf. Jan P. Schinhan, "The Music of the Papago and Yurok," a dissertation submitted to the Philosophical faculty of the University of Vienna, 1933. Now in process of publication. Here the method of measuring the frequency is extended by means of a chart which gives the exact physical outline of each melody, recording each progression according to its movement in time as well as that with regard to pitch. Since horizontal as well as vertical lines are used, both can serve for this purpose. The horizontals are divided in sixteenths of an inch representing duration, the verticals in equal distances representing halfsteps. This is, of course, far more accurate than merely projecting the general outline of a melody in a graph. The latter method is nothing new in itself, having already been used by Madame E. Linev of Russian fame (1905), as well as by Miss Frances Densmore of this country and some other scholars. In 1933 I discussed this method with Joseph Schillinger of Teacher's College (Columbia University), who seemed very much interested in it. It is perhaps regrettable that, in his posthumously published work, his editors, evidently not informed, gave credit to him for having evolved this method. Cf. *The Schillinger System of Composition*, New York, 1946, p. xix.

2. Range. The range in which the melodies of the ballads move varies considerably. The most extended is a thirteenth or an octave and a sixth, which occurs in one song. The smallest range, that of a fourth, likewise occurs only in one song. Numerically, the highest in frequency is the range of an octave, with that of the ninth next in rank.[24] The idea expressed by several writers that a limited tonal range indicates the great age of a song should be regarded with caution.

Among the various tables given in Appendix A will also be found an account of the frequency of all the different tonal ranges. An interesting comparison could be made with regard to the preferences shown in the older ballads (mostly British) as against that to be found in the native American and North Carolina ballads.

3. Melodic Line, or Interval Succession in Pitch. It is convenient to speak of a melody as 'interval succession in pitch' and of meter as 'interval succession in time' (see p. xix above), but these two factors should really not be separated, as indeed they cannot be, for the reason that, when dealing with Western music, no melody can be found which does not have the characteristics of moving in 'measured time.' Nevertheless, for the purpose of our analysis, they must be considered separately.

Melody is a succession or series of either conjunctly or disjunctly ascending or descending tones which differ not only in pitch, but, owing to their varying duration, also in time. It is not, however, a haphazard series of unrelated sounds of varying pitch and duration, but a rhythmical organism which consists of clearly defined accentual groups. "It is a basic, primordial coherence and relationship evolved by the kinetic sense of energy."[25] "The fundamental being of the creative mind is essentially rhythmic. All great art which moves in time, springs direct from this primal impulse."[26] Melody then is the product of this impulse, its tones varying in pitch and duration according to the basic law of unity in variety, which underlies all expression. There is a theory that melody evolved from the natural inflections of speech, since both have two constituents in common, pitch variation and rhythm. As a melody, however, in contrast to what is called a motif or even a phrase, is a fully rounded and balanced tonal structure, it would not be exactly correct to compare it with a complete sentence or statement in language, but rather to such a structure as we know by the term stanza or strophe. Melody is tonal movement in time, but it "has to express a motion, in such a manner that the hearer may easily, clearly, and certainly appreciate the character of that motion by *immediate perception.*"[27] As Ernst Kurth puts it, "melody is flowing power. The real basic content of a melodic line is the 'becoming,' the onward urge which, through its inherent motion and propelling

[24] A survey of 203 English ballads contained in books I-VII of the *Folk-Song Sight Singing Series* published by Oxford University Press shows the same preference for the octave and ninth as against all other intervals.
[25] Cf. Ernst Kurth, *Grundlagen des Linearen Kontrapunkts*, Berlin, 1922, pp. 15-16.
[26] Cf. Margaret H. Glyn, *Theory of Musical Evolution*, London, 1934, p. 2.
[27] Helmholtz, 5th ed., p. 252.

power, takes a particular form that can be perceived and felt. Melody is based on the energy which produces the coherence between the individual tones, combines them into larger groups, and rounds them out into the total imagery of the progression."

Melody is a living thing, an organism,[28] which in given circumstances may change in some ways without, however, losing its individuality or inherent characteristics—as shown in the variations given below the music score. There are, of course, cases like that of the so-called 'character-variation,' where the listener sometimes is hard put to recognize the original idea, and the theorist to explain how such an idea could have sprung from this original. This is not unlike what happens in the human family, where the offspring are often very different from their progenitors. In fact one might liken a melody to a community in which each individual has its own dynamic force or drive, but which does not exist as an independent factor manifesting itself without regard to its surroundings. Each member with his own individual qualities and characteristics brings something to the whole, is in a certain relationship to the whole, which, in each case, is again governed and determined by the relative position the individual occupies in the total structures. And the same is true of an individual tone in the community of what we call a melody. The quality and character of a melodic line is determined not only by each individual tone and its pitch, duration, and position—its dynamic or rhythmical force—but by the varying relationships to the other tones which make up the whole and especially to what is called tonal center.[29] And as in a community, where a few outstanding individuals can shape and control the activities of their fellows by the sheer force of their personalities, their ideals, their integrity and character, so in a melody, tones will be found which take on a dominant importance in comparison with some others which, more or less, function as willing co-workers for the benefit of the whole.

This very fact is the basic reason why the editor decided to tabulate his findings in Appendix A. In a brief introduction there is obviously no room for an extended melodic study of each of the more than 1250 ballads and songs.[30] This would be most interesting and bring out some points which it is not possible to cover in a general survey. One of these, and an important one, would be a discussion of the melodic progressions with regard to their direction; for there is a great difference between a progression used ascendingly or descendingly.—A very telling example, one which is well known, is the beginning of "I know that my redeemer liveth" from Handel's *Messiah*. Just take the ascending fourth (b'-e")

[28] Ernst Kurth has called it "the total or sum of a psychodynamic occurrence."

[29] "The character of every melody is, in part, derived from the mode in which it is cast" (EFSSC, p. 47).

[30] See, however, the tables in Appendix A showing the numerical occurrences of the various interval-progressions for the beginnings as well as the endings of all melodies, and also the characteristics of repeated tones and ascending versus descending tendencies, and showing also whether the melodies start with the up-beat or not.

and invert it to the descending fifth(b'-e'). The result? Nobody will give you credit for knowing much, and certainly not for being very sure about it.

Another important point that must here be omitted concerns the cadential features of each melody. Cadences have a tendency to fall into a more or less stereotyped pattern, either half or full cadences. There is likewise a tendency to mitigate this sameness by varying the beginnings of the melodies. And some airs refuse to conform, especially those that end on a degree other than the tonal center. This phenomenon is frequently to be found in songs which come from Scotland,[31] but occurs also in songs of other peoples like those of the Swiss.

"In European folk song it has frequently been noticed that the French and Italians prefer narrow steps and ranges, as distinguished from the northern races, English, Germans, etc."[32] Let us overlook the "narrow steps," which no doubt should read "narrow intervals," and examine our ballads with this statement in mind. Since the range of the tunes has already been discussed, there are only the interval-progressions and other melodic characteristics left to be considered here.

In 512 tunes, the preferred melodic progression by skips shows a majority of 701 as against that by steps. Likewise, there is a decided favoritism shown towards beginning with the up-beat (322) as against the down-beat (29), not including the 161 songs which begin with a repeated first tone. The latter, in 144 ballads, is repeated one or more times followed by ascending progressions, while in only 37 it is followed by descending motion. In all songs, the one-time repetition of the initial tone is by far the most frequent. Next in frequency come the two- and three-times repeated initial tone. It is interesting to observe that the repetition of the first (161), as compared with that of the final tone (28), stands in the ratio of only slightly higher than 2:1, if the last tones which are anticipated (44) are also counted. It should be noted also that repeated tones other than the initial and final are quite frequent as well as characteristic of most of the songs. Besides favoring a start with the up-beat, the majority of the songs (226) begin with the fifth degree, with the first degree next in frequency (182). With the exception of the endings, the dominant factor in all progressions seems to be the ascending motion. The ratio between ascending versus descending movements is almost 4:1. Of all the 512 ballads, 415 end on the strong beat, which, in 343 cases, is arrived at descendingly.

In discussions of Western music the term *climax* refers to the highest tone occurring in the piece. Normally, and certainly in shorter compositions, this climactic tone should occur but once and is usually found on the accented beat. But this is almost never true in folk song. Such a climax has definitely something of a dramatic character, and that is possibly the very reason why the folk singer, having an objective point of view, does not use it. It would be incorrect, however, to assume that there are no

[31] Cf. William Dauney, *Ancient Scotish Melodies,* Edinburgh, 1838, p. 321; also Margaret Glyn, *Theory of Musical Evolution,* London, 1934, p. 152.
[32] *Harvard Dictionary,* p. 437.

culmination points within the individual phrases, but the latter being very frequently repeated (in 340 tunes), any climax in our sense of the word is prevented. The reason for these frequent repetitions can easily be seen when one realizes that there must be some means of achieving unity. In some songs having the abcd and similar patterns, the unit, besides some small similarities, will have to be brought about by the story. This is a similar problem to that faced by a composer when writing a motet or madrigal. The climax (not repeated) somewhere near the middle of the song occurs in 101 ballads. More details regarding all these points will also be found in Appendix A.

As was the case in our discussion of the modes, it is unfortunately necessary here to deplore the careless or inexpert language of certain editors. Phillips Barry, for example, says that "Scots singers have a liking for melodies cast in the so-called gapped scales, having but five or six tones, . . . as well as for melodic progressions admitting the skip of a full octave, or even of a larger interval." He cites 'The Trooper and the Maid' as musical illustration and continues: "Such structural peculiarities, as well as the Irish cadence, that is, the twice repeated iteration of the closing note of a melody, are of the class of musical archaisms."[33] Since when has a melodic interval been a structural peculiarity? Certainly, specific intervals, for example the fourth, can by repeated occurrences become *melodic peculiarities* of a structure, but they do not constitute either a structure or a structural peculiarity. As for the "melodic progressions admitting the skip of a full octave," one need only refer to Cecil Sharp: "The interval of the octave is a common one in folk-airs of all countries."[34] And what should one say about the tautology "twice repeated iteration of the closing note of a melody"? The very example cited shows the final tone repeated but once!

For another example, take this from Horace Beck: ". . . the tune varies slightly throughout the song to fit the words in the various stanzas. This would indicate perhaps that it is not the original tune."[35] Such a deduction would be equivalent to saying that, inasmuch as the second stanza of 'The *Flying Cloud*' does not conform in its third line to the metrical pattern used in the first stanza, therefore it cannot be the original poem. The reasoning is specious. In the first place, where and what is the *original* tune? In folk music, which is forever in flux, there is no original; there can only be a better or less good version, musically speaking. And the judgment about this is usually that of the people who either do or do not sing the melodies and thus preserve them for later times.

4. Meter, or Interval Succession in Time. Neither in purely monophonic music like Plain Chant ("a single melodic line without any additional parts or accompaniment")[36] nor in the music of our own day has there ever been a melody without rhythm. But, as in Plain Chant, the melodies

[33] BBM, p. xxiii.
[34] EFSSC, p. 83.
[35] Horace P. Beck, "The Riddle of 'The *Flying Cloud*,'" JAFL LXVI (1953), 123-33; 130.
[36] *Harvard Dictionary*, p. 455.

of the troubadours, the Minnesingers and Mastersingers, there was, and in the Orient still is, music without meter.

One thing is certain, however: *rhythm is not meter,* nor is the term meter a substitute for rhythm.[37]

In poetry as in music we have two distinct types of accentuation, the rhythmical and the metrical. The opening lines of Milton's *Paradise Lost* are in the familiar five-foot iambic meter, but no intelligent person would ever think of reading them accordingly, because, in doing so, he would improperly emphasize the metrical accents at the expense of both the natural rhythm and the normal stress of the words. Likewise, in music anyone following the general belief that each first beat in any measure must receive an accent, will not only prove that he does not understand the music, but will at the same time deprive any listener of the possibility of grasping the musical idea expressed by the composer. Yet, although you may not hear the meter in the poetry nor the meter in the music, the metrical scheme is always present. Sometimes the rhythmical and the metrical accents will coincide; at other times they may differ. The right balance between them has been defined "as any organized and intelligible relationship between the individual items of a series of sounds or motions, such relationship being organized with respect to emphasis and duration. No repetition of a set pattern is implied."[38]

What we must realize, then, is that in music as in poetry there is a double system of accentuation. We must also realize that the barline in music is merely a convenience to the eye with a purely metrical significance but with no control whatever over the rhythmical accent. But whereas in verse the syllables and feet vary considerably in length or duration, in music, the quantitative relationships between whole, half, quarter, and eighth notes, etc., are mathematically exact. Therefore, a longer note value, preceded and followed by shorter values, is very likely to draw attention to itself and thus to be felt as the accentual center of the group.

In poetry or rhythmic prose there may be divergence of opinion with regard to stress or the lack of it, just as there is, in the field of music, in the singing of Plain Chant. But in any concerted rendition of either it is necessary to come to an agreement, and this is most naturally reached on the basis of the text. Only in the development of polyphonic music, with several independent melodic lines, did the situation change. When there was a concerted effort of several people singing different melodic lines, there arose the consequent necessity of keeping them together. Then measured music came into being. Whether we observe the stamping of feet or clapping of hands in contemporary popular entertainment or that of so-called primitive societies, not to mention the drums heard in both, the use of the same means is evident, as it likewise is in the hep-two-three-four of more recent times. The performance of concerted music is pos-

[37] It should go without saying that meter and rhythm are not the same thing. Cf. Aurelius Augustinus, *Musik,* transl. by Carl Johann Perl, Strassburg, 1937, p. 167: "By which rhythm, meter and verse differ."

[38] Calvin S. Brown, *Music and Literature,* Athens, Georgia, [1948], p. 15.

sible only by the strict observance of these time-proportions, whatever they may be.

"The realization of rhythmic progression is the natural appreciation of the principle of periodicity which is inherent in the very constitution of the human mind. It is the perception of equality in duration of consecutive mental states."[39] According to the general law of response to a stimulus, every impression, in extent and character, sets up a similar and proportionate movement which tends to recur and keep on doing so.[40] A periodic succession is felt "as progression in cycles (weak-strong, or strong-weak)." "If a long series of quarternotes were played with absolute uniformity in time and stress, the listener would inevitably hear the appropriate notes accented. Such is one of nature's beneficent illusions."[41] A single act of attention which embraces the whole group (feeling of unit), involves the apprehension of this duality: positive—and negative. "An object that does not change cannot be attended to for more than a few seconds."[42] This is due to the fact that attention is discontinuous and intermittent. Through varying the renewal of the act of attention, "undifferentiated sounds can be thought into a variety of rhythms." But, since "the feeling of regular accent is in strict relation to the points at which there is a purposeful renewal of the act of attention,"[43] it should be evident that, when this renewal is carried on *regularly*, it will give rise to the feeling of meter.

One thing, however, should be kept in mind, namely, that all this "renewal of the act of attention" as well as the feeling of meter is purely an activity of mind. The Greek philosopher Demokritus twenty-three centuries ago said: "Sweet and bitter, cold and warm as well as all the colors, all these things exist but in opinion and not in reality; what really exists, are unchangeable particles, atoms, and their motion in space." Bishop Berkeley of more recent times expressed similar ideas. The sixteenth-century mathematician Galileo was perfectly aware of this and Leibniz, the great German mathematician, said that he was able to prove that all these things "were mere apparent qualities." Our own great contemporary Albert Einstein included even space and time as forms of intuition. According to him, the only objective reality of space is the order, grouping, or arrangement of the objects in space, and that of time likewise in the order of events by which we measure it.

Thus, meter first came into music when it was found necessary in concerted music to make sure that the different 'events' as represented by the individual lines of a polyphonic composition would occur in their proper 'order.' Meter was and still is a mere convenience which, on one hand, enables the composer to convey, at least approximately, his ideas and intentions, and on the other, makes it possible for the performer to arrive at an understanding of the music, and thereby to realize the intentions of

[39] John B. McEwen, *The Thought in Music*, London, 1912, p. 9.
[40] *Ibid.*, p. 10.
[41] Carl E. Seashore, "The Sense of Rhythm as a Musical Talent," *Musical Quarterly*, IV (1918), 507-15.
[42] E. W. Scripture, *The New Psychology*, London, 1905, p. 179.
[43] McEwen, pp. 15, 14.

the composer. Rhythm always was first and meter second. It is therefore senseless to state in a definition of meter that it "serves as a skeleton for the rhythm."[44] Meter is the constant basic unit of measurement which, in its various forms and combinations, serves to delineate movement in time. As in our ordinary use of numbers, this basic unit can be subdivided into its smaller constituents as well as fused with others into a larger whole. But one must strongly protest against such misleading as well as erroneous statements as "that $\frac{6}{8}$ 'rhythm' may be duple as well as triple in character, and that $\frac{3}{4}$ may be both, or may be only triple."[45] The confusion comes from the mistaken idea that six eighth-notes in $\frac{3}{4}$ are the same as six eighth-notes in $\frac{6}{8}$ time. There is a decided difference between the latter and what is called a divided triplet. Two dotted quarters, which in both cases look alike, in $\frac{3}{4}$ imply a syncopated effect; in $\frac{6}{8}$ they certainly do not.

In Appendix A are listed all the varied types of meter that occur in the tunes of the ballads in this volume.

5. *Structure or Gestalt: Over-all Rhythm.* It should be quite clear that, if a definite way of measuring is predetermined, there must first be something to be measured, that is, something that can be subdivided into the smallest unit of the measuring device. In music, this something to be measured is a melody, a progression of tones varying not only in pitch, but also in relative time values. This something or the totality of this something may be called structure, *Gestalt,* or over-all rhythm.

St. Augustine, when discussing the role of reason, said: "First it followed its own feelings and formed structures with proportions and divisions. According to its judgment, it delimited these forms and so created verse. What, however, did not conform to these limits but was nevertheless built of reasonably ordered values, it termed rhythm."[46] Both Remigius d'Auxerre[47] and Martianus Capella[48] define rhythm as a combination of sounds which are connected in a well-ordered mutual relationship. Quintilian says: The Greeks named rhythm the masculine element; and he continues, "without rhythm, the melody is without life and form, similar to any matter that can assume the most varied forms. The rhythm gives life to it and moves it in a well-ordered manner. It is the active element which creates; the melody is the passive element which manifests the creation."[49]

Rhythm then is the primordial, creative, emotional force which manifests itself under the control and guidance of logic. Rhythm closely unites a series of heterogeneous but balanced values and impresses upon that entity a distinct character. To quote Mathis Lussi: "Rhythm is the

[44] *Harvard Dictionary,* p. 442.
[45] George Herzog, *Folktunes from Mississippi,* National Play Bureau, No. 25, Works Progress Administration, New York City, 1937.
[46] Cf. Aurelius Augustinus, *De Ordine,* pp. 12-15.
[47] Cf. Remigius d'Auxerre, *De Rhythmus,* p. 80.
[48] Cf. Martianus Capella, *De Nuptiis Philologiae et Mesurii,* Cambridge, Mass., 1939, p. 190.
[49] Cf. Quintilian, *De Musica,* ed. Meibom, p. 43.

moving, driving principle through which music becomes understandable for us. It is rhythm which transforms a series of tones otherwise not logically connected into an aesthetic whole. Thus is formed a musical idea, an understandable element, and thereby a series of tones is removed from a purely sensory realm into that of understanding: rhythm lifts music into the sphere of spirit."[50] George Coleman Gow has so aptly described rhythm "as psychologically the apotheosis of the act of attention,—attention at its greatest tension."[51]

So we find rhythm is the *Gestalt* which an idea assumes in the mind when it finds its most complete and perfect expression. And *Gestalt* has form, outline, strength, beauty, character, and an inherent motion. In music we perceive rhythm as events or movements in time, the character of which is determined by the variable succession of its component homogeneous or heterogeneous parts. But, although rhythm occurs in time, it is not *subject* to time. Nevertheless, "the forever Now" shares the same fate as rhythm. As the latter without a succession of events is unthinkable, so time, the πάντα ῥεῖ of Heraclitus and the "all is in flux" of Bergson, is divided into larger or smaller units which through their numerical relationships convey a given idea in understandable terms. The total unit then is what is meant here by structure, *Gestalt*, or over-all rhythm. And each musical idea, according to its nature, will take on its own individual form—as can readily be seen from the tables in Appendix A.

To give an idea of this *Gestalt* or over-all rhythm of the various melodies, the build-up of each is given in detail, broken down into its smaller parts which together make up the whole. Inasmuch as most of the melodies contained in this Collection are of very small dimensions, the individual parts will necessarily be equally circumscribed. Nevertheless, the germinal idea which, in later periods, found its fruition in forms of considerable proportions, is unmistakably present. The analysis of the individual melodies will show an astounding wealth of imagination and resourcefulness as well as prove that, with all of that, old and tried friends are not forsaken. An interesting phenomenon should be noted, namely that the different versions of a song, though melodically often greatly varied, in most cases adhere to the identical structure of the other related tunes.

It is only natural that, among all the ballads presented here, there should be forms which are familiar to everyone who is informed about folk song. The common strophic form aa¹ (variation form), with all its different combinations, accounts for 155 tunes. The next in frequency is another strophic favorite, ab, which almost reaches the hundred mark. In addition, 107 songs use 29 different combinations of this basic tonal material. In many cases, this fundamental form is broken down into its smaller constituents between some of which one can frequently observe a more or less close relationship. From these smaller subdivisions, given in almost every case, it will be easy to ascertain all the relevant details

---

[50] Mathis Lussi, "The Correlation between Meter and Rhythm," *Vierteljahrschrift für Musikwissenschaft*, 1 (1885), 141-3.
[51] "Rhythm; The Life of Music," *Musical Quarterly*, 1 (1915), 637.

which could not be seen from an analysis taking larger units as structural parts of the whole, like ab. This more detailed analysis shows that, while a goodly number of songs partake of this basic material, they do, to some degree, differ from their close relatives, a fact which is equally borne out by other basic patterns like abc, abcd, abcde, etc.

The simple pattern abcd, which Cecil Sharp instances to show that the makers of English folk-tunes "more frequently squander their ideas than husband them,"[52] is represented by 60 tunes, not counting a few occurrences of abcdd, etc. Two types of structure that go back to early mediaeval times are the patterns aab, baa, and aaba. The former, Alfred Lorenz calls "barform and inverted barform," the latter "Reprisenbar."[53] There are 29 examples of barforms and 36 of "Reprisenbar." One lone survival of a structure which had its ancestral home in Provence and its "canzo," as well as in some songs of the Minnesingers and Mastersingers,[54] is found in the 'Riddle Song' (No. 34 of this Collection) ababcb = ‖ : a + x : ‖ + (b + x). The form aba, which Robert O. Morris[55] declared he never found in English folk songs, occurs six times. To be sure, we must not think here of the fully grown three-part song form. In addition, there are many forms of very low frequency, among them, the lowest, one occurrence only. This happens to be the case in 48 songs, each of which presents its individual variation in the use of otherwise basic material.

Besides variety, there is always the important factor of unity, and it is enlightening to see how the uninstructed mind handles this problem in a masterly even though unconscious manner. The solution is achieved by repetition of some parts of the melody in the total structure. Although Cecil Sharp says that "The frequent iteration of one short phrase cannot be said to be so characteristic of the English folk-tune as it undoubtedly is of the French folk-air,"[56] it appears nevertheless quite frequently in the tunes of this Collection, especially in the various combinations resulting from such basic material as the simple aa and ab. It is quite likely, however, that Cecil Sharp had in mind a motif when he said "short phrase." In that case, his statement would also hold true for our songs.

In Appendix A will be found three different tables dealing with the forms as found in the 512 ballads of the present volume. One table shows the total of each basic material comprising not only the latter, but all its varied combinations. The second shows the most frequent structural combinations, and the third all the varied groupings of otherwise basic material as they were found in the study of all the ballads.

6. *Rendition.* Not much need be added to what Cecil Sharp has previously

---

[52] EFSSC, pp. 76-77 : "It is mostly the text which gives unity to the heterogeneous material."
[53] Alfred Lorenz, pp. 191-2. Friedrich Gennrich calls this last form a "rounded chanson" (*Rundkanzone*)—*Grundriss einer Formenlehre des mittelalterlichen Liedes,* Halle (Saale), 1931, p. 245.
[54] *Harvard Dictionary,* pp. 74 f.
[55] R. O. Morris, *The Structure of Music,* London, 1935, p. 8.
[56] EFSSC, p. 76.

said about mountain singers and their manner of performance.[57] The extensive repertory of these untutored people who owe their knowledge to their earlier association with older people who handed down to them what they in turn had inherited from their predecessors, is astounding. Besides many mountain singers, this editor has known several old Indians, each of whom could sing several hundred songs without any effort. There were, however, a number of the former as well as the latter who were not willing to have their songs taken down in any form whatever.

The manner of singing is quite well known. The mountain singer, in contrast to some so-called folk singers on the concert platform, forgets about himself and sings the story, without actually being affected by any of the less agreeable details. In many cases the tone quality is quite nasal and the articulation of the words pure wishful thinking.[58] There are exceptions, of course, and some of the singers, besides having an excellent natural voice, have a native ability to tell a story in song which would put many of the would-be artists to shame.

Some of the singers, while succumbing to the general manner of singing their songs on a rather high pitch level, find themselves confronted by the human limitations we all share. It is then quite possible to hear them, sometimes in the middle of a phrase, adjust this uncomfortable situation by simply transposing (unconsciously, of course) the remainder of the song to a lower key. It is quite an achievement. But it may have an unfortunate aspect; for if there is no second stanza available in the recording, the person trying to transcribe the song is hard put to arrive at a correct answer.

While it generally holds true that the folk singer, if recalling the tune, will readily be able to proceed with the words, and vice versa, there are a few cases to be found in this Collection in which the singer did recall the tune, but in place of the words, had to have recourse to nonsense-syllables, like la-la-la. As so many people while singing hymns will for various reasons not observe the true value of the notes, especially those of longer duration, so the mountain singers will, without hesitation, shorten time values, especially at the end of phrases. This results many times in rather irrational structures.[59]

Finally, it is interesting to observe the subtle variations which occur in the rendering of the several stanzas of a ballad or song. It is in these variations that the unlearned and unsophisticated art of the folk singer shows itself. With sovereign mastery, difficulties in accommodating different metric values of the text to the same tune are overcome. As in so-called art music, there are masters as well as those who "also run," but the product will always and unmistakably show with which one is dealing. And the same may be said with reference to the singing also.

[57] EFSSC, chap. ix, pp. 104-18.
[58] The editor, while transcribing the records of this Collection, has often wished that the singers had lived up to the statement of Cecil Sharp (EFSSC, p. 109), with regard to the attitude of the singers toward the words.
[59] Cf. EFSSC, p. 79.

Conclusion

This ends the discussion of the different approaches to an analytical study of folk song as presented in the following pages. It is, however, well to remember that, with all the value any analysis can and does have, neither this nor any other process will uncover the alchemy of the creative act in music or in any of the other arts, any more than it will demonstrate why of the thousands of leaves on an oak tree, none are ever exactly alike, nor why two roses growing on the same bush will graciously display their individual charm and beauty. If nothing else, though, such analysis may show forth the unending, inexhaustible creative power manifest throughout the universe.

ABBREVIATIONS

ABFS	*American Ballads and Folk Songs.* By John Avery Lomax and Alan Lomax. New York, 1934.
ABS	*American Ballads and Songs.* By Louise Pound. New York, [1922].
AFM	*American Folk Music.* By George Pullen Jackson. Boston, [1947].
AFSC	*American Folk Songs for Christmas.* By Ruth Crawford Seeger. New York, 1953.
AFSCh	*American Folk Songs for Children.* By Ruth Crawford Seeger. New York, 1948.
AMS	*American Mountain Songs.* By Ethel Park Richardson and Sigmund Spaeth. New York, [1927].
ANFS	*American Negro Folk-Songs.* By Newman I. White. Cambridge [Mass.], 1928.
APPS	*The American Play-Party Song.* By Benjamin A. Botkin. Lincoln, Nebraska, 1937.
AS	*American Speech.* Baltimore, 1926—.
ASb	*The American Songbag.* By Carl Sandburg. New York, [1927].
ASB	*Ancient Songs and Ballads.* By Joseph Ritson. London, 1829. 2 v. Vol. 1.
ASM	*Ancient Scotish Melodies.* By William Dauney. Edinburgh, 1838.
BB	*Ballads of Britain.* By John Goss. London, 1937.
BBM	*British Ballads from Maine.* By Phillips Barry, Fannie H. Eckstorm, [and] Mary W. Smyth. New Haven, 1929.
BISB	*The Burl Ives Songbook.* New York, [1953].
BMFSB	*Twenty-Nine Beech Mountain Folk-Songs and Ballads.* By Mellinger Henry and Maurice Matteson. New York, 1936.
BMNE	*Ballads Migrant in New England.* By Helen Hartness Flanders and Marguerite Olney. New York, 1953.
Botkin	See APPS.
BSI	*Ballads and Songs of Indiana.* By Paul G. Brewster. Bloomington, Indiana, [1940].
BSM	*Ballads and Songs Collected by the Missouri Folk-Lore Society.* By H. M. Belden. Columbia, Missouri, 1940.

BSO	*Ballads and Songs from Ohio.* By Mary O. Eddy. W.P.A., Cleveland, 1939.
BSSB	*Ballads and Songs of the Shanty-Boy.* By Franz L. Rickaby. Cambridge, [Mass.], 1926.
BSSM	*Ballads and Songs of Southern Michigan.* By Emelyn E. Gardner and Geraldine J. Chickering. Ann Arbor, 1939.
BSSN	*Ballads and Sea Songs from Newfoundland.* By Elizabeth Greenleaf [and] Grace Y. Mansfield. Cambridge, [Mass.], 1933.
BSSNS	*Ballads and Sea Songs from Nova Scotia.* By W. Roy MacKenzie. Cambridge, [Mass.], 1928.
BT	*The Ballad Tree.* By Evelyn Kendrick Wells. New York, [1950].
BTBNA	*The British Traditional Ballad in North America.* By Tristram P. Coffin. Philadelphia, 1950.
CH	*Church Harmony.* By William Walker. Chambersburg, Penna., 1841.
CLRS	Check-list of Recorded Songs in the English Language in the Archive of American Folk Song through July 1940. Library of Congress, Music Division, Washington, D. C., 1942.
CRS	*Cooperative Recreation Service Publications.* Delaware, Ohio, 1939.
CS	*Cowboy Songs and Other Frontier Ballads.* By J. A. Lomax and Alan Lomax. New York, 1938.
CSV	*Country Songs of Vermont.* By Helen H. Flanders [and] Helen Norfleet. New York, [1937].
DD	*Devil's Ditties.* By Jeannette Thomas. Chicago, 1931.
DESO	*Down-East Spirituals, and Others.* By George Pullen Jackson. New York, [1943].
DL	*Deutscher Liederhort.* By Ludwig C. Erk and Franz M. Böhme. Leipzig, 1925. 3 v.
DTOe	*Denkmäler der Tonkunst in Oesterreich.* Wien, 1894-1938. 83 v.
EAS	*Early American Songs.* By Margaret and Travis Johnson. New York, [1943].
EFSSC	*English Folk-Song, Some Conclusions.* By Cecil J. Sharp. London, 1907.
ESPB	*The English and Scottish Popular Ballads.* By Francis James Child. Folklore Press [reprint], New York, 1956. 5 v. in 3.
ETWVMB	*East Tennessee and Western Virginia Mountain Ballads.* By Célestin P. Cambiaire. London, [1934].

FB	*Frontier Ballads.* By Charles J. Finger. New York, 1927.
FMA	*Folk Music in America.* By Phillips Barry. National Service Bureau, [New York], 1939.
FMNEE	"Folk Music of Northeastern England," in *Collected Essays.* By W. Gillies Whittaker. London, 1940.
Ford	*Traditional Music of America.* By Ira W. Ford. New York, 1940.
FSA	*Folk-Songs of America.* By Robert W. Gordon. National Service Bureau, [New York], 1938.
FSCSG	*Folk Songs, Chanteys and Singing Games.* By Charles H. Farnsworth and Cecil J. Sharp. New York, 1909-1912.
FSE	*Folk-Songs of England.* Ed. Cecil J. Sharp. Books I, II, III, IV, V, various editors. London, 1908-1912.
FSEK	*Folk Songs of Europe.* Ed. Maud Karpeles. For the International Folk Music Council. London, [1956].
FSF	*Folksongs of Florida.* By Alton C. Morris. Gainesville, 1950.
FSKM	*Folk-Songs of the Kentucky Mountains.* By Josephine McGill. New York, [1917].
FSmWV	*Folk-Songs Mainly from West Virginia.* By John H. Cox. National Service Bureau. New York, 1939.
FSoA	*Folksongs of Alabama.* By Byron Arnold. University, Ala., 1950.
FSONE	*Folk Songs of Old New England.* By Eloise Hubbard Linscott. New York, 1939.
FSRA	*Folk-Songs of Roanoke and the Albemarle.* By Louis W. Chappell. Morgantown, W. Va., 1939.
FSS	*Folk-Songs of the South.* By John Harrington Cox. Cambridge, [Mass.], 1925.
FSSH	*Folk-Songs from the Southern Highlands.* By Mellinger E. Henry. New York, [1938].
FSSM	*30 and 1 Folk Songs from the Southern Mountains.* By B. L. Lunsford and L. Stringfield. New York, 1929.
FSSom	*Folk Songs from Somerset.* By Cecil J. Sharp and Charles L. Marson. London, 1904-1909. 5 v. in 1.
FSUSA	*Folk Song U. S. A. 111 Best American Ballads.* By John A. Lomax and Alan Lomax. New York, 1948.
FSV	*Folk-Songs of Virginia. A Descriptive Index.* By Arthur Kyle Davis. Durham, N. C., 1949.
FTM	*Folk Tunes from Mississippi.* By Arthur Palmer Hudson and George Herzog. National Play Bureau Publ. No. 25, 1937.
Gomme	*The Traditional Games of England, Scotland, and Ireland.* By Alice Bertha Gomme. London, 1894-1898. 2 v.

GOS   *The Good Old Songs.* By C. H. Cayce. Martin, Tenn., 1913.

GSAC   *Games and Songs of American Children.* By William Wells Newell. New York, 1883; new and enlarged ed., 1903, 1911.

HVZ   *Historische Volkslieder der Zeit von 1756 bis 1871.* By Franz W. von Ditfurth. Berlin, 1871-1872. 6 v. in 2.

JAFL   *Journal of American Folklore.* 1888—.

JFSS   *The Journal of the Folk-Song Society.* London, 1899-1931.

Malcolm Laws, Jr. See NAB.

McLendon   "A Finding List of Play-Party Games." By Altha Lea McLendon. SFLQ VIII (1944), 201-34.

MFER   *McGuffey's New Fifth Eclectic Reader.* By William H. McGuffey. New York, 1866.

MSFSH   "More Songs from the Southern Highlands." By Mellinger E. Henry. JAFL XLIV (1931), 61-115.

MSHF   *More Songs of the Hill Folk.* By John J. Niles. New York, [1936].

MSNC   *Mountain Songs of North Carolina.* By Susannah Wetmore and Marshall Bartholomew. New York, 1926.

MSON   *Minstrel Songs Old and New.* Oliver Ditson Company, Boston. n.d.

NAB   *Native American Balladry.* By G. Malcolm Laws, Jr. Philadelphia, 1950.

Newell   See GSAC.

NGMS   *The New Green Mountain Songster.* By Helen Hartness Flanders, Elizabeth Flanders Ballard, George Brown, and Phillips Barry. New Haven, 1939.

NS   *The Negro and His Song.* By Howard W. Odum and Guy B. Johnson. Chapel Hill, N. C., 1925.

NWS   *Negro Workaday Songs.* By Howard W. Odum and Guy B. Johnson. Chapel Hill, N. C., 1926.

OBC   *The Oxford Book of Carols.* By Percy Dearmer, R. Vaughan Williams, and Martin Shaw. London, 1928, 1951.

OFS   *Ozark Folksongs.* Collected and Edited by Vance Randolph. Columbia, Missouri, 1946, 1948, 1949, 1950. 4 v.

OHEFS   *One Hundred English Folk Songs.* By Cecil J. Sharp. New York and Boston, [1916].

OSC   *Our Singing Country.* By John A. Lomax, Alan Lomax, and Ruth Crawford Seeger. New York, 1941.

OSSG   *Old Songs and Singing Games.* By Richard Chase. Chapel Hill, N. C., [1938].

Owens	*Swing and Turn: Texas Play-Party Songs.* By William A. Owens. Dallas, 1936.
PMOT	*Popular Music of the Olden Time.* By W. Chappel. London, [1859]. 2 v.
PSB	*People's Song Book.* By Waldemar Hille. New York, 1948.
PSL	*Pennsylvania Songs and Legends.* By George G. Korson. Philadelphia, 1950.
Roberts	See ZVMW.
SCB	*South Carolina Ballads.* By Reed Smith. Cambridge, [Mass.], 1928.
SCFS	*A Selection of Collected Folk-Songs.* Vol. 1. Arr. by Cecil J. Sharp and R. Vaughan Williams. London, 1951.
SCSM	*A Song Catcher in Southern Mountains.* By Dorothy Scarborough. New York, 1937.
SFLQ	*Southern Folklore Quarterly.* Gainesville, Fla., 1937—.
SFSEA	*Spiritual Folk-Songs of Early America.* By George Pullen Jackson. New York, [1937].
SharpK	*English Folk Songs from the Southern Appalachians.* By Cecil J. Sharp and Maud Karpeles. London, 1932. 2 v.
SHF	*Songs of the Hill-Folk.* By John J. Niles. New York, [1934].
SHMC	*Southern Harmony and Musical Companion.* By William Walker. W.P.A. repr., New York, 1939.
SHP	*Songs of the Hills and Plains.* By Harry Robert Wilson. Chicago, [1943].
SMBFS	"Still More Ballads and Folk-Songs from the Southern Highlands." By Mellinger Henry. JAFL XLV (1932), 1-176.
SMLJ	*Songs of the Michigan Lumberjacks.* By Earl C. Beck. Ann Arbor, 1941.
SO	*Scottish Orpheus.* By Adam Hamilton. Edinburgh, n.d.
SOCH	*The Social Harp.* By John G. McCurry. Philadelphia, 1855, 1859.
SRA	*Songs of the Rivers of America.* By Carl Carmer and Dr. Albert Sirmay. New York, 1942.
SS	*Slave Songs of the United States.* By William F. Allen. New York, 1867 (reprinted 1929).
SSLKFS	*A Selection of Some Less Known Folk-Songs.* Vol. 2. Arr. by Cecil J. Sharp, R. Vaughan Williams, and others, compiled by Cyril Winn. London, 1951.
SSSA	*Songs Sung in the Southern Appalachians.* By Mellinger E. Henry. London, [1934].

SWPH	*Southern and Western Pocket Harmonist.* By William Walker. Philadelphia, 1846.
TAFL	*A Treasury of American Folklore.* By B. A. Botkin. New York, [1944].
TBmWV	*Traditional Ballads Mainly from West Virginia.* By John Harrington Cox. National Service Bureau, 75 S, 1939. (American Folk Song Publications No. 3; mimeographed.)
TBV	*Traditional Ballads of Virginia.* By Arthur Kyle Davis. Cambridge, [Mass.], 1929.
TexasFS	*Texas Folk Songs.* By William A. Owens. Austin, Texas, 1950.
TFS	*A Treasury of Folk Songs.* By Sylvia and John Kolb. New York, 1948.
TNFS	*On the Trail of Negro Folk-Songs.* By Dorothy Scarborough. Cambridge, [Mass.], 1925.
TSFL	*A Treasury of Southern Folklore.* By B. A. Botkin. New York, [1949].
TSNS	*Traditional Songs from Nova Scotia.* By Helen Creighton and D. H. Senior. Toronto, 1950.
TT	*Traditional Tunes.* By Frank Kidson. Oxford, 1891.
VBFB	*The Viking Book of Folk Ballads.* By Albert B. Friedman. New York, 1956.
VGS	*Vocal Gems of Scotland.* By Ernest Haywood. London, 1938.
VTWL	*266 Volks- Trink- und Wanderlieder.* By Hugo Hartmann. Darmstadt, n.d.
Whittaker	See FMNEE.
WMA	*The Waning of the Middle Ages.* By J. Huizinga. London, 1927.
WNS	*White and Negro Spirituals.* By George Pullen Jackson. New York, [1944].
WSSU	*White Spirituals in the Southern Highlands.* By George Pullen Jackson. Chapel Hill, N. C., 1933.
ZVMW	*Zeitschrift für Vergleichende Musikwissenschaft,* ed. by R. Lachmann. Berlin, 1934.

THE
MUSIC OF THE BALLADS

OLDER BALLADS—MOSTLY BRITISH

I

THE ELFIN KNIGHT
(Child 2)

A

'The Cambric Shirt.' Sung by Mrs. James York of Olin, Iredell county. Recorded at Boone, September 14, 1941, by Dr. W. A. Abrams. For additional titles to those given in BTBNA 30, cf. BB 2-3: 'Whittingham Fair'; also AFM No. 9: 'Parsley and Sage.' The latter is also the refrain of the former.

I

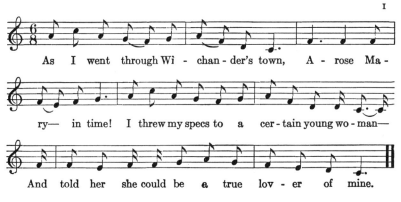

As I went through Wi - chan - der's town, A - rose Ma -
ry— in time! I threw my specs to a cer - tain young wo - man—
And told her she could be a true lov - er of mine.

For melodic relationship, cf. **SharpK 1, No. 1A.

Scale: Hexatonic (4), plagal. Tonal Center: f. Structure: aa¹ (4,4). Circular Tune (V).

B

'Rose de Marian Time.' Sung by Mrs. Fannie Norton of Norton, Jackson county. Recorded at Chapel Hill, 1936, by Professor Richard Chase.

2

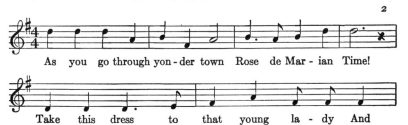

As you go through yon - der town Rose de Mar - ian Time!
Take this dress to that young la - dy And

tell   her   she   is   a   true   lov - er   of   mine.

Variant text of stanza 2:

> Tell her to make me a cambric shirt,
> Rose de Marian time!
> Without any seam or seamster's work,
> Then she'll be a true lover of mine.

For melodic relationship, cf. ***OSSG 18, No. 8.

Scale: Mode III.   Tonal Center: d.   Structure: ab (4,4).

2

LADY ISABEL AND THE ELF-KNIGHT
(Child 4)

A

'Pretty Polly.'   Sung by Mrs. Myra Barnett Miller, Lenoir, Caldwell county. Recorded at Lenoir, August 1936.   There is another, very similar recording by the same singer (record XXXA²-4), with the additional titles 'The Seventh King's Daughters' and 'The Seven Sisters.'   The variations are those of this second recording, also in score No. 140.

3

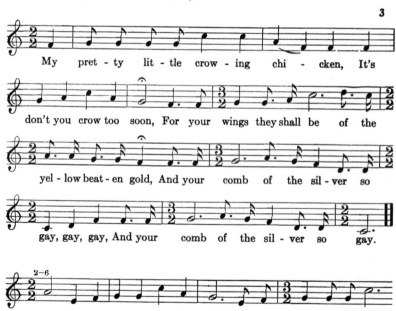

My   pret - ty   lit - tle   crow - ing   chi - cken,   It's

don't you crow too   soon,   For   your   wings they shall be   of   the

yel - low beat - en gold, And your   comb   of   the   sil - ver   so

gay, gay, gay, And your   comb   of   the   sil - ver   so   gay.

2–6

For melodic relationship, cf. ***SharpK 1, No. 3 A, D, G; **OFS 1, No. 2A; *BBM 24, F; ASb 60-61; PSL 30; TBV 549-50; and FSS No. 1B.

Scale: Mode III, plagal. Tonal Center: f. Structure: $aa^1a^2bb^1$ (2,2,2,2,2) = aa^1b (4,2,4). Circular Tune (V).

B

'The Seven Sisters.' Sung by Mrs. Rebecca (Aunt Becky) Gordon. Recorded at Tuxedo, Henderson county, July 19, 1939. In another recording (VIA^{1}-3) the same singer uses this tune with but slight changes for her version of 'The House Carpenter' (No. 40; II, 171).

He fol-lowed her up - stairs and down And in - to her cham-ber -
maid; She had no arms for to force him a - way, No
tongue to tell him nay, nay, No tongue to tell him nay.

For melodic relationship, cf. *TNFS 43 measures 5-6.

Scale: Heptachordal, plagal. Tonal Center: g. Structure: $abca^1d$ (2,2,2,2,2) = ab (4,6); b is terminally incremented.

C

'The Seventh King's Daughters.' Sung by Mrs. James York. Recorded by Dr. W. A. Abrams at Olin, Iredell county, 1940, from original at Boone, August 8, 1940. This tune very closely resembles Mrs. Myra Barnett Miller's tune for 'Pretty Polly' (2A) and has the same approach to the final.

He fol - lowed me up, he fol - lowed me down, He

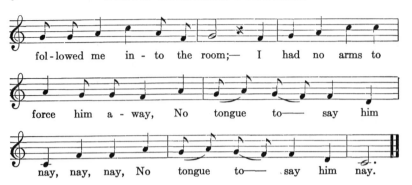

fol-lowed me   in - to   the room;—   I   had   no   arms   to

force   him   a - way,   No   tongue   to——   say   him

nay,   nay,   nay,   No   tongue   to——   . say   him   nay.

For melodic relationship, cf. ***SharpK 1 5-12, No. 3 A, B, D, E, G; FSS 521, No. 1B; **FSF 268, No. 157B; OFS 1 67, No. 6A ('Edward'); *OFS 1 41, No. 2A; SCSM 400, A, first four measures; OFS 1 48, No. 3, the first eight measures there are like the first four in our version; PSL 30, measures 3-4; TBV 550, No. 3D; FSoA 54.

Scale: Mode III, plagal.   Tonal Center: f.   Structure: aa^1acc^1 (2,2,2,2,2) = aa^1 (4,6); a^1 is terminally incremented.   Circular Tune (V).

D

'Pretty Cold Rain.' Sung by Miss Hattie McNeill. Recorded at Ferguson, Wilkes county, 1921 or 1922. Originally there was no text given in the MS score No. 141. The text from Miss Edith Walker, Boone, fits the tune perfectly, however. The score also gives the title as 'Six Fair Maids.' Melodically quite closely related to 'Pretty Polly,' 2A. Same approach to final as 'Pretty Polly,' 2A and 'The Seventh King's Daughters,' 2C.

6

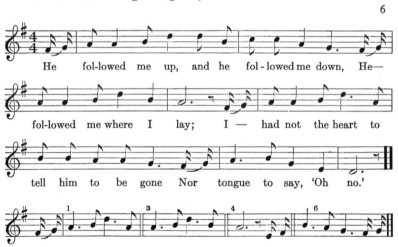

He   fol-lowed me   up,   and he   fol - lowed me down,   He—

fol-lowed   me where   I   lay;   I —   had not   the heart   to

tell   him   to   be   gone   Nor   tongue   to   say,   'Oh   no.'

For melodic relationship, cf. ***SharpK 1, 5, 8, 9, No. 3 A, D, (E); PSL 30; FSS 521, No. 1B; **OFS 141, No. 2, first four measures and ending; FSF 268, No. 157B; *FSoA 54.

Scale: Mixolydian. Tonal Center: d. Structure: $aa^1a^2a^3$ (2,2,2,2) = aa^1 (4,4).

D(1)

'My Pretty Cold Rain.' Sung by Mrs. Nora Hicks. Recorded at Sugar Grove, Watauga county, August 28, 1940. Mrs. Hicks learned it from her grandmother, Mrs. Fannie Hicks. Same approach to final as 'Pretty Polly,' 2A, 'The Seventh King's Daughters,' 2C, and 'Pretty Cold Rain,' 2D.

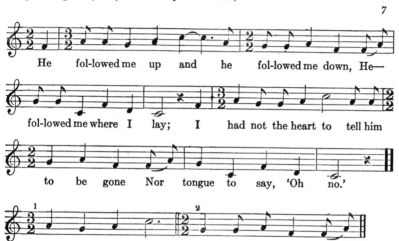

For melodic relationship cf. *BSO 6, No. 2A, first two measures.

Scale: Mode III, plagal. Tonal Center: f. Structure: aa^1 (4,4). Circular Tune (V).

G

'Seventh King's Daughter.' Sung by Mrs. J. Church. Recorded at Heaton, Avery county, July 30, 1939. There is no recording of Pat Frye's singing as mentioned in II, 25; only the text was taken down. Same approach to final as 'Pretty Polly,' 2A, 'The Seventh King's Daughters,' 2C, 'Pretty Cold Rain,' 2D and 'My Pretty Cold Rain,' 2D(1).

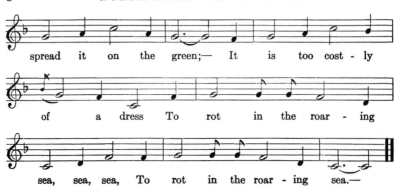

spread   it   on   the   green;—   It   is   too   cost - ly

of   a   dress   To   rot   in   the   roar - ing

sea,   sea,   sea,   To   rot   in   the   roar - ing   sea.—

For melodic relationship cf. ***SharpK 1, No. 3A; **FSS 521, No. 1B; and PSL 30; *FSF 268, beginning and ending; TBV 550, No. 3D, last four measures.

Scale: Hexachordal, plagal. Tonal Center: f. Structure: aa^{1}acc^1 (2,2,2,2,2) = aa^1 (4,6); a^1 is terminally incremented. Circular Tune (V).

3

EARL BRAND

(Child 7)

For the versions of this song which follow it should be said that, with the exception of the versions by I. G. Greer, 3B, and Mrs. Nancy Prather, 3D(1), all have the identical cadence, measures 7-8. This is in addition to the individual relationships between the various tunes which will be mentioned in connection with each version.

B

'Sweet William and Fair Ellen.' Sung by Dr. I. G. Greer. Recorded at Boone, Watauga county, 1913. Also score No. 55.

9

Sweet   Wil - liam   rode   to   the   Old   Man's   gate   And

bold - ly   he   did   say: 'The   young - est daugh-ter   she   may

stay   at   home   But   the   old - est   I'll   take   a - way.'

For melodic relationship, cf. **BMFSB 10, the first four measures; *SharpK
1 14, No. 4A.

Scale: Heptachordal, plagal. Mode III very evident. Tonal Center: f. Structure: abcd (2,2,2,2). Circular Tune (V).

B(1)

'Sweet William and Fair Ellen.' No evidence of singer, date, or place of recording. Melodically very similar to Prather 3D(1), Byers 3D, Johnson 3C,
and less so to Sutton version 3G. The general outline of the M. B. Miller version also shows considerable relationship.

10

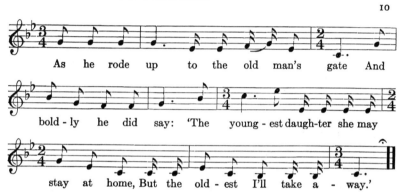

As he rode up to the old man's gate And
bold - ly he did say: 'The young - est daugh-ter she may
stay at home, But the old - est I'll take a - way.'

For melodic relationship, cf. *BMFSB 10.

Scale: Mode II, plagal. Tonal Center: c. Structure: abcb^1 (2,2,2,2) = ab
(4,4).

B(2)

'Sweet William and Fair Ellen.' Contributed by Mrs. Sutton. Score only, taken
down at Lenoir, Caldwell county, 1921 or 1923. Mrs. Sutton rarely, if ever,
gives the name of the singer, but it may be assumed to be Myra, i.e., Mrs. Miller.
The beginning shows some melodic relationship to the Johnson 3C, Byers 3D,
and Prather 3D(1) versions.

11

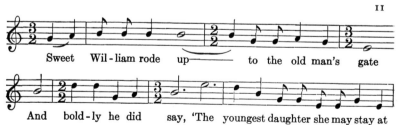

Sweet Wil - liam rode up to the old man's gate
And bold - ly he did say, 'The youngest daughter she may stay at

home,   But   the   old - est   I'll   take   a - way.'

For melodic relationship, cf. *BMFSB 10, first four measures.

Scale: Mode II, plagal. Tonal Center: e. Structure: ab (5,3) ; a is internally
incremented, b is contracted.

C

'Seven Brothers.' Sung by Mrs. Anna Johnson. From the recording of Dr.
W. A. Abrams in North Wilkesboro, Wilkes county, September 14, 1941. At
least in the first four and somewhat in the last measures this version is related
to the Sutton version 3G; likewise to some extent to the anonymous 3B(1),
Byers 3D, Prather 3D(1) and M. B. Miller 3F versions. The text is varied,
combining B and F versions. For further text variants cf. BB 6-7 ('The Doug-
las Tragedy').

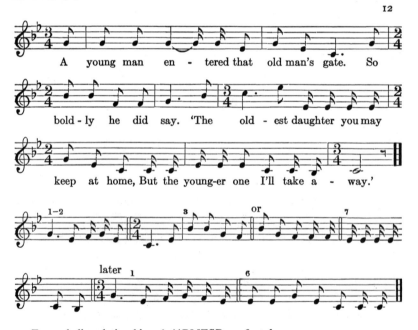

A young man en - tered that old man's gate. So

bold - ly he did say. 'The old - est daughter you may

keep at home, But the young-er one I'll take a - way.'

For melodic relationship, cf. **BMFSB 10, first four measures.

Scale: Mode II, plagal. Tonal Center: c. Structure: abcb^1 (2,2,2,2) = ab
(4,4).

D

'As He Rode Up to the Old Man's Gate.' Contributed by Mrs. N. T. Byers. Score No. 56, dated 1922, Zionville, Watauga county. Originally the MS score with words gives exactly the Smith text (version C) with regard to the youngest and oldest girl. Judging from the printed text (II 30) 3D, there must have been another text furnished later which changed all this. Measures 3-4 of Greer version 3B are practically the same as in this version.

13

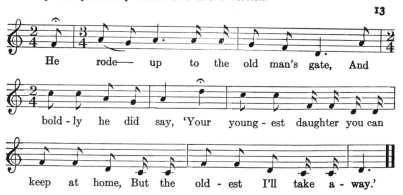

He   rode— up   to   the   old   man's   gate,   And

bold - ly   he   did   say, 'Your   young - est   daughter you can

keep   at   home, But   the   old - est   I'll   take   a - way.'

For melodic relationship, cf. **BMFSB 10, first four measures.

Scale: Mode II, plagal.   Tonal Center: d.   Structure: abcb¹ (2,2,2,2) = ab (4,4).

D(1)

'As He Rode Up to the Old Man's Gate.' Sung by Mrs. Nancy Prather, recorded at Milam, Ashe county, August 5, 1939. Noteworthy are the cadences, which are practically identical, the second being merely transposed a fifth down. A close melodic relationship is found in the Miller 3F and the Byers 3D versions. Only partly related is the Sutton version 3G.

14

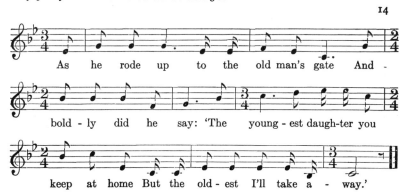

As   he   rode   up   to   the   old man's   gate   And -

bold - ly   did   he   say: 'The   young - est daugh-ter you

keep   at   home But   the   old - est   I'll   take a - way.'

For melodic relationship, cf. **BMFSB 10.

Scale: Hexatonic (6), plagal. Mode II is evident. Tonal Center: c. Structure: abcb¹ (2,2,2,2) = ab (4,4).

F

'Sweet Willie.' Sung by Mrs. Myra Barnett Miller. Recorded by Mrs. Sutton in the Brushies of Caldwell county. This tune is very similar to that of the Johnson 3C and the Sutton 3G versions. Both the Miller and Sutton versions show how fundamentally identical structures can be altered through the incrementation of some sort. Basically, both structures are identical with those of the previous versions. The shift of time values in the individual case accounts for the different aspects.

For melodic relationship cf. **BMFSB 10.

Scale: Mode II, plagal. Tonal Center: c. Structure: abcb¹ (2,2,2,2) = ab (4,4).

G

'Sweet Willie.' Sung by Mrs. Maude Minish Sutton, May 15, 1921. As far as the text is concerned, we have here a combination of the C and D versions. Melodically, this tune is more or less related to the Miller 3F, anonymous 3B(1), Byers 3D, and Prather 3D(1) versions.

16

For melodic relationship, cf. *BMFSB 10.

Scale: Mode II, plagal. Tonal Center: c. Structure: abcb¹ (2,2,2,2) = ab (4,4).

4

THE TWA SISTERS

(Child 10)

A

'The Two Sisters.' There is no recording of this version, but the Collection contains two manuscript copies, in different hands but otherwise identical, of the words and tune. It is included here, though it is probably not of North Carolina provenience.

17

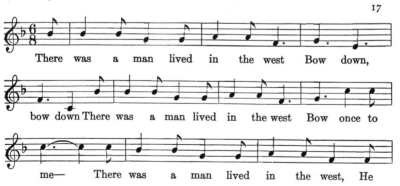

had two daugh - ters of the best. I will be true,

true to my love, And my love will be true to me.—

For melodic relationship cf. *FSF 243-4, No. 147A. The melodic intervals of the first three measures of our version are the same.

Scale: Heptachordal, plagal.   Tonal Center: f.   Structure: aa^{1}a^{2}b (4,4,4,4).

B

'Old Man from the North Countree.' Sung by Otis S. Kuykendall. Recorded at Asheville, Buncombe county, in 1939.

18

There was an old man from the North coun-tree— Bow down—

There was an old man from the North coun - tree Bow down and

bal-ance me. There was an old man from the North coun - tree,

He had daugh - ters one two three— I'll be

true to you my love if you'll be true to me.

Stanza 2
1-2   4-6

Stanza 3

Stanza 4

Continue like 2nd stanza, 11—

For melodic relationship cf. *SharpK ı 33, No. 5I, first three measures, and likewise BSM 2ı, version E.

Scale: Hexatonic (4), plagal. Tonal Center: e-flat. Structure: aa¹a²b (4,4, 4½,3½). This is a rather sophisticated structure (a² is terminally incremented); this brings about the elision between a² and b.

E

'Twa Sisters.' Sung by Pat Frye, of East Bend, Yadkin county, in 1945. From the original recording by Dr. W. A. Abrams. It is quite evident that the singer has shortened the melody at vital cadential points, measures 3 and again 11.

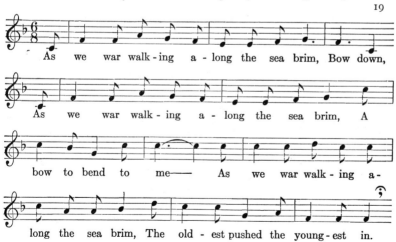

As we war walk-ing a-long the sea brim, Bow down,
As we war walk-ing a-long the sea brim, A
bow to bend to me—— As we war walk-ing a-
long the sea brim, The old-est pushed the young-est in.

Prove   true,   true   to   my   love,   prove true   to   me.——

For melodic relationship cf. *BSM 18, version A, last two measures; version B, our measures 6-7 with 7-8; *ibid.* 21, version E, our measures 3-4 and 6-7 with 3-4 and 7-8; also SharpK 1, No. 5B, measures 6-7 and possibly 5K, the latter, however, being in minor key. The general melodic outline of the first four measures has points in common with FMNEE 37: 'Binnorie.'

Scale: Heptachordal, plagal. Tonal Center: f. Structure: aa^{1}bb^1 (3,4,4,3), or ab (7,7), an unusual build-up.

F

'Twa Sisters.' Sung by Horton Barker. Record contributed by Dr. W. A. Abrams to the present editor in 1951; also sung to the latter personally by the same singer at his home in Chilhowie, Virginia, June, 1952. Cf. FSS 521, 'The Miller's Two Daughters,' to show how different ideas of various songs can be combined to form a new version.

20

There was   an   old   wom-an   lived   on   the   sea   shore,

Bow and bal-ance to   me—   There was   an   old wom-an lived

on   the sea-shore,   Her num-ber   of daughters one,   two, three, four,

And   I'll   be   true   to my   love,   If my love will be true to——   me.—

5   also   10

For melodic relationship cf. ***JAFL, XLV, 1932, 2-3, No. 175; **FSSH 39, No. 4A. Beginning with the third measure, there is considerable similarity; also SharpK 1, No. 5B, measures 8-9 with 5-6 in our version; *ibid.*, first two measures in both, and 5L, our measures 9-12 with 13-16 there.

Scale: Mode III, plagal. Tonal Center: e-flat. Structure: abcdb^{1}a^1 (2,2,2, 2,2); b^1 and a^1 are considerably varied.

2 There was a young man came there to see them,
   Bow and balance to me.
   There was a young man came there to see them,
   And the oldest one got struck on him,
   And I'll be true to my love, dear,
   If my love will be true to me.

The remaining stanzas follow the same pattern.

3 He bought the youngest a beaver hat
   And the oldest got mad at that.

4 'O sister, o sister, let's walk the seashore
   And see the ships as they sail o'er.'

5 While these two sisters were walking the shore
   The oldest pushed the youngest o'er.

6 'O sister, o sister, please lend me your hand
   And you may have Willie and all of his land.'

7 'I never, I never will lend you my hand,
   But I'll have Willie and all of his land.'

8 Sometimes she sank and sometimes she swam
   Until she came to the old mill dam.

9 'O father, o father, come draw your dam,
   Here's sister a mermaid or a swan.'

10 'O miller, o miller, here's five gold rings
   To put me safe on shore again.'

11 The miller received those five gold rings
   And pushed the maiden in again.

12 The miller was hung on his old mill gate
   For drowning little sister Kate.

G

'The Twa Sisters.' Sung by Mrs. Anna Johnson. Recorded from the original procured by Dr. W. A. Abrams at North Wilkesboro, Wilkes county, September 14, 1941. The last four measures of our version show some relationship with those of the Horton Barker version.

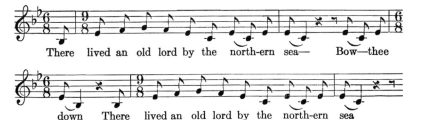

There lived an old lord by the north-ern sea— Bow—thee down There lived an old lord by the north-ern sea

Down and bal-ance to   me   There lived an old lord by the   north-ern

sea   And he   had   daugh-ters one   two   three—   I'll   be

true to   my love,   If   my love will be   true   to   me——

For melodic relationship cf. **SharpK 1, 31, No. 5G, almost throughout; FSSH 39, No. 4A and AMS 27. *DD 70-71: compare our 'Down and balance to me' with 'Bowes down' and 'Bow and balance to me'; also the beginning in both which recurs when the phrase is repeated. Likewise our last 6 measures with the last five of the other version. OFS 1, 60, No. 4G. Compare the phrase 'daughters one, two, three.'

Scale: Mode II, plagal. Tonal Center: c. Structure: abaca^{1}dea^2 (2,1,2,1,2,2,2,2) = aa^{1}a^{2}b (3,3,4,4).

5

THE CRUEL BROTHER

(Child 11)

A

'Oh, Lily O.' Sung by "Granny" Houston, of Bushy Creek, in Avery county. There is no record, only a score procured by Mrs. Sutton. No date given.

22

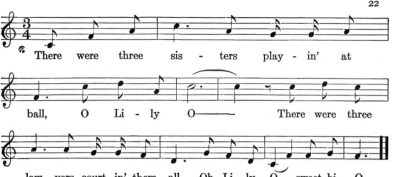

There   were   three   sis - ters   play - in'   at

ball,   O   Li - ly   O———   There were three

law - yers court - in' them   all,   Oh Li - ly   O— sweet hi— O—.

For melodic relationship cf. *SharpK 1, 36, No. 6A, measures 4-5 with 3-5 in our version.

Scale: Mode III, plagal. Tonal Center: f. Structure: ab (4,4).

B

'Lily O.' Sung by Mrs. Rebecca (Aunt Becky) Gordon. Procured by Mrs. Sutton at Saluda Mountain, Henderson county, July, 1928.

For melodic relationship cf. *SharpK 1 37, No. 6B, measures 9-10 with 4-5 of this version.

Scale: Mode III. Tonal Center: c. Structure: aa¹ (3,4).

In this connection should be observed the irregular structure that results from the elision in the third measure. Normally, "ball" would occupy one whole measure and "Oh, Lily" another. As the singer sang it exactly as noted, it is anyone's guess why this shortening of values took place. Perhaps it was due to lack of breath.

6

LORD RANDAL

(Child 12)

A detailed discussion of the relationship of this ballad with European, particularly Italian versions, and others can be found in BBM 64-5.

A

'Tiranti, My Son.' Sung by Mrs. N. T. Byers. Contributed by Miss Amy Henderson of Worry, Burke county, in 1914. The MS score gives the place as Silverstone, Watauga county, and the date as 1915.

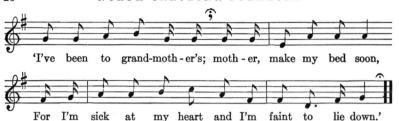

'I've been to grand-moth-er's; moth-er, make my bed soon,

For I'm sick at my heart and I'm faint to lie down.'

For melodic relationship cf. our version, measures 2 and 6, with *BB12, version B, measures 3-4 and 15-16. In the A version this same progression occurs only once, measure 2.

Scale: Heptachordal, plagal. Tonal Center: g. Structure: abab (2,2,2,2) = aa (4,4).

B

'Lord Randall.' Sung by anonymous singer. Contributed by Mrs. Sutton without indication of singer, place, or date.

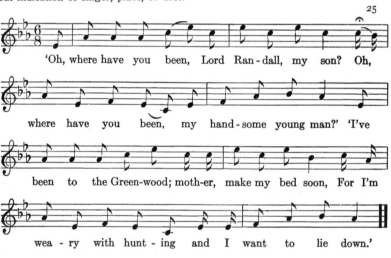

'Oh, where have you been, Lord Ran-dall, my son? Oh,

where have you been, my hand-some young man?' 'I've

been to the Green-wood; moth-er, make my bed soon, For I'm

wea-ry with hunt-ing and I want to lie down.'

Scale: Mode III, plagal. Tonal Center: a-flat. Structure: aba¹b¹ (2,2,2,2) = aa¹ (4,4).

B(I)

'Lord Randall.' Sung by Miss Pearle Webb. Recorded at Pineola, Avery county, September 6, 1941.

'Oh, where have you been, Lord Ran-dall my son?— Oh,

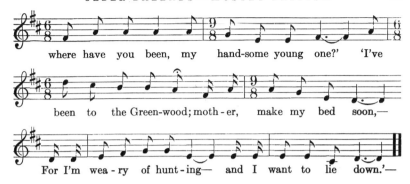

where have you been, my   hand-some young one?'   'I've

been   to   the Green-wood; moth - er,   make my   bed   soon,—

For I'm   wea - ry   of hunt - ing—   and   I   want to   lie   down.'—

Scale: Heptachordal, plagal. Tonal Center: d. Structure: abcd (2,2,2,2). The second measure of d is related to that of b.

B(2)

'Johnny Randall.' Sung by Mrs. Nancy Prather, the aunt of Frank Proffitt. Recorded at Milam, Ashe county, August 5, 1939. Our text is most certainly not the first stanza.

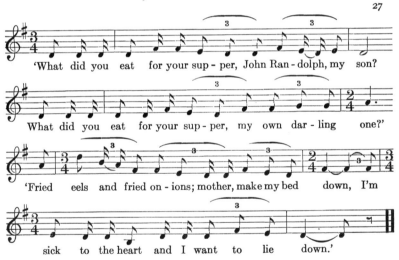

'What did you   eat   for your sup - per, John Ran - dolph, my   son?

What did you   eat   for your sup - per, my   own   dar - ling   one?'

'Fried   eels   and fried on - ions; mother, make my bed   down,   I'm

sick   to the heart   and   I   want   to   lie   down.'

For melodic relationship cf. *BB 51, version D, measures 2, 4, and 8. Scale: Hexachordal, plagal. Tonal Center: d. Structure: aa¹bc (2,2,2,2), possibly aa¹b (2,2,4) or in Alfred Lorenz' terminology mm¹n = barform.

C

'Willie Ransome.' Sung by Myra Barnett (Mrs. J. J. Miller). Recorded by Mrs. Sutton in Caldwell county in 1928. Note the simple "I want to lie down" for "I'd fancy lie down" of the printed text.

28

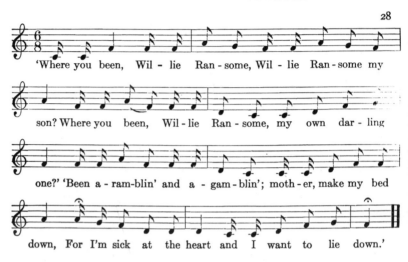

'Where you been, Wil - lie Ran - some, Wil - lie Ran - some my

son? Where you been, Wil - lie Ran - some, my own dar - ling

one?' 'Been a - ram-blin' and a - gam-blin'; moth - er, make my bed

down, For I'm sick at the heart and I want to lie down.'

Scale: Mode III, plagal. Tonal Center: f. Structure: abb¹b² (2,2,2,2). A variation of measures 2-4 serves for measures 6-8.

c(I)

'Willie Ransome.' Sung by Mrs. Rebecca (Aunt Becky) Gordon, July 19, 1939. Place is not given. Other titles quoted: 'Lord Randal' and 'Lord Ransome.'

29

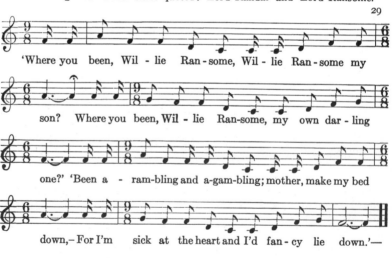

'Where you been, Wil - lie Ran - some, Wil - lie Ran - some my

son? Where you been, Wil - lie Ran-some, my own dar - ling

one?' 'Been a - ram-bling and a-gam-bling; mother, make my bed

down,– For I'm sick at the heart and I'd fan - cy lie down.'—

Scale: Mode III, plagal. Tonal Center: f. Structure: aa¹aa¹ (2,2,2,2) = aa (4,4).

7

EDWARD

(Child 13)

Of all the versions in SharpK only No. 8H, 51 refers to the "hazel-nut tree." All others have "holly-bush."

B

'Dear Son.' Contributed by Miss Jewell Robbins (later Mrs. C. P. Perdue) now of Gastonia. She learned this song from her grandmother, Mrs. Belinda Morton, born in Moore county of English parents.

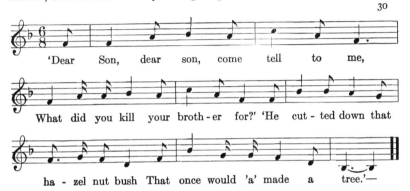

30

'Dear Son, dear son, come tell to me, What did you kill your broth-er for?' 'He cut-ted down that ha-zel nut bush That once would 'a' made a tree.'—

For melodic relationship cf. *SharpK 1 49, No. 8B, measures 1-4.

Scale: Hexatonic (4). Tonal Center: b-flat. Structure: mm^1n (2,2,4) = barform. Observe how the main melodic element of measures 5-6 is combined to form the penultimate measure.

C

'Edward.' From Dr. W. A. Abrams' recording of the singing of Horton Barker from Chilhowie, Virginia, September 14, 1941. The same singer sang this song again to the present editor, who visited the blind singer in Virginia in the summer of 1952. The title is that given by this singer. The recording of Pat Frye's singing referred to in II, 43 was not found. The textual variants should be noted.

31

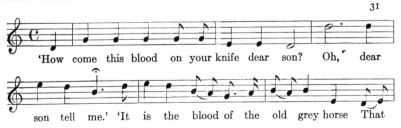

'How come this blood on your knife dear son? Oh, dear son tell me.' 'It is the blood of the old grey horse That

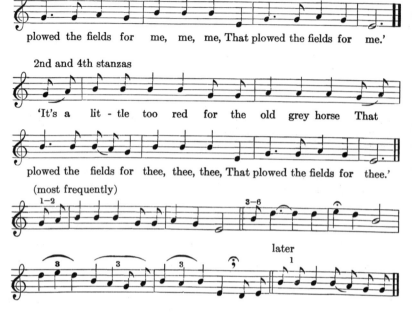

plowed the fields for   me,   me,   me, That plowed the fields for   me.'

2nd and 4th stanzas

'It's a   lit - tle   too   red   for   the   old   grey horse   That

plowed the   fields for   thee, thee, thee, That plowed the fields for   thee.'

(most frequently)

later

For melodic relationship cf. ***SharpK 1 47-8, No. 8D. Our version is very closely related to Sharp's, especially in the variations. They are practically identical in the second stanza, where both are melodically different as well as shorter than the first. As in the Sharp version the singer alternates these two stanzas ABAB. A like relationship will be found (measures 3-10) with SCSM 405, version B, and BT 103.

Scale: Mode II, plagal. Tonal Center: e. Structure: abcdd[1] (2,2,2,2,2).

Text as sung by Horton Barker

3 How come that blood on your knife, dear son?
   Oh, dear son, tell me!
   It is the blood of the guinea grey hound
   That ran the deer for me, me, me,
   That ran the deer for me.

4 How come that blood on your knife, dear son?
   Oh, dear son, tell me!
   It is the blood of my youngest brother
   Who went away with me, me, me,
   Who went away with me.

5 And what did you fall out about?
   Oh, dear son, tell me!
   Because he cut a little apple bush
   That soon would've made a tree, tree, tree,
   That soon would've made a tree.

6 And what will you do now, dear son?
Oh, dear son, tell me!
I'll set my foot into yonder ship
And I'll sail across the sea, sea, sea,
And I'll sail across the sea.

7 And when will you come back, dear son?
Oh, dear son, tell me!
When the sun sets in beyond the sycamore tree,
And that will never be, be, be,
And that will never be.

8 And what will become of your dear little boy?
Oh, dear son, tell me!
The world to wander in up and down,
For he never shall know of me, me, me,
For he never shall know of me.

9 And what will become of your wife, dear son?
Oh, dear son, tell me!
Sorrow and trouble all of her life,
For she'll see no more of me, me, me.
For she'll see no more of me.

10 And what will you leave to your mother, dear son?
Oh, dear son, tell me!
The curse of God I leave to you
For bringing this trouble on me, me, me.
For bringing this trouble on me.

12

CAPTAIN WEDDERBURN'S COURTSHIP

(Child 46)

The author of BBM 93-5 gives as his first version the complete ballad, including the story of the courtship.[1] None of our versions, as stated in II, 48-9, includes this story. One of our versions, however, does include the refrain "Perri Merrie Dictum Domine," but comes from a different singer. For a European relationship refer to VTWL 53 'Ach, Jungfer, ich Will Ihr.' Another title is given in BSSNS 391, No. 4.

A

'The Riddle Song.' Sung by anonymous singer. Mrs. Sutton procured this song giving neither singer, place, nor date.

[1] Referring to the source of his version he says: "Mrs. Marston's spirited and *tuneful version* of 'Captain Wedderburn's Courtship' came as a surprise; . . . ." It should have been, for a little later he says: "Mrs. Marston *cannot sing,* so we are unable to give an air for this text." In fact, the melody to this song, this time with the title 'Bold Robbington,' was written down and later sent to the editor by Mrs. Marston, June 28, 1929. Cf. BBM 481.

32

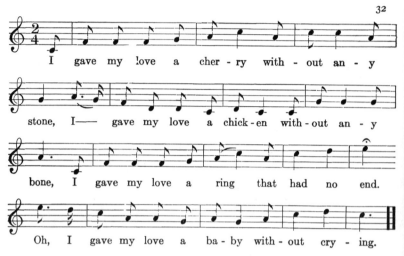

I gave my love a cher - ry with - out an - y
stone, I—— gave my love a chick - en with - out an - y
bone, I gave my love a ring that had no end.
Oh, I gave my love a ba - by with - out cry - ing.

For melodic relationship cf. *SharpK 1 223 and 229, No. 31B and H ('Sir Hugh!'), measures 1-2. Some similarity with FSSH 141, No. 31A.

Scale: Hexatonic (4), plagal. Tonal Center: f. Structure: aba¹b¹ (4,4,4,4). Circular Tune (V).

B

'I Gave My Love a Cherry.' Sung by Obadiah Johnson. Recorded at Cross-nore, Avery county, July, 1940.

33

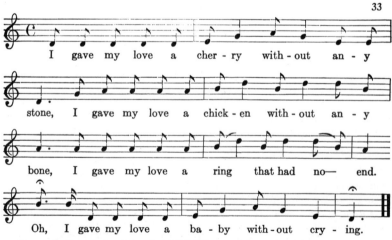

I gave my love a cher - ry with - out an - y
stone, I gave my love a chick - en with - out an - y
bone, I gave my love a ring that had no— end.
Oh, I gave my love a ba - by with - out cry - ing.

For melodic relationship cf. ***FSSH 141, No. 31A; SharpK 11 190, No. 144A; and BT 175.

Scale: Mode I. Tonal Center: d. Structure: aa¹a¹a² (2,2,2,2).

C

'The Riddle Song.' Sung by Horton Barker. Taken from a recording of Dr. W. A. Abrams at Boone, September 14, 1941. The variations noted below are from another rendition made for the present editor in June 1952 at Barker's home in Chilhowie, Virginia. Besides the melodic changes, the singer also made changes in the text. In the first recording by Dr. Abrams he changes "Dictum" to "Dixie." In the second rendition he sang "Pere" for "Perri," "Mare" for "Merri," and "Domini" for "Domine." A Kentucky version given in MSHF 12 gives the refrain as "Piri-Miri-Dictum Domine." On this song see also BBM 99, paragraph 2.

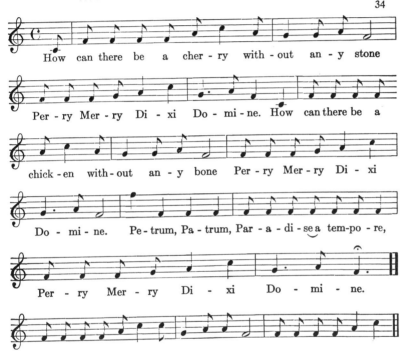

How can there be a cher - ry with - out an - y stone

Per - ry Mer - ry Di - xi Do - mi - ne. How can there be a

chick - en with - out an - y bone Per - ry Mer - ry Di - xi

Do - mi - ne. Pe - trum, Pa - trum, Par - a - di - se a tem-po - re,

Per - ry Mer - ry Di - xi Do - mi - ne.

For melodic relationship cf. **FSONE 268; BSO 25; MSHF 12; *SharpK 1 222 and 229, No. 31B and H, measures 1-2.

Scale: Tetratonic, (4,6,7), plagal. Tonal Center: f. Structure: ababcb (2,2, 2,2,2,2). It is noteworthy that our singer extends the structure by inserting a rather premature "Perry Merry Dixi Domine" (measures 7-8).

14
YOUNG BEICHAN
(Child 53)

E

'Susan Price.' Sung by Mrs. Nora Hicks and granddaughter, Addie Hicks. Recorded at Mast's Gap, Sugar Grove, August 28, 1940.

35

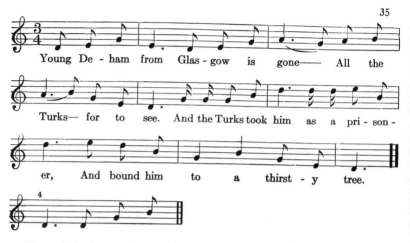

Young De - ham from Glas - gow is gone—— All the

Turks— for to see. And the Turks took him as a pri - son -

er, And bound him to a thirst - y tree.

4

For melodic relationship cf. *FSSH 55, No. 9A.

Scale: Mode III, plagal. Tonal Center: g. Structure: abcd (2,2,2,2). Both cadences are closely related. Measure 6 is merely a variation of measure 3. Circular Tune (V).

F

'Lord Batesman.' Sung by Mr. and Mrs. James York. Recorded at Olin, Iredell county, August 14, 1939. For textual variations cf. BB 30-1.

36

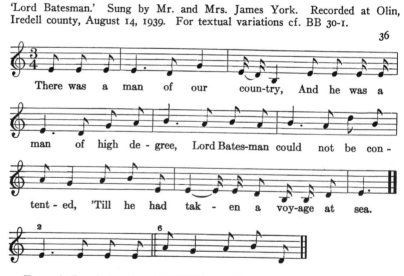

There was a man of our coun-try, And he was a

man of high de - gree, Lord Bates-man could not be con -

tent - ed, 'Till he had tak - en a voy-age at sea.

2   6

For melodic relationship cf. *SFSEA 215, No. 214.

Scale: Mode II, plagal. Tonal Center: e. Structure: aa¹a²a³ (2,2,2,2). The a³ is considerably varied.

16
SIR PATRICK SPENS
(Child 58)

'Sir Patrick Spence.' Sung by Miss Clara J. McCauley. Recorded by Professor E. C. Kirkland at Sewanee, Tenn., August 1937.

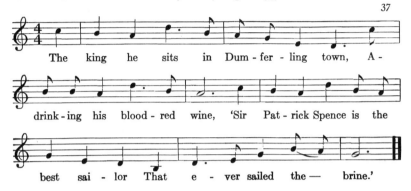

Scale: Hexachordal, plagal. Tonal Center: g. Structure: aa^1a^2b (2,2,2,2) = aa^1 (4,4). This is the second stanza.

17
CHILD WATERS
(Child 63)

Mrs. Sutton evidently contributed two versions of this song. There is, however, no recording of the version reported in II 65 "from the *singing* of Mrs. Rebecca Gordon." The other version, evidently rather salacious, Mrs. Sutton collected from an old woman who lived once near the falls of Gregg's Prong of Wilson's Crest, but felt it was unsuitable for publication. It is unfortunate that we have no tune available for either version.

18
YOUNG HUNTING
(Child 68)

'Lord Bonnie.' Sung by James York. Recorded at Olin, Iredell county in 1939.

round   his— neck And his   sword— by   his—   side.

For melodic relationship cf. *SharpK 1 107, No. 18F, measures 1-2 and 5-6; ASb 64, measure 6 with measure 5 in this version; FSoA 60, measure 1.

Scale: Mode III, plagal. Tonal Center: f. Structure: abac (2,2,2,2) = aa¹ (4,4).

18(1)

'Young Hunting.' Sung by Mrs. J. Trivette. Recorded at Heaton, Avery county, August 10, 1939. Another title given by the singer is 'Oh Henery.' In BT 152 and in BBM 122 our stanza is the ninth.

39

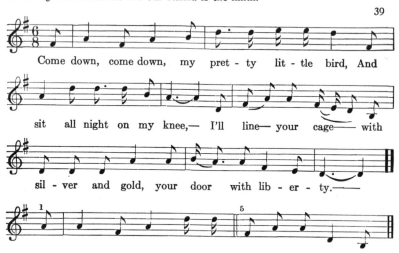

Come down, come down, my pret - ty lit - tle bird, And

sit all night on my knee,— I'll line— your cage—— with

sil - ver and gold, your door with lib - er - ty.——

For melodic relationship cf. **SharpK 1 112, No. 18J, measures 4-8; *OFS 1 90, No. 14, measures 4-5 and very end.
Scale: Mode III, plagal. Tonal Center: d. Structure: abcd (2,2,2,2).

19
LORD THOMAS AND FAIR ANNET
(Child 73)

A

'Lord Thomas and Fair Annet.' Sung by anonymous singer. Secured in Rockingham county, Virginia, 1898-99. Cf. note, II 69.

40

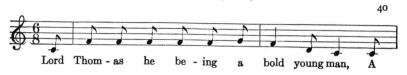

Lord Thom - as he be - ing a bold young man, A

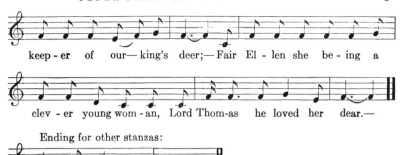

keep - er of our— king's deer;— Fair El - len she be - ing a

clev - er young wom - an, Lord Thom-as he loved her dear.—

Ending for other stanzas:

For melodic relationship cf. *SharpK 1 115, No. 19A, measures 1-2, especially measure 2. The identical progressions of the latter occur in the same measure of 8 versions in Sharp's volume, but in only 3 of our Collection. ASb 156, measures 1-4.

Scale: Irrational, plagal. Tonal Center: f. Structure: abab^1 (2,2,2,2) = aa^1 (4,4).

A(1)

'Lord Thomas and Fair Annet.' Sung by Mrs. Nora Hicks. Recorded at Mast's Gap, Watauga county, August 28, 1940. Also entitled 'Lord Thomas and Fair Ellinger.' With one minor exception measures 1, 3, and 4 are identical with those of the Miller, Greer, Cooke, and Brown versions. In the Greer version even measure 5 is identical melodically.

41

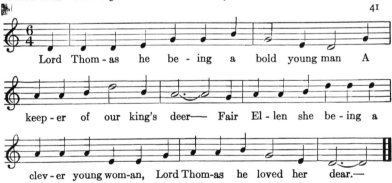

Lord Thom - as he be - ing a bold young man A

keep - er of our king's deer— Fair El - len she be - ing a

clev - er young wom-an, Lord Thom-as he loved her dear.—

For melodic relationship cf. *SharpK 1 115, No. 19A, measures 1-4; TBV 570, No. 18R; FSoA 108, measure 1.

Scale: Mode III, plagal. Tonal Center: g. Structure :aa^{1}a^{2}a^3 (2,2,2,2) = aa^1 (4,4). Circular Tune (V).

This song shows an interesting use of the melodic material. Measures 3-4 are a contraction of 1-2. The second half of the first measure is omitted in the third, but this resulting deficiency is made up by lengthening the values in the fourth. The following two measures (5-6) basically represent a varied repetition of the two preceding them, well exemplifying the general tendency towards balance and also characteristic of musical expression. This is here accomplished by compensating for any upward movement with one in the opposite direction and vice versa. This can be observed up to the end of the song. The limited tonal material certainly has been used to the best advantage. This is particularly noteworthy when it is realized that these creations are not the product of a highly trained musical imagination.

D

'Lord Thomas.' Sung by Miss Ida Wilson. Secured by Thomas Smith of Zionville, Watauga county, in or before 1914. A note on the MS score, however, mentions Sam Flannery as having also contributed the text and tune.

42

Scale: Hexatonic (4), plagal. Tonal Center: d. Structure aba¹b¹ (5,3,4,4). This shows a rather unusual structure, which nevertheless comes about in quite a normal way. Both the cadences of the first and second phrases were shortened to the extent of one measure. Another possibility would be to assume that the first phrase was internally incremented. But this would still demand another measure at the end of the second phrase. This second manner of analysis has one factor to recommend it; e.g., the first phrase would thereby take on the form of the third and the smooth progression into the second phrase would be very much like that from the third to the fourth.

E

'Lord Thomas and Fair Ellender.' Sung by D. E. Holder. Procured by D. W. Fletcher of Durham, RFD 4.

This is the melody to 'Lord Thomas and Fair Annet' mentioned together with 'Barbara Allen' as having probably been sent in by Dr. I. G. Greer. The assumption of the editor, as expressed in II 131, to the effect that one tune had to do double duty for both texts, is not borne out by the facts. There are actually two separate and distinct melodies, one for each song. Perhaps the fact that both melodies were written on a single small sheet of manuscript paper was responsible for this deduction.

43

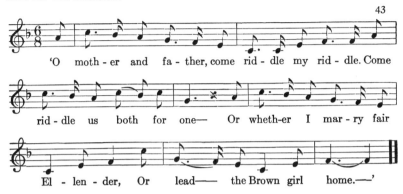

'O moth - er and fa - ther, come rid - dle my rid - dle. Come
rid - dle us both for one— Or wheth-er I mar - ry fair
El - len - der, Or lead—— the Brown girl home.——'

Scale: Irrational, plagal. Tonal Center: f. Structure: aba¹b¹ (2,2,2,2) = aa¹ (4,4). Interesting here again is the use of the melodic material. The second half of measure 1 plus the first half of measure 2 serve to furnish the last two measures. Naturally, we find again the rhythmic shift.

E(I)

'Lord Thomas and Fair Ellender.' Sung by Mrs. Myra Barnett Miller. Recorded probably at Lenoir in August of 1939, 1940, or 1941. Another title is 'Brown Girl.' The first four measures are identical with those of the Greer and Cooke versions. The close relationship with the Brown version is pointed out also in the latter. There is also some melodic relationship with the Hicks version. Measures 1-4 of this version are also related to those of 'The Seven Sisters' by Mrs. James York, and 'Pretty Cold Rain' by Miss Hattie McNeill.

44

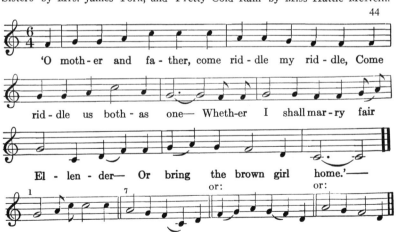

'O moth - er and fa - ther, come rid - dle my rid - dle, Come
rid - dle us both - as one— Wheth-er I shall mar - ry fair
El - len - der— Or bring the brown girl home.'——
                                    or: or:

For melodic relationship cf. **SharpK 1 119-20, No. 19F and H; BSM 45, as well as TBV 570, No. 18R, and OFS 1 94, No. 15A. Likewise FSF 268, No. 157B, and BSSM 37, No. 4.

Scale: Mode III, plagal. Tonal Center: f. Structure: aa¹bb¹ (2,2,2,2) = ab (4,4). The identical approach to both cadences should be mentioned. Circular Tune (V).

G

'Lord Thomas and Fair Eleanor.' Sung by I. G. Greer. Recorded probably in 1915. Sung again for the present editor at Chapel Hill in 1952. The first four measures are practically identical with those of the Miller version. Considerable similarity with 'The Seven Sisters' by Mrs. James York and 'Pretty Cold Rain' by Hattie McNeill.

45

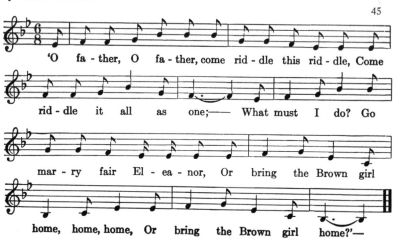

'O fa - ther, O fa - ther, come rid - dle this rid - dle, Come rid - dle it all as one;— What must I do? Go mar - ry fair El - ea - nor, Or bring the Brown girl home, home, home, Or bring the Brown girl home?'—

For melodic relationship cf. **SharpK 1 119-20, No. 19 F and H; BSM 45; TBV 570, No. 18R; FSF 268, No. 157B; BSSM 37, No. 4.

Scale: Mode III, plagal. Tonal Center: e-flat. Structure: aa¹abb¹ (2,2,2,2,2) = ab (4,6). The second phrase is terminally incremented. Circular Tune (V).

H

'Lord Thomas.' Sung by Miss Fannie Grogan. Recorded at Silverstone, Watauga county, 1919.

46

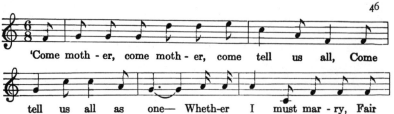

'Come moth - er, come moth - er, come tell us all, Come tell us all as one— Wheth-er I must mar - ry, Fair

El - 'nor dear, Or bring the Brown girl home?'—

Scale: Hexatonic (4), plagal. Tonal Center: f. Structure: abcd (2,2,2,2).
Circular tune (V).

I

'Lord Thomas.' Sung by Mrs. Alice Cooke. Recorded at Boone, Watauga county, in 1922. This is a compound of parts of two versions: a variation of the first two lines of stanza 1, version E and a variation of the third stanza of version M. No doubt the original version was in quatrains. The original eight measures, whichever they were, followed this pattern. When the textual corruption took place, enlarging the stanza to six lines, the tune had to be lengthened also. It is easy to see that the first eight measures constitute what we usually consider a normal tune, even if, as in this case, it is a circular tune; and that by omitting measures 7-10 we should have a perfect cadence. But the tune as given here is adapted to the change of text. It should be noted that the first four measures of this version are almost identical with those of the Miller version.

47

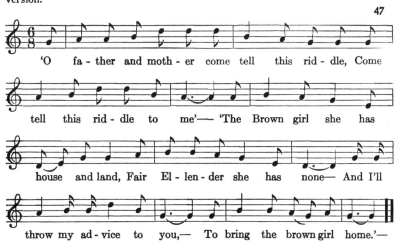

'O fa - ther and moth - er come tell this rid - dle, Come

tell this rid - dle to me'— 'The Brown girl she has

house and land, Fair El - len - der she has none— And I'll

throw my ad - vice to you,— To bring the brown girl home.'—

For melodic relationship cf. **BSM 45; TBV 570, No. 18R; FSF 268, No. 157B; and BSSM 37, No. 4.

Scale: Mode III, plagal. Tonal Center: g. Structure: aa^{1}bb^{1}a^{2}c (2,2,2,2,2,2) = abc (4,4,4); the c is partially related to a; and b, although considerably altered, is derived from measures 2-3 of a.

J

'The Brown Girl.' Sung by Mrs. Brown. Contributed by Mrs. Sutton at Beech Mountain, Watauga county, no date. (One catalogue gives 1921-25.)

Excepting the slightly varied measures 5-6, this tune is identical with that of the Miller version. Measures 1-4 are practically the same as those in the Cooke version.

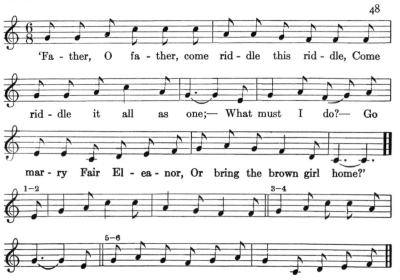

'Fa - ther, O   fa - ther, come   rid - dle   this   rid - dle, Come

rid - dle   it   all   as   one;— What must   I   do?—   Go

mar - ry   Fair   El - ea - nor, Or   bring the brown girl   home?'

For melodic relationship cf. **BSM 45; TBV 570, No. 18R; FSF 268, No. 157B; and BSSM 37, No. 4.

Scale: Hexachordal.   Tonal Center: c.   Structure: aa^1bb^1 (2,2,2,2) = ab (4,4).

K

'Lord Thomas and Fair Ellinor.'   Sung by C. K. Tillett.   Recorded on Roanoke Island, December 29, 1922.

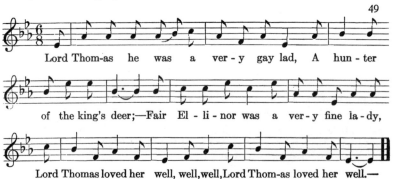

Lord Thom-as   he   was   a   ver - y   gay lad,   A   hun - ter

of the king's deer;—Fair   El - li - nor was   a   ver - y fine la - dy,

Lord Thomas loved her   well, well,well,Lord Thom-as loved her   well.—

For melodic relationship cf. **SharpK 1 115, No. 19A.   The basic melodic tendency is closely related.

Scale: Mode III, plagal. Tonal Center: a-flat. Structure: abcdd[1] (2,2,2,2,2).
The second phrase b is terminally incremented. Circular Tune (V).

M

'Lord Thomas and Fair Eleanor.' Sung by anonymous female singer. Contributed by Mrs. R. D. Blacknall of Durham: catalogue gives 1921? This version is melodically related to that of Horton Barker. These two songs share in a melodic idiom (measure 2) which in songs of the same name occurs likewise in only two versions. The idiom is known by the popular term 'Scotch snap' otherwise known as *alla lombardo*. The two songs in the Sharp collection can be found in SharpK 1 121-25, Nos. 19 J and Q. Our tune has in common with the Miller version, E1, another melodic peculiarity, a downward skip of a sixth. While this skip is found in only two of our versions, in Sharp's collection it occurs quite frequently, although in different measures. Cf. SharpK 1 115-31, Nos. 19 A, C, D, F, G, I, J, S, and Ee.

50

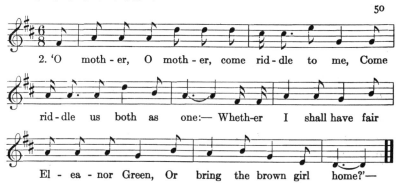

2. 'O moth - er, O moth - er, come rid - dle to me, Come

rid - dle us both as one:— Wheth-er I shall have fair

El - ea - nor Green, Or bring the brown girl home?'—

For melodic relationship cf. **SharpK 1 125, No. 19P, measures 3-4 and 7-8, and No. 19H, measures 1 and 3-4; Also TBV 569, No. 18 (D) II. *BSSM 37, No. 4.

Scale: Heptachordal. Tonal Center: d. Structure: aa[1]bc (2,2,2,2) = ab (4,4).
Possibly mm[1]n (2,2,4) = barform.

M(1)

'Lord Thomas and Fair Eleanor.' Sung by Mrs. J. J. Miller. Recorded at Silverstone, Watauga county, no date.

51

Lord Thom-as, Lord Thom-as, he was a brave man, He

count-ed the King's high dame— She had but one own

fair   daugh - ter,   Fair   El - ean - or   was   her   name.—

For melodic relationship cf. **SharpK 1 127, No. 19V; the main points in the melodic tendency coincide.

Scale: Hexachordal, plagal.   Tonal Center: a.   Structure: aa¹bc (2,2,2,2) = ab (4,4).   Perhaps also mm¹n (2,2,4) = barform.   Circular Tune (V).

O

'Lord Thomas and Fair Annet.'   Sung by Horton Barker.   From record made by Dr. W. A. Abrams at Boone, September 14, 1941.   At his home in Chilhowie, Virginia, Barker sang the same version for the present editor in the summer of 1952.

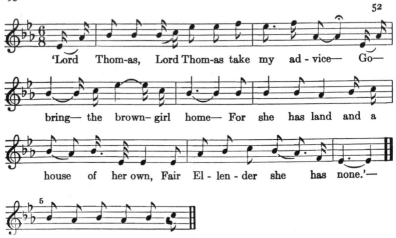

'Lord   Thom-as,   Lord Thom-as take   my   ad - vice—   Go—

bring— the   brown- girl   home— For   she   has   land   and   a

house   of   her own,   Fair   El - len - der   she   has   none.'—

For melodic relationship cf. **SharpK 1 127, No. 19U.   Coincidence of the basic melodic line.   *TBV 569, No. 18 (D) II.

Scale: Mode III, plagal.   Tonal Center: a-flat.   Structure: aa¹bc (2,2,2,2) = ab (4,4).   Circular Tune (V).

P

'Lord Thomas and Fair Annet.'   Sung by Mrs. Rebecca (Aunt Becky) Gordon. Recorded at Asheville, July 19, 1939.   Mrs. Gordon learned her songs from her mother, who was born and reared near Tuxedo, Henderson county.   Another title given is 'O, Lily O.'   There is no first stanza on the recording; the text of the remainder can only partially be understood.   Textually, the form reminds one of version K, particularly in the repetition of the penultimate line.

For melodic relationship cf. *SharpK 1 115, No. 19A, measures 1-2 and 5. In the latter, the daring ascending skip of a sixth leading into the upper octave is, in our version, more cautiously undertaken: first a fourth, then a third, and again a third.

Scale: Mode III, plagal. Tonal Center: e-flat. Structure: abcdd^1 (2,2,2,2,2); the second phrase is terminally incremented.

    3   And .... a sharp knife
        That'd just lately ....
        He .... it through ... heart.
        And the blood came tinkling, tinkling down.
        And the blood came tinkling, tinkling down.

    4   Lord Thomas, Lord Thomas, don't you see
        And don't you ....
        ....
        Your heart's blood came tinkling down,
        Your heart's blood came tinkling down.

    5   Go dig my grave both deep and wide
        And paint my coffin black,
        ....

Q

'Lord Thomas and Fair Eleanor.' Sung by Mrs. Ephraim Stamey. Recorded at Altamont, Avery county, July 14, 1940.
    The stanza is closely related to the fourth stanza of our version M.

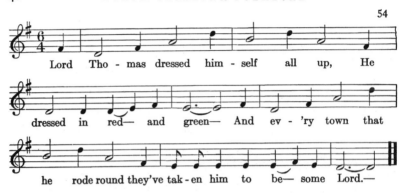

Lord Tho - mas dressed him - self all up, He
dressed in red— and green— And ev - 'ry town that
he rode round they've tak - en him to be— some Lord.—

For melodic relationship cf. *SharpK 1 124, No. 19M, measures 3-4.
Scale: Mode III. Tonal Center: d. Structure: abab¹ (2,2,2,2) = aa¹ (4,4).

20

Fair Margaret and Sweet William
(Child 74)

A

'Lady Margaret.' Sung by Mrs. Nora Hicks. Recorded at Mast's Gap, Sugar
Grove, Watauga county, August 28, 1940. The first stanza was not recorded.

2. 'It's I know noth-ing of La - dy Mar - g'ret, La - dy
Mar - g'ret knows noth-ing of me. And to - mor - row
morn-ing at eight o' clock A— new bride she shall see.'

5-6 (later)

For melodic relationship cf. **SCSM 390; *SharpK 1 140, No. 20H, only, however, in its most basic melodic points.

Scale: Mode III, plagal. Tonal Center: g. Structure aa^1bc (3,3,2,2) = ab (5, 5); possibly also mm^1n (3,3,4) = barform. Circular Tune (V).

C

'Sweet Willie.' Sung by Mrs. Brown. Procured by Mrs. Sutton at Beech Mountain, Watauga county. No date.

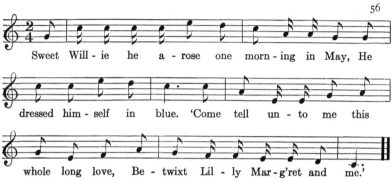

For melodic relationship cf. **SharpK 1 139, No. 20E; *BBM 134.

Scale: Hexachordal. Tonal Center: c. Structure: mm^1n (2,2,4) = barform.

D

'Sweet Willie.' Procured by Mrs. Maude M. Sutton. Singer, date, and place not given.

The MS score No. 2 gives the same text as that of the C version. The text used here, however, was taken from the recording of Mrs. Sutton's second version as found on cylinder 9-X. The tune is almost identical with that of her first version.

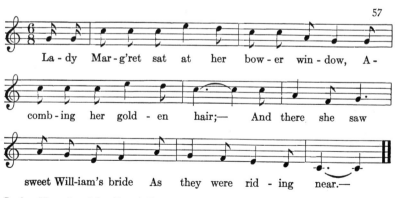

Scale: Hexachordal. Tonal Center: c. Structure: mm^1n (2,2,4) = barform.

H

'Fair Margaret and Sweet William.'   Sung by Mrs. L. H. Palmer.   Recorded at
Senia, Avery county, August 26, 1939.
    Another title given is 'Margaret and William.'   The text is similar to the
20B version, stanza 4.

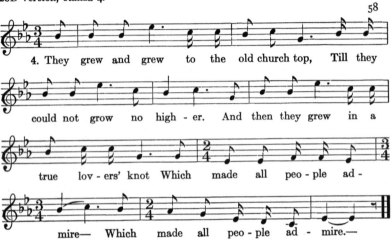

4. They grew and grew   to   the   old church top,   Till they
could not grow   no   high - er.   And then they grew   in   a
true   lov - ers' knot Which   made   all   peo - ple   ad -
mire— Which   made   all   peo - ple   ad - mire.—

    For melodic relationship cf. **TBV 572, No. 19K.

    Scale: Heptachordal, plagal.   Tonal Center: e-flat.   Structure: aa¹a²bc (2,2,2,
2,2) ; c is rhythmically related to b.

I

'Fair Margaret and Sweet William.'   Sung by Mrs. James York.   From the
record of Dr. W. A. Abrams at Boone, September 14, 1941.   Another title given
is 'Lady Margaret and Sweet William.'

Sweet   Will - iam   a - rose   one   morn - ing— bright And
dressed him - self   in   blue.   'Come tell   to   me   of   a
long   lost— love Be - tween La - dy Mar - g'ret and   me.'

    For melodic relationship cf. **BSO 34, No. 12A; FSS 523, No. 11C; TBV
572, No. 19K.

Scale: Hexatonic (4), plagal (Mode III). Tonal Center: f. Structure: abcd (2,2,2,2). Circular Tune (V).

21

LORD LOVEL

B

'Lord Lovel and Lady Nancy.' Sung by Miss Madge Nichols. Recorded at Trinity College, Durham, in the early 1920's.

The first four measures could well pass as variation of Mrs. James York's 'Fair Margaret and Sweet William' (20I) as well as her 'The Seven Sisters' (2B 1). Our text resembles the third stanza of the C version.

60

'When will you come back, Lord Lov - el?' said she, 'When

will you come back?' said she. 'In a year or two, or

three' said he, 'I'll re - turn to my la - dy Nan -

cy, cy, cy, I'll re - turn to my la - dy Nan - cy.'

For melodic relationship cf. **OFS 1 112, No. 16C; our measures 6-7 with FSRA 27, No. 11, measures 2-3.

Scale: Mode III, plagal. Tonal Center: f. Structure: aa1bcc1 (2,2,2,2,2) = ab (4,6); b is terminally incremented.

C

'Lord Lovel.' Sung by Mrs. Myra Barnett Miller. Recorded probably at Lenoir, August 1939, 1940, or 1941. This tune reminds one very much of some Bavarian or Alpine peasant dance.

61

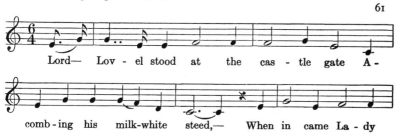

Lord— Lov - el stood at the cas - tle gate A -

comb - ing his milk-white steed,— When in came La - dy

Nan - cy Bell   A - wish - ing   her   lov - er   good   speed.—

Scale: Pentachordal.   Tonal Center: c.   Structure: aba¹b (2,2,2,2) = aa¹ (4,4).

c(1)

'Lord Lovel.'   Sung by Mrs. G. L. Bostic.   Recorded at Boiling Springs, P. O.
Mooresboro, Cleveland county, August 7, 1939.   Another title is 'Lord Lover.'

62

Lord   Lov - el   stood   at   the   cas - tle   gate   A -

comb - ing   his   milk - white   steed,   When   in—   came   La - dy

Nan   -   cy   Bell   A - wish - ing   her   lov - er   good

speed,—   A - wish - ing   her   lov - er   good   speed.—

Scale: Hexatonic (4).   Tonal Center: c.   Structure: aa¹abb (2,2,2,2,2) = aa¹
(4,6).

F

'Lord Lovel.'   Sung by Otis Kuykendall.   Recorded at Asheville in 1939.   This
melody is a fine example to show what can be done with a minimum of invest-
ment.

63

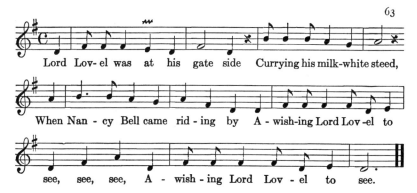

Lord Lov-el was at his gate side Currying his milk-white steed,

When Nan - cy Bell came rid - ing by A - wish-ing Lord Lov -el to

see, see, see, A - wish - ing Lord Lov - el to see.

For melodic relationship cf. **SharpK 1 146, No. 21A, general melodic trend; FSF 273, No. 158A, measures 3-4.

Scale: Hexachordal. Tonal Center: d. Structure: aa^{1}a^{2}bb^1 (2,2,2,2,2).

H

'Lord Lovel.' Sung by anonymous singer. Recorded in August 1939, 1940, or 1941. No place given. Melodically related to Mrs. James York's 'The Seven Sisters' 2B; also very similar to the Nichols version, 21B.

64

'When will you be back Lord Lov - el?' she said, 'when

will you be back?' said she— 'In a year or two or

three,' he said, 'I'll re - turn to my La - dy Nan - cy cy, cy,

I'll re - turn to my La - dy Nan - cy.'—

1-3

Scale: Mode III, plagal. Tonal Center: e-flat. Structure: aa^1bcc^1 (2,2,2,2,2) = mm^1n (2,2,6) = barform; the n is terminally incremented.

I

'Lord Lovel.' Sung by Mrs. Henry S. Hanford. Recorded at Chapel Hill. Set down by Professor J. H. Hanford, May 3, 1915.

65

For melodic relationship cf. ***BSO 41, No. 13D.
Scale: Heptachordal. Tonal Center: e-flat. Structure: $aa^1bb^1a^2$ (4,4,2,2,4).

J

'Lord Lovel.' Sung by Mrs. Nora Hicks. Recorded at Mast's Gap, Sugar Grove, Watauga county, in September 1940.

F. C. Brown says: "More like Earl Brand." Not much of the text can be understood owing to poor recording, but in the last stanza there is a distinct "Lord Lovel."

66

Come home my Lord, la - dy Mar - g'ret she said.

For melodic relationship cf. **SharpK 1 146, No. 21A, basic melodic tendency in first four measures; BT 108; SCB 122; WSSU 177, 3a; ASb 70; FSoA 124; *BSO 43, No. 13E, measures 1-2.

Scale: Mode III. Tonal Center: e-flat. Structure: abb¹c (2,2,2,2) = ab (4,4).

22

THE LASS OF ROCH ROYAL

(Child 76)

A

'The Storms Are on the Ocean.' Sung by Mrs. L. H. Palmer. Recorded at Senia, Powder Mill Creek, Avery county, August 26, 1939. The singer gave the title as 'Lass of Rock Royal.' The melodic variations are taken from a second recording (XIV A¹-4), the textual variations will be found below. For others cf. BB 44-5.

67

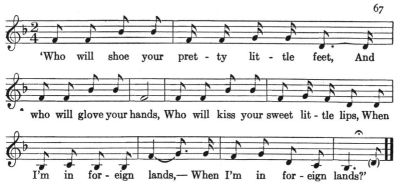

'Who will shoe your pret - ty lit - tle feet, And who will glove your hands, Who will kiss your sweet lit - tle lips, When I'm in for - eign lands,— When I'm in for - eign lands?'

Scale: Mode III. Tonal Center: b-flat. Structure: aa^{1}a^{2}bc (2,2,2,2,2) = ab (6,4). The second phrase is internally incremented.

3 My father will shoe my pretty little feet,
My mother will glove my hands,
And he will kiss my sweet little lips
When he comes from the foreign lands,
When he comes from the foreign lands.

23
Sweet William's Ghost
(Child 77)

'Sweet Willy.' MS score only; no name, no place, no date. The melody perfectly fits the text printed in II 93.

68

The dead man came to his true love's door And jin-gled at the ring. Loud he sobbed and— loud he—groaned, But she would not let him in.

Scale: Mode II, plagal. Tonal Center: c. Structure: aba^{1}b (2,2,2,2) = aa^1 (4,4).

25
The Wife of Usher's Well
(Child 79)

It was difficult to decide whether or not to include the following tunes, for some of them partially, others very closely, resemble one or more of the other versions. It seemed best, however, to print them as illustrating the fact that one of the main characteristics of folksong is the constant flux of a basic material. The close relationship of the majority of these tunes to 'Barbara Allen' is quite evident.

A

'The Three Little Babes.' Sung by Mrs. Ewart Wilson. Recorded at Pensacola in September 1929. The last five measures are almost identical with those of the Lloyd Church, N. Hicks, I. G. Greer (2nd), and Anonymous versions.

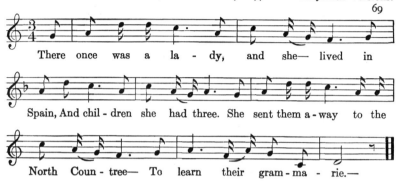

For melodic relationship cf. **FSKM 5; *SharpK 1 153, No. 22D. Considering only the basic idea, we find that the Sharp version, measures 4-6, seems to furnish our first phrase a and the former's measures 2-4 our second phrase. Scale: Mode II, plagal. Tonal Center: d. Structure: aa¹ab (2,2,2,2).

C

'The Three Little Babes.' Sung by Lloyd Church. From the recording of Dr. W. A. Abrams. No place or date given. There is considerable melodic relationship with Mrs. Hicks' version, 25J.

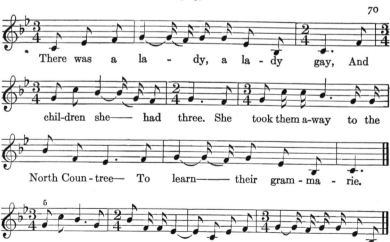

For melodic relationship cf. **SharpK 1 152, No. 22B, also beginning of F, J, K, M, and almost all of P; OFS 1 122, No. 19A; BT 155; FSKM 5, measures 5-8; BB 17, version E; BSO 46, No. 14; *FSoA 56 (the version printed there is quite impossible).

Scale: Mode II, plagal.   Tonal Center: c.   Structure; abb¹a¹ (2,2,2,2).

c (1)

'The Three Little Babes.' Sung by anonymous female singer; no place or date. Very closely related to 25J and 25 E(1).

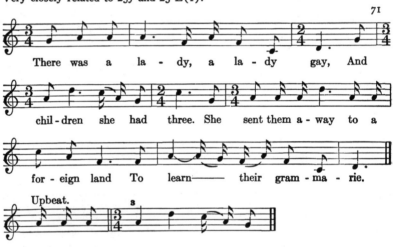

For melodic relationship cf. **SharpK 1 151-9. Nos. 22 B, F, G, and P, and most of the basic melodic line also in I, K, M, N. Similarly in BB 17, version E and BT 155; FSF 280; FSKM 5; *OFS 1 122, No. 19A.

Scale: Mode II, plagal.   Tonal Center: d.   Structure: abb¹a¹ (2,2,2,2).

(D)

'The Three Little Babes.' Sung by Thomas Smith; no place or date. The basic melodic tendency is closely related to the Greer version (first version, cylinder 6-VII), 25E.

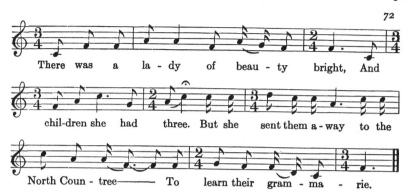

There was a la-dy of beau-ty bright, And chil-dren she had three. But she sent them a-way to the North Coun-tree—— To learn their gram-ma - rie.

Scale: Mode III, plagal. Tonal Center: f. Structure: abcd (2,2,2,2).

E

'The Wife of Usher's Well.' Recorded as MS score from I. G. Greer of Boone, Watauga county, 1915 or 1916. Basically, this version is related to the Smith version, 25D. For variants of text cf. BB, 50-1.

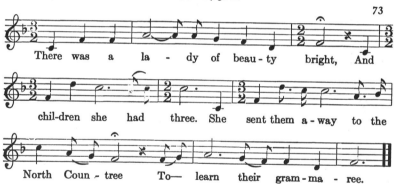

There was a la - dy of beau-ty bright, And chil-dren she had three. She sent them a-way to the North Coun - tree To— learn their gram-ma - ree.

For melodic relationship cf. *SharpK I 160, No. 22Q, first and second cadences and measures 6-7.

Scale: Hexachordal, plagal. Tonal Center: f. Structure: abb¹a¹ (2,2,2,2).

E(1)

'Three Little Babes' or 'Lady Gay.' Sung by Dr. I. G. Greer. Likewise recorded as MS score at Boone, Watauga county, 1915 or 1916. The singer stated that the same tune goes for this version as for the first. Melodically speaking, there are only negligible deviations in the second recording. The metrical distribution, however, differs in the basic values.

74

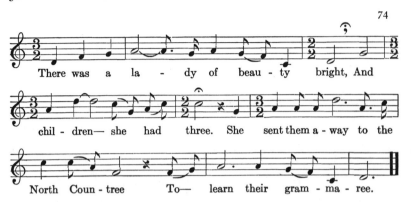

There was a la - dy of beau - ty bright, And

chil - dren— she had three. She sent them a - way to the

North Coun - tree To— learn their gram - ma - ree.

For melodic relationship cf. **SharpK I 151-9, No. 22 B, F, I, K, M, N, and some measures of P. Our first three measures are like those of version G. Others are BT 155, and FSKM 5.

Scale: Mode II, plagal. Tonal Center: d. Structure: abb¹a¹ (2,2,2,2).

J

'The Three Little Babes.' Sung by Mrs. Nora Hicks. Recorded at Mast's Gap, Watauga county. No date. The singer is the mother of Mrs. Calvin Hicks and the daughter of Aunt Becky Hicks, who lived back of Willowdale Church near Sugar Grove. This song resembles very closely the Lloyd Church version (25C) as well as Greer's second version (25E(1)). The text is the same as for the latter.

75

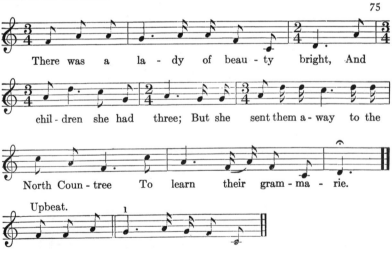

There was a la - dy of beau - ty bright, And

chil - dren she had three; But she sent them a - way to the

North Coun - tree To learn their gram - ma - rie.

Upbeat.   1

For melodic relationship cf. **SharpK I 151, No. 22B; OFS I 122, No. 19A; BT 155; FSKM 5; *BSO 46, No. 14.

Scale: Mode II, plagal. Tonal Center: d. Structure: abb¹a¹ (2,2,2,2).

26
LITTLE MUSGRAVE AND LADY BARNARD
(Child 81)

A

'Lord Daniel's Wife.' MS score written by Thomas Smith of Zionville, Watauga county, from the singing of Bennett Smith. Besides other similarities, the first three measures are practically identical with those of the Walker version, 26B.

76

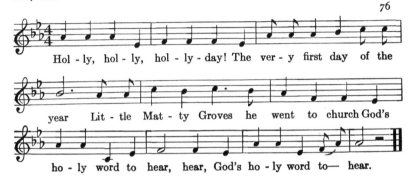

Hol - ly, hol - ly, hol - ly - day! The ver - y first day of the

year Lit - tle Mat - ty Groves he went to church God's

ho - ly word to hear, hear, God's ho - ly word to— hear.

For melodic relationship cf. **SharpK 1 161-82. Although our tune is in ¼ time, it is, in its basic melodic outline closely related to versions No. 23 L and N. Measure 8 of our version is identical with the same of versions A, C, E, G, I, and O.

Scale: Mode III, plagal. Tonal Center: a-flat. Structure: abcdd¹ (2,2,2,2,2).

B

'Little Mathey Grones.' MS score from Miss Edith Walker, of Boone, Watauga county. No date.

The first three measures, as mentioned above, are almost identical with those of 26A. The first two measures are identical with the well known song 'Old MacDonald Had a Farm,' and measures 3-4 and 7-8 remind one very much of 'Yankee Doodle.' For textual variants cf. BB 52-3.

77

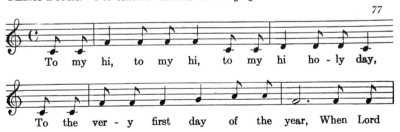

To my hi, to my hi, to my hi ho - ly day,

To the ver - y first day of the year, When Lord

Ar - nold went down to King Hen - ry's The Ho - ly Word for to

hear, hear, The Ho - ly Word for to hear.

For melodic relationship cf. **SharpK 1 181, No. 23 L, N, measures 1-3; OFS 1 126, No. 20C, the first four measures are rhythmically identical, melodic relationship is insignificant.

Scale: Mode III, plagal. Tonal Center: f. Structure: aba[1]bc(2,2,2,2,2) = aa[1]b (4,4,2).

B(1)

'Little Mathey Groves.' Sung by Mrs. James York. From previous recording of Dr. W. A. Abrams, Boone, August 8, 1940.

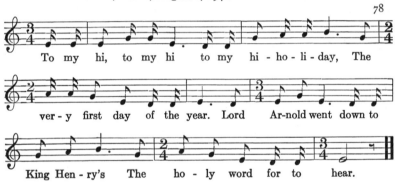

To my hi, to my hi to my hi - ho - li - day, The

ver - y first day of the year. Lord Ar-nold went down to

King Hen - ry's The ho - ly word for to hear.

For melodic relationship cf. **SharpK 1 168, No. 23E, measures 1-4, but only in a very basic way of melodic tendency.

Scale: Mode II, plagal. Tonal Center: e. Structure: abab (2,2,2,2) = ab (4,4).

C

'Lord Daniel' or 'Little Mathigrew.' MS score from I. G. Greer, of Boone, Watauga county, probably in 1913 or 1914.

It was on one day, it was on one day, The

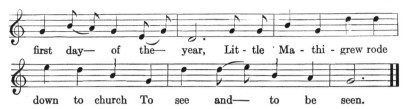

first day— of the— year, Lit - tle ˙ Ma - thi - grew rode

down to church To see and— to be seen.

For melodic relationship cf. *SharpK 1 182, No. 23O. Our first two measures might be called a variation of the same in the Sharp version.

Scale: Mode III, plagal. Tonal Center: g. Structure: aba¹c (2,2,2,2) = aa¹ (4,4).

F

'Lord Daniel's Wife.' Sung by Mrs. J. Church. Recorded at Heaton, Avery county, July 30, 1939.

80

2. First came down all dressed in red,— Next came down in green,

Next came down was Lord Dan - iel's wife, As fine as an - y a

queen, queen, As fine as an - y a queen.

For melodic relationship cf. **SharpK 1 164, No. 23C.

Scale: Pentachordal, plagal. Tonal Center: f. Structure: abcdd¹ (2,2,2,2,2).

G

'Little Musgrove and Lady Barnard.' Sung by Mrs. Nora Hicks. Recorded at Mast's Gap, Watauga county, in September 1940. Our stanza is the second.

81

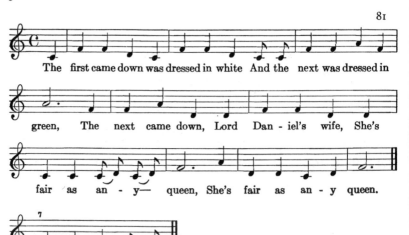

The   first came down was dressed in white And the   next was dressed in

green,   The   next   came down, Lord   Dan - iel's   wife,   She's

fair   as   an - y—   queen, She's   fair   as   an - y   queen.

For melodic relationship cf. **SharpK 1 168, No. 23 F and K, measures 1-4;
BSM 58; *SharpK 1 172, No. 23H, only the beginning; OFS 1 126, No. 20C;
and BBM 177.

Scale: Tetratonic (2,4), plagal. Tonal Center: f. Structure: abcdd¹ (2,2,2,2,2).

H

'Little Mathey Groves.' Sung by Mrs. Nancy Prather. Recorded at Milam,
Ashe county, August 5, 1939.

The recording is so poor that not all the words are recoverable. The text
is garbled, for the first two lines evidently belong to the first, the next two to
the second stanza (see below). The words with the tune correspond to stanza 3.

82

She passed by   and   he passed by And she cast her   eyes   on

him   say - ing, 'Come, come   a - long   lit - tle   Ma - thi - grove,

You   must   go   home with   me   for   to   lie.'

Scale: Mode III, plagal.   Tonal Center: e-flat.   Structure: abcd (2,2,2,2).
Measure 5 is derived from measure 2.

1   .... boy and the .... girl
    The very first day of the year.

2   The first came down was a kingly bride,
    And the other was a gaily girl.

27
BONNY BARBARA ALLAN
(Child 84)

To avoid unnecessary repetition it should be stated for almost all of
our eighteen versions of this song that there is a general coincidence of
the musical idiom connected with some parts of the text.   To quote but
two instances: "There was a fair maid dwelling," and "Every man cried,
'Well away.'"   What the imagination of a real singer can do with such
standard phrases to create a new tonal picture is remarkable, to say the
least.   There are some textual changes in the other stanzas.

A
'Barbara Allen.' Sung by anonymous singer.   Taken possibly from recordings
by Dr. W. A. Abrams in 1940.   The last six measures are quite closely related to
the Eggers (27A(1)) and the Pittman (27A(3)) versions.

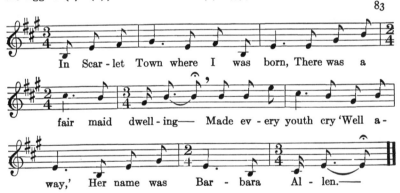

For melodic relationship cf. **SCB 132, version B; and FSSH 81, No. 15A.

Scale: Mode III, plagal.   Tonal Center: e.   Structure: abcd (2,2,2,2).

A(1)
'Barbara Allen.' Sung by H. Eggers.   Recorded at Boone, August 23, 1939.
The last six measures are quite closely related to those of the Anonymous (27S)
and the Pittman (27A(3)) versions.

84

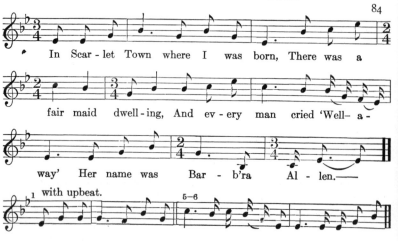

In Scar - let Town where I was born, There was a
fair maid dwell - ing, And ev - ery man cried 'Well- a -
way' Her name was Bar - b'ra Al - len.——

1 with upbeat. 5-6

For melodic relationship cf. **MSHF 6; Sharp K 1, 194-5, No. 24 M and P, basic melodic tendency of the very beginning.

Scale: Mode III, plagal. Tonal Center: e-flat. Structure: abb¹c (2,2,2,2) = ab (4,4).

A(2)

'Barbara Allen.' Sung by Mr. and Mrs. Nathan Hicks, with dulcimer. Recorded at Matney, Watauga county, July 28, 1939. This version makes use of the basic 'George Collins' tune.

85

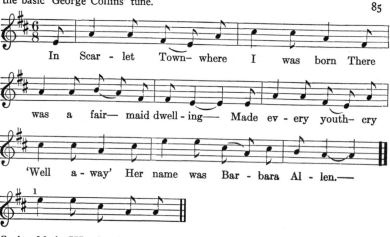

In Scar - let Town— where I was born There
was a fair— maid dwell - ing— Made ev - ery youth— cry
'Well a - way' Her name was Bar - bara Al - len.——

1

Scale: Mode III, plagal. Tonal Center: a. Structure: abac (2,2,2,2) = aa¹ (4,4).

A(3)

'Barbara Allen.' Sung by the Pittman brothers. Recorded at Handy, Davidson county, August 21, 1939. The last six measures are quite closely related to

those of the Eggers (27A(1)) and the Anon. (27S) versions. Text variants in
the other stanzas.

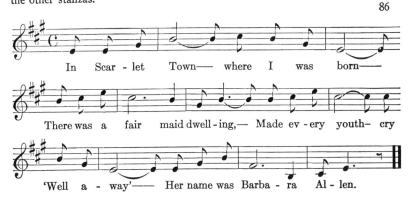

For melodic relationship cf. **SharpK 1 192 and 195, No. 24K, measures 3-6
and version O, measures 2-4, basic melodic relationship only; MSHF 6, beginning and ending.

Scale: Mode III, plagal. Tonal Center: e. Structure: abb¹c (2,2,2,2) = ab
(4,4).

A(4)

'Barbara Allen.' Sung by Mrs. Laura Timmons. From previous recording of
Dr. W. A. Abrams, Boone, August 8, 1940. Only the first three measures differ
from the Horton Barker version. These are given below as variations. There
is a partial relationship with 27O, 27S, 27S(1), 27V, 27FF, 27GG, 27HH,
27II.

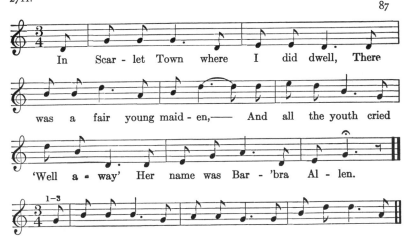

For melodic relationship cf. **SharpK 1 183, No. 24A and 194, No. 24L, measures 3-6; also, SFSEA 150, No. 131; SCSM 387, version C; FSoA 8; FSF 285, No. 161B.

Scale: Mode III, plagal. Tonal Center: g. Structure: abcd (2,2,2,2).

A(5)

'Barbara Allen.' Sung by Mrs. J. Trivette. Recorded at Heaton, Avery county, July 30, 1939. The melodic ending is like that of version 270.

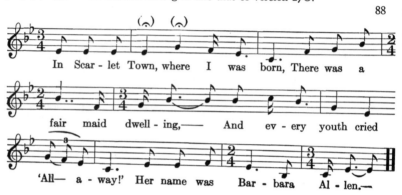

For melodic relationship cf. **SharpK 1 184, No. 27B, measures 1-4, also No. 27I, measures 2-5. Partial resemblance FSoA 8.

Scale: Mode III, plagal. Tonal Center: e-flat. Structure: abcd (2,2,2,2); measures 5-6 are derived from 1-2.

A(6)

'Barbara Allen.' Sung by James York. From the previous recording of Dr. W. A. Abrams at Boone, July 8, 1940. This tune, in parts, resembles the melody to 'Lord Ullin's Daughter,' No. 329 (music score 506) below.

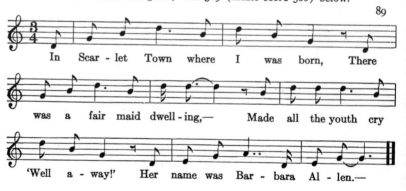

For melodic relationship cf. **SharpK 1 194, No. 27M, less in 192 J and K. Excepting the major versus the minor triad, the melodic trend in our version and that of Sharp is the same. FSF 285, No. 161B.

Scale: Mode III, plagal. Tonal Center: g. Structure: abb¹c (2,2,2,2) = ab (4,4).

B

'Barbara Allen.' Sung by Frank Proffitt. Recorded at Pick Britches, Sugar Grove, Watauga county, July 24, 1939. The skip of a descending diminished fifth (measure 15), revealing a more recent influence, is not to be found in any of the songs of this name contained in the Sharp collection.

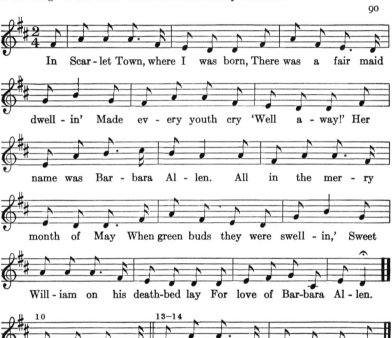

For melodic relationship cf. **FSF 287, No. 161C, first four and last two measures; *SharpK 1 194, No. 27L, measures 2 and 5. This latter version is the only occurrence of this type of progression in all the versions of this song found in the Sharp collection.

Scale: Heptachordal, plagal. Tonal Center: d. Structure: aba¹ca¹ba²d (2,2,2 2,2,2,2) = aa¹a²a³ (4,4,4,4).

E

'Barbara Allen.' Sung by Mrs. C. K. Tillett, at Wanchese, Roanoke Island, December 29, 1922.

91

In Scarborough town where I was born, There was a fair maid dwell-ing—

And ev - ery youth cried 'Well a-way,' Her name was Bar-bara Al - len.—

For melodic relationship cf. **SharpK 1 183, No. 24A and 185, No. 24C, ending; SOCH 23, 'Heavenly Dove.'

Scale: Mode III, plagal. Tonal Center: g. Structure: abcd (2,2,2,2).

G

'Barbara Allen.' Sung by Mrs. G. L. Bostic. Recorded at Mooresboro, Cleveland county, August 7, 1939.

92

One day, one day in the month of May, When the

green leaves were a - swell - ing, When John - nie Graves from

West Ten - nes - see Fell in love with Bar - bara Al - len.

1   6

For melodic relationship cf. **FSF 289, No. 161D (first five measures); SharpK 1 188, No. 24 E, F, G, and H (first four measures); also SCSM 387, version F. Although rhythmically totally different, there is a surprising similarity in the purely melodic line. This is also true of BB 54, version B; BSM 63, version K; BSI 106, version D; TBV 578, version 24U, 580 versions 24 HH, II, and JJ; also FSS 523, No. 16F; FSKM 40, the very beginning; BSO 52, No. 16A, interesting comparison.

Scale: Mode III, plagal. Tonal Center: a. Structure: aa1bc (2,2,2,2) = ab (4,4). Circular Tune (V).

O

'Barbara Allen.' Sung by Dr. I. G. Greer. Recorded as MS score from I. G.

Greer of Boone, Watauga county. No date given. The text was given to the present editor by Dr. Greer in 1953. Basic melodic points in common with other versions are ingeniously employed to create a new version.

93

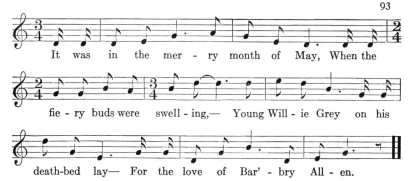

It was in the mer - ry month of May, When the fie - ry buds were swell - ing,— Young Will - ie Grey on his death-bed lay— For the love of Bar' - bry All - en.

For melodic relationship cf. **SharpK 1 183, No. 24A; TBV 579, No. 24DD, first three measures; *MSHF 6; SFSEA 150, No. 131.

Scale: Mode III, plagal. Tonal Center: g. Structure: abcd (2,2,2,2).

2 He sent his servant to the town
To tell her to come and see him.
And slowly, slowly she arose,
And slowly went to see him.

3 And when she got there, all she said,
'Young man, I think you're dying.
And die, oh die, oh die you may!
You can't get Barbara Allen.'

4 'I'm low, I'm low, I'm low indeed,
And death is in me dwelling.
But never better will I be
If I can't get Barbara Allen.'

5 'Don't you remember the other day
When we were at the tavern drinkin',
You drank a toast to the ladies all
And slighted Barbara Allen?'

6 'Yes, I remember the other day
When we were at the tavern drinkin';
I drank a toast to the ladies all
And three to Barbara Allen.'

7 'Do you remember the other night
When we were at the ballroom dancing,
You gave your hand to the ladies all
And slighted Barbara Allen?'

8 'Yes, I remember the other night
When we were at the ballroom dancing,
I gave my hand to the ladies all
And my heart to Barbara Allen.'

S

'Barbary Allen.' Sung by anonymous singer. Procured by Mrs. Sutton. No mention of singer, date, or place. In a second MS text, the second line reads "When all the flowers were blooming." Likewise "fur" instead of "for."

94

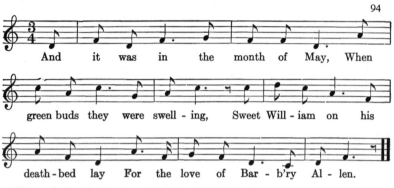

And   it   was   in   the   month   of   May,   When

green buds they   were   swell - ing,   Sweet Will - iam   on   his

death - bed   lay   For   the   love   of   Bar - b'ry   Al - len.

For melodic relationship cf. *FSoA 8; MSHF 6.

Scale: Mode III, plagal. Tonal Center: f. Structure: abcd (2,2,2,2); the third measure is derived from the first, and the seventh from the fifth.

S(I)

'Barbara Allen.' I. G. Greer? Dr. White attributes this to Mrs. Sutton. There is, in either case, no place or date given.

At the end of the section dealing with Barbara Allen, No. 27, in vol. II, 131 there is mention of a sheet "on which is written a tune set to the first stanza of 'Barbara Allen' and the stanza of 'Lord Thomas and Fair Annet' ...." There is such a sheet, but it contains two distinct melodies, one for 'Barbara Allen,' the other for 'Lord Thomas and Fair Annet.' Our version here is the first on that sheet. Both tunes are given with their texts.

95

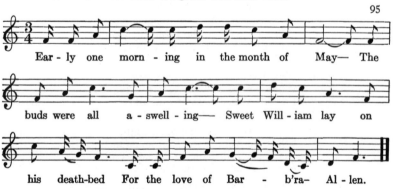

Ear - ly   one   morn - ing   in   the month of   May—   The

buds were   all   a - swell - ing—   Sweet Will - iam   lay   on

his   death-bed   For   the   love   of   Bar   -   b'ra-   Al - len.

For melodic relationship cf. **SharpK 1 183, No. 24A, measures 4-8, 185, No. 24C, measures 3-8; 191, No. 24I, measures 3-6; 195, No. 24N, general tendency, and No. 24P, beginning; FSoA 8; OFS 1 127, No. 21A; BSM 62, version G; FSF 285, No. 161B; and SFSEA 150, No. 131. *FSKM 40.

Scale: Mode III, plagal. Tonal Center: f. Structure: abcd (2,2,2,2).

V

'Barbara Allen.' Sung by Otis Kuykendall. Recorded at Asheville in 1939.

For melodic relationship cf. *SharpK 1 184, No. 24B, measures 2-8; SFSEA 150, No. 131. SCSM 387, version C. This is the only one of all other versions in which the fifth measure is entirely the same as that of our version.

Scale: Mode III, plagal. Tonal Center: f. Structure: abcd (2,2,2,2).

AA

'Barbara Allen.' Vol. II, 129 says, "The air accompanying this text. . . ." No record or score came to the present editor.

FF

'Barbara Allen.' Sung by H. J. Beaker. Recorded in August 1939, 1940, or 1941. No place given. There is partial but considerable similarity with 27GG and the Horton Barker versions. Cf. also 27A(1), 27A(4), as well as 27S(1).

97

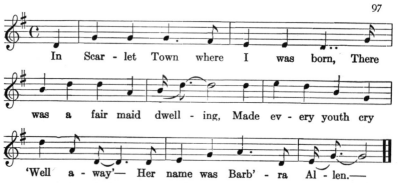

In Scar - let Town where I was born, There was a fair maid dwell - ing, Made ev - ery youth cry 'Well a - way'— Her name was Barb' - ra Al - len.—

For melodic relationship cf. **SCB 132, version B; BSM 62, version G; SharpK 1 191, No. 24I, and 195, N, measures 5-7 similar to our 3-5; TBV 577, No. 24G, similar beginning; SFSEA 150, No. 131; and MSHF 6.

Scale: Hexatonic (4), plagal. Tonal Center: g. Structure: abcd (2,2,2,2).

2 It was all in the month of June,
    All things there were bloomin'.
    Sweet William lay on his death bed
    For the love of Barb'ra Allen.

3 And death was painted on his face,
    O'er his heart was stealin'.
    Oh, hasten away to comfort him,
    O lovely Barb'ra Allen.

4 He sent his servant to the town
    Where Barb'ra was a dwellin'.
    'My Master's sick and sends for you,
    If your name be Barb'ra Allen.'

5 Slowly, slowly she got up,
    Slowly she came nigh him.
    And all she said when she got there,
    'Young man, I think you're dyin'.'

6 'Oh, I am sick, very sick,
    Death on me is stealin'.
    No better, no better I never can be
    If I can't have Barb'ra Allen.'

7 'Oh, yes you're sick, very sick,
    Death on you is stealin',
    No better, no better you never can be
    For you can't have Barb'ra Allen.'

8 'Oh, don't you remember in yonder town
    You were at the tavern,
    You drank a health to the ladies all around,
    But slighted Barb'ra Allen.'

9 As she was on her highway home,
The birds they kept a-singing'.
They sang so clear and seemed to say,
'Hard-hearted Barb'ra Allen.'

10 She looked to the east, she looked to the west
And spied his corpse a-comin'.
'Lay, lay down that corpse o' clay
That I may look upon him.'

11 'Oh, mother, oh, mother, go make my bed,
Make it long and narrow.
Sweet William died for pure, pure love,
And I shall die for sorrow.'

12 She was buried in the old church yard,
He was buried nigh her.
On William's grave there grew a red rose,
On Barb'ra's grew green briers.

13 The rose and the brier they grew so high
They could grow no higher.
They met and formed a true love-knot,
The rose wrapt around the brier.

GG

'Barbara Allen.' Sung by H. R. Buchanan. Recorded at Minneapolis, Avery county, September 7, 1939.

This tune is the basic melody underlying the lovely variation given in the following version by Becky Tarwater (27HH). There is likewise only little difference between this version and that of Wiseman (27II). There is only partial but considerable resemblance with 27FF, measures 3-5 and 7-8, and 27A(4).

98

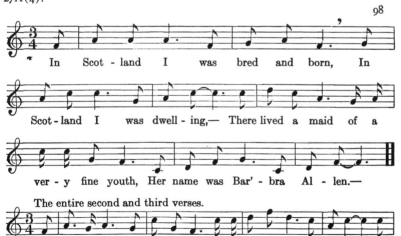

In Scot - land I was bred and born, In
Scot - land I was dwell - ing,— There lived a maid of a
ver - y fine youth, Her name was Bar' - bra Al - len.—

The entire second and third verses.

For melodic relationship cf. ***TAFL 820; FSF 285, No. 161B; **SCSM, 387, version C and 388, version H; FSoA 8; OFS 1 127, No. 21A; SCB 132, version B; BSM 62, version G; TBV 577, No. 24H; SFSEA 150, No. 131. SharpK 1 185, No. 27C, basic melodic line.

Scale: Mode III, plagal. Tonal Center: f. Structure: abcb¹ (2,2,2,2) = ab (4,4).

HH

'Barb'ry Allen.' Sung by Becky Tarwater. Recorded in August 1939, 1940, or 1941. No place given. This tune is a perfect example of the intuitive art of variation which the true folk singer has as his native endowment. Actually this version is only a variation of the Buchanan version (27GG), but what a difference that makes.

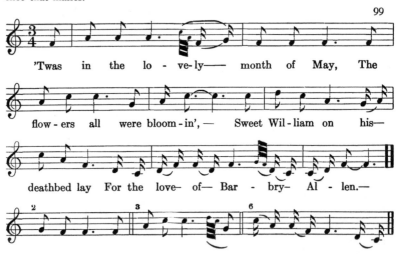

'Twas in the lo - ve- ly—— month of May, The

flow - ers all were bloom - in', — Sweet Wil - liam on his—

deathbed lay For the love— of— Bar - bry— Al - len.—

For melodic relationship cf. **SharpK 1 185, No. 27C for basic melodic outline; also SFSEA 150, No. 131.

Scale: Mode III, plagal. Tonal Center: f. Structure: abcb¹ (2,2,2,2) = ab (4,4).

> 2 He sent his servant to her door,
>   He sent him to her dwellin'.
>   'My master's sick and he calls for you
>   If your name be Barb'ry Allen.'

3 Then slower, slower got she up
Unto his bedside going.
My master's sick and he calls for you
If your name be Barb'ry Allen.

4 He turned his pale face to the wall
And bursted out a-cryin',
'Adieu, adieu to all beloved,
Adieu to Barb'ry Allen.'

5 Sweet William died on Saturday night
And Barb'ry died that Sunday.
Their parents died for the love of the two,
They was buried on a Easter Monday.

6 A white rose grew on William's grave,
A red rose grew on top of it,
They climbed and they climbed in a true lover's knot
A-warning young people to marry.

II

'Barbara Allen.' Sung by Mrs. Manassa Wiseman. Recorded at the foot of Buck Hill, September 1, 1939. Mrs. Wiseman was 79 years old. Only a slight variation of the 27GG and very similar to 27A(4).

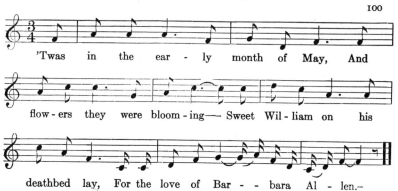

100

'Twas in the ear-ly month of May, And flow-ers they were bloom-ing— Sweet Wil-liam on his deathbed lay, For the love of Bar - - bara Al - len.—

For melodic relationship cf. ***SCSM 387-8., versions C and H; **FSF 284, No. 161A and 285, No.161B; FSoA 8; OFS 1 127, No. 21A; SCB 132, version B; BSM 62, version G; TBV 577, No. 24H and SFSEA 150, No. 131. Scale: Mode III, plagal. Tonal Center: f. Structure: abcd (2,2,2,2).

28

LADY ALICE

(Child 85)

B

'George Collins.' Sung by Frank Proffitt. Recorded at Sugar Grove, Watauga county, on July 24, 1939. There are two recordings, but only one slight textual variation. The singer sings "drove" instead of "rode." For the musical variations, see below.

101

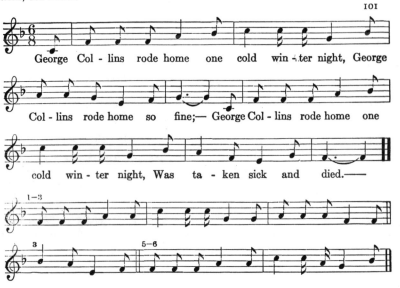

For melodic relationship cf. *TBV 582, No. 25E, measures 1 and 5.

Scale: Hexatonic (6), plagal. Tonal Center: f. Structure: abab¹ (2,2,2,2) = aa¹ (4,4).

B(1)

'George Collins.' Sung by Mr. and Mrs. Nathan Hicks, with dulcimer. Recorded at Matney, Watauga county, July 28, 1939. Quite similar to 28B.

102

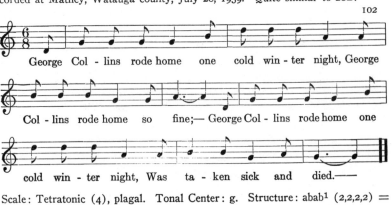

Scale: Tetratonic (4), plagal. Tonal Center: g. Structure: abab¹ (2,2,2,2) = aa¹ (4,4).

B(2)

'George Collins.' Sung by James York. From the previous recording by Dr. W. A. Abrams. No date nor place given. Measures 2 and 6 are the same as in 28E(1), 28E(2), and 28G.

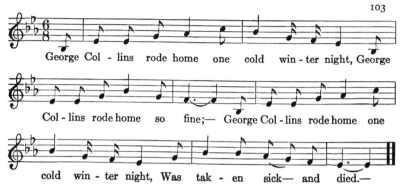

103

George Col - lins rode home one cold win - ter night, George Col - lins rode home so fine;— George Col - lins rode home one cold win - ter night, Was tak - en sick— and died.—

For melodic relationship cf. **SharpK 1 199, No. 25E; *FSF 292, No. 162B measure 2 only.

Scale: Hexachordal, plagal. Tonal Center: e-flat. Structure: abab[1] (2,2,2,2) = aa[1] (4,4).

D

'George Collins.' Sung by D. E. Holder. Recorded March 9, 1915, near Durham. There is also an anonymous version which differs only slightly from this tune (measures 2 and 6). These deviations are given below.

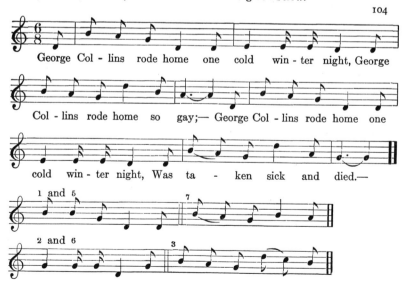

104

George Col - lins rode home one cold win - ter night, George Col - lins rode home so gay;— George Col - lins rode home one cold win - ter night, Was ta - ken sick and died.—

1 and 5   7

2 and 6   3

For melodic relationship cf. *SCSM 394, version B; FSRA 33, No. 14, measures 3-4.

Scale: Mode III, plagal. Tonal Center: g. Structure: abab¹ (2,2,2,2) = aa¹ (4,4).

E

'George Collins. Sung by Mrs. Sallie Eggers. Recorded at Zionville, Watauga county, before May 1, 1915. Of all our versions and all others with one exception (cf. melodic relationship) this tune alone has the melodic progression found in measures 2 and 6.

105

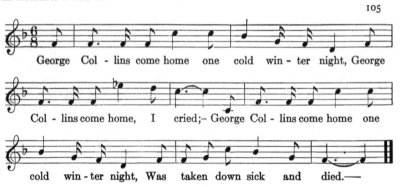

George Col - lins come home   one   cold   win - ter   night, George
Col - lins come home,   I   cried;– George Col - lins come home   one
cold   win - ter night, Was   taken down sick   and   died.—

For melodic relationship cf. *SharpK 1 198, No. 25D, measure 2; FSF 291, No. 162, measure 1.

Scale: Hexatonic (3), plagal. Tonal Center: f. Structure: abac (2,2,2,2) = aa¹ (4,4).

E(1)

'George Collins.' Sung by Mrs. J. Church. Recorded, but no date or place given. The basic melodic relationship to 28E(2) can readily be seen.

106

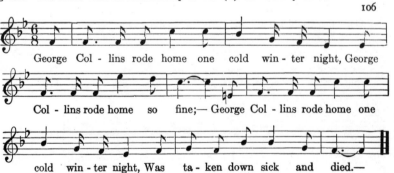

George Col - lins rode home   one   cold   win - ter   night, George
Col - lins rode home   so   fine;— George Col - lins rode home   one
cold   win - ter night, Was   ta - ken down sick   and   died.—

For melodic relationship cf. *SCSM 394, version E, measures 2 and 6; FSF 291, No. 162, measure 1; *ibid.* 292, No. 162B, measure 2.

Scale: Hexatonic (3), plagal. Tonal Center: f. Structure: abac (2,2,2,2) = aa¹ (4,4).

E(2)

'George Collins.' Sung by Mrs. Nora Hicks. Recorded, but no date or place given.

107

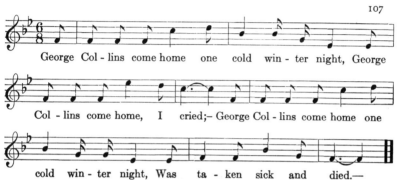

George Col - lins come home   one   cold   win - ter   night, George

Col - lins come home,   I   cried;– George Col - lins come home   one

cold   win - ter   night, Was   ta - ken   sick   and   died.—

For melodic relationship cf. *SharpK 1 199, No. 25E, measures 1-2; FSF 291, No. 162, measure 1; *ibid.* 292, No. 162, measure 2.

Scale: Hexatonic (3), plagal. Tonal Center: f. Structure: abac (2,2,2,2) = aa¹ (4,4).

G

'George Collins.' Sung by Miss Pearle Webb. Recorded at Pineola, Avery county, in 1939. There are greater (measures 1-2 and 5-6) similarities with 28E(2) and lesser (measures 2 and 6) with 28E(1) and 28B(2).

108

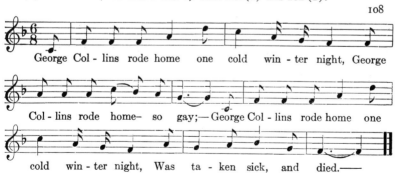

George Col - lins rode home   one   cold   win - ter   night, George

Col - lins rode home– so   gay;— George Col - lins rode home   one

cold   win - ter   night, Was   ta - ken   sick,   and   died.——

For melodic relationship cf. **SharpK 1 199, No. 25E, basic melodic outline only; *ibid.* 197, No. 25B, measure 6; FSF 292, No. 162B, measure 2.

Scale: Hexachordal, plagal. Tonal Center: f. Structure: abac (2,2,2,2) = aa¹ (4,4).

O

'Lady Alice.' Sung by Miss Nancy Maxwell. Recorded as MS score; no date or place given.

109

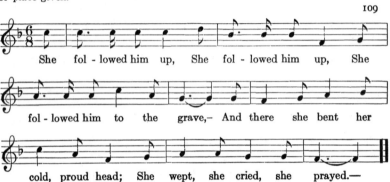

She   fol - lowed him   up,   She   fol - lowed him   up,   She

fol - lowed him   to   the   grave,--   And there   she bent   her

cold, proud head;   She   wept,   she   cried,   she   prayed.--

For melodic relationship cf. **SharpK 1 196, No. 25A; FSRA 33, No. 14, measures 2 and 7-8.

Scale: Hexachordal. Tonal Center: f. Structure: abcd (2,2,2,2).

29

LAMKIN

(Child 93)

A

'Beaulampkins.' Sung by Mrs. Emma Smith. Recorded as MS score at Zionville, Watauga county, in March 1914. As in other songs with numerous versions, one can also here find some musical idioms which seem to be standard. Note particularly the ending, which is alike in all four versions. Both 29A and 29A(1) differentiate their cadences, while in 29A(2) and 29B both cadences are alike.

110

Beau - lamp-kins was as   fine   a   ma - son   As   ev - er   laid

stone. He built a fine cast - le And pay he got none.

1-6   Stanza 5.

For melodic relationship cf. ***SharpK 1 201, No. 27A, measures 1-4, last four in the basic outline; *ibid.* 205, No. 27D, last two measures; **FSSH 9 (from the impossible notation of the tune nobody would suspect any melodic relationship with our version) ; BMFSB 20, especially the cadences, besides other similarities.

Scale: Mode III, plagal. Tonal Center: a-flat. Structure: abcb^1 (2,2,2,2) = ab (4,4).

A(1)

'Beaulampkins.' Sung by Mrs. Nancy Prather. Recorded at Milam, Ashe county, August 5, 1939. Very closely related to 29A, especially in both cadences, which are alike in each one of the two songs.

III

Beau - lamp-kins was as fine a ma - son As e - ver laid-

stone. He built a fine cast - le And- pay he got none.

For melodic relationship cf. ***SharpK 1 201, 204, No. 27A, C, excepting the final cadence; *ibid.* 205, No. 27D, where the last two measures are identical; **FSSH 91 (same remarks as made in previous version apply here also) ; BMFSB 20, cadences are alike besides other similarities.

Scale: Mode III, plagal. Tonal Center: a-flat. Structure: aa^{1}ba^2 (2,2,2,2) = Reprisenbar.

A(2)

'Beaulampkins.' Sung by anonymous singer. Recorded, but no date or place given. Excepting one minute difference, this tune, beginning with the third measure, is identical with 29B. In contrast to the preceding two versions, both the first and second cadences in this and the following version are alike.

112

Beau - lamp-kins was as fine a ma - son As ev - er laid a

stone. He built a fine cast - le And pay he got none.

For melodic relationship cf. *BMFSB 20, last two measures.

Scale: Hexatonic (4), plagal. Tonal Center: f. Structure: aba¹b (2,2,2,2) =
aa¹ (4,4).

B

'Bo Lamkin.' Sung by Frank Proffitt, Sugar Grove, Watauga county. Recorded, but no date or place given. In a second recording of the same singer the
tonal material is strictly pentatonic.

113

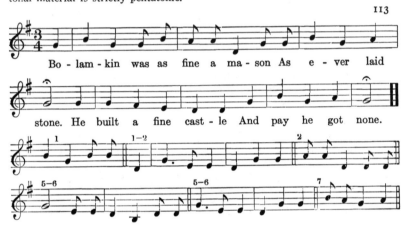

For melodic relationship cf. *BMFSB 20, last two measures.

Scale: Hexatonic (4), plagal. Tonal Center: g. Structure: aa¹ba¹ (2,2,2,2)
= Reprisenbar.

30
The Maid Freed from the Gallows
(Child 95)

A

'The Maid Freed from the Gallows.' From the collection of Miss Isabel Rawn.
Sung by Miss Belvia Hampton. Recorded at Warne, Clay county, in 1915.
The first two measures with up-beat are identical with those of the Nora Hicks'
version of 'Little Musgrove and Lady Barnard' (26G) as well as the E. Sanders'
version of 'Leap Frog John' (vol. V). The fourth and fifth measures remind
one of 'Oh, Susanna.'

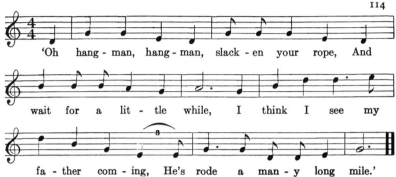

'Oh   hang - man,   hang - man,   slack - en   your   rope,   And

wait   for   a   lit - tle   while,   I   think   I   see   my

fa - ther   com - ing,   He's   rode   a   man - y   long   mile.'

For melodic relationship cf. *SharpK 1 No. 28A, measures 1-2.

Scale: Mode III, plagal.   Tonal Center: g.   Structure: abca¹ (2,2,2,2) = ab (4,4).

B

'Maid Freed from the Gallows.' From the same collection as A and with the same tune, but by an anonymous singer.

C

'The Gallows Tree.' Sung by Mrs. Walter. Recorded as MS score; no date or place given. Measures 2 and 6 are practically the same as in 30O.

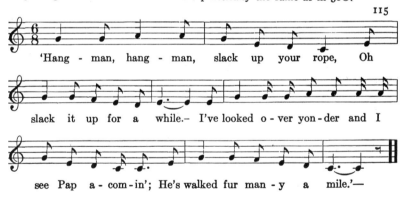

'Hang - man,   hang - man,   slack   up   your   rope,   Oh

slack   it   up   for   a   while.—   I've looked o - ver yon - der   and   I

see   Pap   a - com - in';   He's walked fur man - y   a   mile.'—

For melodic relationship cf. *FSSH 95, version A, melodic outline only.

Scale: Hexachordal.   Tonal Center: c.   Structure: abab¹ (2,2,2,2) = aa¹ (4,4).

H

'True Love.' Sung by Miss Jean Holeman. Recorded at Durham in July 1922, Other titles given are 'Maid Freed from the Gallows' and 'Hangman, Hangman.

The first four measures are the initial phrase of 'Iam Christus astra ascenderat,' which is a Whitsuntide church melody from the eleventh century. The same tune is also used in the German hymn 'Christ der du bist der helle Tag,' which dates from 1568. As our singer changed the melody for the second stanza, "Oh did you bring me gold," the two stanzas are given consecutively.

116

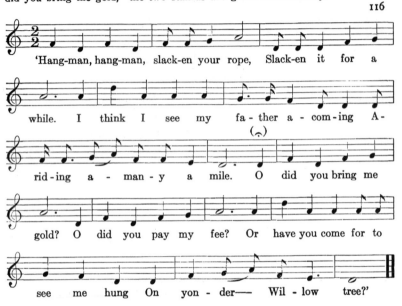

'Hang-man, hang-man, slack-en your rope, Slack-en it for a while. I think I see my fa-ther a-com-ing A-rid-ing a-man-y a mile. O did you bring me gold? O did you pay my fee? Or have you come for to see me hung On yon-der— Wil-low tree?'

For melodic relationship cf. ***SFSEA 159, No. 142, measures 8-10, and 237, No. 245, measures 1-4 with our measures 9-12. **SharpK 1 162, No. 28B, measures 5-6, melodic tendency only.

Scale: Pentachordal. Tonal Center: d. Structure: (1st stanza) abcd (2,2,2,2); (2nd stanza) $b^1b^2c^1d^1$ (2,2,2,2).

N

'Hangman, Hangman.' Sung by Steve Church. From previous recording of Dr. W. A. Abrams, Boone, September 14, 1941. Our stanza is the third. Neither sweetheart nor father brings gold.

117

'Oh Georg-ie, hold-up— your- head, And hold it fur a while. I think I see your

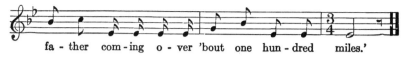

fa - ther   com - ing   o - ver 'bout   one   hun - dred   miles.'

For melodic relationship cf. **SharpK 1 162, No. 23B ('Little Musgrave and Lady Barnard'), measures 1-2.

Scale: Hexatonic (4), plagal. Tonal Center: e-flat. Structure: abb¹a¹ (2,2,2,2).

O

'Hangman's Song.' Sung by Belvia Hampton. Recorded as MS score, no date or place given. There is no text for Belvia Hampton's second version. On the other hand, there is no tune for John Duncan's text (version 30G) sent in by Miss Cora Lee Wyatt. Since the latter, however, fits the former perfectly, it was so used. Measures 2 and 6 are practically the same as those in 30C.

118

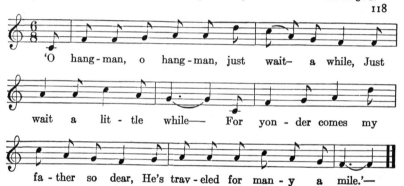

'O   hang - man,   o   hang - man,   just   wait—   a   while,   Just

wait   a   lit - tle   while——   For   yon - der comes   my

fa - ther   so   dear,   He's trav - eled   for   man - y   a   mile.'—

For melodic relationship cf. ***FSoA 68, measures 3-4 only.

Scale: Mode III, plagal. Tonal Center: f. Structure: abab¹ (2,2,2,2) = aa¹ (4,4).

P

'Maid Freed from the Gallows.' Sung by Frank Proffitt, with guitar. Recorded at Pick Britches, Sugar Grove, Watauga county, July 24, 1939. Another title given is 'Hangman, Hangman.' The melodic material of measures 2, 5, and 6 of this version is the same as that of 30A, but what a difference in the use made of it! The harmony inflicted upon this melody by the guitar player is a fine example of experimentation with a totally unknown quantity!

119

'Have   you   got   an - y   mon - ey   for   me,   And

gold   to   pay   my   fee?   For   I   stole   a   sil - ver - y

cup,   And   hang - ed   I   must   be.'————

For melodic relationship cf. *SharpK 1 208, No. 28A, only the main points of the melody.

Scale: Heptachordal, plagal.   Tonal Center: g.   Structure: abc (2,2,4).

Q

'Hangman's Tree.' Sung by Miss Pearle Webb. Recorded at Pineola, Avery county, August 24, 1939. There is also a second recording of a version sung by Mrs. Anna Johnson, which differs only in a few points from this version, and from which the first set of variations are taken.

120

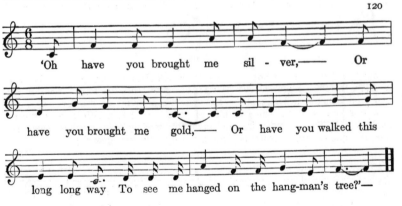

'Oh   have   you brought   me   sil - ver,———   Or

have   you brought me   gold,——   Or   have   you walked this

long   long   way   To   see   me hanged on   the hang-man's tree?'—

Scale: Hexatonic (4), plagal. Tonal Center: f. Structure: abcd (2,2,2,2).

R

'The Gallows Tree.' Sung by Mrs. James York. Recorded at Olin, Iredell county, August 24, 1939. Melodic deviations in another recording are given in the variations below.

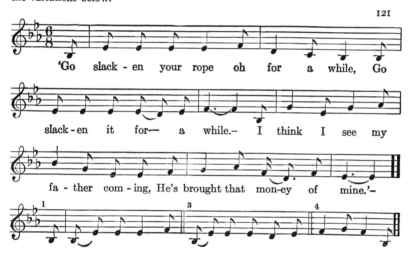

For melodic relationship cf. **SharpK 1 214, No. 28K, measures 1-4; FSF 297.

Scale: Heptachordal. Tonal Center: e-flat. Structure: aa^1bc (2,2,2,2) = ab (4,4).

33

ROBIN HOOD RESCUING THREE SQUIRES

(Child 140)

'Bold Robing.' Sung by Mrs. Calvin Hicks, of Mast's Gap, Watauga county. Recorded, but no date or place given. There is a second recording, the melodic deviations of which are given in the variations below.

122

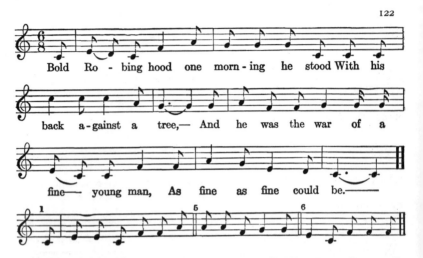

Bold Ro - bing hood one morn - ing he stood With his

back a - gainst a tree,— And he was the war of a

fine— young man, As fine as fine could be.——

For melodic relationship cf. **TBV 592, No. 40C ('The House Carpenter').
Scale: Hexachordal. Tonal Center: c. Structure: aba¹c (2,2,2,2) = ab (4,4).

34
Sir Hugh; or, the Jew's Daughter
(Child 155)

B

'It Rained a Mist.' Sung by the mother of Cleophas Bray. From previous recording of Dr. W. A. Abrams, Boone; no date. Measures 2-4 are closely related to Mrs. Calvin Hicks's 'Bold Robing' (No. 33); measures 7-10 are very similar.

123

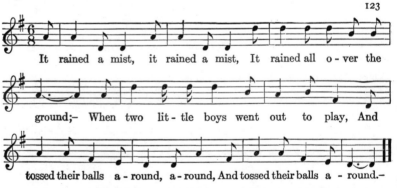

It rained a mist, it rained a mist, It rained all o - ver the

ground;– When two lit - tle boys went out to play, And

tossed their balls a - round, a - round, And tossed their balls a - round.–

For melodic relationship cf. ***BB 67, version D; SCB 148-49, first two measures only; **BMFSB 22; JAFL xxxix (1926), 213; BSO 66, No. 20; BB 66-7.

Scale: Mode III. Tonal Center: d. Structure: abb¹cc¹ $(2,2,2,2,2) =$ ab $(4,6)$; b is terminally incremented.

D

'The Jewish Lady.' Sung by the mother of Miss Margaret Johnson. MS score received by the present editor in 1952 through the kindness of Professor Hudson. The melodic line of this tune is only a variation of that sung by Mrs. Bray (34B).

124

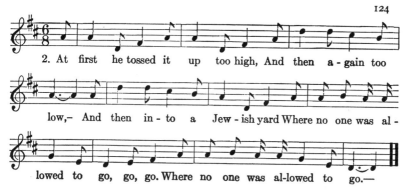

2. At first he tossed it up too high, And then a-gain too

low,– And then in-to a Jew-ish yard Where no one was al-

lowed to go, go, go. Where no one was al-lowed to go.—

For melodic relationship cf. **BSO 66, No. 20; JAFL xxxix (1926), 213; BMFSB 22.

Scale: Heptachordal. Tonal Center: d. Structure: abb¹cc¹ $(2,2,2,2,2) =$ ab $(4,6)$; b is terminally incremented.

36
THE BONNY EARL OF MURRAY
(Child 181)

'The Earl of Moray.' Sung by Aunt Becky Gordon. Recorded as MS score at Stateline Hill, Henderson county; no date given. The old Scotch version in *Ballads of Britain*, 80-1, gives the last line as "lay'd him on the green." Similar also in BMNE 133 and BBM 468.

125

Ye High-lands and ye Low-lands, it's where have ye been? Oh, they've

slain the Earl of Mo - ray and laid him on the ground.

Scale: Mode III, plagal. Tonal Center: f. Structure: aa¹bc $(2,2,2,2) =$ ab $(4,4)$.

37

THE GYPSY LADDIE

(Child 200)

A

'Black Jack David.' Sung by Mrs. Nora Hicks. Recorded at Mast's Gap, Watauga county, September 1940. Measures 1-2 and 5-6 are closely related to those in 37B, 37B(1), and 37I. These have astonishingly much in common with the melody 'Der mey hat menig Herze hoch ersteiget,' which was composed by Neithart von Reuenthal (1180-1240). Cf. DTOe, vol. 37, I.

126

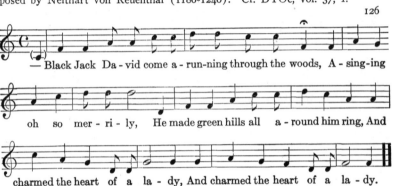

— Black Jack Da - vid come a - run-ning through the woods, A - sing-ing

oh   so   mer - ri - ly,   He made green hills all   a - round him ring, And

charmed the heart of a la - dy, And charmed the heart of a la - dy.

For melodic relationship cf. **SharpK 1 144, No. 20N, measures 1-2, and 31G, 31H, measures 1-2 with our 1-2 and 5-6, melodic outline only; BMFSB 6.

Scale: Mode III, plagal. Tonal Center: f. Structure: aba^1 cc^1 (2,2,2,2,2) = ab (4,6). The b is related to a; the second phrase is internally incremented.

B

'Black Jack David.' Sung by Mrs. Julia Grogan. Recorded at Zionville, Watauga county; no date given. "Written as sung by a neighbor" (II 162) evidently pertains to the text, since we have a recording. Measures 1-2 and 5-6 correspond very closely to those of 37A. There were two more recordings, one of the Michael version, the other anonymous, both of which differ from this version to a lesser or greater degree. The differences are given below in the variations.

127

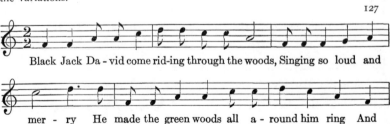

Black Jack Da - vid come rid-ing through the woods, Singing so loud and

mer - ry   He made the green woods all   a - round him ring   And

charmed the heart of a la - dy, And charmed the heart of a la - dy.

For melodic relationship cf. ***TBV 590-1, No. 37A, last two measures, stanza as well as refrain; **BMFSB 6.

Scale: Mode III, plagal. Tonal Center: f. Structure: aba^{1}cc^1 (2,2,2,2,2) = ab (4,6). The second phrase is terminally incremented.

B(1)

'Black Jack David.' Sung by Mrs. J. Church. Recorded at Heaton, Avery county, August 10, 1939. Dr. Brown notes: "The Churches live at foot of Oak Ridge, on End of Nowhere Branch, Beech Creek, near Pogy Mountain." The first six measures of this melody are practically identical with those of 37B.

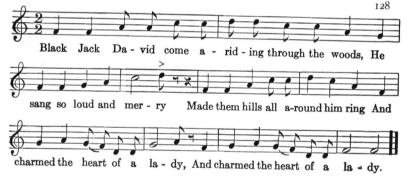

Black Jack Da - vid come a - rid - ing through the woods, He

sang so loud and mer - ry Made them hills all a-round him ring And

charmed the heart of a la - dy, And charmed the heart of a la - dy.

For melodic relationship cf. ***SharpK 1 228-9, No. 31G and H (the melodic line of measures 1-2 and 5-6 only).

Scale: Mode III, plagal. Tonal Center: f. Structure: aba^{1}cc^1 (2,2,2,2,2) = ab (4,6); the second phrase is internally incremented.

C

'The Egyptian Davy O.' Sung by Mrs. Ephraim Stamey. Recorded at Alta-

mont, Avery county, July 14, 1940. Another title given is 'Gypsy Daisy.' There
is a general relationship in the melodic line with that of 37G. The variations
for measure 1 are from a second recording.

129

There were three gyp-sies in this town, There were three gyp-sy
Da - vys, There were three gyp-sies in this town, That
charmed the heart of a la - dy. Ram-ding a ding o
ding o die Ram-ding a ding o Dai - sy, Ram-ding a
ding o ding a die o, Ram-ding a ding o Dai - sy.

For melodic relationship cf. *SharpK 1 235, No. 33D, measures 1-3; BB 95,
version D.

Scale: Hexatonic (4), plagal. Tonal Center: f. Structure: (stanza) aa^{1}a^{2}b
(2,2,2,2); (refrain) cc^{1}c^{1}b^1 (2,2,2,2); (both together) aa^{1}bb^1 (4,4,4,4). Circular Tune (V).

D

'Black-Eyed Davy.' Sung by Mrs. Peggy Perry. Recorded at Silverstone,
Watauga county, March 11, 1915. The beginning on the seventh degree is most
unusual.

130

'How old are you, my pret - ty Pol - ly? How

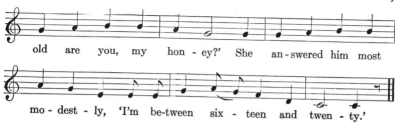

old   are   you,   my   hon - ey?'   She   an - swered   him   most

mo - dest - ly,   'I'm   be-tween   six - teen   and   twen - ty.'

For melodic relationship cf. *SharpK 1 236, No. 33E, measure 1, otherwise only rhythmically.

Scale: Heptachordal. Tonal Center: c. Structure: abb¹c (2,2,2,2) = ab (4,4).

D(1)

'Black-Eyed Davy.' Sung by Mrs. N. T. Byers. No date or place given. This and the following two versions by Dr. I. G. Greer, all of which are basically the same melody, serve as fine examples of the intuitive and spontaneous artistry of the folksinger in varying tonal material to suit the occasion.

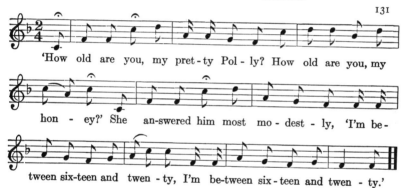

131

'How   old   are   you,   my   pret - ty   Pol - ly?   How   old   are   you,   my

hon - ey?'   She   an-swered   him   most   mo - dest - ly,   'I'm   be-

tween six-teen and   twen - ty,   I'm   be-tween   six - teen   and   twen - ty.'

For melodic relationship cf. *SharpK 1 239, No. 33J, measures 1-2.

Scale: Hexachordal, plagal. Tonal Center: f. Structure: abacc¹ (2,2,2,2,2) = ab (4,6); the second phrase is internally incremented.

E

'Black Jack David. Sung by Dr. I. G. Greer. Recorded at Boone in 1915. Sung again for the present editor at the singer's home in Chapel Hill, 1952. Cf. note to the preceding version, 37D(1). Measures 5-7 remind one slightly of 'Oh, Susanna!'

132

Black   Jack   Da - vid   come   a - rid - in' through the woods,

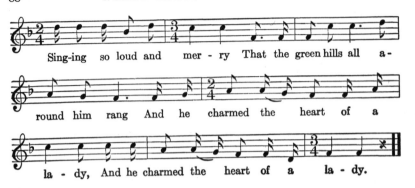

Sing-ing so loud and mer - ry That the green hills all a-
round him rang And he charmed the heart of a
la - dy, And he charmed the heart of a la - dy.

Scale: Hexachordal, plagal. Tonal Center: f. Structure: aba¹cc¹ (2,2,2,2,2) =
ab (4,6); the second phrase is internally incremented.

E(1)

'Black Jack David.' Sung by Dr. I. G. Greer. No date or place given. This
second version, like the first, was again sung for the present editor at the
singer's home in Chapel Hill in 1952. Cf. note to 37D(1).

133

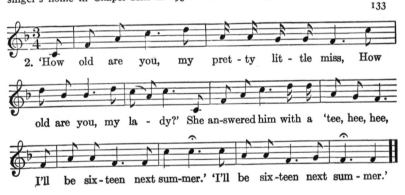

2. 'How old are you, my pret - ty lit - tle miss, How
old are you, my la - dy?' She an-swered him with a 'tee, hee, hee,
I'll be six - teen next sum-mer.' 'I'll be six - teen next sum - mer.'

Scale: Hexachordal, plagal. Tonal Center: f. Structure: abacc¹ (2,2,2,2,2) =
ab (4,6); the second phrase is internally incremented.

F

'The Gypsy Davy.' Sung by Mrs. J. J. Miller. Recorded at King's Creek,
Caldwell county; no date. This stanza is the fifth of version B, in II, 162-3.

134

5. So late in the night when the land - lord came In-

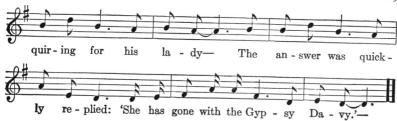

quir - ing for his la - dy— The an - swer was quick -

ly re - plied: 'She has gone with the Gyp - sy Da - vy.'—

Scale: Hexachordal. Tonal Center: d. Structure abb¹a¹ (2,2,2,2).

G

'How Old Are You, My Pretty Little Miss?' Sung by Mrs. James York. Recorded in Iredell county in August 1939. There is a general melodic resemblance with 37C. Measures 7-8 are identical with those of 'What Shall We Do with a Drunken Sailor?' as sung by T. F. Leary in this collection; cf. V.

135

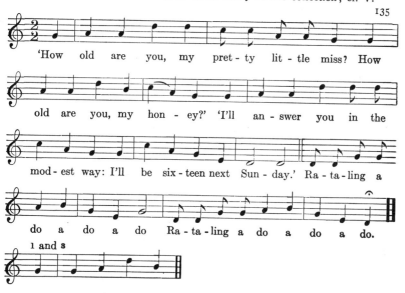

'How old are you, my pret - ty lit - tle miss? How

old are you, my hon - ey?' 'I'll an - swer you in the

mod - est way: I'll be six - teen next Sun - day.' Ra - ta - ling a

do a do a do Ra - ta - ling a do a do a do.

1 and 3

For melodic relationship cf. **SharpK 1 234, No. 33B, measures 1-8 for basic melodic tendency only.

Scale: Hexachordal, plagal. Tonal Center: g. Structure: aa¹a²bcc¹ (2,2,2,2,2,2) = abc (4,4,4). Circular Tune (V).

G(1)

'Gypsy Laddie.' Sung by Mrs. Nancy Prather. Recorded at Milam, Ashe county, August 5, 1939. Another title given is 'Gypsy Davy.' The steady use of the one-measure pattern throughout is noteworthy.

136

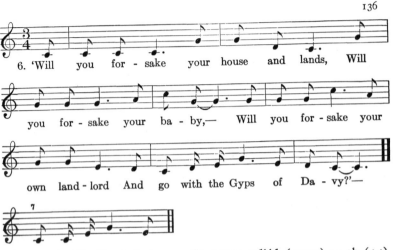

6. 'Will you for - sake your house and lands, Will
you for - sake your ba - by,— Will you for - sake your
own land - lord And go with the Gyps of Da - vy?'—

Scale: Mode III. Tonal Center: c. Structure: aa¹bb¹ (2,2,2,2) = ab (4,4).

H

'Black Jack David.' Sung by anonymous singer. No date or place given.

137

Black Jack Da-vid come a - rid-ing through the woods, All so gay and
mer - ry. And the green trees all a - round him stood— And he
charmed the heart of a la - dy, Charmed the— heart of a la - dy.

Scale: Mode III, plagal. Tonal Center: g. Structure: abb¹cc¹ (2,2,2,2,2) = ab (4,6); the second phrase is internally incremented.

I

'Black Jack David.' Sung by Frank Proffitt. Recorded at Sugar Grove, Watauga county, July 24, 1939. See note to 30A.

138

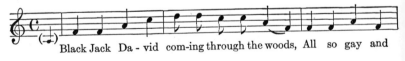

Black Jack Da - vid com-ing through the woods, All so gay and

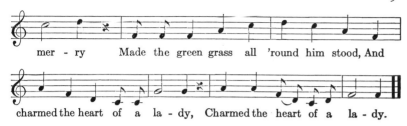

mer - ry   Made the green grass all 'round him stood, And

charmed the heart of a la - dy, Charmed the heart of a la - dy.

Scale: Mode III, plagal. Tonal Center: f. Structure: aba¹cc¹ (2,2,2,2,2) = ab (4,6); the second phrase is internally incremented.

38
Geordie
(Child 209)

'Georgie.' Sung by Mrs. James York. No date or place given, but probably the same as next version. Mrs. York said that this was her mother's version, with the title 'Georgie.'[1]

As   I   went   o - ver   Lon - don's bridge   So

---

[1] During a visit at their home, June 17, 1956, Mr. and Mrs. York asked the present editor to make the corrections in the text as given below:

1   As I crossed over London's bridge
    So early in the morning,
    'Twas there I spied a pretty fair maid
    Lamenting o'er her lover.

3   When she got to the Oxford Court
    So early in the morning,
    And down upon her bended knees
    She pled for the life of Georgie.

4   He has not robbed the king's highway
    Nor took the life of any,
    But he stold fifteen of the queen's best steeds
    And conveyed them away to Ghelenay.

7   Georgie was hanged with a white silk cord
    And hung where there were many,
    Because he was of noble blood
    And loved by the royal lady.

ear - ly in the morn - ing, It was there I spied a
pret - ty fair maid La - ment - ing o'er her lov - er.

For melodic relationship cf. *SharpK 1 240, No. 34A, measures 1-2 and merely some points of melodic coincidence; also SFSEA, 226, No. 229, measures 1-4.

Scale: Pentachordal, plagal. Tonal Center: a-flat. Structure: abb¹c (2,2,2,2) = ab (4,4). The varied use of tonal material of measures 1-2 in the last three measures is interesting.

38 (1)

'Geordie.' (2nd tune.) Sung by Mrs. James York. Recorded at Olin, Iredell county, August 14, 1939. This is given by the singer as Mrs. York's father's version. Dr. Brown says: "Mrs. York's 'Little Mohee' air."[1] In contrast to the second version by Miss Pearle Webb, 38(3) below, this can justifiably be called a second version.

140

'O judge, o judge, I've killed a man And al - so have robbed man - y—— And stole six - teen of the queen's best steeds, And sold them in the val - ley.'—— 'My true love, you are too late For the jud - ge's tri - al's all o - ver—

---

[1] On a recent visit to the home of Mr. and Mrs. York, the present editor was informed that this was not correct. The additional stanza was obtained at that time.

My true love, you are too late For the judg-e's tri-al's all o - ver.'–

2 The youngest judge well he spoke up,
Says Georgie, 'I'm sorry for you.
But unless you confess to what you've done
You'll be hung for murder.'

4 Oh judge, oh judge, I've killed a man
And also have robbed many.
I stole sixteen of the queen's best steeds
And sold them in the valley.

Refrain:
'My pretty Miss, you are too late,
For Georgie's trial's all over.
My pretty Miss, you are too late,
For Georgie's trial's all over.'

For melodic relationship cf. *SFSEA 226, No. 229, measures 1-2.

Scale: Hexachordal, plagal. Tonal Center: d. Structure: ababca^{1}ca^1 (2,2,2,2,
2,2,2,2) = aabb (4,4,4,4). Circular Tune (III).

38(2)

'Geordie.' Sung by Miss Pearle Webb. From the previous recording of Dr.
W. A. Abrams at Boone, August 8, 1940. There is a resemblance with some
'Barbara Allen' versions.

141

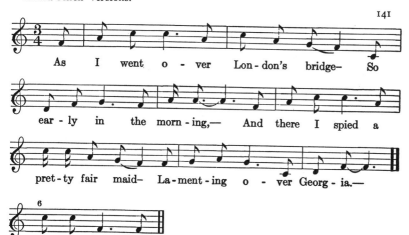

As I went o - ver Lon - don's bridge– So
ear - ly in the morn - ing,— And there I spied a
pret - ty fair maid– La - ment - ing o - ver Georg - ia.—

Scale: Mode III, plagal. Tonal Center: f. Structure: abac (2,2,2,2) = aa¹ (4,4).

38(3)

'Geordie.' (2nd version) Sung by Miss Pearle Webb. From the previous recording of Dr. W. A. Abrams, Boone, August 8, 1940. If all the variations occurring in the six stanzas are considered, it will be found that only one measure of the first version, the seventh, does not occur in the second version. This takes somewhat away from the importance usually attached to a second version. There is, however, an interesting rhythmic shift in the fifth stanza as given for measures 6-7. The tune for the first stanza serves without change for the second and third.

Scale: Mode III, plagal. Tonal Center: f. Structure: abab¹ (2,2,2,2) = aa¹ (4,4).

38(4)

'Georgie.' Sung by Miss Hattie McNeill. Recorded at Ferguson, Wilkes county, 1921. Another title given is 'I'd Fight for the Life of Georgie.' The

MS score has no more of the text, and the words of the recording cannot be recovered.

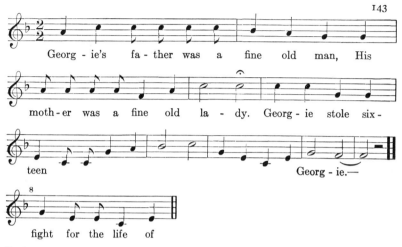

Georg - ie's fa - ther was a fine old man, His

moth - er was a fine old la - dy. Georg - ie stole six -

teen Georg - ie.—

fight for the life of

Scale: Hexatonic (6), plagal. Tonal Center: f. Structure: abcb¹ (2,2,3,3) = ab (4,6). The ending of both phrases is related.

40
JAMES HARRIS (THE DAEMON LOVER)
(Child 243)

A

'The Housecarpenter.' Sung by Mrs. Nora Hicks. Recorded at Mast's Gap, Watauga county, August 28, 1940. This, together with the Myra B. Miller and the Greer versions, shows a remarkable melodic relationship to the second half of 'Cross of Christ,' No. 504 in *Good Old Songs* (Cayce). Measures 1 and 3 identical with those of 40H, and measures 2 and 3 are identical with those of 40C.

'We've met, we've met, my own true— love,' 'We've

met, we've met,' said he;—'And I'm just re - turn-ing from the

salt,   salt—   sea   And its all   for the love   of   thee.'

For melodic relationship cf. ***TBV 593, No. 40H and 594, No. 40V, measures 1-4; FSF 313, No. 168B; FSS 524, No. 25L, measures 3-4 only; **SharpK I 251, No. 35H, measures 1-4; *ibid.* J, measures 1-5; P, measures 1-4; FSSH 115, No. 23B; SCSM 400, A ('James Harris') ; *FSRA 38, No. 18.

Scale: Hexachordal, plagal. Tonal Center: b-flat. Structure: aa¹bb¹ (2,2,2,2) = ab (4,4). Circular Tune (V).

A(I)

'The House Carpenter.' Sung by Mrs. G. L. Bostic. Recorded at Mooresboro, Cleveland county, August 7, 1939; another title given is 'Banks of Citoree.'

2. 'I   could have— mar - ried the king's daught-er, dear, I'm

sure she'd 'a' mar - ried me; But I re - fused the

crown of gold, And it's all for the sake of— thee.'

For melodic relationship cf. *SharpK I 252, No. 35K, basic melodic outline only.

Scale: Heptachordal, plagal. Tonal Center: g. Structure: aba¹c (2,2,2,2) = aa¹ (4,4).

A(2)

'The House Carpenter.' Sung by Myra Barnett Miller. Recorded probably at Lenoir, August 1939, 1940, or 1941. Another record is identical with this version, and it contains all the stanzas. Towards the end, however, the singer gradually rises in pitch, and finishes a whole tone above the level on which she started.

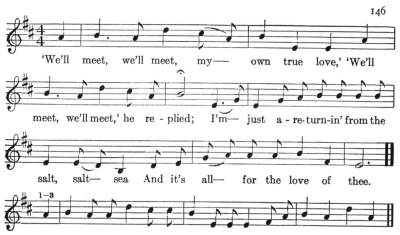

For melodic relationship cf. ***FSF 313, No. 168B, measures 3-4; **ibid., No. 168A, measure 7 with 6 in our version; SharpK 1 245, No. 35B and 252, No. 35J; TBV 593, No. 40H and more so, 594, No. 40V, measures 1-4; SCSM 400, version A ('James Harris'), measures 3-4; FSS 524, No. 25L, measures 3-4; *FSSH 116, No. 23C, measures 1-2; SharpK 1 209, No. 28B ('The Maid Freed from the Gallows'), measure 6; FSRA 38, No. 18.

Scale: Dorian, plagal. Tonal Center: e. Structure: aa¹bb¹ (2,2,2,2) = ab (4,4).

B

'The House Carpenter.' Sung by Aunt Becky Gordon. No date or place given. This tune, with but slight changes, is the same this singer uses for her version of 'The Seven Sisters' (2B). For her first stanza she uses the third and fourth lines of stanza 1 and the first and second lines of stanza 2 as given in II 173.

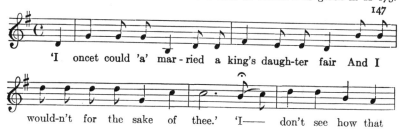

you could fault me, For– I mar - ried a house car - pen -

ter, er, For I mar - ried a house car - pen - ter.'

3-4   3   7   9

For melodic relationship cf. **BSM 82, version D; FSF 311, No. 168A: *SharpK 1 249, No. 35E, measures 3-5.

Scale: Heptachordal, plagal.   Tonal Center: g.   Structure: abca¹d (2,2,2,2,2) = abc (4,4,2), or ab (4,6) where b is internally incremented.

C

'The House Carpenter.' Sung by Dr. I. G. Greer. Recorded as MS score at Boone, 1913. Except for a few deviations, which are shown in the variations below, this tune is the same as that used by Mrs. Rebecca Icenham, version D. For an interesting and subtle use of tonal material observe the combination of measures 5 and 2 in the last two measures.

148

'We've met, we've met, my— own true— love,' 'We've

met, we've met,' he cried; 'For I'm just– re - turn-ing from the

salt, salt— sea And it's all for the love— of thee.'

1-2

6-7

For melodic relationship cf. ***SharpK 1 251, No. 35H, measures 1-4 and 6-8, No. 35 J, L, measures 6-8, and P, measures 1-4; FSF 313, No. 168B, measures 3-4, same in FSSH 115, No. 23B and SCSM 400, version A ('James Harris') ; TBV 594, No. 40V, measures 1-4 (basic melodic line) ; *FSRA 38, No. 18; SharpK 1 209, No. 28B, measure 6 ('Maid Freed from the Gallows').

Scale: Hexatonic (3) plagal. Tonal Center: f. Structure: aa¹bc (2,2,2,2) = ab (4,4).

D

'The House Carpenter's Wife.' Sung by Mrs. Rebecca Icenham. Recorded at Silverstone, Watauga county, in February 1915. See the note to the preceding version.

E

'The House Carpenter.' Sung by Miss Chloe Michael. Recorded at Boone, Watauga county, July 29, 1939. For almost the identical stanza, textually, see II 425, No. 162, 'The One Forsaken.'

149

'I will come– in, but I won't sit— down, I

have but a mo - ment of time; I heard you're en-gaged to an -

oth - er young man Your heart is no long - er— mine.'

For melodic relationship cf. *SharpK 1 244, No. 35 A, (B), H, J, L, P.

Scale: Hexatonic (6), plagal. Tonal Center: d. Structure: aa¹bc (2,2,2,2) = ab (4,4).

2 Where man, where man may I long to love,
Where may ....
I just returned from the South, South Sea
All for the love of thee.

3 Were you .... house carpenter
And coming .... of me?
I take you where the grass grows ....
On the banks of the green ....

4 You find for .... house carpenter
And .... of thee.

What have you to maintain me on
And keep me from slavery?

5   I have three ships ... are on the sea
    A-sailing ....
    .... gentlemen
    That will be at your command.

6   And (taking?) up her three little babes
    .... three,
    They stay at home, my three little babes
    And keep your papa company.

7   There hadn't been a soul ...... to reach
    I'm sure that it was .... through (three?)
    ...... about a week and then her true lover's arms
    And she wept most bitterly.

8   Are you .... silver or gold,
    Or is it for my cargo ....
    Or are you awakened for my three little babes
    Whose face you have seen no more?

H

'The House Carpenter.' Sung by C. K. Tillett. Recorded on Roanoke Island,
December 29, 1922. Measures 1 and 3 are identical with those of 40A. There
is some Negro influence noticeable in the flattening of the seventh degree.

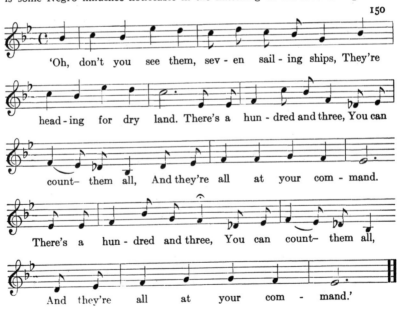

For melodic relationship cf. ***FSS 524, No. 25L, measures 3-4; SharpK 1 251-6, No. 35H and J, measures 1 and 3; **ibid., No. 35P and somewhat less, version B; FSF 313, No. 168B, and FSSH 115, No. 23B, measures 3-4; TBV 593-4, No. 40M and N, measures 1-4; *FSRA 38, No. 18.

Scale: Hexatonic (4), plagal. Tonal Center: e-flat. Structure: aa¹bcb¹c¹ (2,2,2,2,2,2) = abb (4,4,4) or, to use Alfred Lorenz' terminology, nmm¹ = inverted barform.

J

'The House Carpenter.' Sung by Miss Jessie Hauser. Recorded as MS score; no date or place given. Since this tune, excepting one measure, is identical with that of 40C, only that one (measure 6) is given here. The score, signed by Mrs. James Thomas, fits the A text of the first stanza (II 171) and not that of her garbled first stanza (II 176).

151

Scale: Hexatonic (3), plagal. Tonal Center: f. Structure: aa¹bc (2,2,2,2) = ab (4,4).

L

'The House Carpenter.' Sung by Mrs. James York. Recorded at Olin, Iredell county, in 1939. The portamenti are primitive indeed; the Negro influence is quite evident in the flattened third and seventh.

152

'We have met, we've met my own true— love; We've met, we've met,' said he. 'I once could have mar - ried a king's daughter fair, And— she would have mar - ried me.'—

Scale: Mixolydian, plagal. Tonal Center: f. Structure: abac (2,2,2,2) = aa¹ (4,4).

41
THE SUFFOLK MIRACLE
(Child 272)

'Richest Girl in Our Town' ('Lucy Bound'). Sung by Pat Frye. From previous recording of Dr. W. A. Abrams in 1945, no place given.

Here is a counterpart to the Hauser version of 'The House Carpenter' (40J), only in this case the melody, as recorded, takes in not only the first two lines of stanza 1, but also all of the second stanza. This, however, is all the recording contains. Any of the remaining stanzas of four lines each could possibly start with the up-beat in the fourth measure, as the second stanza actually does in the recording. Or, it could begin with the up-beat to the first measure and end with the eighth measure. The latter would seem preferable. Since the recording stops with the conclusion of the second stanza, no definite decision can be made. Both are possible.

Something should be said with reference to the analysis given below. It is only too evident that the whole melody is built from the material of the first two measures. Following this, we would arrive at an analysis like this: aa^1a^2 $a^3a^4a^5$, which would state the simple fact mentioned above. It would, however, not give any idea how the individual variations of this primary idea were used and so it was decided to mark the first subsidiary phrase b, realizing full well, that it actually is a^1. But the chosen procedure should give a clearer picture of the structure.

153

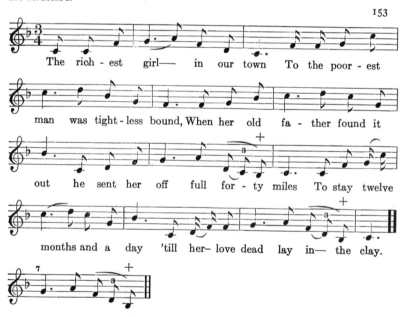

For melodic relationship cf. *SharpK 1 261, No. 37A, measure 1 with up-beat.

Scale: Hexachordal, plagal. Tonal Center: f. Structure: $abb^1a^1b^2a^2$ (2,2,2,2,2,2)

for the whole melody. If eight measures are considered as suggested above, this
would be: 1) aba¹b¹, and 2) abb¹a. Circular Tune (V).

42
OUR GOODMAN
(Child 274)

A

'Kind Wife.' Sung by anonymous singer. Procured by Thomas Smith, Zionville, Watauga county, in 1914. Here, this stanza of twenty-four measures is
produced by sheer exploitation of the melodic material of eight measures. This
is an excellent example for showing how a melody is adapted to a varying text
and just what happens in the process.

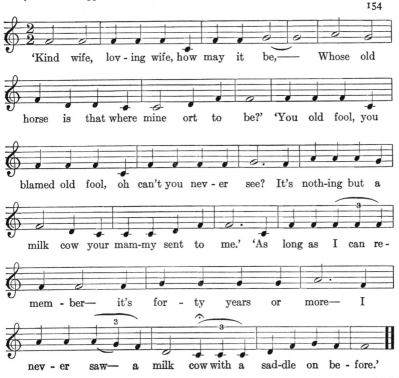

For melodic relationship cf. **SharpK 1 270, No. 38E, measures 13-20 which
are, more or less, the basic material of our version.

Scale: Mode III, plagal. Tonal Center: f. Structure: aba¹b¹a²b² (4,4,4,4,4,4)
= aa¹a² (8,8,8).

A(1)

'Kind Wife.' Sung by Myra Barnett Miller. Recorded, probably at Lenoir,

August 1939, 1940, or 1941. These eight measures are repeated twice to take care of the six lines of the stanza.

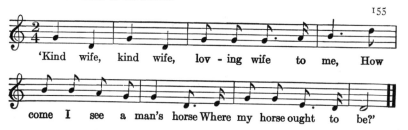

155

'Kind wife, kind wife, lov - ing wife to me, How come I see a man's horse Where my horse ought to be?'

For melodic relationship cf. **SharpK, I 270, No. 38E, measures 13-20, which as in the above version, contribute the basic material of this version.

Scale: Mode III, plagal. Tonal Center: g. Structure: abcd (2,2,2,2). Circular Tune (V).

B

'Arrow Goodman.' Sung by anonymous singer. No date or place given. Another title given is 'Our Goodman.'

156

2. Last—night when I come home as drunk as I could be. There was a horse stand - in' in the sta - ble where my horse ought to be. 'Come here— my lit - tle wife and ex - plain this thing to me: How come a horse stand-in' in the sta - ble where my horse ought to be?' 'You old fool, you cra - zy fool, Can't you nev - er see? It's noth-ing but a

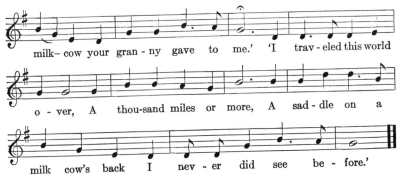

milk– cow your gran - ny gave to me.' 'I trav - eled this world

o - ver, A thou-sand miles or more, A sad - dle on a

milk cow's back I nev - er did see be - fore.'

For melodic relationship cf. *SharpK 1 270, No. 38E, measures 7-8 and 15-16, which are like our 3-4.

Scale: Hexatonic (4), plagal. Tonal Center: g. Structure: $aa^1a^2a^3$ (8,8,8,8).

B(1)

'Arrow Goodman.' Sung by H. J. Beaker. No place given; dated August 1939, 1940, or 1941. Other titles given are: 'Our Goodman' and 'Good Wife.'

157

2. Last Sat - ur - day night when I came home as drunk as

I could be, I saw a horse in the sta - ble, where

my horse ought to be.— 'Come my wife, my dear lit - tle wife, Come

'splain this thing to me: How come a horse in the sta - ble where

my horse ought to be?' 'Oh, you old fool, you blind fool, you're

drunk as you can be; That's noth - ing but a milk cow my

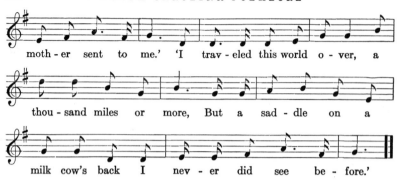

moth - er sent to me.' 'I trav - eled this world o - ver, a

thou - sand miles or more, But a sad - dle on a

milk cow's back I nev - er did see be - fore.'

For melodic relationship cf. ***ASb 312, 'The Roving Gambler,' measures 1-4; FSF 317, No. 170, measures 3-4 and recurrences.

Scale: Hexatonic (4), plagal. Tonal Center: g. Structure: aa^{1}a^{2}a^3 (8,8,8,8).

B(2)

'Arrow Goodman.' Sung by Otis Kuykendall. Recorded at Asheville, July 18, 1939. Another title given: 'Our Goodman.'

2. I came in the oth - er night as drunk as I could be. —

I found a horse in the sta - ble where my—horse ought to

be.— 'Come here my lit - tle wife and 'splain this thing to me:—

How come this horse in the sta - ble where my—horse ought to

be?' 'You drunk fool, you cra - zy fool, you sure - ly can - not

see. That's on - ly a milk cow your gran - ny sent to me.' 'I've

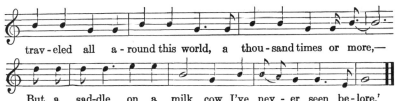

trav-eled all a-round this world, a thou-sand times or more,—

But a sad-dle on a milk cow I've nev-er seen be-lore.'

For melodic relationship cf. ***BMFSB 14, measures 1-2.

Scale: Mode III, plagal. Tonal Center: g. Structure aa^{1}a^{2}a^3 (8,8,8,8).

B(3)

'Arrow Goodman.' Sung by Miss Millie Saunders. Recorded at Jonas Ridge (Rip Shin Ridge), Burke county, June 30, 1940. Other title given: 'Our Goodman.'

159

3. The oth-er night when I came home as drunk as I could

be, Found a head a-lay-ing on a pil-low where

my head ought to be. 'Come here my lit-tle wife and ex-

plain this thing to me. How come an-oth-er head lay-ing

on a pil-low where my head ought to be?' 'Blind fool, you

cra-zy fool, Can't you nev-er see? It's noth-ing

but a cab-bage head your gran-ny sent to me.'

For melodic relationship cf. ***SharpK 1 270, No. 38E, measures 7-8 and 15-16, and our 3-4.

Scale: Mode III, plagal. Tonal Center: g. Structure: aa¹a²a³ (8,8,8,8).

B(4)

'Arrow Goodman.' Sung by Miss Pearle Webb. Recorded at Pineola, Avery county, August 24, 1939. Another title given: 'Our Goodman.'

160

2. I came home the oth - er night, as drunk as I could be.

Found a horse stand-in' in the sta - ble where my horse ought to be.

'Come here lit - tle wi - fie, ex - plain this thing to me:

How come a horse stand - in' in the sta - ble where my horse

ought to be?' 'You old fool, cra - zy fool, can't you ev - er

see, It's noth - ing but a milk cow my gran'-ma gave to me.'

'I've trav-eled this wide world o - ver, I've trav-eled from shore to shore,

but a sad - dle on a milk cow I nev - er did see be-fore.'

For melodic relationship cf. ***FSF 317, No. 170, measure 2 and its repetitions.

Scale: Mode III, plagal. Tonal Center: g. Structure: aa¹a²a³ (8,8,8,8).

B(5)

'Arrow Goodman.' Sung by Miss Pearle Webb. From a previous recording of Dr. W. A. Abrams at Boone, Watauga county, August 8, 1940. This second recording does not greatly differ from her earlier version. The variations are such as one would certainly expect.

161

I came in the oth-er night as drunk as I could be—
Found a coat a-hang-in' on the wall where my coat ought to
be. 'Come here, my lit-tle wi-fie; Ex-plain this thing to
me: How come a coat a-hang-in' on the wall Where
my coat ought to be?' 'You fool, you cra-zy fool,
Can't you ev-er see— It's noth-ing but a bed-quilt My
gran'-ma gave to me.' 'I've trav-eled the wide world
o-ver, I've trav-eled from shore to shore, But pock-ets
on a bed-quilt I nev-er did see be-fore.'

For melodic relationship cf. ***FSF 317, No. 170, measure 2 and its repetitions.

Scale: Mode III, plagal. Tonal Center: a. Structure: aa¹a²a³ (8,8,8,8).

B(6)

'Arrow Goodman.' Sung by Mrs. Ewart Wilson. Recorded at Pensacola, Yancey county, September, 1929. Another title given: 'Our Goodman.'

162

When I come home the oth - er night just as drunk as

I could be, I found a hat a - hangin' on the rack where

my hat ought to be. 'Oh come here my lit - tle wif - ey, and ex -

plain this thing to me, Oh how come a hat a - hang - in'

on the rack where my hat ought to be?' 'You blind old fool, you

cra - zy fool, Can't you plain - ly see, that that is on - ly a

fry - ing pan that my ma gave to me?' 'I've— trav - eled this

world o - ver a thou - sand miles or more, But I

nev- er saw a fry - ing pan, with a hat band on be - fore.'

For melodic relationship cf. ***FSF 317, No. 170, measures 3-4 and their repetitions.

Scale: Mode III, plagal. Tonal Center: a. Structure: aa¹a²a³ (8,8,8,8). Circular Tune (V).

C

'Our Goodman.' Sung by Frank Proffitt. No date or place given.

Thurs-day night when I come home as drunk as I could be—
Found a coat a - hang-ing on the rack where my coat ought to
be. 'Come here, my lit - tle wi - fie, And 'splain this thing to
me, How come— this coat a - hang-ing on the rack where
my coat ought to be?' 'Oh y'old cra - zy fool you, Oh
can't you nev - er see? It's noth - ing but a bed-quilt my
gran - ny give to me.' 'I trav - eled— all o - ver this
world a thou - sand miles or more, But pock - ets on a
bed - quilt I nev - er did see be - fore.'

For melodic relationship cf. **SharpK 1 270, No. 38E, measures 7-8 and
15-16.

Scale: Heptachordal, plagal. Tonal Center: f. Structure: aa¹a²a³ (8,8,8,8).

43
GET UP AND BAR THE DOOR
(Child 275)

B

'Get Up and Bar the Door.' Sung by James York, with guitar. Recorded at Olin, Iredell county, September 14, 1941. Our text is almost identical with that of BBM 318, version A. Anyone who has ever attempted to recover a text, even from a good recording, will know that it is sometimes impossible to understand the words as they were sung. What the present editor gave to the editors of the ballad texts was simply what he was able to recover from the recording by careful listening. During a recent visit at the home of the singer, however, he was given the corrected version which follows below.

164

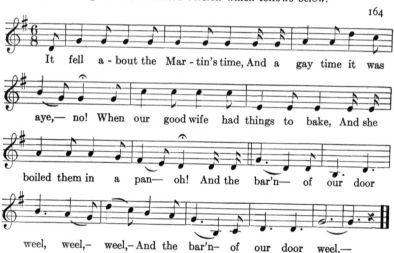

It fell a-bout the Mar-tin's time, And a gay time it was aye,— no! When our good wife had things to bake, And she boiled them in a pan— oh! And the bar'n— of our door weel, weel,— weel,—And the bar'n— of our door weel.—

1 It came about the Martimer's time,
   A gay time it was then, O,
   When our good wife had puddings to make
   And she boiled 'em in a pan, O,

2 The wind's so cold, blew south and north,
   And blew into the floor, O,
   Said our good man to our good wife,
   "Gang out an' bar the door, O."

3 "My hand is in my sausage meat,
   Good man, as ye may see, O,
   And it shouldna' be barred these hundred years;
   It'll never be barred by me, O."

For melodic relationship cf. ***BB 122B, measures1-10; *ibid.* A, measures 1-2; **BBM 320, B; FSF 320, No. 171 (has no refrain, however).
Scale: Heptachordal, plagal. Tonal Center: g. Structure: abcd (4,4,4,4).

44
THE WIFE WRAPT IN WETHER'S SKIN
(Child 277)

A

'Danyou.' Sung by Mrs. Ada Rayfield. Recorded in MS score by Mrs. Rayfield at Zionville, Watauga county, March 14, 1915. For another title, coming from the folk-music of Northeastern England, 'Broom, Green Broom,' cf. FMNEE 21.

165

There was an old man that lived in the West, Dan - you. There
was an old man that lived in the West, And he
had him a wife that was none of the best.
Dan - you Um - te did - dle - te, Dan - you.

For melodic relationship cf. ***SharpK 1 271-2, No. 39B; measures 1, 5, 13, 14 are identical with our fifth measure; also 2-4 and 6 are closely related; *ibid.* 274, version E and 275, No. 40A, first verse; PSL 41, measure 1.

Scale: Mode III, plagal. Tonal Center: f. Structure: abb¹c (3,2,2,3). This unusual structure comes about through elision: measures 3-4 and 8-9.

C

'Dandoo.' Sung by Frank Proffitt, with guitar. Recorded at Sugar Grove, Watauga county, in 1937. The motive of a descending fourth is quite in evidence here, as it is in all of our versions.

166

This good lit - tle man come in at noon, Dan - doo,
Dan - doo, This good lit - tle man come in at noon:

'Have you got my din - ner soon?' To my high - land,
to my low-land, To my crish crash, to my clin - go.

For melodic relationship cf. **SharpK I 271, No. 39B, measures 1-4; FSF 322, No. 172, measures 1-2.

Scale: Tetratonic (2,4), plagal. Tonal Center: g. Structure aba¹a²a³b¹ (2,2,2, 2,2,2) = aba¹ (4,4,4).

2 He laid the hide all on her back,
   Dandoo, dandoo.
   He laid the hide all on her back
   And the way he made that hick'ry crack
   To my highland, to my lowland.
   To my crish crash, to my clingo.

D

'The Wife Wrapped in a Wether Skin.' Sung by Miss Edith Walker. Recorded at Boone, no date given. For some unknown reason, the singer repeats the first two lines before proceeding with the song as printed. In the next stanza, the singer exchanges measures 7-8 for that given in the variations below; then these eight measures are repeated. There seems to be 'method in the madness.'

167

There was an old man who lived in the West, Dan - u,
dan - u, There was an old man who lived in the West,
Dan - u, dan - u, There was an old man who lived in the West
Um - phy - doo - dle - u - dan - u There was an old man who

lived in the West Had him a wife, she was

none of the best. To my ha - rem - ga - rem -

gi - rem - la - rem, Um - phy - doo - dle - u - dan - u.

Measure 12 of variation continues the same as measure 12 in stanza.

Scale: Mode III, plagal. Tonal Center: f. Structure: ababacaa^{1}c (2,2,2,2,2, 2,2,2,4) = aa^1 (8,12).

D(1)

'Wife Wrapped in Weather's Skin.' Sung by Mrs. Laura B. Timmons. From the previous recording of Dr. W. A. Abrams, Boone, August 8, 1940. Observe the singular spelling of "Weather's." The constant interplay between the ascending and descending fourths should be noted. It seems to be almost a musical illustration of what is going on.

168

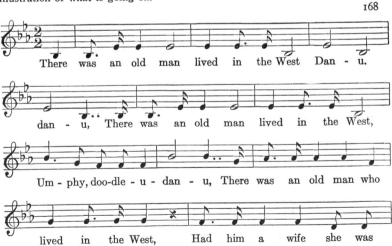

There was an old man lived in the West Dan - u.

dan - u, There was an old man lived in the West,

Um - phy, doo-dle - u - dan - u, There was an old man who

lived in the West, Had him a wife she was

none   of   the   best,   To   my   ha - rem,   ga - rem

gi - rem   la - rem,   Um - phy - doo - dle - u - dan - u.

Scale: Heptachordal, plagal.   Tonal Center: e-flat.   Structure: abacdd¹d²c¹
(2,2,2,2,2,2,2,2) = ab (8,8).

45

THE FARMER'S CURST WIFE

(Child 278)[1]

'Farmer's Curst Wife.' Sung by Horton Barker. From the previous recording
of Dr. W. A. Abrams, Boone, no date given. The first four measures are very
much like those of 45(1).

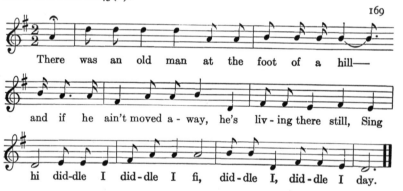

There   was   an   old   man   at   the   foot   of   a   hill—

and   if   he   ain't moved a - way,   he's   liv - ing there still,   Sing

hi   did - dle   I   did - dle   I   fi,   did - dle   I,   did - dle   I   day.

For melodic relationship cf. **SharpK 1 278, No. 40D; BB 126, version A,
measures 1-2.
Scale: Mode III. Tonal Center: d. Structure: abcd (2,2,2,2).

2   He hitched up his horse, and he went out to plow,
    But how to get around he didn't know how.

3   The devil came to his house one day,
    Saying, 'One of your family I'm gona take away.'

4   'Then,' said the old man, 'I am outdone,
    For I'm afraid you've come for my oldest one.'

5   'It's neither your son nor your daughter I crave,
    But your old scolding woman I now must have.'

_____
[1] BTBNA 166. The author gives Child 276.

6   'Take her, oh take her, with the joy of my heart,
    I hope, by golly, you'll never part.'

7   The devil put her in a sack,
    And he slung her up across his back.

8   When the devil came to the forks of the road,
    He says, 'Old lady, you're a terrible load.'

9   When the devil came to the gates of hell,
    He says, 'Punch up the fire, I'm gona scorch her well.'

10 Here came the devil a-draggin' a chain,
    She up with a hatchet and split out his brains.

11 And the old devil went climbing the wall,
    Says,' Take her back, Daddy, she's a-murdering us all.'

12 The old man was peeping outa the crack,
    And saw the old devil come a-wagging her back.

13 She found the old man sick in the bed,
    And up with the butter-stick and paddled his head.

14 The old woman went whistling over the hill,
    'The devil wouldn't have me, so I wonder who will.'

15 There's one advantage women have over men,
    They can go to hell and come back again.

45(1)

'The Farmer's Curst Wife.' Sung by Mrs. J. Church. Recorded at Heaton,
Avery county, August 10, 1939. Another title given: 'The Woman and the
Devil.' Not only a different singer but also a varied text. The first four
measures are very much like those of 45 above.

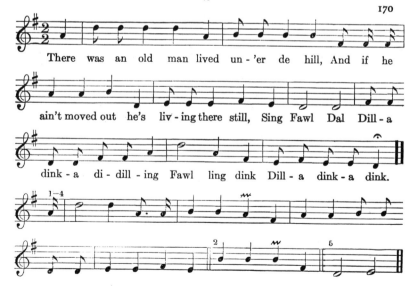

There was an old man lived un-'er de hill, And if he
ain't moved out he's liv-ing there still, Sing Fawl Dal Dill-a
dink-a di-dill-ing Fawl ling dink Dill-a dink-a dink.

For melodic relationship cf. **SharpK 1 278, No. 40D; BB 126, version A, measures 1-2.

Scale: Mode III. Tonal Center: d. Structure: abc (2,2,4).

45(2)

'The Farmer's Wife.' Sung by Mrs. Laura B. Timmons. From previous re- cording of Dr. W. A. Abrams, Boone, August 8, 1940. The text begins like several of Sharp's versions, but the reference to "hard times" seems not to occur in any of the known collections.

Magnificently sung. What a spirit! What can notes convey?

171

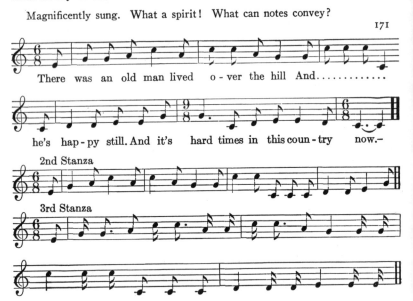

There was an old man lived o - ver the hill And............

he's hap - py still. And it's hard times in this coun - try now.—

2nd Stanza

3rd Stanza

For melodic relationship cf. **SharpK 1, 277, No. 40C, measures 1-2.

Scale: Mode III. Tonal Center: c. Structure: abc (2,2,2).

2 He took her to the gates of hell,
   He kicked her over and then she fell,
   And its hard times in this country now.

3 The little young devil peeping over the wall,
   'Take her out, take her out, or she'll kill us all,'
   And its hard times in this country now.

4 He ....
   And here he come a-waggin' her back
   And its hard times in this country now.

45(3)

'Farmer's Curst Wife.' Sung by Mrs. James York. From previous recording of Dr. W. A. Abrams, Boone, August 8, 1940. For a melodic likeness compare the beginning of 'Edward,' 7C.

172

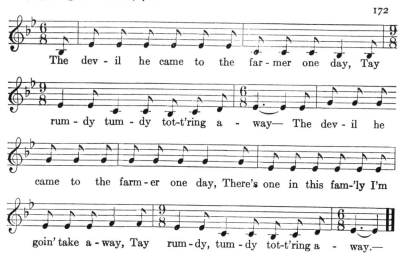

For melodic relationship cf. **BB 126, version A, measures 1-2.

Scale: Hexatonic (4), plagal. Tonal Center: e-flat. Structure: aba¹a²b¹ (2,2,2,2) = aa¹ (4,6); the second phrase is initially incremented.

2 'Its neither you nor your son, Johnny, I want,
   Tay rumdy, tumdy tott'ring away.
   Its neither you nor your son, Johnny, I want,
   The drunken old wife, the drunken old sot,
   Tay rumdy, tumdy tott'ring away.'

46

THE CRAFTY FARMER

(Child 283)

A

'A Yorkshire Bite.' Sung by anonymous singer. Recorded as MS score, no date or place given.
   This song is Child 283, not 278 as in II 188.
   For other texts and versions cf. BB 130, No. 1. Melodically, the beginning reminds one of 'Turkey in the Straw.'

173

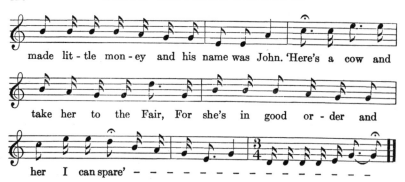

made lit - tle mon - ey and his name was John. 'Here's a cow and

take her to the Fair, For she's in good or - der and

her I can spare' – – – – – – – – – – – – – – – – –

Scale: Hexachordal, plagal. Tonal Center: g. Structure: abcb¹d (2,2,2,2,2) = ab (4,6) ; the second phrase is internally incremented.

47
THE SWEET TRINITY (THE GOLDEN VANITY)
(Child 286)

A

'The Turkish Revoloo.' Sung by Mrs. Nora Hicks. Recorded at Mast's Gap, Watauga county, August 28, 1940. Only slight changes in text. It is noteworthy that all versions except 47D have the same structure. But in general, all the versions (except 47D) resemble one another a great deal.

174

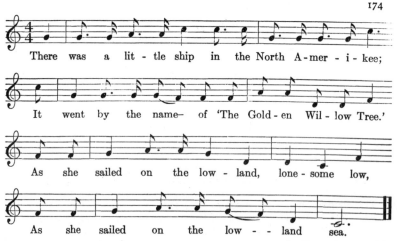

There was a lit - tle ship in the North A - mer - i - kee;

It went by the name— of 'The Gold - en Wil - low Tree.'

As she sailed on the low - land, lone - some low,

As she sailed on the low - - land sea.

For melodic relationship cf. **SharpK 1 284, No. 41C; SharpK 1 339, No. 52B ('The Boatsman and the Chest').

Scale: Mode III, plagal. Tonal Center: f. Structure: abcc¹ (2,2,2,2) = ab (4,4). Possibly nmm¹ (4,2,2) = inverted barform. Circular Tune (V).

A(1)

'The Turkish Revoloo.' Sung by Mrs. James York. From previous recording of Dr. W. A. Abrams, Boone, September 14, 1941. Other titles given are 'The Sweet Trinity' and 'The Golden Willow Tree.'

175

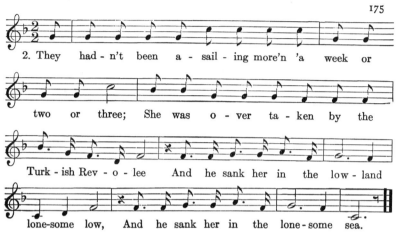

For melodic relationship cf. **SharpK 1 284 and 288, No. 41C and G, measures 1-2; *ibid.* 289, No. 41H, last three measures with our last six.

Scale: Hexachordal, plagal. Tonal Center: f. Structure: abcc¹ (2,2,2,2) = ab (4,4). Possibly nmm¹ (4,2,2) = inverted barform. Circular tune (V).

B

'The Golden Willow Tree.' Sung by Dr. I. G. Greer. Recorded, but no date or place given. Other titles given are: 'Cabin Boy,' 'The Golden Trinity,' 'The Golden Vanity,' 'Lowland Lonesome Low,' and 'Turkish Revoloo.'

176

As   she   sailed   on   the   salt   wa - ter   sea.

For melodic relationship cf. *SharpK 1 289, No. 41H, measures 7-8.

Scale: Mode III, plagal. Tonal Center: f. Structure: abcc[1] (2,2,2,2) = ab (4,4). Possibly nmm[1] (4,2,2) = inverted barform. Circular Tune (V).

c

'The Lonesome Low.' Sung by Myra Barnett Miller. Recorded as MS score, but no date or place given.

There was a lit - tle ship a - sail - ing on the sea,

And she went by the name of 'The Gold - en Wil - low Tree.'

As she sailed on the low - land, lone - some low,

As she sailed on the lone - some sea.

For melodic relationship cf. ***SharpK 1 339, No. 52B, measures 1-4; *ibid.* 284, No. 41C.

Scale: Hexachordal. Tonal Center: c. Structure: abcc[1] (2,2,2,2) = ab (4,4). Possibly nmm[1] (4,2,2) = inverted barform.

c(1)

'The Lonesome Low.' Sung by Myra Barnett Miller. Recorded probably at Lenoir, August 1939, 1940, or 1941. This is a second version by this singer, a recording against which the score of the previous version could be checked. The second melody proved to be merely a variation of the first. Other titles given are 'The Sweet Trinity,' and 'The Golden Willow Tree.'

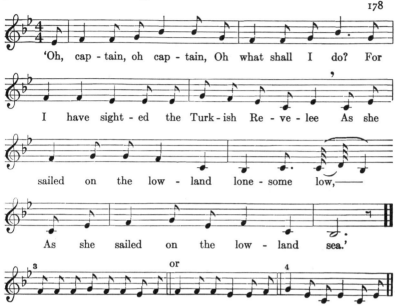

178

'Oh, cap - tain, oh cap - tain, Oh what shall I do? For

I have sight - ed the Turk - ish Re - ve - lee As she

sailed on the low - land lone - some low,——

As she sailed on the low - land sea.'

or

For melodic relationship see references to 47C above.

Scale: Mode III, plagal. Tonal Center: e-flat. Structure: abcc^1 (2,2,2,2) = ab (4,4). Possibly nmm^1 (4,2,2) = inverted barform. Circular Tune (V).

D

'Cabin Boy.' Sung by C. K. Tillett. Recorded at Wanchese, Roanoke Island, in 1923. The tune for the second stanza begins with the eight measures given in the variations, which in themselves represent merely unimportant changes in the melodic line of the initial eight measures of the original melody. Instead, however, of continuing with the remainder of the latter, the second stanza repeats for the remaining eight measures the initial phrase of the first stanza.

179

Up steps the cab - in boy an' the cab - in boy said

he: 'What will you give— me to sink the Re - ve -

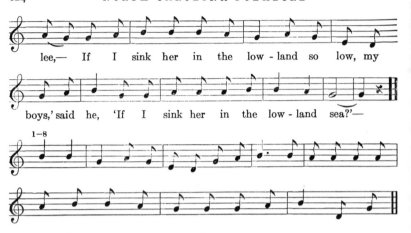

lee,— If I sink her in the low - land so low, my

boys,' said he, 'If I sink her in the low - land sea?'—

For melodic relationship cf. **FSRA 43, No. 23, measures 5-8.

Scale: Hexachordal, plagal. Tonal Center: g. Structure: (1st stanza) aba^{1}c (4,4,4,4) = aa^1 (8,8). (2nd stanza) a^{2}c^{1}ab^1 (4,4,4,4) = aa^1 (8,8).

48

THE MERMAID

(Child 289)

'Stormy Winds.' Sung by C. K. Tillett. Recorded at Wanchese, Roanoke Island, December 29, 1922. Other titles given are 'Mermaid' and 'The Wreck.' There is another version by the same singer printed in FSRA 46, which is a considerably later recording. The more surprising is it to find the latter almost identical in the general outline.

180

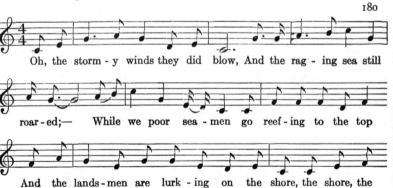

Oh, the storm - y winds they did blow, And the rag - ing sea still

roar - ed;— While we poor sea - men go reef - ing to the top

And the lands - men are lurk - ing on the shore, the shore, the

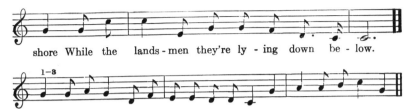

shore While the   lands - men they're ly - ing down   be - low.

For melodic relationship cf. ***FSRA 46; *SharpK i 291, No. 42A, measures 1-5 and 293, version D, measures 1-4.

Scale: Heptachordal.   Tonal Center: c.   Structure: abca¹a² (2,2,2,2,2) = ab (4,6).

> 2   Oh, up spoke the captain of our gallant ship,
> A well spoken man was he,
> Saying, 'I have a family in fair New York town,
> And this night they'll be looking for me, for me,
> And this night they'll be looking for me.'

49
TROOPER AND MAID
(Child 299)

'The Bugle Boy.' Sung by Mrs. Peggy Perry. Recorded as MS score at Zionville, Watauga county, in 1915. This is the ballad concerning which in II 199 (footnote 1) Professor Belden says, "It should be observed that the last six lines are metrically of a different pattern from the preceding stanzas. They fit the situation well enough, but belong really to a different song." This "different song" we have here. Incidentally, the page given for BSI is not 188, but 167.

181

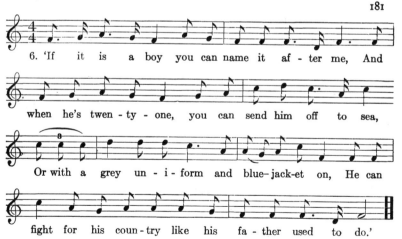

6. 'If   it   is   a boy you can name it   af - ter me,   And

when he's twen - ty - one, you can send him off   to   sea,

Or with a   grey   un - i - form and blue-jack-et   on,   He can

fight   for   his coun - try like   his   fa - ther used   to do.'

Scale: Mode III, plagal. Tonal Center: f. Structure: aa¹ba² (2,2,2,2) =
Reprisenbar.

49(1)

'The Bugle Boy.' Sung by C. K. Tillett. Recorded at Wanchese, Roanoke
Island, December 29, 1922. The last two lines of a varied third stanza are here
repeated, thereby extending the melody.

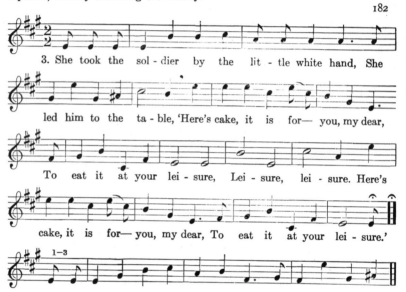

For melodic relationship cf. **TBV 606, No. 51A, measures 7-10 and 13-15
with our 5-7 and 11-13.

Scale: Hexachordal, plagal. Tonal Center: e. Structure: nmm¹ (4,6,4) =
inverted barform. The m is terminally incremented.

> 2   She took the soldier's horse by the bridle rein,
>   She led him to the stable,
>   . . . .

(The record breaks off here.)

50
THE DILLY SONG

A

'Singing the Ten Commandments.' Sung by Miss Mattie Dobson. Recorded as
MS score, but no date or place given. Another title given is 'The Twelve
Apostles.' Cf. FSmWV 44-45. For other titles see AFSC 66. For the sixth
stanza, measure a (see below), is inserted after the fourth measure. For the
seventh stanza, measure b (see below), is added preceding measure a.

183

'I will— sing.' 'What will you sing?' 'I'll sing the fifth.'

'What is the fifth?' 'Five is the fire - man in the boat,

And two of them were stran - gers; Two of them were

lit - tle white babes, All dressed in morn - ing gran - ger;

One of them was God a - lone, Shout ev - 'ry na - tion!'

a

The sixth is the gos - pel preach - er.

b

Sev - en is the sev - en stars in the sky.——

Scale: Pentachordal, plagal. Tontal Center: f. Structure: aaaabb^{1}b^2 (1,1,1,1, 2,2,2) = ab (4,6). Circular Tune (V).

B

'Come and I Will Sing You.' Sung by Miss Edith Walker. Recorded at Boone, no date given. The various stanzas are taken care of by interpolating inter- mittently a and b (see below), independently, and only once combined. Like- wise, the last four measures are repeated as the text requires. Sometimes, either a or b is interpolated, but there is no stereotyped procedure in this.

184

'Come and I will sing you.' 'What will you sing?'

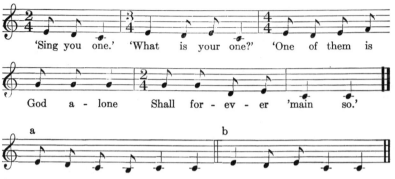

'Sing you one.' 'What is your one?' 'One of them is
God a - lone Shall for - ev - er 'main so.'

Scale: Pentachordal. Tonal Center: c. Structure: aa¹bb¹ca² (2,1,1,1,2).

51

THE TWELVE BLESSINGS OF MARY

'The Twelve Blessings of Mary.' Sung by Mrs. Arizona Hughes. Recorded
at Henson Creek, Avery county, in 1939. Only stanza 5 differs in ending as
given below (measures 12-16).

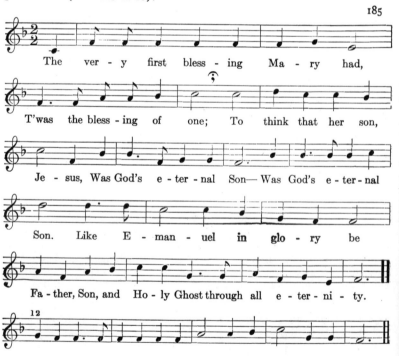

The ver - y first bless - ing Ma - ry had,
T'was the bless - ing of one; To think that her son,
Je - sus, Was God's e - ter - nal Son— Was God's e - ter - nal
Son. Like E - man - uel in glo - ry be
Fa - ther, Son, and Ho - ly Ghost through all e - ter - ni - ty.

Scale: Heptachordal, plagal. Tonal Center: f. Structure: abcdb¹c¹b²d¹ (2,2,2, 2,2,2,2,2) = abcb¹b² (2,4,2,4,4).

52

The Twelve Days of Christmas

B

'The Twelve Days of Christmas.'[1] Sung by Mrs. Ervilla Chamberlain. Recorded at Raleigh in 1924. The first two measures are used for all twelve days. With each day, however, the presents increase as given below under 1st, 2nd, 3rd, and 4th. The fifth begins, of course, with "Five gold rings," the sixth with "Six geese a-laying," and the 12th day shows how all the previous days are to be treated. Cf. FSEK 130, No. 87.

186

The first day of Christ-mas my true love sent to me

1st A par-ter-idge up-on a pear tree. 2nd Two tur-tle doves

3rd And a par-ter-idge up-on a pear tree. Three French hens,

Two tur-tle doves And a par-ter-idge up-on a pear tree.

4th Four Corn-ish birds, Three French hens, Two tur-tle doves And a

par-ter-idge up-on a pear tree. Five gold rings,

Four Cor-nish birds, Three French hens, Two tur-tle

---

[1] For the game, see 1 70 f.

doves And a   par - ter - idge up - on   a   pear tree.

Six geese a - lay - ing,   Five gold rings,   Four Cor - nish birds,

Three French hens,   Two tur - tle doves And   a   par - ter - idge up -
                                              12th Day

on a   pear tree.   Twelve hunt - ers   hunt - ing, Eleven la - dies

leap - ing, Ten   tail - ors stitch - ing, Nine fid - dlers fid - dling,

Eight Lords a - danc - ing, Seven swans a - swim-ming, Six geese a -

lay - ing,   Five gold rings,   Four Cor-nish birds, Three French hens,

Two tur - tle doves And   a par - ter - idge   up - on   a pear tree.

The following analysis of the scale as well as the structure is based on the
first two measures plus the '12th day' stanza.

Scale: Pentachordal, plagal.   Tonal Center: g.   Structure: abb¹cd (2,4,4,2,3).

D

'The Twelve Days of Christmas.' Sung by Mrs. G. Watson. Recorded at
Boone, August 14, 1939. The measure "Three French hens" is used throughout
for all presents.

187

The   first   day   of Christ-mas my true love sent to me   A

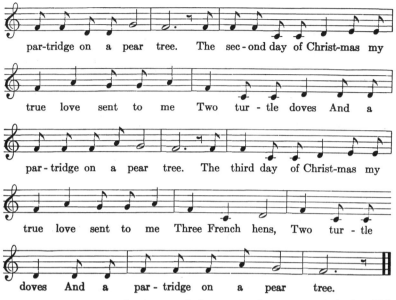

par-tridge on a pear tree. The sec-ond day of Christ-mas my

true love sent to me Two tur - tle doves And a

par - tridge on a pear tree. The third day of Christ-mas my

true love sent to me Three French hens, Two tur - tle

doves And a par - tridge on a pear tree.

Scale: Hexatonic (4) plagal. Tonal Center: f. Structure: aa¹ (3,3). This
is based on 'The third day' phrase of six measures.

53
I Saw Three Ships Come Sailing In

'On Christmas Day.' Sung by anonymous singer. Recorded MS score, but no
date or place given.

188

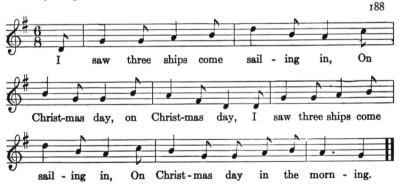

I saw three ships come sail - ing in, On

Christ-mas day, on Christ-mas day, I saw three ships come

sail - ing in, On Christ-mas day in the morn - ing.

For melodic relationship cf. ***OBC 36; *AFSC, measures 1-2 and 5-6.

Scale: Hexatonic (6), plagal. Tonal Center: g. Structure. abab¹ (2,2,2,2) =
aa¹ (4,4).

54

DIVES AND LAZARUS I

'The Rich Man and Lazarus.' Sung by Dr. I. G. Greer. Recorded as MS score at Boone, no date, but about 1915-16. The text is almost identical with that of SharpK II 29, No. 84A; the tune, however, is different from either of the versions given there.

189

There was a man in an-cient time, The Scrip-ture doth– in-form–us, Whose pomp and gran-deur and his crimes Were great and ver-y nu-mer-ous. This rich man fared sump-tuous-ly each day, And was dressed in pur-ple lin-en; He ate and drank, but scorned to pray, And spent his day— in sing-ing.

For melodic relationship cf. **DESO 48, No. 31; to a lesser degree, *ibid.* 27, No. 11.

Scale: Hexatonic (3), plagal. Tonal Center: e-flat. Structure: aba^{1}b^{1}cb^{2}a^{1}b^1 (2,2,2,2,2,2,2,2) = aa^{1}ba^1 (4,4,4,4) = Reprisenbar.

56

THE ROMISH LADY

'The Romish Lady.' Sung by Miss Jewell Robbins. Recorded at Pekin, Montgomery county, in 1921. This is only slightly different from the anonymous version, which follows.

190

There was a Rom-ish la-dy Brought up in po-pe-ry,

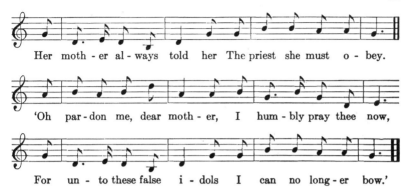

Her moth - er al - ways told her The priest she must o - bey.

'Oh par - don me, dear moth - er, I hum - bly pray thee now,

For un - to these false i - dols I can no long - er bow.'

For melodic relationship cf. ***WSSU 141, No. 37, last four measures; **FSoA 19, our measures 3-4, which occur twice there.

Scale: Mode III, plagal. Tonal Center: g. Structure: aa¹ba $(4,4,4,4)$ = Reprisenbar.

56(1)

'The Romish Lady.' Sung by anonymous singer. Recorded as MS score, but no date or place given. There are only slight differences here from the previous version. These insignificant changes occur in measures 2, 6, 10-11, and 14.

191

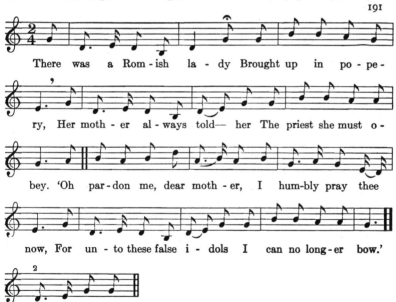

There was a Rom - ish la - dy Brought up in po - pe -

ry, Her moth - er al - ways told— her The priest she must o -

bey. 'Oh par - don me, dear moth - er, I hum-bly pray thee

now, For un - to these false i - dols I can no long - er bow.'

2

For analysis, see preceding, 56.

56(2)

'The Romish Lady.' Sung by Myra Barnett Miller. Recorded probably at Lenoir, August 1939, 1940, or 1941.

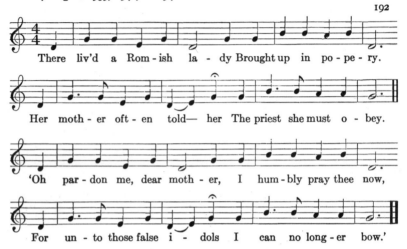

There liv'd a Rom - ish la - dy Brought up in po - pe - ry.

Her moth - er oft - en told— her The priest she must o - bey.

'Oh par - don me, dear moth - er, I hum - bly pray thee now,

For un - to those false i - dols I can no long - er bow.'

For melodic relationship cf. **SHMC 82, basic melodic points only.

Scale: Mode III, plagal. Tonal Center: g. Structure: aa^{1}aa^1 (4,4,4,4) = aa (8,8).

61

NANCY OF YARMOUTH

'Jimmy and Nancy.' Sung probably by Mrs. R. E. Barnes at Taylorsville, Alexander county. MS score, dated 1853. The tune requires two stanzas of the text as given in II 223 ff. Text and tune are identical with those of the Greer version, which is therefore omitted.

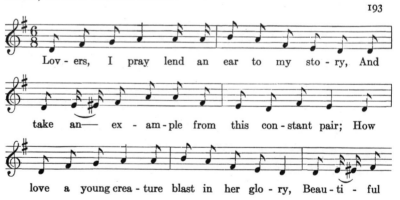

Lov - ers, I pray lend an ear to my sto - ry, And

take an— ex - am - ple from this con - stant pair; How

love a young crea - ture blast in her glo - ry, Beau - ti - ful

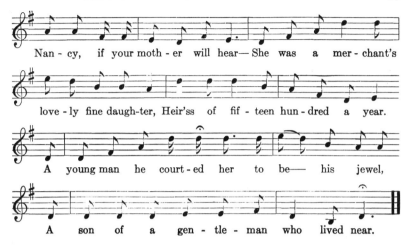

Nan - cy, if your moth - er will hear— She was a mer - chant's
love - ly fine daugh-ter, Heir'ss of fif - teen hun - dred a year.
A young man he court - ed her to be— his jewel,
A son of a gen - tle - man who lived near.

Scale: Hexachordal, plagal. Tonal Center: d. Structure: ababcdc¹e (2,2,2,2, 2,2,2,2) = aabb¹ (4,4,4,4).

62
THE BRAMBLE BRIAR

B

'The 'Prentice Boy.' Sung by Aunt Becky Gordon. Recorded on July 19, 1939, but no place given. The title given by the singer is 'The Silk Merchant's Daughter.' The story is practically identical with 'In Seaport Town.' Cf. SharpK 1 313, No. 48E. As frequently in these re-recordings, the first stanza does not begin with the initial measures.

194

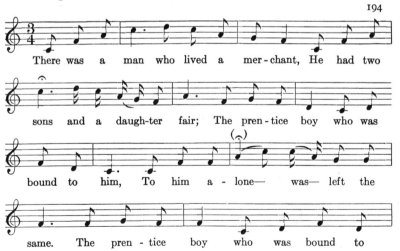

There was a man who lived a mer - chant, He had two
sons and a daugh-ter fair; The pren - tice boy who was
bound to him, To him a - lone— was— left the
same. The pren - tice boy who was bound to

him,   To   him   a - lone—   was—   left   the   same.

For melodic relationship cf. **SharpK 1 313, No. 48E, measures 1-2; *ibid.* 310, version A, last two measures; OFS 1 381, No. 100, measures 1-4.

Scale: Mode III, plagal.   Tonal Center: f.   Structure: aa¹bcbc (2,2,2,2,2,2) = abb (4,4,4) = nmm (inverted barform).

C

'The Ditch of Briars.'   Sung by Mr. and Mrs. James York.   From previous recording of Dr. W. A. Abrams, Boone, August 8, 1940.   Owing to the condition of the record it is not possible to understand the words of the first stanza. The story in general is the same as in the previous version, 'The 'Prentice Boy' (62B).   G. Malcolm Laws in NAB classifies this as derived from British broadsides.

195

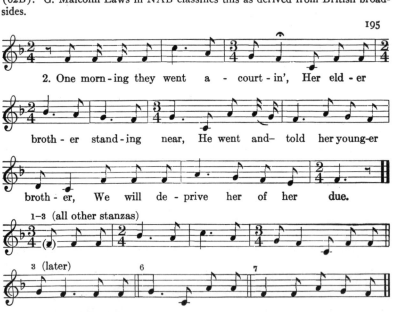

2. One morn-ing they went   a - court-in',   Her eld - er

broth - er stand-ing   near, He went and— told   her young-er

broth - er,   We   will   de - prive   her   of   her   due.

1–3 (all other stanzas)

3 (later)   6   7

Scale: Heptachordal, plagal.   Tonal Center: f.   Structure abcd (3,3,2,2).

3   Early, early the next morning,
    Hunting, hunting they would go.
    Little did he think of bloody murder,
    So a-hunting they did go.

4   When they returned late in the evening,
    She inquired of where he went.
    The brothers ...... and whispered lowly,
    'Brother, tell me if you can.'

5 We left him in the wild woods hunting,
  And his face on earth you no more shall see.
  He's crossing o'er the deep blue ocean.
  He'll return no more to thee.

6 That night as she lay on her bed a-weeping,
  His ghost to her it did appear.
  'Then go unto yon ditch of briars,
  There you will my body find.'

7 She rose early the next morning,
  Gave .... at home.
  She went till she came to the ditch of briars
  Where her true love'd been killed and thrown.

8 His face was gray and ....
  Tears in his eyes ....
  She took his pale, cold lips a-cryin',
  'You were the dearest dear of mine.'

9 'Since my two brothers have been so cruel
  As to take your good, sweet life away,
  One grave shall hold us both together,
  While on this earth I'll no longer stay.'

64

THE GOSPORT TRAGEDY

C

'Polly.' Miss Pearle Webb. No date or place given. Although the tune is totally different, the text is very closely related to that of 'The Cruel Ship's Carpenter.' Cf. SharpK 1 317, No. 49A.

196

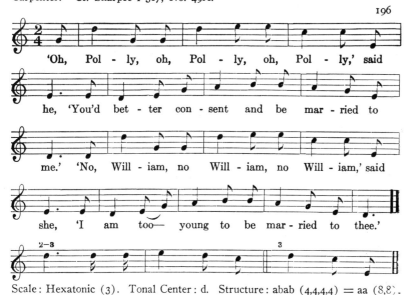

'Oh, Pol - ly, oh, Pol - ly, oh, Pol - ly,' said he, 'You'd bet - ter con - sent and be mar - ried to me.' 'No, Will - iam, no Will - iam, no Will - iam,' said she, 'I am too— young to be mar - ried to thee.'

Scale: Hexatonic (3). Tonal Center: d. Structure: abab (4,4,4,4) = aa (8,8).

E

'Pretty Molly.' Sung by Mrs. James York. From previous recording of Dr. W. A. Abrams, Boone, August 8, 1940. This is the last stanza. Owing to the condition of the record, the words of the other stanzas cannot be understood. The only thing certain is that the name 'Polly' does occur. The text is closely related to that of SharpK 1 324, No. 49L; also, FSUSA 304-5, No. 84.

197

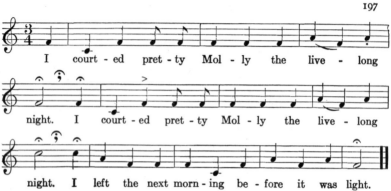

Scale: Triadic, plagal. Tonal Center: f. Structure abab¹cb (2,2,2,2,2,2) $=$ aab (4,4,4) $=$ mmn $=$ barform; the b is partly related to a.

E(I)

'Pretty Polly.' Sung by Mrs. J. Church. Recorded at Heaton, Avery county, August 10, 1939. This text is very closely related to that of SharpK 1 321 and 325, No. 49 F and N; cf. also MSHF 3, No. 1.

198

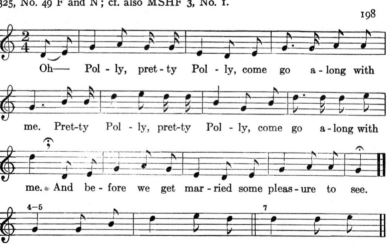

For melodic relationship cf. **SCSM 397, version E, melodic line; SharpK 1 324, No. 49L, measures 1-4, melodic progression only. Since the tune of this version is in ¾ and that of the former in ¾, the rhythmic shift produces an entirely different melody despite the tonal material.

Scale: Mode III, plagal. Tonal Center: g. Structure: aba¹b¹ab (2,2,2,2,2,2) = aa¹a (4,4,4).

65
THE LEXINGTON MURDER

The story of all the versions that follow is very much like that of SharpK I 407, No. 71A: 'The Miller's Apprentice,' or 'The Oxford Tragedy'; also BSO 233-5, version C, 'The Murdered Girl.'

A

'The Lexington Murder.' Sung by anonymous singer. Recorded, but no date or place given. The text of this version is a combination of versions A and F.

199

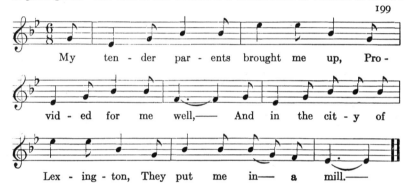

My ten - der par - ents brought me up, Pro -

vid - ed for me well,— And in the cit - y of

Lex - ing - ton, They put me in— a mill.—

For melodic relationship cf. **SCSM 402, version A, general melodic line.

Scale: Tetratonic (4). Tonal Center: e-flat. Structure: abac (2,2,2,2) = aa¹ (4,4).

2 Last Saturday night three weeks ago,
   Oh, cursed be the day,
   The devil put it in my mind
   To take her sweet life away.

3 I went down to her sister's house
   At eight o'clock last night,
   And she, the poor girl, seemed not to think
   For her I had a spite.

4 I asked her if she'd take a walk
   A little way with me,
   That we might have a little talk
   About our wedding day.

5 We walked along a-side by side
   'Till we came to a silent place;
   I picked me up a stick from the ground
   And struck her in the face.

6 She fell upon her bended knee,
   'Have mercy!' she did cry,
   'For Heaven's sake, don't murder me,
   I'm not prepared to die.'

7 I heeded not the mercy cry,
   But struck her all the more
   Until I could see that innocent blood,
   The blood I could not restore.

8 I covered my hands in her cold black hair
   To cover up my sin,
   I dragged her to the river bank,
   And there I plunged her in.

9 I started on my way back home,
   And I met my servant, John,
   'Why do you look so very weak,
   And yet you are so warm?'

10 'And what is the cause of all that blood
   Upon your hands and clothes?',
   And as the innocent one replied,
   'The bleeding of my nose.'

11 I lit my candle and I went to bed
   A-thinking I could rest.
   It seemed as if the flames of hell
   Was burning on my breast.

A(1)

'Lexington Murder.' Sung by Mrs. G. L. Bostic. Recorded near Mooresboro, Cleveland county, August 7, 1939. There is some melodic relationship with the anonymous version (65A), and the Dunnegan version of 'Nellie Cropsey' (307C), measures 2-4.

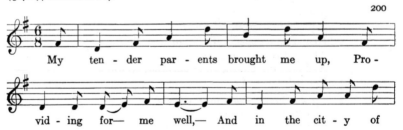

My ten - der par - ents brought me up, Pro -
vid - ing for— me well,— And in the cit - y of

Lex - ing - ton   They   placed–   me   in —   the   mill.—

Scale: Hexachordal.   Tonal Center: d.   Structure: abac (2,2,2,2) = aa¹ (4,4).

2   I went down to her mother's house,
Just half past eight o'clock.
But little did the .... think
That I had a spite at her.

3   I said, 'Come, take a little walk,
For just a little way,
So we can have a little talk
About our wedding day.'

4   So, walking .... side by side,
'Till we came to a silent place,
I drew a slat from off the fence
And struck her in the face.

5   Down on her bended knees she fell,
And cried, 'For mercy sake,
For heaven's sake, don't murder me.
For I'm not prepared to die.'

6   But little did I heed her cry;
I only struck her more
Until the blood was overflowed
All on her handsome face.

7   I hid my hands in her black hair
And tried to hide my sin,
And drug her back to the river-side,
And there I throwed her in.

A(2)

'The Lexington Murder.'   Sung by Mrs. J. Trivette.   Recorded at Heaton,
Avery county, August 10, 1939.   Other titles given are 'The Bloody Miller' and
'The Cruel Miller.'   Melodically, there is some relationship (measures 2-4) with
the Dunnegan version of 'Nellie Cropsey' (307C).

201

3. Last   Sat - ur - day night three weeks a - go, Ac - curs - ed   be   the   day—

The dev - il put it in my heart To take her life— a - way.–

Scale: Mode III. Tonal Center: d. Structure: abcd (2,2,2,2,).

B

'The Bloody Miller, or The Murdering Miller.' Sung by Dr. I. G. Greer. Recorded as MS score at Boone in 1915 or 1916. With stanza 9 of this version cf. George Petrie, The Petrie Collection of the Ancient Music of Ireland, 134, and the *Complete Petrie Collection,*' 693-694:

> 'Oh, Johnnie, dearest Johnnie,
> What dyed your hands and clothes?'
> He answered him, as he thought fit,
> 'By a bleeding at the nose.'

202

One month a - go since Christmas last, That most un-hap-py day,

The dev - il he per - suad-ed me To take her life a - way.

Scale: Dorian (plagal.) Tonal Center: e. Structure aba¹c (2,2,2,2) = aa¹ (4,4).

D

'Lexington Murder.' Sung by Mrs. R. C. Vaught. Recorded at Taylorsville, Alexander county, in June 1923. Measures 3-8 are closely related to those of the 65A and 307C versions.

203

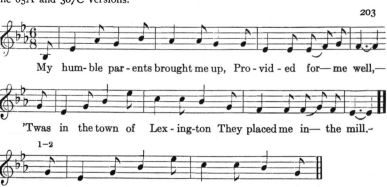

My hum- ble par - ents brought me up, Pro - vid - ed for— me well,—

'Twas in the town of Lex - ing-ton They placed me in— the mill.–

1–2

Scale: Hexachordal, plagal. Tonal Center: e-flat. Structure: abcd (2,2,2,2).

G

'The Knoxville Girl.' Sung by anonymous female singer with guitar. Recorded, but no date or place given. The only thing in common between this text and that given in II 244 f. is the "dark and rolling eyes" of stanza 6, line 2. Besides this, the structure of our tune definitely requires two stanzas as given in the printed text.

Scale: Hexatonic (4), plagal. Tonal Center: f. Structure: abacabac¹ (2,2,2, 2,2,2,2,2) = aa¹aa² (4,4,4,4).

2 We went to take an evening walk,
  About a mile from town;
  I picked up a stick from off the ground
  And knocked that fair child down.
  She fell upon her bended knees,
  And 'Mercy,' she did cry.
  Said, 'Willie, dear, don't kill me here,
  For I'm unprepared to die.'

3 I did not listen to her words,
  I beat her more and more
  Until the ground around her
  Was but a bloody pour.
  I took her by her golden curls,
  And dragged her 'round and 'round,
  And threw her in the water deep
  That flows through Knoxville town.

4 I started back to Knoxville,
   Got there about midnight.
   My mother was so worried,
   She woke up in a fright,
   Says, 'Son, oh, son, what have you done?
   You've blood . . . . '
   The answer that I gave her
   Was 'Bleeding at the nose.'

5 They took me to the Knoxville jail
   And locked me in a cell.
   My friends they tried to get me out,
   But none could go my bail.
   Her sister swore my life away,
   She swore without a doubt
   That I was the very man
   That laid her sister out.

M

'Poor Nell.' Sung by B. C. Reavis. Recorded, but no date or place given.
Measures 1-2 and 5-6 are strongly reminiscent of 'Home, Sweet Home.'

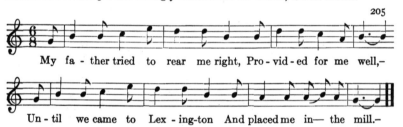

My fa - ther tried to rear me right, Pro - vid - ed for me well,—

Un - til we came to Lex - ing-ton And placed me in— the mill.—

Scale: Hexachordal. Tonal Center: g. Structure: abac (2,2,2,2) = aa^1 (4,4).

66

ON THE BANKS OF THE OHIO

G

'On the Banks of the Ohio.' Sung by Miss Addie Hardin. Recorded as MS
score at Rutherwood, Watauga county, in 1922. Although the MS gives only
the last two lines of the chorus, it was possible to recapture the stanza and
complete chorus from a cylinder record. Another title given is 'The Wexford
Girl.'

I asked my love to take a walk Just to be a - lone with

me,   And   as   we   walked   we'd   have   a   talk   A - bout   our

wed - ding   day   to   be.   On - ly   say   that   you'll   be

mine,   Hap - py   in   my   home you'll   find,   Down   be - side

where   the   wa - ters   flow   On   the   banks   of   the   O - hi - o.

For melodic relationship cf. ***BMFSB 44.

Scale: Hexatonic (6), plagal.   Tonal Center: f.   Structure: aba^{1}a^{2}aba^{1}a^2
(2,2,2,2,2,2,2,2) = aa^{1}aa^1 (4,4,4,4).

67
ROSE CONNALLY

A

'Rose Connally.' Sung by Frank Proffitt and Nathan Hicks, with dulcimer and
guitar. Recorded at Sugar Grove, Watauga county, in 1939. This melody is
closely related to 'Old Rosin the Beau' of this collection. The second stanza
given in II 249 is a part of the first stanza in the version given in FSUSA 302,
No. 83.

207

Down   in   the   wil - low   gar - den,   Where me and my love did   be—

There   we   sit—   a - court - ing;   My— love dropped off—   to   sleep.—

Upbeat and first measure   2

3—4   1 also

For melodic relationship cf. ***FSUSA 302, No. 83, compare with our variations, occurring in the stanza; also *ibid.* ** our stanza without the variations.

Scale: Hexatonic (4), plagal. Tonal Center: f. Structure: abac (2,2,2,2) =
aa¹ (4,4).

B

'Down in the Willow Garden.' Sung by anonymous male singer. Recorded,
but no date or place given. This is also closely related to 'Old Rosin the Beau'
and to 67B(1), which follows.

208

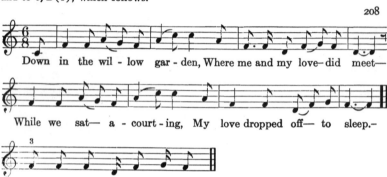

Down in the wil - low gar - den, Where me and my love– did meet—

While we sat— a - court - ing, My love dropped off— to sleep.-

For melodic relationship cf. ***FSUSA 302, No. 83; compare with our
variations occurring in the stanza.

Scale: Mode III, plagal. Tonal Center: f. Structure: abac (2,2,2,2) = aa¹
(4,4).

B(1)

'Down in the Willow Garden.' Sung by Miss Edith Walker. From the previous
recording of Dr. W. A. Abrams, Boone, August 8, 1940. This is closely related
to 'Old Rosin the Beau' and to 67A and 67B. For the variations see note on
67A.

209

Down in the wil - low gar - den Where me and my love– did meet–

were court - ing, My love dropped off— to sleep.-

Scale: Mode III, plagal.   Tonal Center: e-flat.   Structure: abac (2,2,2,2) =
aa¹ (4,4).

70

THE LANCASTER MAID

'Pretty Betsey.'   Sung by Jewell Robbins.   Recorded, but no date or place given.
The story is very much like 'Betsy,' SharpK 11 4, No. 74, but the tune is totally
different.

210

Pret - ty   Bet - sy   was   of   a   beau - ty   clear;   She   had

late - ly   come   from Au - gus - ta   here,   A   wait - ing - maid   she

came   to   be.   Oh   Bet - sy   was   of   a   high   de - gree.

Scale: Hexachordal, plagal.   Tonal Center: g.   Structure: abb¹a¹ (2,2,2,2) =
ab (4,4); b and b¹ are rhythmically closely related.   Circular tune (V).

71

THE DROWSY SLEEPER

A

'Awake, Arise.'   Sung by anonymous singer.   Recorded as MS score by Mrs.
Sutton, but no date or place given.   Songs like this one, and Mrs. Sutton's
remark, "It is like a gypsy song, *all wailing minors*" (italics by this editor),
make one sincerely doubt Mrs. Sutton's qualifications and judgment in musical
matters.   There is of course no minor quality in this song, "wailing" or otherwise.   The text of this version is a contraction of SharpK 1.359, No. 57B,
stanzas 1 and 3.

211

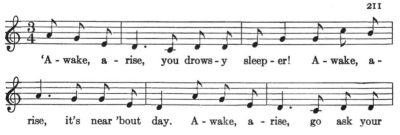

'A - wake, a - rise,   you drows - y   sleep - er!   A - wake,   a -

rise,   it's   near 'bout   day.   A - wake, a - rise,   go   ask   your

fa - ther, If you're my bride— to— be. And if you're not, come

back and tell me; It's the ver - y last time I'll both-er thee.'

Scale: Hexatonic (4). Tonal Center: c. Structure: aba¹b¹a¹b¹ (2,2,2,2,2,2) = aa¹a¹ (4,4,4).

$$\text{Scale: Hexatonic (4). Tonal Center: c. Structure: } aba^1b^1a^1b^1\ (2,2,2,2,2,2) = aa^1a^1\ (4,4,4).$$

B

'Charlie and Bessie.' Sung by Mrs. B. Greene. Recorded at Zionville, Watauga county, September 11, 1939. Other titles given are 'The Silver Dagger' and 'Wake Up, You Drowsy Sleeper.'

212

'Bes - sie, oh, Bes - - sie, go and ask your fa - ther

If you can be a bride of mine, And if he says

'No' please come and tell me And I'll no long - er— both - er you.'

1 With upbeat

For melodic relationship cf. *SharpK 1 358, No. 57A, measures 2-8, general melodic outline.

Scale: Mode III, plagal. Tonal Center: g. Structure: aba¹b¹ (2,2,2,2) = aa¹ (4,4).

$$\text{Scale: Mode III, plagal. Tonal Center: g. Structure: } aba^1b^1\ (2,2,2,2) = aa^1\ (4,4).$$

D

'Oh, You Drowsy Sleeper.' Sung by Mrs. James York. Recorded probably at Olin, Iredell county, in 1939.

213

'Wake up, wake up you drow-sy sleep-er, Wake up, wake up;

'tis al - most day. How can— you lie there and—

slum - ber When your true love is going a - way?'

Scale: Hexatonic (2), plagal. Tonal Center: g. Structure: aa¹bc (2,2,2,2) = ab (4,4). Rhythmically, the four subphrases are practically identical.

E

'O Drowsy Sleeper.' Sung by Otis Kuykendall. Recorded at Asheville in 1939. This tune is quite similar to 'The 'Prentice Boy' sung by Aunt Becky Gordon (62B).

214

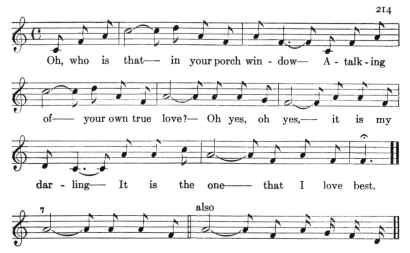

Oh, who is that— in your porch win - dow— A - talk - ing

of— your own true love?— Oh yes, oh yes,— it is my

dar - ling— It is the one—— that I love best.

also

For melodic relationship cf. **SharpK 1 360, No. 57C.

Scale: Mode III, plagal. Tonal Center: f. Structure: aabc (2,2,2,2) = ab (4,4).

72
THE SILVER DAGGER

B

'The Dying Lovers.' Sung by Miss Lizzie Lee Weaver. Recorded as MS score at Piney Creek, Alleghany county, about 1915.

215

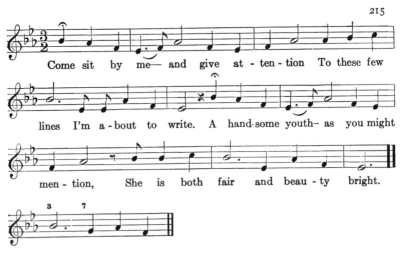

Come sit by me— and give at - ten - tion To these few
lines I'm a - bout to write. A hand-some youth— as you might
men - tion, She is both fair and beau - ty bright.

Scale: Mode I. Tonal Center: e-flat. Structure: abab¹ (2,2,2,2) = aa¹ (4,4).

D

'The Silver Dagger.' Sung by Mrs. James York. From the previous recording
of Dr. W. A. Abrams, probably at Boone; no date given.

216

Young lad - ies, Young lad - - - ies Come lend your at -
ten - tion, To these few lines I'm a - bout to
write; There was a young man court - ed a fair young
maid - en, Who was his joy and his heart's de - light.

For melodic relationship cf. *SharpK II 229, No. 165A, only in general out-line. Scale: Mode II, plagal. Tonal Center: c. Structure: aa¹bb¹ (2,2,2,2) = ab (4,4).

2 And when his parents came to know it
   They pled with him both night and day,
   Saying, 'Will you forsake your loving father?
   She's so very poor, I've heard them say.'

3 And she being near beneath her window,
   She heard that awful, mournful groan.
   She run and she run like one distracted,
   Saying, 'I'm lost, I'm lost, I'm left alone.'

76
MOLLY BAWN

A

'Polly Bonn.' Sung by Miss Jewell Robbins. Recorded at Pekin, Montgomery county. No date given. Another title given is 'Molly Bander.' The phrase "The rain it did fall" leans heavily on "far, far away" of 'Swanee River' fame.

217

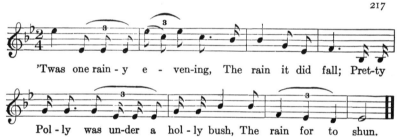

'Twas one rain-y e-ven-ing, The rain it did fall; Pret-ty
Pol-ly was un-der a hol-ly bush, The rain for to shun.

Scale: Hexatonic (4), plagal. Tonal Center: e-flat. Structure: abcd (2,2,2,2).

B

'Mollie Vaunders.' Sung by anonymous singer. Recorded as MS score. No date given; probably at Lenoir, Caldwell county. The text of this version is almost the same as SharpK I 329, No. 50C; the name of the girl in the latter is, however, "Molly Bander." Another name found is "Molly Banding."

218

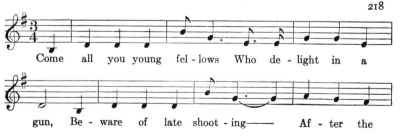

Come all you young fel-lows Who de-light in a
gun, Be-ware of late shoot-ing—— Af-ter the

sun's down. I'll   tell you   a   sto - ry, Which hap-pened of

late,   Con - cern - ing Mol-lie Vaun-ders, Whose beau - ty was great.

For melodic relationship cf. ***FSS 529, No. 102A; *SharpK 1 329 and 332, No. 50 C and F, measures 4, 8, 12, and 16, cadences only.

Scale: Heptachordal, plagal. Tonal center: g. Structure. aba^{1}cdb^{1}ac^1 (2,2,2, 2,2,2,2) = aa^{1}ba^2 (4,4,4,4) = Reprisenbar.

C

'Shooting of His Dear.' Sung by Mrs. Nora Hicks. Recorded at Mast's Gap, Watauga county, September 28, 1940. For another variety of trees ("beech tree") cf. SharpK 1 329, No. 50B and C.

219

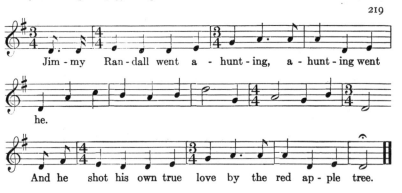

Jim - my   Ran - dall went   a - hunt - ing,   a - hunt - ing went

he.

And he   shot his own true   love by the red ap - ple tree.

For melodic relationship cf. **SharpK 1 328, No. 50A, general melodic line only.

Scale: Mixolydian. Tonal Center: d. Structure: abcda^{1}b (2,2,2,2,2,2) = aba^1 (4,4,4).

78

MARY OF THE WILD MOOR

'Mary of the Wild Moor.' Sung by anonymous singer. Recorded as MS score at Wanchese, Roanoke Island, in May 1920. This song is an excellent example of what can be accomplished with almost nothing to start with. The entire melody is almost completely built of the pattern formed by the first three notes, its inversion and transposition.

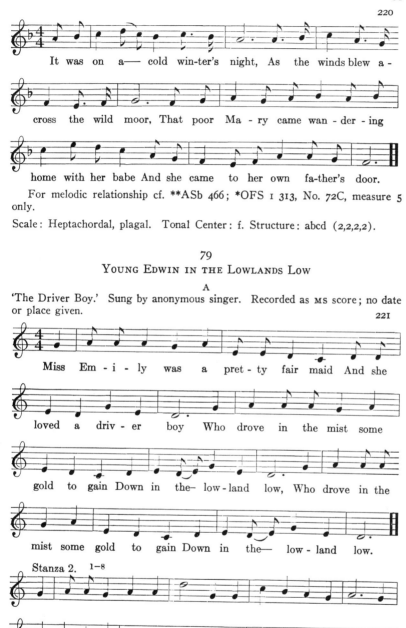

220

It was on a— cold win-ter's night, As   the winds blew a -

cross the wild moor, That poor Ma - ry came wan - der - ing

home with her babe And she came   to her own   fa-ther's door.

For melodic relationship cf. **ASb 466; *OFS 1 313, No. 72C, measure 5 only.

Scale: Heptachordal, plagal.   Tonal Center: f. Structure: abcd (2,2,2,2).

79
Young Edwin in the Lowlands Low

A

'The Driver Boy.'   Sung by anonymous singer.   Recorded as MS score; no date or place given.

221

Miss Em - i - ly was   a   pret - ty fair maid And she

loved   a   driv - er   boy Who drove in   the mist some

gold   to gain Down in   the— low - land   low, Who drove in the

mist some gold   to   gain Down in   the— low - land   low.

Stanza 2.   1—8

For melodic relationship cf. **SharpK 1 351, No. 56B, phrase b (variation), and *ibid.* 354 and 356, versions E and G, measures 5-8. Also 356, No. 7, versions I and J, measures 7-8 with final cadence in our song.

Scale: Mode IV, plagal. Tonal Center: d. Structure: abab^{1}ab^1 (2,2,2,2,2,2) = aa^{1}a^1 (4,4,4).

A(1)

'The Driver Boy.' Sung by Mrs. E. Stamey. Recorded at Altamont, Avery county, July 14, 1940. The singer does not repeat the last two lines as given in the printed text in II 267 f. Our text is very similar to that of SharpK 1 351, No. 56B. The third and fourth measures remind one of 'Oh, Susanna!'

222

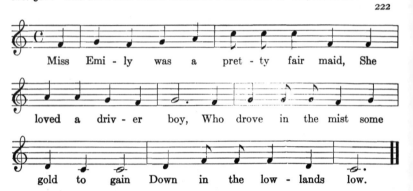

For melodic relationship cf. **SharpK 1 351 and 356, No. 56 B and G.

Scale: Mode III, plagal. Tonal Center: f. Structure: abcd (2,2,2,2). Circular Tune (V).

80

THE THREE BUTCHERS

B

'Good Woman.' Sung by anonymous singer. Recorded probably in Pasquotank county in 1919 or thereabouts.

223

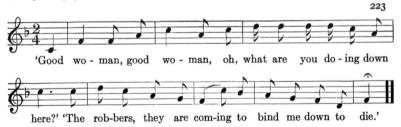

For melodic relationship cf. **FSRA 83.

Scale: Hexachordal, plagal. Tonal Center: f. Structure: abcd (2,2,2,2).

81

THE BUTCHER BOY

A

'In Jefferson City.' Sung by anonymous singer. Recorded as MS score, probably about 1920; no place was given. The initial measures remind one of 'The
Campbells Are Coming'; they are also related to those of the 'Villiken and His
Dinah' (204A) and 'Little Mohee' (110), and somewhat less to 'Orphan Girl,'
(148) in our collection.

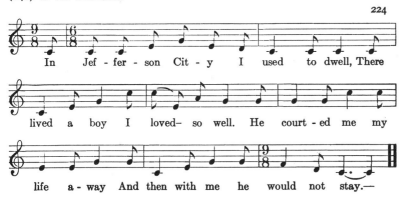

224

In   Jef - fer - son   Cit - y   I   used   to dwell, There
lived   a   boy   I   loved— so   well.   He   court - ed   me   my
life   a - way   And then with me   he   would   not   stay.—

Scale: Hexachordal.   Tonal Center: c.   Structure: abcd (2,2,2,2); the d is
slightly related to a.

K

'London City.' Sung by Edith Walker. Recorded, but no date or place given.
Other titles given are 'Farmer's Boy' and 'Butcher Boy.' The initial measures
are only slightly related to those of 81N, which follows.

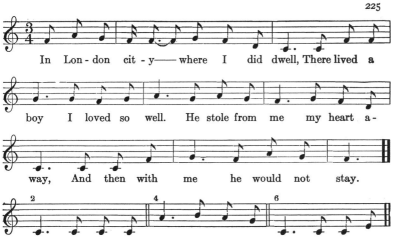

225

In   Lon - don   cit - y —— where   I   did dwell, There lived a
boy   I   loved so   well.   He stole from   me   my   heart a-
way,   And   then   with   me   he   would   not   stay.

Scale: Mode III, plagal. Tonal Center: f. Structure: abab¹ (2,2,2,2) = aa¹ (4,4).

N

'The Forsaken Lovers.' Sung by the Reverend L. D. Hayman. Recorded as MS score at Durham about 1915. Practically the same text as that in the fifth stanza of 'A Wish,' No. 254F, in III 293.

226

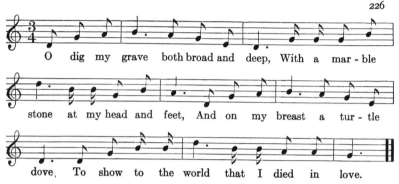

O dig my grave both broad and deep, With a mar - ble stone at my head and feet, And on my breast a tur - tle dove, To show to the world that I died in love.

Scale: Mode III, plagal. Tonal Center: g. Structure: abab¹ (2,2,2,2) = aa¹ (4,4).

82

THE LOVER'S LAMENT

B

'Pretty Polly.' Sung by Mrs. N. T. Byers. Recorded as MS score. No date or place given. The beginning recalls that of the popular song of years ago 'When You Wore a Tulip.' ("Rolling of her eye" seems to be a standard means to describe a certain psychological condition.) Cf. No. 65G, stanza 6; also SharpK II 254, No. 180A, stanza 3. (Here the "rolling" becomes a "movement.") This tune is nearly identical with 82E.

227

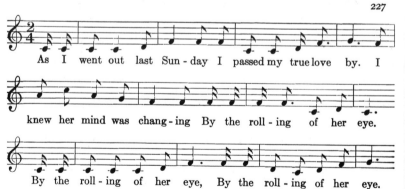

As I went out last Sun - day I passed my true love by. I knew her mind was chang - ing By the roll - ing of her eye. By the roll - ing of her eye, By the roll - ing of her eye.

I   knew her mind was chang-ing By the roll-ing of her eye.

For melodic relationship cf. **SharpK II 254, No. 180A, measures 3-8 with our 11-16.

Scale: Mode III, plagal. Tonal Center: f. Structure: abab[1] (4,4,4,4) = aa[1] (8,8). Circular Tune (V).

E

'Little Molly.' Sung by Alexander Tugman. Recorded as MS score, but no date or place given. From the recording, however, it is possible to supply the missing text in the second stanza as found in II 283. Compare also SharpK II 254, No. 180A, stanza 7.

228

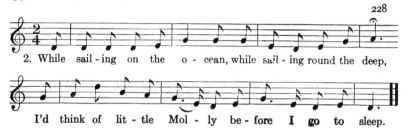

2. While sail-ing on the o - cean, while sail-ing round the deep,

I'd think of lit-tle Mol-ly be-fore I go to sleep.

For melodic relationship cf. **SharpK II 254, No. 180A, measures 3-8. Scale: Mode III, plagal. Tonal Center: g. Structure: abcd (2,2,2,2). Circular Tune (V).

84

LOCKS AND BOLTS

'I Dreamed Last Night of My True Love.' Sung by Pat Frye. From previous recording of Dr. W. A. Abrams, probably in the summer of 1945. For a similar idea from the time of Edward VI and printed in 'Lusty Juventus,' cf. ASB LXXX. Similar text to ours in SharpK II 18, No. 80B.

229

I dreamed last night of my true love, My

arms they came—— a-round her;— But when I waked 'twas

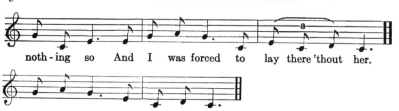

noth-ing so And I was forced to lay there 'thout her.

For melodic relationship cf. **SharpK ii No. 8oB, measures 5-8.

Scale: Hexatonic (4). Tonal Center: c. Structure: abcc¹ (2,2,2,2) = ab (4,4).

85
NEW RIVER SHORE

'New River Shore.' Sung by C. K. Tillett. Recorded at Wanchese, Roanoke Island, probably on December 29, 1922. G. Malcolm Laws, Jr. mentions this among a number of songs "many of which have been traced to British broadsides." Cf. NAB. The tune to this version requires two stanzas as printed in II 286.

230

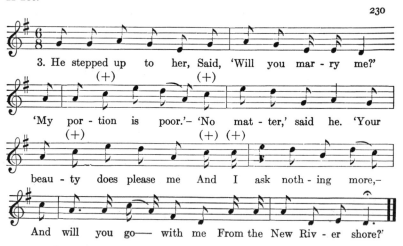

3. He stepped up to her, Said, 'Will you mar - ry me?'
(+)   (+)
'My por - tion is poor.'– 'No mat - ter,' said he. 'Your
(+)   (+) (+)
beau - ty does please me And I ask noth - ing more,–
And will you go— with me From the New Riv - er shore?'

Scale: Heptachordal, plagal. Tonal Center: g. Structure: abb¹c (2,2,2,2) Circular Tune (V).

86
THE SOLDIER'S WOOING
A

'The Rich Lady from London.' Sung by Mrs. Nora Hicks. Recorded at Mast's Gap, Watauga county, August 28, 1940. This tune also furnishes a fine example of what difference the use of a given material can make. Much of the melodic material is the same as in one of Cecil Sharp's version (see below), but what a difference in the result!

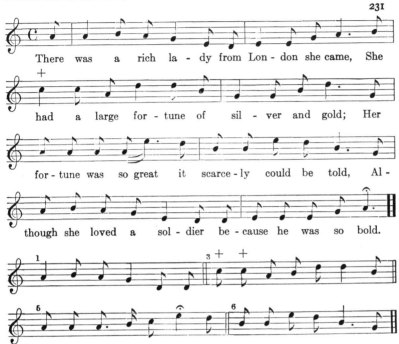

231

There was a rich la - dy from Lon - don she came, She had a large for - tune of sil - ver and gold; Her for - tune was so great it scarce - ly could be told, Al - though she loved a sol - dier be - cause he was so bold.

For melodic relationship cf. **SharpK I 355, No. 51E, general melodic line.

Scale: Hexatonic (6), plagal.   Tonal Center: a.   Structure: abca¹ (2,2,2,2).

A(1)

'The Soldier's Wooing' or 'Yankee Soldier.' Sung by C. K. Tillett. Recorded at Wanchese, Roanoke Island, December 29, 1922. Another title given is 'The Lady Held the Horse of a Soldier.' The first stanza is a compound of two others; the second is the same as stanza 4 of version 86C, II 289. For another version by the same singer, but sung two years later, cf. FSRA 88, No. 50.

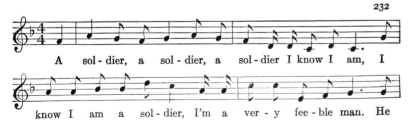

232

A sol - dier, a sol - dier, a sol - dier I know I am, I know I am a sol - dier, I'm a ver - y fee - ble man. He

drew his sword and pis - tol, And caused them to rat - tle, As the

la - dy held the horse 'till the sol - dier fought the bat - tle.

Scale: Heptachordal, plagal. Tonal Center: f. Structure: abb¹a¹ (2,2,2,2).
Circular Tune (V).

D

'The Bold Soldier.' Sung by M. T. Barnes. Recorded at Alliance, Pamlico
county, in 1927. Another title given is 'A Jolly Soldier.' The story and text
are very similar to SharpK I 333-7, No. 51 A, C, E, and G.

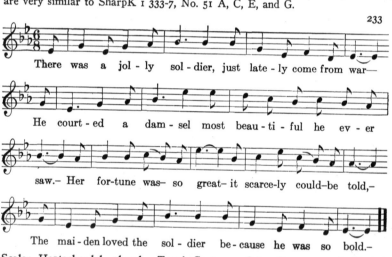

There was a jol - ly sol - dier, just late - ly come from war—

He court - ed a dam - sel most beau - ti - ful he ev - er

saw.– Her for-tune was– so great– it scarce-ly could–be told,–

The mai - den loved the sol - dier be - cause he was so bold.–

Scale: Heptachordal, plagal. Tonal Center: e-flat. Structure: abab¹cc¹a¹b
(2,2,2,2,2,2,2,2) = aa¹ba² (4,4,4,4) = Reprisenbar.

87
EARLY, EARLY IN THE SPRING

A

'Early, Early in the Spring.' Sung by Mrs. James York. Recorded at Olin,
Iredell county, May 1917. This version is identical with another from Ruth
Weatherman, collected by Dr. W. A. Abrams; also very closely related to 87C.
The text is similar to that of SharpK II 152 and 154, No. 125 B and E.

234

Ear - ly, ear - ly in the spring— I shipped on board— to serve my king— And left my dear - est dear be - hind— Who oft - time said— her heart was mine,— Who oft - time said— her heart was mine.—

Scale: Heptachordal, plagal. Tonal Center: c. Structure: abb¹a¹a¹ $(2,2,2,2,2)$.

B

'Early in the Spring.' Sung by C. K. Tillett. Recorded at Wanchese, Roanoke Island, in 1922.

235

Ear - ly, ear - ly in the spring I shipped on board— to serve my king, I left my dar - ling girl— be - hind, She has of - ten told me her— heart was mine.

Scale: Mode II, plagal. Tonal center: f-sharp. Structure: abb¹c $(2,2,2,2)$ = ab $(4,4)$.

C

'It Was Early.' Sung by James York. Recorded at Olin, Iredell county, in 1939. Very closely related to 87A. The singer asked the present editor to make the following corrections: stanza 3, "And loudly for her I did call"; stanza 5, "And all fair girls who won't prove true"; stanza 7, "Don't split the waves where the billows fly."

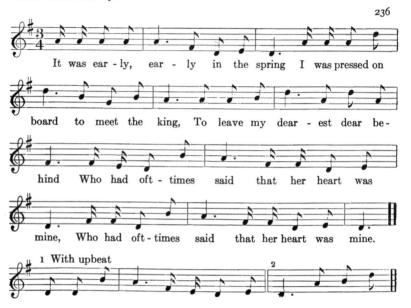

It was ear - ly, ear - ly in the spring I was pressed on board to meet the king, To leave my dear - est dear be - hind Who had oft - times said that her heart was mine, Who had oft - times said that her heart was mine.

1 With upbeat   2

For melodic relationship cf. ***OFS I 336, No. 81D, measures 2-4 and 14-16 and our measures 1-2 and 9-10.

Scale: Mode III. Tonal Center: d. Structure: abb¹a¹a¹ (2,2,2,2,2).

88

CHARMING BEAUTY BRIGHT

A

'The First Girl I Courted.' Sung by Mrs. Peggy Perry. Recorded as MS score in March 1915. No place given.

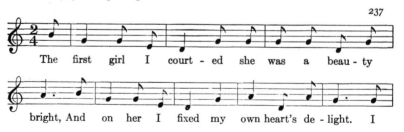

The first girl I court - ed she was a beau - ty bright, And on her I fixed my own heart's de - light. I

court - ed her for love, for love I did in - tend,

And nev - er - more— could I have love to com - plain.

For melodic relationship cf. **SCSM 439 ('The Lover's Lament'), measures 1-3.

Scale: Mode III, plagal. Tonal Center: g. Structure: $aba^1b^1cdc^1a$ (2,2,2,2, 2,2,2,2) $=aa^1ba^2$ (4,4,4,4) = Reprisenbar. Circular Tune (V).

B

'Seven Year Song.' Sung by Mrs. Myra Barnett Miller. Recorded as MS score in the Brushies, in Caldwell county. No date given. This is a remarkable example of how one and the same singer will handle the same tonal material (almost) of the same song, but at different times. The following version was probably recorded at a later date (but not in score), 88B(1). She did not say that she considered it another version.

238

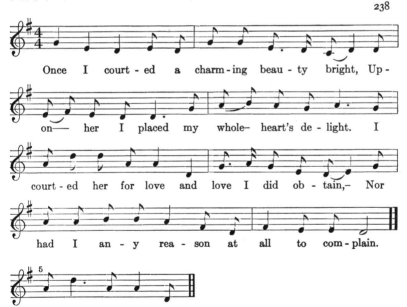

Once I court - ed a charm - ing beau - ty bright, Up -

on— her I placed my whole— heart's de - light. I

court - ed her for love and love I did ob - tain,— Nor

had I an - y rea - son at all to com - plain.

For melodic relationship cf. **SCSM 439 ('The Lover's Lament'), measures 1-3.

Scale: Mixolydian, plagal. Tonal Center: d. Structure: $abb^1 cc^1$ (2,1,1,2,2) = abc (2,2,4).

B(1)

'Seven Year Song.' Sung by Mrs. Myra Barnett Miller. Recorded at Lenoir, dated August 1939, 1940, or 1941. There are only very few songs where the accurate notation of what the singer actually sang results in so irregular a structure as a fifteen-measure phrase.[1] The singer held the last note somewhat longer, but not long enough to suffice for two half measures, nor for the remainder of the last measure. The last four measures are like those of 'Sweet William.'

239

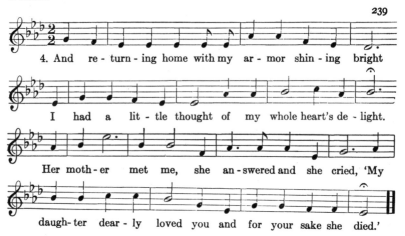

4. And re-turn-ing home with my ar-mor shin-ing bright
I had a lit-tle thought of my whole heart's de-light.
Her moth-er met me, she an-swered and she cried, 'My
daugh-ter dear-ly loved you and for your sake she died.'

Scale: Mixolydian, plagal. Tonal Center: e-flat. Structure: abcd (3,4,4,4).

B(2)

'Seven Years Song.' Sung by Mrs. Vivian Blackstock. Recorded, but no place given. There is a note from Dr. White: "Words and music given on score, dated November 6, 1923, from a letter of Maude Minnish."

240

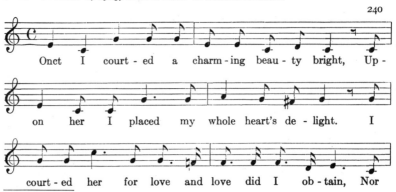

Onct I court-ed a charm-ing beau-ty bright, Upon her I placed my whole heart's de-light. I
court-ed her for love and love did I ob-tain, Nor

[1] It would, of course, have been easy to note measures 3-5 simply in two 3/2 measures, which would make the total number 14 measures. But, since the first version did not change its gait, it seems best to leave this one as it is.

had   I   an - y   rea - son   at   all   to   com-plain.

Scale: Hexachordal. Tonal Center: c. Structure: aa¹bc (2,2,2,2). If bc is taken as one unit, this would be: mm¹n = barform; otherwise, ab (4,4).

Scale: Hexachordal. Tonal Center: c. Structure: aa^1bc (2,2,2,2). If bc is taken as one unit, this would be: mm^1n = barform; otherwise, ab (4,4).

C

'The First Girl I Courted.' Sung by C. K. Tillett (*not* Mrs. Tillett, as in II 294). Recorded at Wanchese, Roanoke Island, in 1922.

241

The   first   one   I   court - ed   was   a   charm-ing   beau - ty

bright,   And   on   her   I   pressed   my   own   heart's de - light;   I

court - ed   her   for   love   and   love   I   did   in - tend.—   And

why's   there   an - y   rea - son   why   I   should   com - plain?

Scale: Hexachordal. Tonal Center: c. Structure: $aba^1b^1cdc^1a^2$ (2,2,2,2,2,2,2,2) = aa^1bb^1 (4,4,4,4) = ab (8,8).

D

'Charming Beauty Bright.' Sung by Mrs. James York. Recorded, probably at Olin, Iredell county, August 1939. This title evidently was given by the singer, since it is so listed in the catalogue.

242

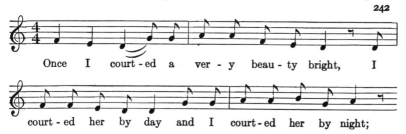

Once   I   court - ed   a   ver - y   beau - ty   bright,   I

court - ed   her   by   day   and   I   court - ed   her   by   night;

I court-ed her for love and love I did ob-tain,—

There's where she had no—— right to com-plain.

Scale: Hexachordal. Tonal Center: d. Structure: aa¹bc (2,2,2,2) = ab (4,4).

89
THE GLOVE

B

'The Lion's Den.' Sung by Mrs. J. Trivette. Recorded, but no date or place given. The text is quite similar to, and the story the same as, that in SharpK I 398, No. 67C.

243

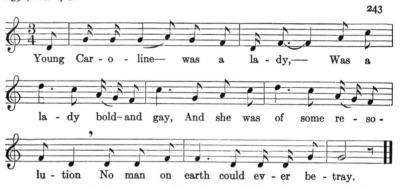

Young Car-o-line— was a la-dy,— Was a

la-dy bold-and gay, And she was of some re-so-

lu-tion No man on earth could ev-er be-tray.

For melodic relationship cf. **SharpK I 398, No. 67C, general melodic line.

Scale: Mode II, plagal. Tonal Center: g. Structure: abb¹c (2,2,2,2).

90
A BRAVE IRISH LADY

A

'New Ballad.' Sung by Horton Barker. From the previous recording of Dr. W. A. Abrams, probably at Boone. No date given. (In II 299 for BSSM 250-1 read 150-1.)

244

There was—— a lit-tle la-dy, From

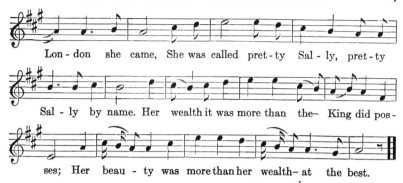

Lon - don   she   came,   She was called   pret - ty   Sal - ly,   pret - ty

Sal - ly   by name.   Her   wealth it was more than   the—   King did pos -

ses;   Her   beau - ty   was   more than her   wealth— at   the best.

For melodic relationship cf. **SharpK 1 299, No. 44G, the main points in the general melodic progressions.

Scale: Heptachordal, plagal.   Tonal Center: a.   Structure: abcc^1 (4,4,4,4) = ab (8,8).

c

'Sweet Sally.' Sung by Mrs. G. L. Bostic. Recorded at Mooresboro, Cleveland county, August 7, 1939. Other titles given are 'Brown Girl,' 'Irish Girl,' and 'Pretty Girl.'

245

A   no - ble   young   law - yer   from   Lon - don   he   came   To

court   this   fair   dam - sel   and   Sal - ly   by   name.   Her

be - ing   so   loft - y   and   a   for - tune   so   high

That   'twas   on   this   young   law - yer   she   scarce cast   her   eye.

For melodic relationship cf. **SharpK 1 299, No. 44G, measures 2-3 and 7-8 with our 5-6 and 7-8.

Scale: Mode I.   Tonal Center: c.   Structure: abacacdb^1 (2,2,2,2,2,2,2,2) = aa^{1}a^{1}b (4,4,4,4).

D

'Sally Dover.' Sung by C. K. Tillett. Recorded at Wanchese, Roanoke Island, December 29, 1922. Other titles given are 'Sally,' 'Fair Sally,' and 'Brown Girl.' The tune of this version is almost identical with that of 'The Sheffield Apprentice' (120B) by the same singer. For similar texts cf. JAFL xxviii (1914), 67-76 (stanza 3), and SharpK ii 210, No. 155 (stanza 2). This recording was made two years prior to that printed in FSRA 74-5 by the same singer. The second stanza of the latter is that given here. The word "aching" may possibly be incorrect, as the recording is very poor.

246

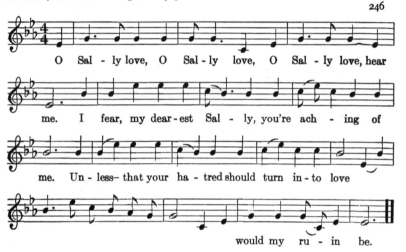

O Sal - ly love, O Sal - ly love, O Sal - ly love, hear me. I fear, my dear - est Sal - ly, you're ach - ing of me. Un - less— that your ha - tred should turn in - to love would my ru - in be.

For melodic relationship cf. **FSRA 74-5.

Scale: Irrational. Tonal Center: e-flat. Structure: abb¹a¹ (4,4,4,4).

91

SERVANT MAN

'Servant Man.' Sung by Mrs. J. J. Miller and Mrs. Polly Rayfield. Recorded as MS score, probably at Lenoir in 1915. Our text is practically identical with that of SharpK ii 96, No. 109A.

247

I once— knew a lit - tle girl, I loved her as my life; I would free - ly give my heart and

hand To make– her my wife, To make– her my wife.

For melodic relationship cf. **FSmWV 39-40; OSC 139.

Scale: Hexachordal. Tonal Center: c. Structure: abcc¹a¹ (2,2,2,2,2). This could be interpreted several ways. First, as aba¹, where b is then an inverted barform. Secondly, a could be called what A. Lorenz terms 'Rahmensätze.'

92
A Pretty Fair Maid Down in the Garden

A

'Gay Young Sailor.' Sung by Mrs. Grogan. Recorded as MS score, but no date or place given. Our text is very similar to that of SharpK II 71, No. 98B.

248

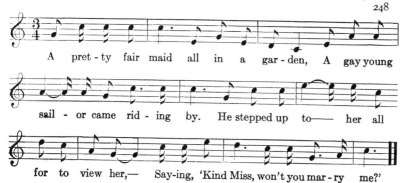

A pret - ty fair maid all in a gar - den, A gay young

sail - or came rid - ing by. He stepped up to—— her all

for to view her,— Say-ing, 'Kind Miss, won't you mar - ry me?'

For melodic relationship cf. **SCSM 423, version A; SharpK II 71, No. 98B, only the musical equivalent of 'A pretty fair maid.'

Scale: Mode III. Tonal Center: c. Structure: aba¹c (2,2,2,2) = aa¹ (4,4).

A(1)

'Gay Young Sailor.' Sung by Mrs. N. Prather. Recorded at Milam, Ashe county, August 8, 1939. The words given correspond to stanza 2 in II 305.

249

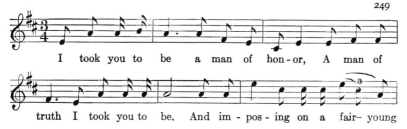

I took you to be a man of hon - or, A man of

truth I took you to be, And im - pos - ing on a fair– young

la - dy   Which were   not   fit - ten your bride   to   be.

For melodic relationship cf. **SCSM 424-5, versions D and E; FSF 346. No. 186A; SharpK ɪɪ 70, No. 98A.

Scale: Mode III, plagal.   Tonal Center: a.   Structure: abcd (2,2,2,2).

3   I have a true love on the ocean,
     Seven long years been gone from me;
     .... make no alteration,
     But seven more makes none with me.

4   Supposin' he's in some river drownded,
     Supposin' he's on a battlefield slain,
     Supposin' he's married to a foreign young lady.
     That you'll never see his face again.

5   If he's dead, I'm ....
     And if he's married, I love his lady,
     And if .... return again,
     ....

A(2)

'The Single Sailor.' Sung by Miss Ada Wilson. Recorded as ᴍꜱ score, either 1914 or 1915. No place given. The melodic variations given below are from two other recordings, B(1) and B(2). The first stana of B(2) reads:

1   A pretty fair maid out in the garden,
     A gallant soldier riding by,
     And in these words he did address her,
     Saying, 'Pretty fair maid, won't you marry me?'

250

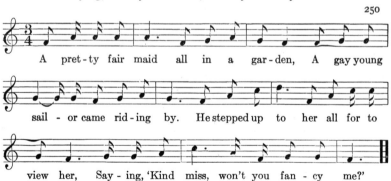

A   pret-ty   fair   maid   all   in   a   gar-den,   A   gay young

sail - or came   rid-ing   by.   He stepped up   to   her   all   for to

view her,   Say - ing, 'Kind   miss,   won't you   fan - cy   me?'

Scale: Mode III.   Tonal Center: f.   Structure: abcd (2,2,2,2).

B(1)

'There Was a Lady in the Garden.'   Sung by anonymous singer.   Recorded as
MS score, but no date or place given.

For melodic relationship cf. **OFS I 258, No. 55A.

Scale: Hexatonic (4), plagal.   Tonal Center: d.   Structure: aba¹c (2,2,2,2)
= aa¹ (4,4).

B(2)

'Pretty Fair Maid in the Garden.' Sung by H. R. Eggers. From a previous recording of Dr. W. A. Abrams, probably 1940. This tune resembles a cowboy song more than anything else. The third measure of the variations brings back memories of 'When You and I Were Young, Maggie.'

Pret-ty fair Miss was in the gar - den,— A brave young sol-dier came rid - ing by. Rode up to where she were dress - ing,— 'Pret-ty fair Miss, won't you mar - ry me?'

Stanza 3 1–3

bring back the one hap - py

Scale: Heptachordal, plagal. Tonal Center: c. Structure: aba¹b¹ (2,2,2,2) = aa¹ (4,4).

B(3)

'A Pretty Fair Maid.' Sung by Aunt Becky Gordon. Recorded July 19, 1939. No place given. Mrs. Gordon learned her songs from her mother, who was born and reared near Tuxedo, Henderson county. This melody is very similar to 92K and 92L.

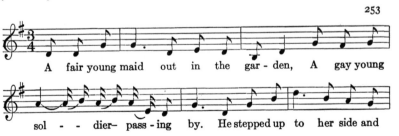

A fair young maid out in the gar - den, A gay young sol - - dier- pass - ing by. He stepped up to her side and

asked   her,   He   said,   'Fine   miss,   will   you   mar - ry   T?'

For melodic relationship cf. **SCSM 424-5, versions D and E; SCB 162, No. xv; FSF 346, No. 186A; SharpK II 70, No. 98A.

Scale: Heptachordal, plagal.   Tonal Center: g.   Structure: abcd (2,2,2,2).

B(4)

'The Returning Soldier.' Sung by Mrs. Thomas, grandmother of Edith Walker. Recorded at Pineola, Avery county, August 24, 1939. Other titles given are 'Pretty Fair Maid,' and 'The Broken Token.' Considerable similarity (measures 4-6) with 92B as well as with 92L.

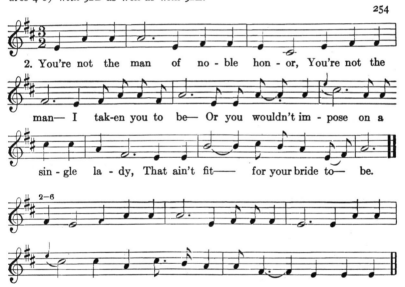

2. You're not   the   man   of   no - ble   hon - or,   You're not the

man— I   tak-en you to   be— Or you   wouldn't im - pose   on a

sin - gle   la - dy,   That ain't fit——   for your bride to—   be.

For melodic relationship cf. **BSM 150, version D. There is a surprising similarity in the basic melodic line.

Scale: Mode III, plagal.   Tonal Center: a.   Structure: abcd (2,2,2,2).

3   I have a true love in the army,
    And he's been gone for seven long years;
    And if he stays there for seven years longer
    No man on earth can marry me.

C

'The Rugged Soldier.' Sung by Miss Hattie McNeill. Recorded as MS score, but no date or place given. The beginning is similar to 92L and 92D(2).

255

A pret-ty fair miss all in the gar-den, A rug-ged sol-dier pass-ing by. 'O say lit-tle miss, don't you want to mar-ry?' 'No, sir, no, sir, Not I, not I.'

For melodic relationship cf. **ASb 68; SCB 162, No. xv; FSF 346, No. 186A; The melodic idiom for 'Miss all in the garden' is the same as in SharpK II 70, No. 98A.

Scale: Hexatonic (4). Tonal Center: c. Structure: abab^1 (2,2,2,2) = aa^1 (4,4).

D

'Pretty Fair Maid.' Sung by C. K. Tillett. Recorded at Wanchese, Roanoke Island in June 1920.

256

Pret-ty fair maid all in a gar-den, Rich young sail-or came pass-ing by. He stepped up to—— her as if he knew her, Say-ing, 'Fair miss can you fan-cy I?'

Scale: Hexatonic (4). Tonal Center: c. Structure: abac (2,2,2,2) = aa^1 (4,4). The b in the smaller subdivision is somewhat related to a.

D(1)

'Pretty Fair Maid.' Sung by Mrs. Ephraim Stamey. Recorded at Altamont, Avery county, July 14, 1940.

257

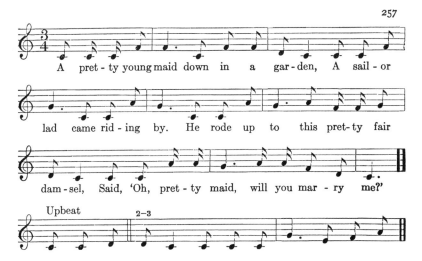

For melodic relationship cf. **SharpK II 70, No. 98A, measure 1 with up-beat.

Scale: Mode III, plagal. Tonal Center: f. Structure: aa¹bb¹ (2,2,2,2) = ab (4,4). Circular Tune (V).

D(2)

'Pretty Fair Maid in a Garden.' Sung by Mrs. Ewart Wilson. Recorded at Pensacola, Yancey county, in September 1929. This tune is very similar to 92L.

258

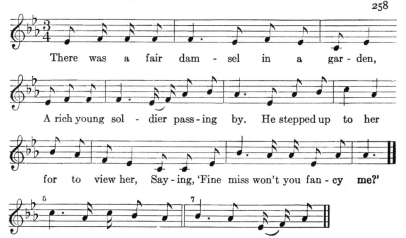

Scale: Mode III, plagal. Tonal Center: a-flat. Structure: aa¹bc (2,2,2,2) = ab (4,4).

I

'Pretty Maid.' Sung by anonymous singer. Recorded as MS score, but no place given. In 1923 or thereabouts. The first measure with up-beat is like that of 92J. The melodic standard for "all in a garden" is used here also.

259

Pret - ty maid, pret - ty maid, All in the gar - den,— A—

sail - or pass - ing by. 'Pret - ty maid, pret - ty maid, Will you

mar - ry a sail - or?' 'Oh, no, no, no,' was the re - ply.

For melodic relationship cf. **ASb 68, measures 1-2.

Scale: Heptachordal, plagal. Tonal Center: g. Structure: abcd (2,2,2,2). The c is slightly related to a.

J

'Seven Long Years He Has Kept Me Waiting.' Sung by Mary Strawbridge. Recorded, but no date or place given.

260

2. He caught a - round her ten - der mid - dle, And gave her

kiss - es one, two, three,- And said, 'I am that brisk young

sail - or, Late - ly I asked you to mar - ry me.'

For melodic relationship cf. *FSF 349, No. 187, first four notes and last two measures; ASb 68, measure 1 with up-beat.

Scale: Mode III. Tonal Center: b-flat. Structure: aa^{1}a^{2}b (2,2,2,2) = aa^1 (4,4).

K

'Pretty Fair Maid.' Sung by Y. F. Church. Recorded at Heaton, Avery county, July 30, 1939. This tune likewise is almost identical with 92L.

261

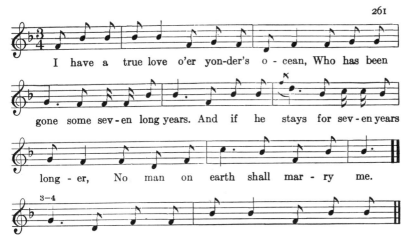

I have a true love o'er yon-der's o - cean, Who has been

gone some sev - en long years. And if he stays for sev - en years

long - er, No man on earth shall mar - ry me.

3—4

For melodic relationship cf. **SCSM 424, version D; SharpK ii 70, No. 98A, as in most of the other versions, measures 1-2 with up-beat.

Scale: Mode III.   Tonal Center: b-flat.   Structure: abcd (2,2,2,2).

L

'Pretty Fair Maid.' Sung by Mrs. B. Greene. Recorded at Zionville, Watauga county, September 11, 1939. F. C. B. says in a note: "She had not sung this song in 35 years." Other titles given are 'Seven Years Song,' and 'The Broken Token.' The singer does not sing 'I,' but 'me' for the last word of the first stanza. This text resembles that of version D.

262

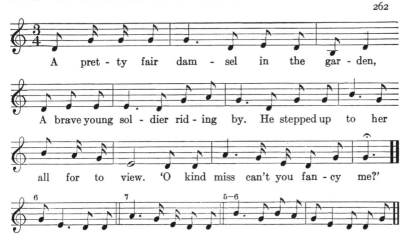

A pret - ty fair dam - sel in the gar - den,

A brave young sol - dier rid - ing by. He stepped up to her

all for to view. 'O kind miss can't you fan - cy me?'

6   7   5—6

For melodic relationship cf: **SharpK ii 70, No. 98A, first two measures with up-beat only.

Scale: Mode III, plagal.   Tonal Center: g.   Structure: aa¹a²a³ (2,2,2,2) = aa¹
(4,4).

2 You're not the man of noble honor,
   You're not the man I've taken you to be,
   Or you would not impose on a single lady.
   No man on earth can marry me.

3 I have a true lover in the army,
   He's been gone for seven long years,
   And if he's gone for seven years longer,
   No man on earth can marry me.

4 Perhaps he's in some river drowned,
   Perhaps he's on some battlefield slain,
   Perhaps he's to some foreign girl married,
   Then your love is all in vain.

5 If he's in some river drowned,
   If he's on some battlefield slain,
   If he's to some foreign girl married,
   I love the girl who married him.

6 He pulled his hands out of his pocket,
   His fingers being very long.
   The engagement ring was on his finger.
   Seeing it, at his feet she fell.

7 He picked her up all in his arms,
   And kisses gave her, one, two, three,
   'I am your sweet way-faring stranger,
   Just returned to marry thee.'

93

JOHN REILLEY

'John Reilley.' Sung by J. F. Spainhour. Recorded as MS score; no date or
place given. The story of this song is similar to that given in SharpK II 22,
No. 82A. G. Malcolm Laws, Jr. includes this ballad among many of those
that were traced to British broadsides. Variations given below are from a
second, anonymous score, which actually notes this tune in ¾ time.

263

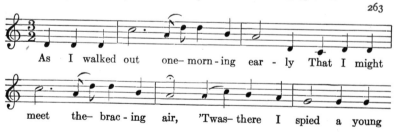

As   I walked out   one- morn-ing   ear - ly   That I might

meet   the- brac - ing   air,   'Twas- there   I   spied   a   young

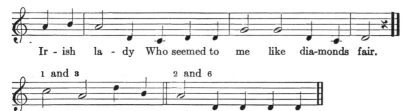

Ir - ish   la - dy   Who seemed to   me   like   dia-monds fair.

1 and 3   2 and 6

Scale: Pentachordal, plagal. Tonal Center: g. Structure: aa¹bb¹ (2,2,2,2); measure 2 of second phrase (bb¹) is the same as that of the first (aa¹). Also ab (4,4); or if bb¹ of the smaller subdivision is considered as one unit, mm¹n (2,2,4) = barform. Circular Tune (V).

$$93(1)$$

'John Reilly.' Sung by C. K. Tillett. Recorded at Wanchese, Roanoke Island. December 29, 1922. This version was recorded eleven years earlier than that noted in FSRA 66. Basically, however, both tunes are alike. For the missing words of the stanza given cf. BSSN 182, No. 90, the words of which fit perfectly. Owing to the condition of the record it is not possible to get the first stanza.

264

John   Reil - ly   is   my   true   love's name

And   if   I   find   this

young man,   My   eyes   have   nev - er   seen.——

Scale: Mode III, plagal. Tonal Center: f. Structure: abcd (4,4,4,4).

94

JOHNNY GERMAN

B

'Johnny German.' Sung by Mrs. Julia Grogan. Recorded as MS score; no date or place given. Both text and tune, however, though not the singer, are version A (cf. II 306 ff.). This song also belongs to the number of ballads which Malcolm Laws, Jr. declares to have been traced to British broadsides. The version given in SharpK II 256, No. 181A combines two of the stanzas of our version into one.

180   NORTH CAROLINA FOLKLORE

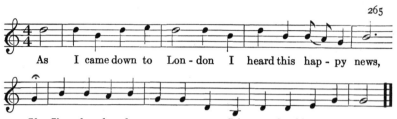

As   I came down to Lon - don   I heard this hap - py news,

If I'm the la - dy un - to you It's you should not re - fuse.

Scale: Mode III, plagal. Tonal Center: g. Structure: aa¹bb¹ (2,2,2,2) = ab (4,4).

95
THE DARK-EYED SAILOR

A

'A Dark-Eyed Sailor.' Sung by C. K. Tillett. Recorded at Wanchese, Roanoke Island; no date given. The chromaticism points to some outside influence.

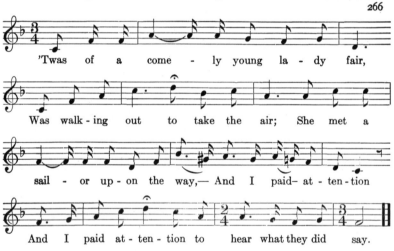

'Twas of a come - ly young la - dy fair,

Was walk - ing out to take the air; She met a

sail - or up - on the way,— And I paid– at - ten - tion

And I paid at - ten - tion to hear what they did say.

For melodic relationship cf. **SCSM 426, measures 3-4 with our 2-4; also NGMS 36, TSNS 144, and BSSM 161, but only for general melodic outline.

Scale: Hexachordal, plagal. Tonal Center: f. Structure: abcd (2,2,3,3).

96
LOVELY SUSAN

'Lovely Susan.' Sung by anonymous singer. Recorded as MS score in Pasquotank county in 1921-1922.

267

He pulled out his pock - et - hand - ker-chief, He tore . it

half in two, Say - ing, 'One half of this I'll keep my -

self And the oth - er I'll give to you. While the can - non

they are roar - ing— ·Like thun - der in the sky I will

think of Love - ly Su - san That I left on yon - der side.

Scale: Hexachordal, plagal.[1] Tonal Center: f. Structure: aba^{1}c (2,2,2,2) = aa^1 (4,4). The a^1 is considerably varied. Circular tune (V).

97

POLLY OLIVER

'Pretty Polly.' Sung by Mrs. Nora Hicks. Recorded at Mast's Gap, Watauga county, August 28, 1940. The missing line of the printed version in II 312 was recovered from the recording. The structure of the melody requires, however, the stanzas as printed to be grouped in pairs. This is along the lines also followed in another version found in SharpK I 345, No. 54B in which our text is the second stanza.

268

Pret - ty Pol - ly lies mus - ing in her down - y

---

[1] Whether or not the transcriber of this song forgot to insert a b-flat as signature is beyond the judgment of this editor. There was a recording besides the MS score, but it was among the records which were destroyed in transit to the Library of Congress. Judging from the general character of the tune, especially the modulation to the dominant in measure 4, the assumption of a simple F major scale as a basic material would seem reasonable.

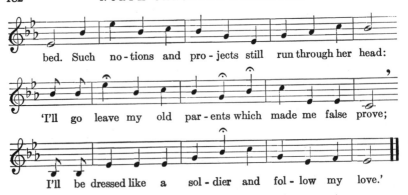

bed. Such   no - tions and pro - jects still   run through her head:

'I'll   go   leave my   old   par - ents which made me false prove;

I'll   be dressed like   a   sol - dier and fol - low my   love.'

Scale: Hexachordal, plagal. Tonal Center: e-flat. Structure: abcdcca^{1}b (2,2,2, 2,2,2,2) = abb^{1}a^1 (4,4,4,4).

99

JACK MUNRO

A

'Jacky, the Sailor Boy.' Sung by Mrs. James Miller. Recorded as MS score; no date or place given. The singer uses the Massey text but with variations. Our version has no tune for the chorus, as given in II 314 ff. This is again one of the ballads which Malcolm Laws, Jr., mentions as having been traced to British broadsides. Cf. 99E, 'British Lady.'

269

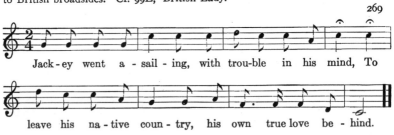

Jack - ey went a - sail - ing, with trou-ble   in his mind, To

leave his   na - tive coun - try, his own   true love be - hind.

For melodic relationship cf. **SharpK 1 394, No. 65Q.

Scale: Mode I. Tonal Center: c. Structure: abb^{1}c (2,2,2,2).

B

'Poor Jack Is Gone a-Sailing.' Sung by James York. Recorded at Olin, Iredell county, September 14, 1941. This version has a chorus. Measures 2-4 are similar to those of 99A. During a visit at the singer's home at Mocksville, N. C., June 17, 1956, Mr. York sang this tune in strict $\frac{2}{2}$ time. He also requested the following correction in the text: "with trouble on his mind."

270

Poor Jack has gone a - sail - ing, with trou - ble in his mind,– To leave his na - tive coun - try and a dar - ling one be - hind. I sing low, you sing low, I sing fair you well my dear.

For melodic relationship cf. **SharpK 1 393-4, No. 650.

Scale: Mode III, plagal. Tonal Center: g. Structure: aaa^1a^2bc $(2,2,2,2,2,2)$ = aa^1b $(4,4,4)$ = mm^1n (barform).

C

'War Song.' Sung by Mrs. Byers. Recorded as MS score; no date or place given. This version also has a chorus.

271

She dressed her - self in men's cloth - ing, an op - u let she put on. She marched in - to the ar - my to face the can - non ball. Sing— lo, so fare you well.—

For melodic relationship cf. **FSoA 50, measures 7-9 with our 6-3; FSF 353, No. 189.

Scale: Mode II, plagal. Tonal Center: e. Structure: abcde (2,2,2,2,4) = abc (4,4,4).

E

'The British Lady.' Sung by Mrs. Ewart Wilson. Recorded at Pensacola, Yancey county, in September 1929. Cf. SMBFS under 'Jackaro,' also JAFL XLV (1932), 76, No. 175. In measure 6, the singer actually sings 'shi-ap." The general, underlying melodic line is quite similar to that of 99B. Measures 2-4 are similar to those in 99A.

272

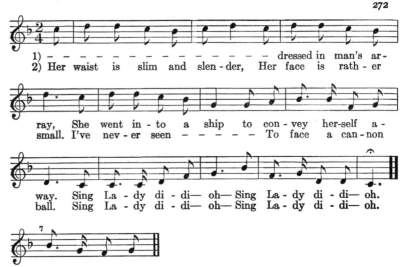

1) – – – – – – – – – – – – – – dressed in man's ar-
2) Her waist is slim and slen-der, Her face is rath-er

ray, She went in-to a ship to con-vey her-self a-
small. I've nev-er seen – – – – – To face a can-non

way. Sing La-dy di-di— oh— Sing La-dy di-di— oh.
ball. Sing La-dy di-di— oh— Sing La-dy di-di— oh.

7

For melodic relationship cf. **SharpK I 392, No. 65K, measures 5-8. The refrain is identical with that of *ibid.* 395, No. 65T, similar to 393 and 395, versions M, N, and S.

Scale: Hexatonic (3), plagal. Tonal Center: c. Structure: aa¹a²bcd (2,2,2, 2,2,2) = ab (6,6). The b, c, and d of the smaller subdivision are rhythmically the same.

100

THE GIRL VOLUNTEER

B

'The War Is A-Raging.' Sung by Miss Jewell Robbins. Recorded at Pekin, Montgomery county, sometime in the years 1921-24.

273

'The war is a-rag-ing; And, John-nie, you must

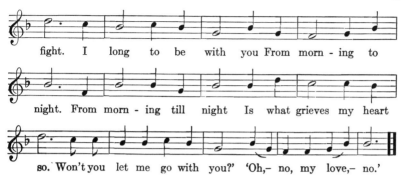

fight. I long to be with you From morn - ing to

night. From morn - ing till night Is what grieves my heart

so. Won't you let me go with you?' 'Oh,– no, my love,– no.'

For melodic relationship cf. ***SharpK ii iii, No. 113A excepting measures 5-6 and 13-14; **FSoA 6.

Scale: Mode III, plagal. Tonal Center: b-flat. Structure: abab (4,4,4,4) = aa (8,8).

C

'War Is Now Raging and Johnny He Must Fight.' Sung by Miss Lura Wagoner. Recorded as MS score, perhaps in Virginia, January 1914. See note in II 318.

War now is rag - ing And John - ny he must fight.

I— want to be with— him From morn - ing till night.

I— want to be with— him, It grieves my heart so.

'Won't you let me go with you?' 'O— no, my love, no.'

For melodic relationship cf. **SharpK ii iii, No. 113A; FSoA 6.

Scale: Mode III, plagal. Tonal Center: g. Structure: aba^{1}b (4,4,4,4) = aa^1 (8,8).

IOI

CHARMING NANCY

B

'Charming Nancy.' Sung by C. K. Tillett. Recorded at Wanchese, Roanoke
Island, no date. This is merely a fragment. The record is particularly poor
and breaks off with "West Indies." (The singer sings "West" instead of "East"
as the printed text gives it.) The same singer sang this song for the FSRA
collectors, but in our version he changes the temporal values of the individual
tones. This is the first time such differences have been encountered in the
numerous versions by this singer. In spite of it all there still remains some
melodic similarity.

275

For melodic relationship cf. **FSRA 68.

Scale: Hexachordal, plagal. Tonal Center: e-flat. Structure: (too fragmentary
for analysis).

C

'Charming Nancy.' Sung by anonymous singer. Recorded at Elizabeth City,
Pasquotank county, no date. Cf. ASM 321. Owing to the fact that there are
two interlinked pentatonic modes (Mode II on d, and Mode III on f as well as
Mode I on c, the latter of which is merely a transposition of the former), this
song is particularly rich in idioms familiar from medieval music as well as
Gregorian Chant: f-g-b-flat; c-b-flat-g, etc.

276

Scale: Hexachordal, plagal. Tonal Center: f. Structure: abcc (2,2,1,1) = abc
(2,2,2).

104

THE SAILOR BOY

A

'Oh, Father, Go Build Me a Boat.' Sung by Mrs. Nora Hicks. Recorded at Mast's Gap, Watauga county, August 28, 1940.

The text of this ballad is practically identical with the third stanza of 'Sweet William,' SharpK II, 84, No. 106A. This version combines the text of the first two lines of version A with the last two of the second stanza of version B.

This tune presents several problems. First, the extraordinary range of one octave and a fifth. Second, the question whether or not something happened to the singer, which made her uncertain about the right pitch or interval. (Unfortunately, only one stanza was recorded.)   Attention is called to the beginning of the repeating phrase "Ev'ry ship that I pass by." The preceding phrase ends on the lowest tone of the total range, but, without much ado, the line jumps twice, via the intervals of a seventh plus that of a sixth, thus traveling the entire range. These most unusual skips raise considerable doubt about the correctness of the melodic line and the pitch level in general. There is one more reason for this. Usually, when a text line is repeated, its musical equivalent is likewise repeated. Compare even here the phrase "And there I'll inquire for my sweet sailor boy" with the phrase which concludes the song, as well as the preceding "that I pass by" with its later repetition.

277

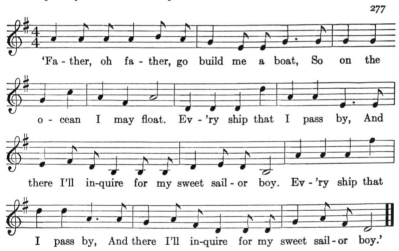

'Fa - ther, oh fa - ther, go build me a boat, So on the o - cean I may float. Ev - 'ry ship that I pass by, And there I'll in-quire for my sweet sail - or boy. Ev - 'ry ship that I pass by, And there I'll in-quire for my sweet sail - or boy.'

For melodic relationship cf. **SCSM 441; SharpK II 84, No. 106A; and OFS I 298, No. 68B, general melodic line.

Scale: Mixolydian, plagal.   Tonal Center: d.   Structure: nmm^1 (4,4,4) = Inverted barform.

C

'Oh, Captain, Captain, Tell Me True.' Sung by anonymous singer. Recorded as MS score; no date or place given. Another title given is 'Sweet Willie.'

The text used did not come with the MS score, but there is another type-written sheet with a text given by Mrs. Nilla Lancaster (Wayne county) which fits the tune perfectly and was therefore used. There are, however, two choruses on this typewritten sheet which do not belong to 'Sweet Willie.' The first is a variation of 'The Blue-Eyed Boy' (with changes in 3rd and 4th lines), while the second chorus, according to Professor Belden, belongs to 'The Inconstant Lover.' The third and fourth lines of the stanza given here are much more like that of 104G.

278

'Cap - tain, cap - tain tell me true, Does my sweet Will - ie sail with you?' 'Oh no, kind mis - sus, he does not sail with— me, They say he's drowned in the sea.'

Scale: Mode II, plagal.   Tonal Center: c.   Structure: aba^{1}b (2,2,2,2) = aa^1 (4,4).

L

'The Prentice Boy.' Sung by C. K. Tillett. Recorded at Wanchese, Roanoke Island; no date given. Dr. Brown says (in a note) "Sea Song."

This is the song referred to earlier (cf. 104A) with regard to intonation, pitch, and similar problems. The maneuvering of the voice from the lowest tone of the total range to the highest using most unusual intervals, to say the least, is probably the more puzzling, as otherwise the whole of the second phrase is practically a verbatim repetition of the first. Whether measures 10-11 can be credited to an emotional outburst conditioned by the thought expressed, will probably never be answered. It is here offered free as a theme for a future doctoral dissertation investigating the pathological depths of an untrained musical mind.

279

The pren-tice boy and he was bound To sail the rag - ing seas a - round; And just be - fore he be - came twen - ty - one

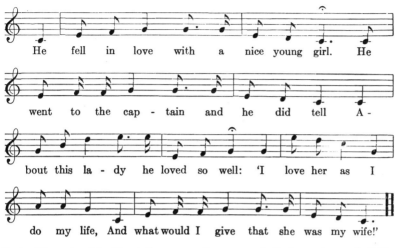

He fell in love with a nice young girl. He

went to the cap - tain and he did tell A -

bout this la - dy he loved so well: 'I love her as I

do my life, And what would I give that she was my wife!'

Scale: Heptachordal. Tonal Center: c. Structure: aba¹b (4,4,4,4) = aa¹ (8,8).

M

'The Forsaken Lover.' Sung by C. K. Tillett. Recorded at Wanchese, Roanoke
Island, probably December 29, 1922.

280

O fa - ther, fa - ther, build me a boat, So a - cross the

O - cean I will float. And— hail thy ship, as they'll pass

by it, 'Quir - ing for my Wil - lie Boy. And— hail thy

ship, as they'll pass by it, 'Quir - ing for my Wil - lie Boy.

Scale: Hexachordal, plagal. Tonal Center: f. Structure: nmm (4,4,4,) =
Inverted barform. Circular tune (V).

N

'Black-Eyed Susan.' Sung by Mrs. G. L. Bostic. Recorded at Mooresboro,

Cleveland county, August 7, 1929. Another title given is 'Sweet Willie.' No text has been found. That given here was taken from the recording. Some of the stanzas omit the up-beat.

281

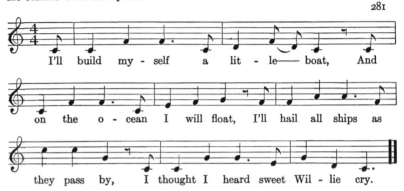

I'll build my - self a lit - le— boat, And on the o - cean I will float, I'll hail all ships as they pass by, I thought I heard sweet Wil - lie cry.

Scale: Hexatonic (4), plagal. Tonal Center: f. Structure: aa¹a²a³ (2,2,2,2) = aa¹ (4,4). Circular Tune (V).

2 'Captain, captain, tell me true,
  Does my Willie sail with you?'
  'No, pretty maid, he don't sail here,
  He's drowned in the deep, I fear.'

105

SCARBORO SAND (ROBIN HOOD SIDE)

'Scarboro Sand.' Sung by C. K. Tillett. Recorded at Wanchese, Roanoke Island, in 1920 and 1923. This is again only a fragment, although somewhat more extended than the previous one. At "But," the record breaks off with a great noise. This ballad is the only one contributed by Tillett which underwent, for unknown reasons, considerable changes, judging from a later recording that was printed in another collection. Cf. FSRA 70. The changes mentioned were, in this case, not for the better.

282

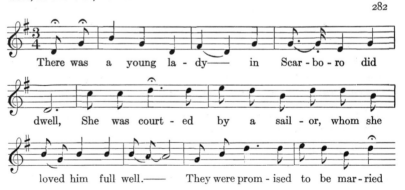

There was a young la - dy— in Scar - bo - ro did dwell, She was court - ed by a sail - or, whom she loved him full well.— They were prom - ised to be mar - ried

when   he——   did   re - turn;——   But——

For melodic relationship cf. **FSRA 70.

Scale: Heptachordal, plagal. Tonal Center: g. Structure: abb[1] (?). It is quite
evident that the scale material, and especially the structure, cannot adequately
be determined from a melody that is only fragmentary.

106

WILLIAM TAYLOR

'William Taylor.' Sung by C. K. Tillett. Recorded at Wanchese, Roanoke
Island, December 29, 1922. This ballad also belongs among a number of songs
'many of which have been traced to British broadsides.' Cf. NAB.

283

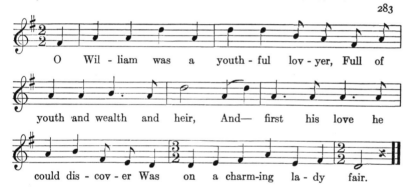

O   Wil - liam   was   a   youth - ful   lov - yer,   Full   of

youth and wealth   and   heir,   And—   first   his   love   he

could dis - cov - er   Was   on   a   charm-ing   la - dy   fair.

Scale: Mode III. Tonal Center: d. Structure: abcd (2,2,2,2).

108

GREEN BEDS

A

'Young Johnny.' Sung by Mrs. Myra Barnett Miller. Recorded probably at
Lenoir, August 1939, 1940, or 1941.

Of all the tunes in this collection, this version probably makes the most
varied use of its tonal material. This will best be seen from the analysis of the
six stanzas available, which is given below. Similarly it may be interesting to
see how this varied use manifests itself likewise in the choice of the material.
This being really an outstanding example in this collection, a full account of
the different scale materials derived from the individual stanzas will also be
given below.

284

'What luck have you, young John - ny, What luck have you at sea?'

'Oh, noth-ing in this world On - ly what you see on me.'

2
'Oh, I've had a jol - ly life with the sail - ors on the sea.

Go bring your daugh - ter Pol - ly And set her on my knee.'

3
'My daugh - ter she is ab - sent; She ain't been seen to - day.

And if she were here, young John - ny, She'd cast you fur a - way.'

5
Young John - ny be - ing wea - ry, He hung down his head

And called for a. can - dle To light him to bed.

6
'All my beds is full of stran - gers And's been fur weeks and more,

And you must find your lod - gin' On some fur - thering shore.'

Scale: (1st stanza) Mode II; (2nd, 3rd and 4th stanzas) Hexatonic (2), plagal; (5th stanza) Mode II; (6th stanza) Hexatonic (6). Tonal Center: (1st stanza) c; (2nd stanza) g; (3rd stanza) c; (4th stanza) c; (5th stanza) g; (6th stanza) c. Structure: (1st stanza) ab (4,4); (2nd stanza) cd (4,4); (3rd stanza) d^1c^1 (4,4); (4th stanza) d^1c^1 (4,4); (5th stanza) dd^1 (4,4); (6th stanza) c^2c^1 (4,4).

A(1)

'Young Johnny.' Sung by anonymous singer. Recorded as MS score; no date or place given. This tune in its melodic outline is very closely related to 108B.

285

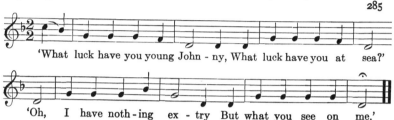

'What luck have you young John - ny, What luck have you at sea?'

'Oh, I have noth - ing ex - try But what you see on me.'

Scale: Mode II, plagal. Tonal Center: g. Structure: aa^1ba^2 (2,2,2,2) = Reprisenbar. Circular Tune (V).

A(2)

'Young Johnny.' Sung by Mrs. Myra Barnett Miller. Recorded as MS score, probably at Lenoir; no date given. Text and tune are identical with a version (MS score 286) by Dr. I. G. Greer.

286

'What luck, what luck, young John-nie, What luck do you bring to me?'

'My luck, it is quite dif - f'rent From what it used to be.'

Scale: Pentachordal. Tonal Center: c. Structure: abb^1c (2,2,2,2) = ab (4,4).

B

'What Luck, Young Johnny?' Sung by S. T. Faulkner. Recorded at Durham, about 1915-16. This is very similar to 108A(1).

287

'What luck have you, young John - ny, What luck have you at sea?'

'Oh,   I   have noth - ing   ex - try   But   what   you see   on   me.'

Scale: Hexatonic (6).   Tonal Center: d.   Structure: abcd (2,2,2,2).

D

'Young Johnny.' Sung by Mrs. James York. Recorded at Olin, Iredell county, in 1939. The structure of the tune requires the stanzas as given in II 336-7 to be grouped in pairs.

288

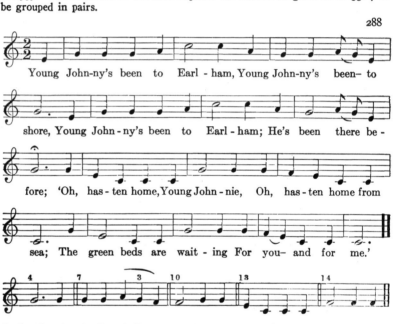

Young John-ny's been to Earl - ham, Young John-ny's been- to

shore, Young John-ny's been to Earl - ham; He's been there be -

fore; 'Oh, has-ten home, Young John-nie, Oh, has-ten home from

sea; The green beds are wait - ing For you- and for me.'

Scale: Irrational.   Tonal Center: c.   Structure: aabb¹ (2,2,2,2) = ab (4,4).

109

POOR JACK

A

'Poor Jack.' Sung by C. K. Tillett. Recorded at Wanchese, Roanoke Island, probably in 1922. Aside from 'The Sailor Boy' 104A sung by Mrs. Hicks, there is only one other song with an extremely wide range, namely this ballad. But, whereas in the former case there were some doubts about the intentional skips, there seems to be no reason in this case to assume any error. The range is, however, extreme, one octave and a sixth. Attention should also be called to some unusual skips (measures 4-5).

289

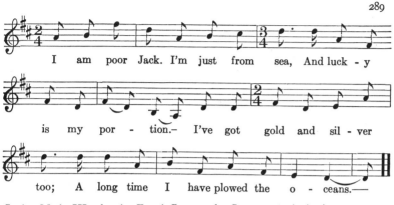

I am poor Jack. I'm just from sea, And luck - y is my por - tion.— I've got gold and sil - ver too; A long time I have plowed the o - ceans.—

Scale: Mode III, plagal.   Tonal Center: d.   Structure: ab (3,5).

110
LITTLE MOHEA

C

'The Little Mohee.'   Sung by anonymous singer.   Recorded as MS score; no date or place given.
Reminds one somewhat of 'On Top of Old Smoky.'

290

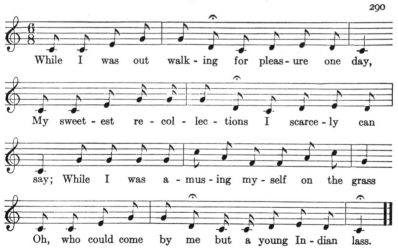

While I was out walk - ing for pleas - ure one day, My sweet - est re - col - lec - tions I scarce - ly can say; While I was a - mus - ing my - self on the grass Oh, who could come by me but a young In - dian lass.

For melodic relationship cf. **FSF 357, No. 190; SHF 2; noteworthy in our version is the shortening of values at the end of each phrase, as compared with the two versions quoted.

Scale: Hexachordal.   Tonal Center: c.   Structure: aaba (2,2,2,2) = Reprisenbar.

D

'The Lass of Mohay.'   Sung by C. K. Tillett.   Recorded at Wanchese, Roanoke Island; no date given.

291

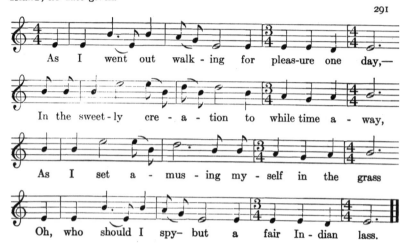

Scale: Mode II, plagal.   Tonal Center: e.   Structure: abb¹a (4,4,4,4).

F

'Indian Mohee.'   Sung by Mrs. L. F. Banks.   Recorded; no date or place given. Fragment only, as the record breaks off with "myself in." The first two measures are identical with those of our version of 'Villikens and His Dinah,' 20A. See notes to the latter.

292

Scale: Hexachordal.   Tonal Center: e-flat.   Structure: abb¹ (4,4,3)? (Naturally, this version being a fragment only, the above analysis is limited and incomplete.)

I

'The Little Mohee.' Sung by Otis Kuykendall. Recorded at Asheville in 1939.
Measures 4-5 consist of the familiar phrase from 'On Top of Old Smoky.'

293

As I went out walk - ing— for pleas-ure one day,—

In sweet re - cre - a - tion as the day– passed a -

way,— As I set a - mus - ing— my - self on the

grass–Pray whom should I spy– but a— young In-dian lass.-

1 with upbeat

2   3

6—7

Scale: Heptachordal, plagal. Tonal Center: e-flat. Structure: aa¹ba¹ (2,2,2,2)
= Reprisenbar.

M

'Little Mohee.' Sung by anonymous female singer with guitar. Recorded; no
date or place given. Similar to 110D. Again measures 13-18 are familiar from
'On Top of Old Smoky.'

294

As I was out walk - ing—— for pleas-ure one day,——

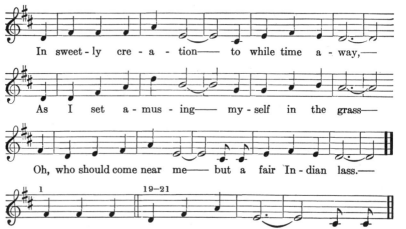

In sweet-ly cre - a - tion—— to while time a - way,——

As I set a - mus - ing—— my - self in the grass——

Oh, who should come near me—— but a fair `In - dian lass.——

1   19—21

For melodic relationship cf. **FSF 357, No. 190; MSNC 16-23; SHF 2.

Scale: Heptachordal, plagal. Tonal Center: d. Structure: aa^{1}ba^2 (6,6,6,6) =
Reprisenbar. This is an unusual structure inasmuch as each phrase contains
six measures. The melody could have been noted in 9/8 or 9/4, which would have
(beginning with the second full measure) made eight phrases of three measures
each.

N

'The Little Mohee.' Sung by Mrs. H. R. Buchanan. Recorded at Minneapolis,
Avery county, September 7, 1939. Similar to 110D.

295

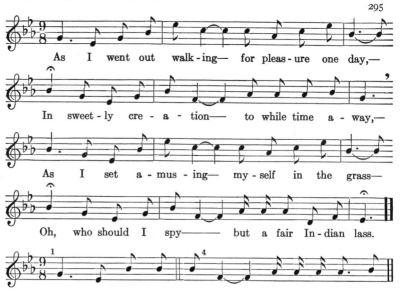

As I went out walk-ing—— for pleas-ure one day,——

In sweet-ly cre - a - tion—— to while time a - way,——

As I set a - mus - ing— my - self in the grass—

Oh, who should I spy—— but a fair In - dian lass.

1   4

For melodic relationship cf. **FSoA 72, measures 1-2 and their repetition; BSO 285, the purely melodic outline (not rhythmical).

Scale: Heptachordal, plagal. Tonal Center: e-flat. Structure: aba^{1}b^1 (2,2,2,2) = aa^1 (4,4).

O

'The Little Mohee.' Sung by anonymous male singer with guitar. Recorded probably at Blowing Rock, Watauga county, in August 1936. As the song progresses, it takes on an extraordinary freedom, almost rhapsodic in character. Similar to 110D.

For melodic relationship cf. **SCSM 448.

Scale: Heptachordal, plagal. Tonal Center: c. Structure: abab^1 (6,6,6,6) = aa^1 (12, 12).

111

THE FAITHFUL SAILOR BOY

A

'The Sailor Boy.' Sung by C. K. Tillett. Recorded at Wanchese, Roanoke Island, in May 1920.

on the ground. A sail - or boy stood on the deck; The

ship was out - ward bound. His sweet-heart, stand - ing by his side,

Shed man - y'a bit - ter tear. At last he pressed her to his heart

And whis-pered in her ear: Fare - well, fare - well, my

own true love; This part - ing gives me pain. You'll be my

own, my guid - ing star Un - til I re - turn a - gain. My

thought shall be of you, my love, While storms are rag - ing high. So,

fare you well! Re-mem - ber me, Your faith-ful sail - or boy.

Scale: Heptachordal, plagal. Tonal Center: g. Structure: aba^{1}caba^{1}c (2,2,2,2, 2,2,2,2) = aa^{1}aa^1 (4,4,4,4).

112
THE SAILOR'S BRIDE

A

'My Soldier Boy.' Sung by Miss Hattie McNeill. Recorded as MS score; no date or place given.

298

Ear - ly in the spring when I was young The

flow-ers were in bloom, the birds they sung, Not a soul was

hap - pier than I When my sol - dier boy was by.

For melodic relationship cf. *OFS IV 268-9, No. 762.

Scale: Mode III, plagal. Tonal Center: g. Structure: abcd (2,2,2,2). Circular Tune (V).

B

'Charlie and Mary.' Sung by C. K. Tillett (not Mrs. Tillett, as in II 345). Recorded at Wanchese, Roanoke Island, in 1922.

Mer - ry spring when I was young, The flow - ers bloom and

the birds did sing; There nev - er was a soul so hap-py as

I When my— sweet sai - lor boy was nigh. Tal la la la

Tal la la tal la tal la la la tal la la la

tal There nev - er was a soul so hap - py as

I When my— sweet— sai - lor boy was nigh.

Scale: Hexachordal. Tonal Center: c. Structure: abcda¹b¹cd (2,2,2,2,2,2,2,2) = aba¹b (4,4,4,4) = aa¹ (8,8).

113
BARNEY McCoy

B

'Nora Darling.' Sung by Miss Jewell Robbins. Recorded at her home in Gastonia, July 31, 1951, by the present editor. The singer, now Mrs. Purdue, told the editor that, when but eighteen months old, she sang some of the old folksongs for the entertainment of a quilting party for her mother. For other listings and texts see BSSM 477; Ford 337-8; OFS IV 291-2.

300

I am go - ing far a - way, Nor - a dar - ling,— And—

leav - ing such an an - gel far be - hind. It would

break my heart in two, which I fond - ly gave to you,

And no oth - er one so lov - ing, kind and true.

Then come to my arms, Nor - a dar - ling,— Bid your

friends and dear old Ire - land good - bye. For it's

hap - py we would be In the dear land of the free

Liv - ing hap - py with your Bar - ney Mc - Coy.

For melodic relationship cf: *OFS IV 291-2, No. 776.

Scale: Heptachordal, plagal. Tonal Center: c. Structure: aba¹c, a²b¹a¹c (2,2,2,2), (2,2,2,2) = ab a¹b (4,4,4,4) = aa¹ (8,8).

117

POOR PARKER

'Poor Parker.' Sung by Miss Jean Holeman. Recorded; no date or place given.

Ye gods a - bove, pro - tect us wid - ows! With eyes of pi - ty look down on us!— Help me, help me out of trou-ble And all this sad— ca - la - mi - ty!— Oh, Park - er was my law - ful hus-band, Though for - tune to me— has proved un - kind; And though poor Park -er was hanged for mu - ti - ny, Worse than him— was left— be - hind.-

Scale: Heptachordal, plagal. Tonal Center: g. Structure: ababa¹b¹cb (2,2,2,2, 2,2,2,2,) = aaa¹b (4,4,4,4).

118

HIGH BARBARY

'High Barbary.' Sung by C. K. Tillett. Recorded at Wanchese, Roanoke Island; no date given.

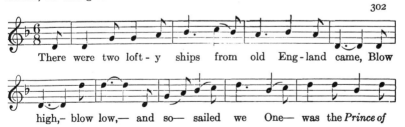

There were two loft - y ships from old Eng - land came, Blow high,- blow low,— and so— sailed we One— was the *Prince of*

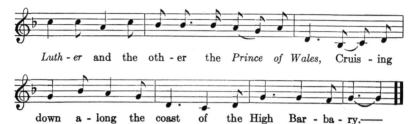

Luth - er and the oth - er   the *Prince of Wales,* Cruis - ing

down   a - long   the   coast   of   the   High   Bar - ba - ry.——

For melodic relationship cf. *FSF 53-4, No. 21, measures 4-5 with our 7-10; FSCSG 24-6, measures 9-10.

Scale: Hexatonic (6), plagal.   Tonal Center: g.   Structure: $abccdee^1b^1ff^1$ $(2,2,1,1,2,1,1,2,2,2) = abcb^1$ $(2,4,4,6)$. The structure is noteworthy: a is terminally, and b internally incremented. The last four measures are a free sequence.

119
THE LORENA BOLD CREW

'Huxter's Bold Crew.' Sung by C. K. Tillett. Recorded at Wanchese, Roanoke Island, December 29, 1922. Like all the other songs of this singer this ballad also was recorded before those given in FSRA. Nevertheless, there still is considerable similarity in these two versions. (See below.) Of numerous stanzas given by Chappell only three are printed in our II 353. Mentioned should be the change in title from 'Buxter's' to 'Huxter's.' Dr. Brown notes: "Chantey?" Cf. SSLKFS 16-17.

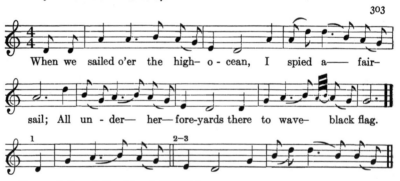

303

When we   sailed o'er   the   high– o - cean,   I   spied a——   fair-

sail; All   un - der—   her—fore-yards there   to   wave–   black flag.

1   2-3

For melodic relationship cf. **FSRA 52.

Scale: Mode II, plagal. Tonal Center: g. Structure: aba^1c $(2,2,2,2) = aa^1$ $(4,4)$.

120
THE SHEFFIELD APPRENTICE
B

'The Sheffield Apprentice.' Sung by C. K. Tillet. Recorded at Wanchese, Roanoke Island, in June 1920.

304

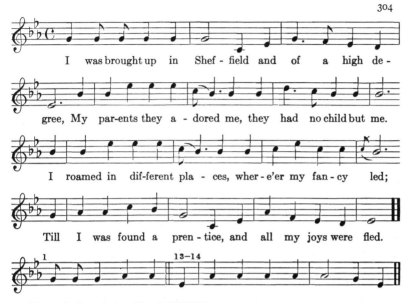

I was brought up in Shef - field and of a high de -
gree, My par-ents they a - dored me, they had no child but me.
I roamed in dif-ferent pla - ces, wher - e'er my fan - cy led;
Till I was found a pren - tice, and all my joys were fled.

For melodic relationship cf. **FSRA 140.

Scale: Heptachordal, plagal. Tonal Center: e-flat. Structure: abb¹a¹ (4,4,4,4).

121

THE RAMBLING BOY

'The Ramblin' Boy.' Sung by anonymous singer. Recorded as MS score; no date or place given. Probably before 1919. Very closely related to the following 121(1).

305

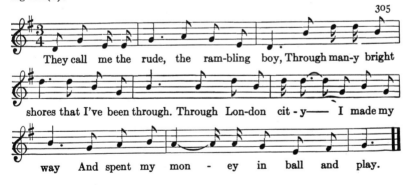

They call me the rude, the ram-bling boy, Through man-y bright
shores that I've been through. Through Lon-don cit - y—— I made my
way And spent my mon - ey in ball and play.

For melodic relationship cf. **OFS II 84.

Scale: Hexatonic (4), plagal. Tonal Center: g. Structure: abb¹c (2,2,2,2).

121(1)

'The Ramblin' Boy.' Sung by Mrs. Myra Barnett Miller. Recorded probably at Lenoir, in 1939, 1940, or 1941. Very closely related to the preceding version.

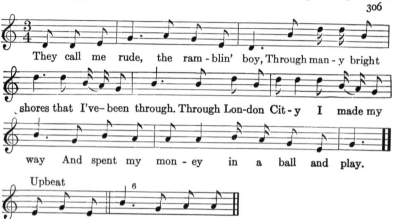

They call me rude, the ram-blin' boy, Through man-y bright shores that I've-been through. Through Lon-don Cit-y I made my way And spent my mon-ey in a ball and play.

For melodic relationship cf. **OFS II 84.

Scale: Mode III, plagal. Tonal Center: g. Structure: abb¹c (2,2,2,2).

121(2)

'The Rambling Boy.' Sung by Mrs. G. L. Bostic. Recorded at Mooresboro, Cleveland county, August 7, 1934.

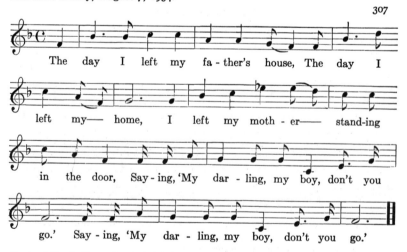

The day I left my fa-ther's house, The day I left my— home, I left my moth-er— stand-ing in the door, Say-ing, 'My dar-ling, my boy, don't you go.' Say-ing, 'My dar-ling, my boy, don't you go.'

Scale: Mixolydian, plagal (with interchangingly flattened and natural seventh). Tonal Center: f. Structure: abcdd (2,2,2,2,2).

121 (3)

'The Rake and Rambling Boy.' Sung by Mrs. James York. Recorded at Olin,
Iredell county, August 14, 1939.

308

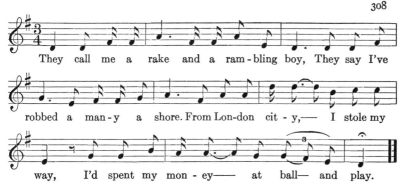

They call me a rake and a ram-bling boy, They say I've
robbed a man-y a shore. From Lon-don cit - y,— I stole my
way, I'd spent my mon - ey— at ball— and play.

Scale: Mixolydian.   Tonal Center: d.   Structure: aa¹bb¹ (2,2,2,2) = ab (4,4).

124

CAROLINE OF EDINBURGH TOWN

B

'Caroline of Eddingburg Town.' Sung by C. K. Tillett. Recorded at Wanchese, Roanoke Island, in June 1920. Our stanza is the fourth of the A version
(II 359).

309

4. O'er lof - ty hills and moun-tains to - geth - er they did
go— Till they ar - rived in En - ge - land, far from her
hap - py home.- She cries, 'My dear - est Hen - ne - ry, pray
nev - er on me frown,— Or you'll break the heart of
Ca - ro - line of Ed - in - bor - ough Town.'—

For melodic relationship cf. **FSONE 183-5; NGMS 79-83, the very beginning and ending only; SharpK 1 404, No. 69, only in main melodic points.

Scale: Heptachordal, plagal (with sometimes chromatically altered 4th and 7th). Tonal Center: e-flat. Structure: abb¹a¹ (4,4,4,4).

128

WILLIAM RILEY

'William Riley.' Sung by Mrs. James York. Recorded at Olin, Iredell county, in 1939. The seventh stanza omits four measures (11-14). The musical structure requires the stanzas as printed in II 363 to be grouped in pairs.

310

It's of a brave young girl That I am goin' to
sing, Way o - ver high hills and moun - tains Their
com - pan - y to re - frain. Her fa - ther fol - lowed
af - ter her With his vile ar - mored men, And so
tak - en was poor Ri - ley— And his pret - ty Pol - ly Bann.

For melodic relationship cf. **SharpK II 81, No. 104A, main melodic points of first four measures only; *OFS 1 419, No. 115.

Scale: Mixolydian, plagal. The b natural is omitted in all other stanzas. This would justify the above classification. Tonal Center: c. Structure: abca¹ (4,4,4,4). The c is slightly related to a.

128(1)

'William Riley.' Sung by Mrs. Nora Hicks. Recorded at Mast's Gap, Watauga county, August 28, 1940. As very frequently, the recording begins after the singer has started. Sometimes the last seven measures are repeated; at one time, the first four measures are repeated twice, thus filling one complete stanza. At other times, measures 5-8 are repeated, with an altered ending for the last line. The text given in OFS I 419, No. 115 seems to supply nicely the missing words at the beginning, but our version omits the third line found in the former. There is some melodic similarity with the preceding version.

311

For melodic relationship cf. **SharpK II 81, No. 104A. Our melody is, however, shortened four measures.

Scale: Hexatonic (6), plagal. Tonal Center: d. Structure: aba¹ (4,4,4).

2   His poor old father followed after her
    With forty bright armed men.
    This lady she was taken back
    And in her closet bound.
    Poor Riley he was taken back
    And chained down to the ground.

130

SWEET WILLIAM AND NANCY

'Sweet William and Nancy.' Sung by Mrs. Rhoda Wilson. Recorded as MS score at Silverstone, Watauga county, February 6, 1915. The structure of the music requires the stanzas as given in II 366, to be grouped in pairs.

312

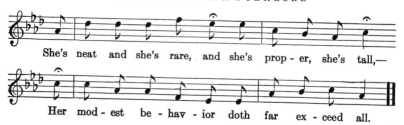

She's neat and she's rare, and she's prop - er, she's tall,—

Her mod - est be - hav - ior doth far ex - ceed all.

Scale: Hexachordal, plagal. Tonal Center: a-flat. Structure: aa¹ba² (2,2,2,2)
= Reprisenbar.

131
THE IRISH GIRL

'As I Walked Out One Morning.' Sung by Miss Jewell Robbins. Recorded at
Pekin, Montgomery county, in 1922. Observe the triadic structure of measures
2, 3, 5, 6, and 7.

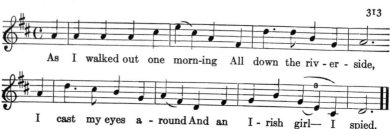

As I walked out one morn-ing All down the riv - er - side,

I cast my eyes a - round And an I - rish girl— I spied.

For melodic relationship cf. ** SharpK ii 255, No. 180B, last five measures;
.also Texas FS 160.

Scale: Heptachordal, plagal. Tonal Center: d. Structure: abb¹c (2,2,2,2).

135
THREE LEAVES OF SHAMROCK

No title. Sung by Miss Eugenia Clarke. Recorded as MS score; no date or
place given. The first measure reminds one of 'When Irish Eyes Are Smiling.'

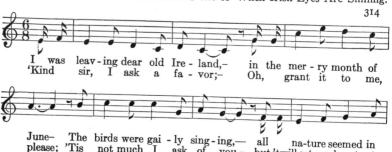

I was leav - ing dear old Ire - land,–   in the mer - ry month of
'Kind sir, I ask a fa - vor;–   Oh, grant it to me,

June—   The birds were gai - ly sing - ing,—   all   na-ture seemed in
please; 'Tis   not much I ask of you,–   but 'twill set my heart at

tune.– An   I - rish girl   ac - cost - ed   me with a   sad tear
ease.–   Take these to   my broth - er   Ned, who is   far a -

in   her   eye,—   And   as   she spoke these words   to   me   she
cross the   sea.—   And don't   for - get   to   tell   him, sir,   that

bit - ter - ly   did   cry.–   Three leaves of   sham-rock, the   I - rish-man's
they were sent   by   me.'–

sham - rock,   From his own dar-ling   sis - ter,–   her bless-ings too   she

gave.   'Take these to   my broth-er,—   for   I   have   no   oth - er.—

And   these   are   the   sham-rock— from his   dear   old moth-er's   grave.'

Scale: Heptachordal. Tonal Center: c. Structure: $aba^1b^1a^2b^2a^3b^3$ (4,4,4,4,4, 4,4,4) $= aa^1a^2a^3$ (8,8,8,8) $= aa^1$ (16, 16).

136
SKEW BALL

'Skew Ball.' Sung by Mrs. Peggy Perry. Recorded as MS score at Zionville, Watauga county, in 1915.

The text of the Thomas Smith version, II 371, gives "tail and cast [*or* least]" in the third line. The MS score gives the text only partially, but this part is complete. The word is clearly "list." This can mean a strip of cloth or other material, or a strip or band of any kind. It can also mean a division of the hair. The latter is quite as probable as the former in this context.

315

Oh,   gen - tle - men,–   la - dies, and   all,   I'll—
A   short drum - mer—   rid - ing a - long   With his

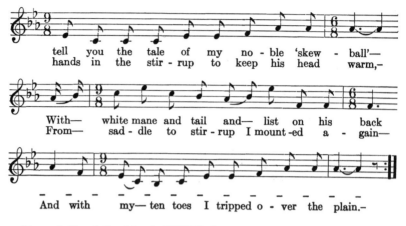

tell   you   the   tale   of   my   no - ble 'skew - ball'—
hands in   the   stir - rup to   keep his   head   warm,—

With—   white mane and tail and— list on   his   back
From—   sad - dle   to   stir - rup I mount -ed a - gain—

And with   my— ten toes I tripped o - ver the plain.—

For melodic relationship cf. **TNFS 63.

Scale: Mode III, plagal. Tonal Center: a-flat. Structure: aa¹ba¹ (2,2,2,2) =
Reprisenbar.

143

ANNIE LEE

B

'Saucy Anna Lee.' Sung by C. K. Tillett. Recorded at Wanchese, Roanoke
Island, in December 1922. Measures 3-5 are melodically the same as 2-3 of
'Turkey in the Straw.'

316

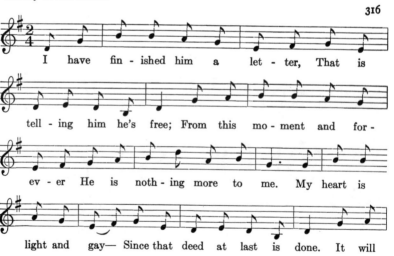

I   have   fin - ished him   a   let - ter, That   is

tell - ing him he's   free; From this   mo - ment and   for -

ev - er   He   is   noth - ing more to   me. My heart is

light and   gay— Since that deed at   last is   done. It will

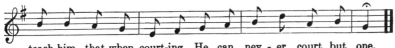

teach him that when court-ing He can nev - er court but one.

Scale: Hexatonic (4), plagal. Tonal Center: g. Structure: aa¹aa¹ (4,4,4,4) aa¹ (8,8).

145
THE GIRL I LEFT BEHIND

B

'The Maid I Left Behind.' Sung by C. K. Tillett. Recorded at Wanchese, Roanoke Island; no date given. Our version has only half of the stanza as given in BSSM 98-100. Mentioned by Malcolm Laws, Jr., as one among numerous songs, many of which have been traced to British broadsides.

317

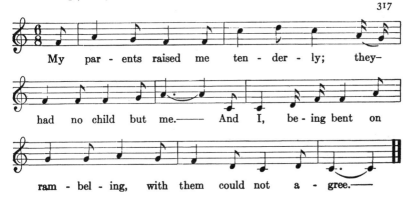

My par - ents raised me ten - der - ly; they—
had no child but me.—— And I, be - ing bent on
ram - bel - ing, with them could not a - gree.——

For melodic relationship cf. ***FSRA 137.
Scale: Mode III, plagal. Tonal Center: f. Structure: abcd (2,2,2,2). Circular Tune (V).

E

'The Girl I Left Behind.' Miss Fannie Grogan. Recorded as MS score at Zionville, Watauga county, in 1922. The text is identical with that of SharpK II 62, No. 96A.

318

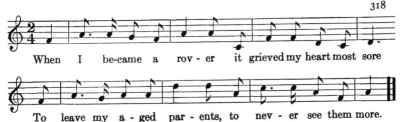

When I be-came a rov - er it grieved my heart most sore
To leave my a - ged par - ents, to nev - er see them more.

For melodic relationship cf. *SharpK II 62, No. 96A, measures 1-2.

Scale: Mode III, plagal. Tonal Center: f. Structure: aa¹ba² (2,2,2,2) = Reprisenbar. Circular Tune (III).

F

'The Girl I Left Behind.' Sung by Miss Fannie Grogan. Recorded at White Rock, Madison county, June 22, 1927. The musical score and comments pertaining to it are the same as for the preceding version.

146

THE ISLE OF ST. HELENA

A

'Napoleon.' Sung by C. K. Tillett. Recorded at Wanchese, Roanoke Island, December 29, 1922. The general melodic outline of the first six measures is very similar to that of 146E. For a Danish version see CRS, Kit O, 16. For a German version considerably different, cf. *Historische Volkslieder der Zeit von 1756-1871* I, part 3, 143.

319

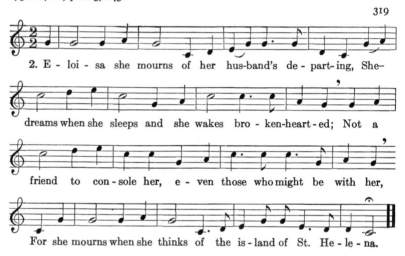

2. E - loi - sa she mourns of her hus-band's de - part-ing, She—

dreams when she sleeps and she wakes bro - ken-heart - ed; Not a

friend to con - sole her, e - ven those who might be with her,

For she mourns when she thinks of the is - land of St. He - le - na.

For melodic relationship cf. ***FSRA 186; **SharpK II 245, No. 173, measures 1-4.

Scale: Mode III. Tonal Center: c. Structure: abb¹a¹ (4,4,4,4). There is a general similarity between b and a.

B

'Bone Part.' Sung by Miss Fannie Grogan. Recorded at Silverstone, Watauga county; no date given. The general melodic outline of the first six measures is quite similar to that of 146A. Cf. WSSU 182 and SOCH 159 for texts.

320

Bone's gone to the war in the bat - tle he is fight - ing, He has gone to a place where he nev - er took no de - light in. Oh,– there he may sit down and tell all that he has seen While for home he doth weep on the Isle of—— St. Tel - len - a.

For melodic relationship cf. **FSRA 186; SharpK II 245, No. 173, measures 1-4, 7-8, and 14-16.

Scale: Hexachordal. Tonal Center: d. Structure: aba^{1}b (4,4,4,4) = aa^1 (8,8).

E

'Napoleon.' Sung by C. K. Tillett. Recorded at Wanchese, Roanoke Island, December 29, 1929. Another title given is 'The Isle of Saint Helena.' This song is totally different from his other versions, *including that in FSRA.*

321

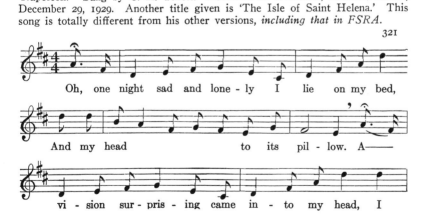

Oh, one night sad and lone - ly I lie on my bed, And my head to its pil - low. A—— vi - sion sur - pris - ing came in - to my head, I

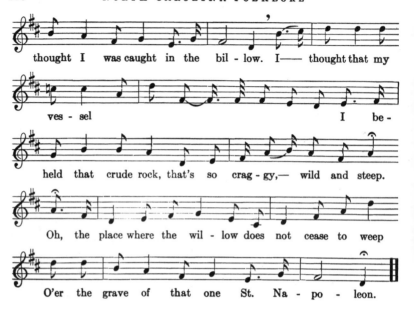

thought I was caught in the bil - low. I—— thought that my

ves - sel I be -

held that crude rock, that's so crag - gy,— wild and steep.

Oh, the place where the wil - low does not cease to weep

O'er the grave of that one St. Na - po - leon.

Scale: Mixolydian, plagal, with alternating sharpened and natural seventh. Tonal Center: d. Structure: aa^{1}ba^1 (4,4,4,4) = Reprisenbar.

148

THE ORPHAN GIRL

B

'The Orphan Girl.' Mrs. Vivian Blackstock. Recorded, probably in 1923, no place given.

The tune is identical with that of 148C, below and all the comments there also apply to this.

C

'The Orphan Girl.' Sung by M. G. Fulton. Recorded as MS score; no date or place given.

All three versions of this collection have basically the same melodic contour, although they all vary in details. In the general melodic outline the first two measures of this version are quite similar to those of 'Villikins and His Dinah' 204A, 'Indian Mohee' 110F and 'Jefferson City' 81A. Cf. SFSEA 48, No. 19.

This tune is identical with the anonymous version, which may be the one said to have been taken down by Mrs. Blackstock, 148B. It is almost identical with 148H.

322

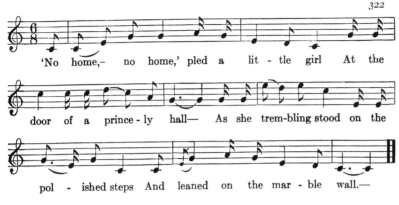

'No home,– no home,' pled a lit - tle girl At the

door of a prince - ly hall— As she trem-bling stood on the

pol - ished steps And leaned on the mar - ble wall.—

For melodic relationship cf. ***ASb 316; FSoA 17; FSF 119-23; SCSM 454; BSM 278, version B; TexasFS 282; OFS IV, 194-6; TT 51, 'The Golden Glove,' second version; *BSI 293-7.

Scale: Mode III. Tonal Center: c. Structure: abcd (2,2,2,2).

The MS score gives for the third and fourth line of stanza 1: "While she trembling stood on the marble steps / And leaned on the polished wall." This is the text of No. 148J.

F

'The Orphan Girl.' Sung by Mrs. Minnie Church. Recorded as MS score at Heaton, Avery county, in October 1930.

323

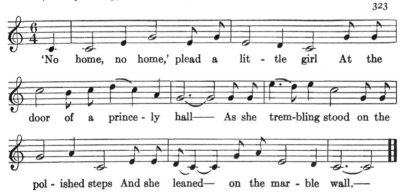

'No home, no home,' plead a lit - tle girl At the

door of a prince - ly hall— As she trem-bling stood on the

pol - ished steps And she leaned— on the mar - ble wall.—

For melodic relationship cf. ***ASb 316-17; FSoA 17; **SCSM 454, version A; FSF 119, No. 58; BSM 278, version B; OFS IV 194, No. 725A; *BSI 296.

Scale: Hexatonic (4). Tonal Center: c. Structure: abcd (2,2,2,2).
One additional stanza is as follows (cf. 148L):

The rich man lay on his bed of down
And dreamed of his silver and gold,
While the little girl lay on her bed of snow
And murmured, 'I'm cold, so cold.'

H

'The Orphan Girl.' Sung by Miss Beulah Walton. Recorded; no date or place given. Basically, this tune is the same as that of 148F. The first four measures are almost identical with those of 148C.

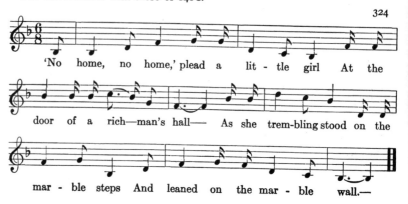

For melodic relationship cf. ***ASb 316-17. FSoA 17; FSF 119, No. 58; SCSM 454, version A; BSM 278, version B; OFS IV 194, No. 725A; *BSI 296.

Scale: Mode III. Tonal Center: b-flat. Structure: abcd (2,2,2,2).

149

THE BLIND GIRL

A

'Blind Girl's Prayer.' Sung by Dr. I. G. Greer. Recorded as MS score at Boone, Watauga county, June 3, 1915. There are two scores of two versions by the same singer, of which the second, however, differs only in measure 7, given as the variation below. As the stanza as printed in II 393 f. consists of eight lines, this melody will have to be repeated for the second half.

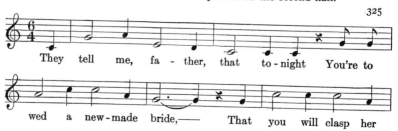

in   your— arms Where   my   dear- moth - er   died.—

For melodic relationship cf. **FSoA 79; OFS IV 191; *FSSH 371.

Scale: Mode III. Tonal Center: c. Structure: abcd (2,2,2,2).

D

'The Blind Child's Prayer.' Sung by Miss Pearle Webb. Recorded as MS score at Pineola, Avery county, in 1922. Basically, this tune is only a melodic variation of 149A.

326

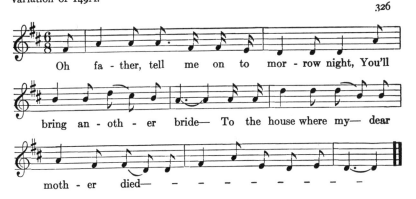

Oh   fa - ther, tell   me   on   to   mor - row night, You'll

bring an - oth - er   bride— To the house where my— dear

moth - er   died— - - - - - - - -

For melodic relationship cf. **FSoA 79; OFS IV 191, version A.

Scale: Hexatonic (4). Tonal Center: d. Structure: abcd (2,2,2,2).

K

'The Blind Child.' Sung by Otis Kuykendall. Recorded at Asheville in August 1939.

327

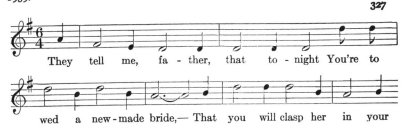

They   tell   me,   fa - ther, that   to - night You're   to

wed   a new - made bride,— That   you   will clasp her   in   your

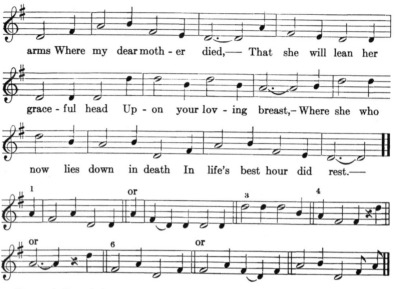

arms Where my dear moth - er died,— That she will lean her

grace - ful head Up - on your lov - ing breast,– Where she who

now lies down in death In life's best hour did rest.—

For melodic relationship cf. **FSoA 79; OFS IV 191, version A; *FSSH 371.

Scale: Mode III. Tonal Center: d. Structure: aba¹b (4,4,4,4) = aa¹ (8,8).

150

TWO LITTLE CHILDREN

A

'The Orphans.' Sung by Miss Estalena Graybeal. Recorded; no date or place given.

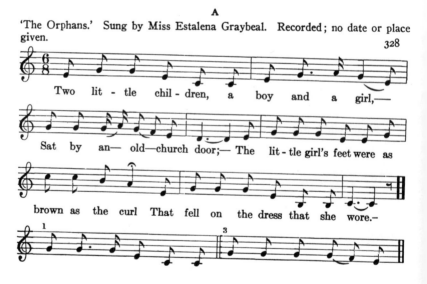

Two lit - tle chil - dren, a boy and a girl,—

Sat by an— old—church door;— The lit - tle girl's feet were as

brown as the curl That fell on the dress that she wore.–

For melodic relationship cf. *TexasFS 288.

Scale: Heptachordal, plagal. Tonal Center: c. Structure: $aa^1a^2a^3$ (2,2,2,2) = aa^1 (4,4).

D

'Two Little Orphans.' Sung by Zilpah Frisbie. Recorded in McDowell county in 1923. The chorus uses the same tune as the stanza.

329

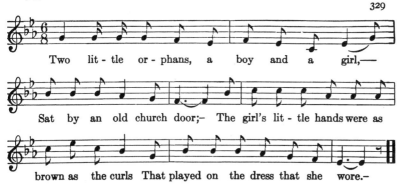

Two lit - tle or - phans, a boy and a girl,—

Sat by an old church door;– The girl's lit - tle hands were as

brown as the curls That played on the dress that she wore.–

Scale: Hexachordal, plagal. Tonal Center: e-flat. Structure: $aa^1a^2a^3$ (2,2,2,2) = aa^1 (4,4). The variations of a are considerable.

151

THE SOLDIER'S POOR LITTLE BOY

A

'Poor Little Sailor Boy.' Sung by C. K. Tillett. Recorded at Wanchese, Roanoke Island in 1922. (In II 396 for BSI 394-6 read BSI 304-6).

330

It was of a dark and— storm - y night, So—

cold— the wind did blow;— It was of a poor lit - tle

sail - or boy Up— to a— la - dy's door. A - set - ting

at her win - dow He lift - ed his eyes with joy, Say -

ing, 'For the Lord's sake some pit - y take On a

poor lit - tle sail - or boy.' Say - ing, 'For the Lord's sake some

pit - y take On a poor lit - tle sail - or boy.'

Scale: Mode II, plagal. Tonal Center: e. Structure: $aa^1ba^1a^1$ $(4,4,4,4) =$ aba $(8,4,8)$.

153
FOND AFFECTION

B

'Once I Loved with Fond Affection.' Sung by Mrs. W. L. Pridgen. Recorded; no date or place given. In II 398 for ASb 232 read ASb 323.)

331

Once I loved with fond af - fec - tion And I

thought that you loved me, But I found that you de -

ceived me And you cared no more for me.

Scale: Heptachordal, plagal. Tonal Center: c. Structure: $abab^1$ $(2,2,2,2) =$ aa^1 $(4,4)$.

E

'Fond Affection.' Sung by Austin E. Elliott. Recorded as MS score in Randolph county in 1919.

332

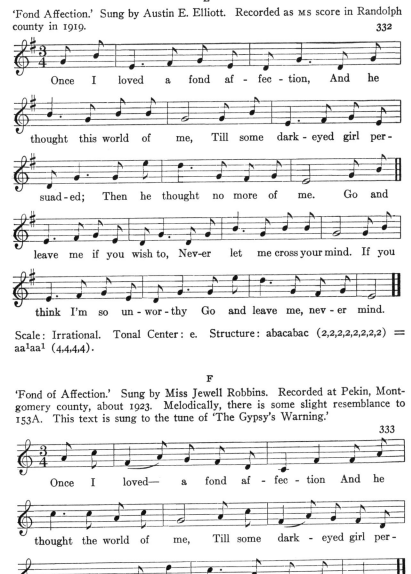

Once I loved a fond af - fec - tion, And he

thought this world of me, Till some dark - eyed girl per -

suad - ed; Then he thought no more of me. Go and

leave me if you wish to, Nev-er let me cross your mind. If you

think I'm so un - wor - thy Go and leave me, nev - er mind.

Scale: Irrational. Tonal Center: e. Structure: abacabac (2,2,2,2,2,2,2,2) = aa¹aa¹ (4,4,4,4).

F

'Fond of Affection.' Sung by Miss Jewell Robbins. Recorded at Pekin, Montgomery county, about 1923. Melodically, there is some slight resemblance to 153A. This text is sung to the tune of 'The Gypsy's Warning.'

333

Once I loved— a fond af - fec - tion And he

thought the world of me, Till some dark - eyed girl per -

suad - ed; Then he thought no more of me.

Scale: Mode III, plagal. Tonal Center: f. Structure: aba¹b¹ (2,2,2,2) = aa¹ (4,4).

H

'Fond Devotion.' Sung by Miss Pearle Webb. Recorded as MS score at
Pineola, Avery county, in 1921.

334

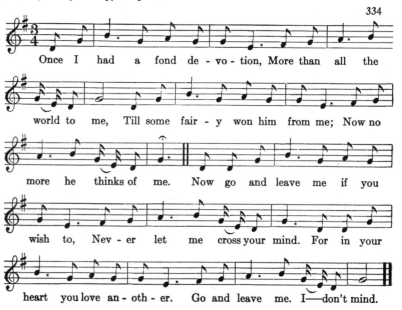

Once I had a fond de - vo - tion, More than all the

world to me, Till some fair - y won him from me; Now no

more he thinks of me. Now go and leave me if you

wish to, Nev - er let me cross your mind. For in your

heart you love an - oth - er. Go and leave me. I——don't mind.

Scale: Hexatonic (4), plagal. Tonal Center: g. Structure: abababab (2,2,2,2,
2,2,2,2) = aaaa (4,4,4,4).

N

'Go and Leave Me If You Wish To.' Sung by Bascom Lamar Lunsford. Recorded at Turkey Creek, Buncombe county; no date given. The chorus of this
version is the second stanza in the following versions: FSSH 250-1, No. 74;
OFS IV 253, No. 755G; BMFSB 52.

335

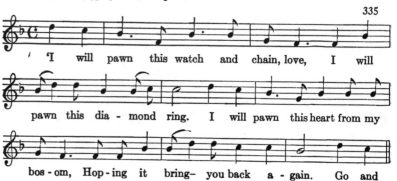

'I will pawn this watch and chain, love, I will

pawn this dia - mond ring. I will pawn this heart from my

bos - om, Hop - ing it bring— you back a - gain. Go and

leave me if you wish to, Nev - er let— me cross your— mind.

If you think I'm too un - wor-thy, Go, my dar - ling, I don't mind.'

Scale: Mode III, plagal. Tonal Center: b-flat. Structure: aa¹aa¹ $(4,4,4,4)$ = aa $(8,8)$.

154
You Are False, but I'll Forgive You

A

'You Are False, but I'll Forgive You.' Sung by Miss Mary Strawbridge. Recorded; no date or place given.

336

Fare thee well, for once I loved you E - ven

more than tongue can tell; Lit - tle did I think you'd leave me;

Now I bid you all fare - well. You have wrecked the heart I

cher - ished, You have doomed me day by day, You are false;

but I'll for - give you. But for -get you I nev - er may.

Scale: Heptachordal, plagal.   Tonal Center: e-flat.   Structure: aa¹ba¹ (4,4,4,4)
= Reprisenbar.

155
WE HAVE MET AND WE HAVE PARTED

A

'We Have Met and We Have Parted.'   Sung by Dr. I. G. Greer.   Recorded as
MS score at Boone, Watauga county, probably during 1915-16.   This text is
almost the second stanza in SSSA 165.   The chorus also is very similar.

337

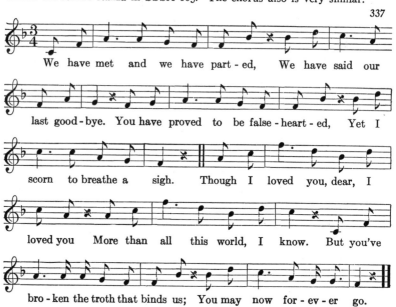

We have met and we have part-ed,   We have said our

last good-bye. You have proved to be false-heart-ed,   Yet I

scorn to breathe a sigh.   Though I loved you, dear, I

loved you More than all this world, I know. But you've

bro-ken the troth that binds us; You may now for-ev-er go.

Scale: Hexachordal, plagal.   Tonal center: f.   Structure: aa¹bb¹a² (4,4,2,2,4)
= aba¹ (8,4,4).

A(1)

'Through the Woods and Through the Bushes.'   Sung by Miss Eugenia Clark.
Recorded as MS score at Colletsville, Caldwell county, June 1921.   With the
exception of the first line, the remainder of the stanza given here is identical
with that of stanza 10 of the preceding 155A.   Compare also the text of 153I,
stanza 8.   With slight variations this tune is also identical with that of 155A;
it lacks, however, the chorus found there.

338

10. Through the woods and through the bush-es——

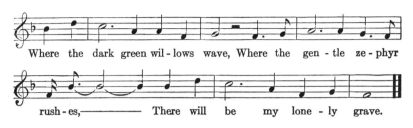

Where the dark green wil-lows wave, Where the gen - tle ze - phyr rush - es,———— There will be my lone - ly grave.

Scale : Hexachordal. Tonal Center : f. Structure : abab[1] (2,2,2,2) = aa[1] (4,4).

B

'The Broken Engagement.' Sung by anonymous singer. Recorded as MS score at Asheville in May 1920.

339

We have met and we have part - ed,— We have said our last good - bye. You have proved to me false-heart - ed,— Though I fain would have a sigh. For I loved you, dear - ly loved you,— More than all this world, I know. But you've bro - ken the trust you plight - ed;— Now you may for - ev - er go.

Scale : Heptachordal, plagal. Tonal Center : f. Structure : aa[1]aa[1] (4,4,4,4) = aa (8,8).

B(1)

'The Broken Engagement.' Sung by Dr. I. G. Greer for the present editor. Recorded at Chapel Hill, 1952. Our stanza is very similar to the first stanza of 'This Night We Part Forever' from Miss Pearle Webb, No. 159 in II 422 f.

340

Though this night we part for-ev-er, You are noth-ing more to me. Brave-ly I each tie will sev-er, All that binds my heart to thee. I have loved you, dear-ly loved you, More than all this world can know. But the bro-ken vows you've plight-ed, Now I say for-ev-er go.

Scale: Heptachordal. Tonal Center: b-flat. Structure: abcdabcd (2,2,2,2,2,2,2,2) = abab (4,4,4,4).

I

'Lovers' Last Farewell.' Sung by Miss Millie Saunders. Recorded at Jonas Ridge (Rip Shin Ridge), Burke county, June 30, 1940. The words of the first stanza are not clear. The remaining stanzas are given below, of which the third is given with the score. For a similar text compare this stanza with the third of 'The Butcher's Boy' (II 273, version 81B) ; also OFS IV 333, No. 811C.

341

3. You love some oth-er and I know why— Be-cause he has— more gold than I.— The gold will melt,— and the sil-ver will fly—— My love for you—— will nev-er die.——

Scale: Hexatonic (4). Tonal Center: c. Structure: abab (4,4,4,4) = aa (8,8).

2 I thought I heard my true love say,
  'I will return and come this way.
  You love some other, you don't love me,
  You care not for my company.'

4 'There is a flower,' I heard them say,
  'That can be seen from day to day.'
  And if that flower I want to find,
  It sure'll be placed in this heart of mine.

5 So, farewell you well, my own true love,
  Oh, meet me in that land above.
  And when we meet there in that land
  We'll take no more this parting hand.

156

BROKEN TIES

B

'Broken Ties.' Sung by Katie S. Russell. Recorded at Roxboro, Person county, probably in 1923. The idiom of this song is very much like that of the well-known cowboy songs. The chromatic changes also point to some influence foreign to the traditional folk idiom. The text of this stanza is almost the same as that of the chorus given in FSSH 235-6.

342

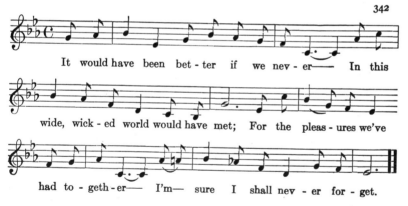

It would have been bet-ter if we nev-er— In this wide, wick-ed world would have met; For the pleas-ures we've had to-geth-er— I'm— sure I shall nev-er for-get.

Scale: Heptachordal, plagal. Tonal center: e-flat. Structure: aba^{1}b^1 (2,2,2,2) = aa^1 (4,4).

157

THEY WERE STANDING BY THE WINDOW

A

'The Broken Heart.' Sung by Dr. I. G. Greer. Recorded as MS score at Boone,

Watauga county; no date given. The rhythmic line of this tune is identical
with that found in BMFSB 56, but there is no melodic relationship whatsoever.

343

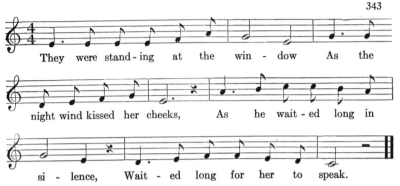

They were stand - ing   at   the   win - dow   As   the

night wind kissed   her cheeks,   As   he wait - ed long in

si - lence,   Wait - ed long for   her   to   speak.

For melodic relationship cf. *OFS IV 283, No. 771; the first, third, and last
cadences are alike.

Scale: Heptachordal. Tonal Center: c. Structure: aa^{1}bb^1 (2,2,2,2) = ab (4,4).

160

PARTING WORDS

'Parting Words.' Sung by Dr. I. G. Greer. Recorded as MS score at Boone,
Watauga county, about 1915. The tune given serves for both stanza and chorus.

344

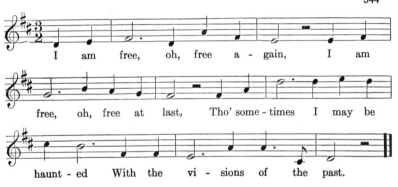

I   am   free,   oh,   free   a - gain,   I   am

free,   oh,   free   at   last,   Tho' some - times   I   may   be

haunt - ed   With   the   vi - sions   of   the   past.

Scale: Heptachordal, plagal. Tonal Center: d. Structure: abcd (2,2,2,2).

163

DON'T FORGET ME, LITTLE DARLING

'Don't Forget Me, Little Darling.' Sung by Bonnie and Lola Wiseman. Recorded at Upper Hinson's Creek, August 26, 1939.

2. Don't for-get me, lit-tle dar-ling,—— When from you I'm far a-way, But re-mem-ber, lit-tle dar-ling,—— We may meet a-gain some day.

Scale: Heptachordal, plagal. Tonal Center: f. Structure: abab (2,2,2,2) = aa (4,4).

165

The Ripest Apple

'The Ripest Apple.' Sung by Dr. I. G. Greer. Recorded as MS score at Boone, Watauga county, probably in 1915. The variations from the printed text are from the MS score.

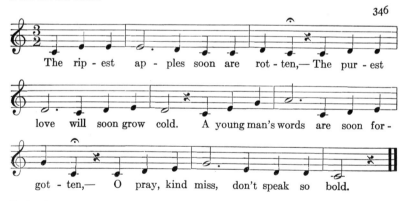

The rip-est ap-ples soon are rot-ten,—The pur-est love will soon grow cold. A young man's words are soon for-got-ten,— O pray, kind miss, don't speak so bold.

Scale: Mode III. Tonal Center: c. Structure: abcd (2,2,2,2).

167

My Little Dear, So Fare You Well

E

'Come All Ye Girls from Adam's Race.' Sung by Miss Jennie Belvin. Recorded at Durham; no date given. Another title has "of" instead of "from."

347

7. Go dig my grave most wide and deep. Place a mar-ble
stone at head and feet; And on my breast place a tur-tle
dove   To   show   to   the   world   I   died   for   love.

Scale: Hexatonic (4), plagal. Tonal Center: f. Structure: abab[1] (2,2,2,2) =
aa[1] (4,4).

170

THE HOMESICK BOY

A

'Homesick Boy.' Sung by Bascom Lamar Lunsford. Recorded at Turkey Creek.
Buncombe county; no date given. Another title given is 'Roanoke River.' After
the traditional regularity of the first eight measures, those making up the chorus
seem strangely confused; and this is also the impression one has on hearing the
song. Judging from internal evidence, there seems to be no doubt but that some
arbitrary handling is at the root of the apparent unbalance.

348

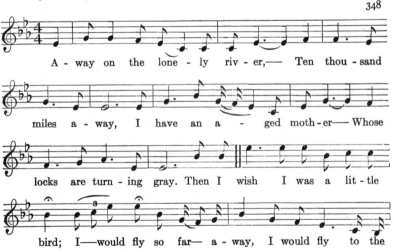

A - way on the lone - ly riv-er,— Ten thou-sand
miles a-way, I have an a - ged moth-er—Whose
locks are turn-ing gray. Then I wish I was a lit-tle
bird; I—would fly so far— a-way, I would fly to the

Ro - anoke Riv - er, Ten thou - sand miles a - way.

Scale: Hexachordal, plagal. Tonal Center: e-flat. Structure: aba^1b^1cd (2,2,2, 2,3,3) = aa^1b (4,4,6) = mm^1n = barform.

B

'I Wish I Were a Little Bird.' Sung by Miss Jewell Robbins. Recorded at Pekin, Montgomery county, between 1921 and 1924.

349

Last night while I was sleep - ing I dreamed a hap - py,

hap - py dream. I dreamed I saw my moth - er A -

pray - ing to God for me. I wish I was a lit - tle

bird, a lit - tle bird; I'd fly, I'd fly far a - way, I'd

fly be-yond the riv - er, Ten thou - sand miles a - way.

Scale: Hexachordal. Tonal Center: d. Structure: $abab^1cb^2ab^1$ (2,2,2,2,2,2,2,2) = aa^1ba^1 (4,4,4,4) = Reprisenbar.

176
THE DERBY RAM

A

'The Great Sheep.' Sung by Mrs. Isenhour, of Zionville, Watauga county. Recorded as MS score; no date or place given. Our text is practically identical with that of the second stanza of SharpK II 186, No. 141C, as well as OFS I 400, No. 106C. There is no chorus in our version.

350

3. The wool on the sheep's back, it growed to the sky;— The

ea - gles built their nests there, for I heard the young ones cry.

For melodic relationship cf. **OFS 1 398, No. 106A, first four measures; BSI 319-21, measures 1-2.

Scale: Hexachordal, plagal. Tonal Center: f. Structure: aa¹bb¹ (2,2,2,2) = ab (4,4).

B

'Darby's Ram.' Sung by Otis Kuykendall. Recorded at Asheville in 1939. The singer gave this title. Note the differences in text. The chorus is sung after every other stanza. The melodic material of measures 4-8 and 12-15 is the same. The use of it, however, is the noteworthy feature.

351

As I went out to Dar - by, sir, All— on a

mur - ky day, I met the big - gest ram, sir, That

ev - er fed— on hay. And he ram - bled, he ram -

bled, And he ram-bled till the butch - er cut him down.———

For melodic relationship cf. *31 FSSM 8-9, stanza only.

Scale: Mode III, plagal. Tonal Center: e-flat. Structure: abcb¹dd¹e (2,2,2,2, 2,2,4) = abcd (4,4,4,4).

2 It had four feet to walk, sir,
   And it had four feet to stand,
   And every foot it had, sir,
   Covered an acre of land.

3 This old ram had horns, sir,
   That reached up to the sky,
   An eagle built a nest there;
   I heard the young ones cry.

4 This old ram had wool, sir,
   That reached up to the moon,
   A nigger went up in January,
   And he didn't come back till June.

C

'Big Sheep.' Sung by Doyle Pruitt. From the previous recording of Dr. W. A
Abrams; no date or place given. Another title is 'Darby's Ram.'

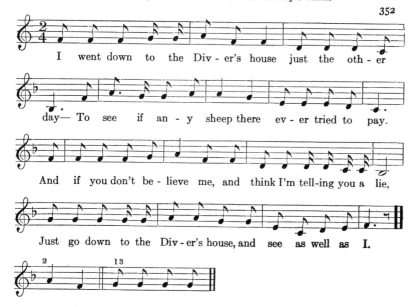

Scale: Heptachordal, plagal. Tonal Center: f. Structure: aba^{1}b^1 (4,4,4,4) =
aa^1 (8,8).

177

THE MILLER AND HIS THREE SONS

A

'The Miller and His Three Sons.' Sung by Dr. E. E. Ericson. Recorded as

MS score at Chapel Hill; no date given. For additional text versions and comments cf. PMOT, I 190-1 and II 772; also Whittaker, 25.[1]

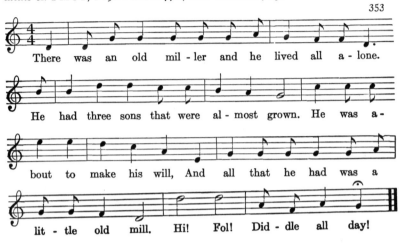

353

There was an old mil - ler and he lived all a - lone.

He had three sons that were al - most grown. He was a -

bout to make his will, And all that he had was a

lit - tle old mill. Hi! Fol! Did - dle all day!

For melodic relationship cf. *BSSM 247, first three notes only; BSO 167,
measure I with up-beat.

Scale: Mixolydian, plagal. Tonal Center: g. Structure: abcd (2,2,2,4). The
last phrase is terminally incremented.

A(I)

'The Miller and His Three Sons.' Sung by Mrs. Ewart Wilson. Recorded;
no date or place given. Another title is 'The Miller.' Textually, the only difference is in the chorus.

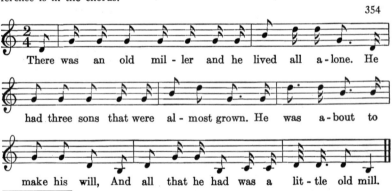

354

There was an old mil - ler and he lived all a - lone. He

had three sons that were al - most grown. He was a - bout to

make his will, And all that he had was a lit - tle old mill.

---

[1] Students of musical history will be interested in a statement by Leah J.
Wolford, *The Play-Party in Indiana* (Indianapolis, 1916), p. 68: "The tune to
'The Jolly Miller' was in 1624 harmonized by Beethoven for George Thomson
(*Pills to Purge Melancholy*, i, p. 169)"—quoted by B. A. Botkin, *The American
Play-Party Song* (Lincoln, Nebraska, 1937), p. 247.

Fol— de did-dle die— You die, you die, Fol de did-dle die.

For melodic relationship cf. **Sharp II 222, No. 161B, measures 2, 4-10;
FSF 382, No. 205A, melodic line of second measure.

Scale: Mixolydian, plagal. Tonal Center: g. Structure: mm¹n op = (2,2,4,2,2)
= Barform plus strophe.

J

'The Miller and His Three Sons.' Sung by Alexander Tugman. Recorded as
MS score at Todd, Ashe county; no date given. The section in 2/4 is considerably slower than the preceding in 3/4. Such change in time signature affecting
a whole section is rather rare.

He called to him his eld - est son And
said, 'My son, my race is run. And if to you these
mills I make, I'd like you to tell me the toll you'd
take.' Oh rec - ko, rek - tum a rin ko ry do.

For melodic relationship cf. **BSO 167, No. 61A, measure 1 with up-beat;
also our measures 9-12 are in the general melodic line an augmentation of the
seventh and eighth measures of the Ohio version.

Scale: Hexatonic (6), plagal. Tonal Center: g. Structure. abcde (4,4,2,2,2).

2 'Father,' he said, 'My name is Jack;
From every bushel I'll take one peck;
And every bushel the mill does grind,
A very good living I will find.'

K

'The Miller's Sons.' Sung by Miss Ruth Miller. From a previous recording
of Dr. W. A. Abrams, Boone, Watauga county; no date given. The text of
this version is totally different from any of those given in II 440-4. There is
also no refrain in this ballad. The identical text can be found in FSCSG 44-5.

356

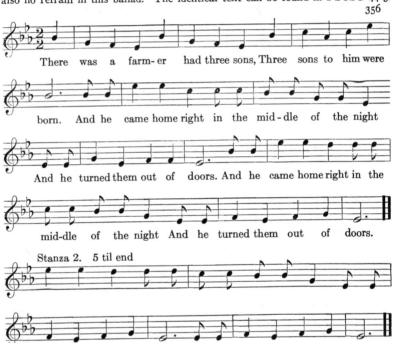

For melodic relationship cf. ***FSCSG 44-5, No. 18.

Scale: Heptachordal. Tonal Center: e-flat. Structure: nmm¹ (4,4,4) = Inverted barform.

179

THE OLD DYER

'The Old Dyer.' Sung by Miss Laura Mathews. Recorded as MS score at
Durham; no date given. The nonsense syllables of the refrain are somewhat
different from those given in the printed text, II 445.

357

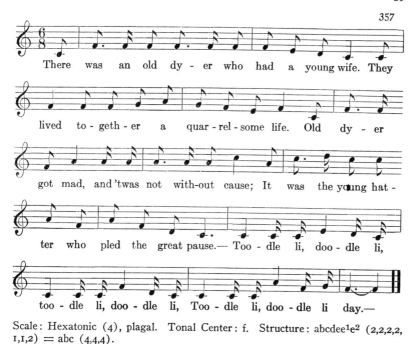

There was an old dy - er who had a young wife. They
lived to - geth - er a quar - rel - some life. Old dy - er
got mad, and 'twas not with-out cause; It was the young hat -
ter who pled the great pause.— Too - dle li, doo - dle li,
too - dle li, doo - dle li, Too - dle li, doo - dle li day.—

Scale: Hexatonic (4), plagal. Tonal Center: f. Structure: abcdee¹e² (2,2,2,2,
1,1,2) = abc (4,4,4).

181

JOHNNY SANDS

B

'Johnny Sands.' Sung by Professor N. I. White. Recorded probably at Durham, but no date given. Malcolm Laws, Jr., includes this among a number of
other songs many of which have been traced to British broadsides.

358

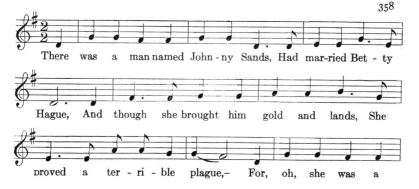

There was a man named John - ny Sands, Had mar-ried Bet - ty
Hague, And though she brought him gold and lands, She
proved a ter - ri - ble plague,— For, oh, she was a

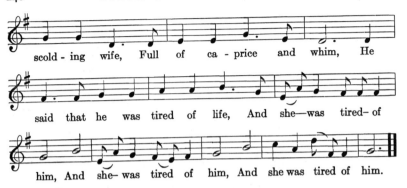

scold - ing   wife,   Full   of   ca - price   and   whim,   He

said   that   he   was   tired   of   life,   And   she—was   tired- of

him,   And   she— was   tired   of   him,   And   she was   tired of   him.

For melodic relationship cf. ***FSF 368, No. 197A, the melodic line of the stanza with the exception of the first cadence. The refrain also is different.

Scale: Heptachordal, plagal.   Tonal Center: g.   Structure: abab¹c (4,4,4,4,4); c is partly related to b¹.

182

THE OLD WOMAN'S BLIND HUSBAND

A

'The Old Woman's Blind Husband.'   Sung by Mrs. O. D. Barnett.   Recorded as MS score at Durham in 1921.

359

There   was   an   old   wo - man   in   our   town,— In

our———   town- did   dwell,–   She   loved- her   dear - est   hus - band

But   an - oth - er   man   quite—   as   well—   Oh!   sing   ti - de -

ree - rum,   ti - de - ree - rum,   Mac - fa - lu - fa - lai.—

For melodic relationship cf. ***OFS IV 246, No. 750, measures 1-4 ('Johnny Sands'); **SharpK I 349, No. 55B, first six measures.

Scale: Hexatonic (4), plagal.   Tonal Center: g.   Structure: abc (4,4,4).

A (I)

'The Old Woman's Blind Husband.' Sung by Horton Barker. From previous recording of Dr. W. A. Abrams, Boone, Watauga county; no date given. Other titles given 'Rich Old Lady' and 'There Was an Old Lady in Our Town.' Although this tune is in Dorian mode, the melodic line, for the first eight measures, is closely related to that of the preceding version, 182A.

360

There was an old la - dy in our town, In

our— town did dwell,— She loved her hus - band dear - ly

But an - oth - er man twice as well.— Sing too - di - um,

Sing too - di - um, Whack fa - la - li day.——

For melodic relationship cf. ***SharpK I 349, No. 55B; **OFS IV 246, No. 750, first four measures.

Scale: Dorian (plagal). Tonal Center: g. Structure: abc (4,4,4).

2 She went down to the butcher shop
To see if she could find,
To see if she could find something
To make her old man blind.

3 She got twelve dozen marrow bones,
She made him sup them all.
Says he, 'Old woman, I am so blind
I cannot see at all.'

4 Said he, 'I'm goin' to drown myself
If I could only see.'
Said she, 'My dearest husband,
I'll go and show you the way.'

5 She bundled him up in his old grey coat,
She took him to the brim;
Said he, 'I cannot drown myself
Unless you push me in.'

6 The old woman took a step or two back
To give her roll and spring;

The old man stepped a little aside
And she went tumbling in.

7   She bubbled and gurgled and squalled out
As loud as she could bawl.
Said he, 'Old woman, I am so blind
I can't see you at all.'

183

THE DUMB WIFE

B

'The Bonnie Blade.'   Sung by Mrs. N. T. Byers.   Recorded as MS score at
Durham in 1921.

361

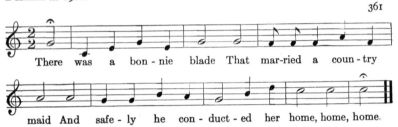

There was   a   bon - nie   blade That mar-ried a   coun-try
maid And   safe - ly   he   con - duct - ed   her home, home, home.

Scale: Heptachordal.   Tonal Center: c.   Structure: aa¹bc (2,2,2,2).

B(1)

'The Dumb Wife.'   Sung by Mrs. Laura B. Timmons.   From previous recording of Dr. W. A. Abrams, at Boone, Watauga county, August 8, 1940.   Another
title is 'Scolding Wife.'   This singer is an artist of the first water.   The structure of the melody requires the stanzas as printed in II 454 to be grouped in
pairs.

362

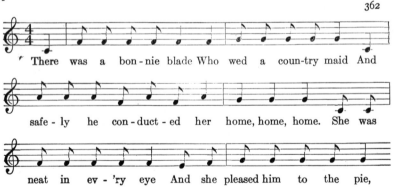

There was   a   bon - nie blade Who wed   a   coun-try maid And
safe - ly   he   con - duct - ed   her   home, home, home.   She was
neat   in   ev - 'ry eye   And she pleased him   to   the   pie,

But a - lack, and a - las! she was dumb, dumb, dumb.

Scale: Hexatonic (4), plagal. Tonal Center: f. Structure: aba^{1}c (2,2,2,2) = aa^1 (4,4).

184

THE HOLLY TWIG

A

'When I Was a Bachelor.' Sung by Miss Penelope Nichols. Recorded as MS score at Durham, May 1920. Our text is a variation of the first stanza (second choice) of 'The Holly Twig' in SharpK I 341, No. 53A. (In II 455 for SharpK II read SharpK I.)

When I was a bach - e - lor bold and young I court - ed a girl with a flat - ter - ing tongue; She said she would have me, but she did - n't say when, And the kiss - es I gave her were a hun-dred and ten, And the kiss - es I gave her were a hun - dred and ten.

Scale: Tetratonic (4) plagal. Tonal Center: f. Structure: aa^{1}a^{2}a^{3}a^4 (2,2,2,2,2) = aa^1 (4,6). The second phrase is terminally incremented.

185

NOBODY COMING TO MARRY ME

'My Father's a Hedger and Ditcher.' Sung by Miss Mary Barbour. Recorded at Raeford, Holt county, in 1922.

364

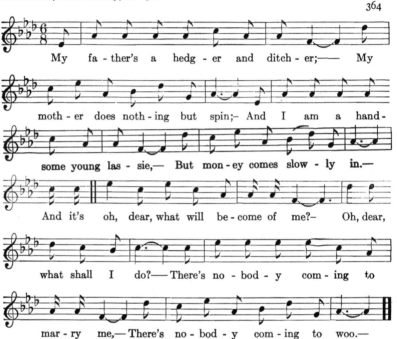

My fa - ther's a hedg - er and ditch - er;—— My

moth - er does noth - ing but spin;– And I am a hand -

some young las - sie,— But mon - ey comes slow - ly in.—

And it's oh, dear, what will be - come of me?– Oh, dear,

what shall I do?—There's no - bod - y com - ing to

mar - ry me,— There's no - bod - y com - ing to woo.—

Scale: Heptachordal, plagal. Tonal Center: a-flat. Structure: ababcdcb (2,2,2, 2,2,2,2,2) = aabb[1] (4,4,4,4).

186

WHISTLE, DAUGHTER, WHISTLE

B

'Whistle, Daughter.' Sung by Miss Lura Wagoner. Recorded at MS score at Vox, Alleghany county; no date given. For a similar story from the Rhineland in Germany cf. VTWL 124, No. 233. Cf. also DL II 640 ('Spinn, spinn, meine liebe Tochter').

365

'Whis - tle, daugh-ter, whis - tle, and I'll give you a pin.' 'I

can - not whis - tle moth - er, and neith - er can I spin.'

Scale: Irrational, plagal. Tonal Center: f. Structure: abab (2,2,2,2) = aa (4,4).

187

HARD OF HEARING

'Old Woman.' Sung by Miss Ethel Burleson and Joe Powles. Recorded; no date or place given. According to the structure of the tune, each line is to be repeated. This is also true of the Cecil Sharp version (see below).

366

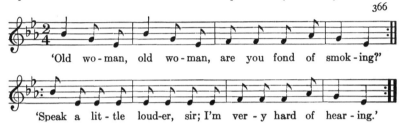

'Old wo - man, old wo - man, are you fond of smok - ing?'

'Speak a lit - tle loud-er, sir; I'm ver - y hard of hear - ing.'

For melodic relationship cf. ***SharpK ii 252, No. 178; SHP 16.

Scale: Pentachordal. Tonal Center: e-flat. Structure: ababcbcb (2,2,2,2,2,2,2,2) = aabb (4,4,4,4) ; b is partly related to a.

187(1)

'Old Woman.' Sung by Miss Pearle Webb. From previous recording of Dr. W. A. Abrams, Boone, Watauga county; no date given.

367

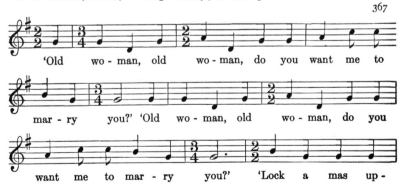

'Old wo - man, old wo - man, do you want me to

mar - ry you?' 'Old wo - man, old wo - man, do you

want me to mar - ry you?' 'Lock a mas up -

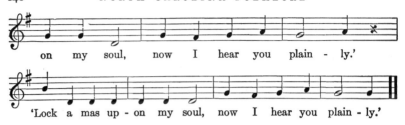

on   my   soul,   now   I   hear   you   plain - ly.'

'Lock a mas up - on my soul, now I hear you plain - ly.'

Scale: Hexatonic (6), plagal. Tonal Center: g. Structure: aabb[1] (4,4,4,4).

188

THE THREE ROGUES

B

'Colony Times.' Sung by Miss Eula Todd. Recorded at Jefferson, Ashe county, in 1921.

368

In   the   good   old   col - o - ny   times,   When   we   were

un - der   the   king,   Three   rog - uish chaps   fell   in - to   mis - haps

Be - cause they could   not   sing.   Be - cause they   could   not   sing,

Be - cause they could   not   sing,   Three   rog - uish chaps   fell

in - to   mis - haps   Be - cause they   could   not   sing.

For melodic relationship cf.**SHP 9; FSONE 213-14, the very beginning only; *BSO 197-8, the very beginning only.

Scale: Hexatonic (4), plagal. Tonal Center: g. Structure: aabcccbc (1,1,1,1, 1,1,1,1) = abb[1] (2,4,2) [the b is terminally incremented].

C

'The Three Rogues.' Sung by Mrs. J. J. Miller. Recorded in Caldwell county in 1921.

369

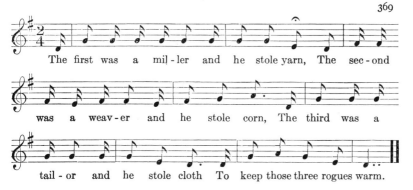

The first was a mil-ler and he stole yarn, The sec-ond
was a weav-er and he stole corn, The third was a
tail-or and he stole cloth To keep those three rogues warm.

Scale: Irrational, plagal. Tonal Center: g. Structure: abac (2,2,2,2) = aa¹
(4,4). Circular tune (V).

192

THE BURGLAR MAN

'The Burglar Man.' Sung by H. J. Beaker. Recorded probably at Boone, Watauga county, August 1939, 1940, or 1941.

370

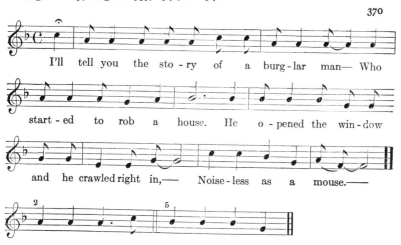

I'll tell you the sto-ry of a burg-lar man— Who
start-ed to rob a house. He o-pened the win-dow
and he crawled right in,— Noise-less as a mouse.—

Scale: Hexatonic (6), plagal. Tonal Center: f. Structure: abcd (2,2,2,2).

193

BILLY GRIMES THE DROVER

A

'Billy Grimes.' Sung by Miss Amy Henderson. Recorded as MS score at Worry, Burke county, in 1914.

371

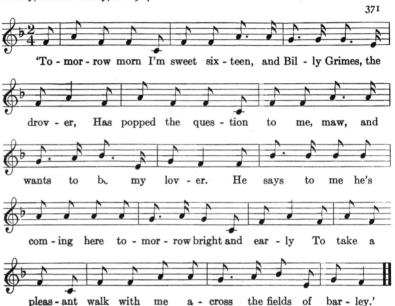

'To - mor - row morn I'm sweet six - teen, and Bil - ly Grimes, the

drov - er, Has popped the ques - tion to me, maw, and

wants to bᴏ my lov - er. He says to me he's

com - ing here to - mor - row bright and ear - ly To take a

pleas - ant walk with me a - cross the fields of bar - ley.'

For melodic relationship cf. **'Maryland, My Maryland,' measures 6-8.

Scale: Hexatonic (6), plagal. Tonal Center: f. Structure: aa¹ba¹ (4,4,4,4) = Reprisenbar.

F

'Billy Grimes.' Sung by Miss Susie Hageman. Recorded at Beech Creek, Watauga county, in 1922. The first, eighth, and ninth measures are identical with those of 193I.

372

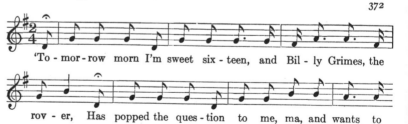

'To - mor - row morn I'm sweet six - teen, and Bil - ly Grimes, the

rov - er, Has popped the ques - tion to me, ma, and wants to

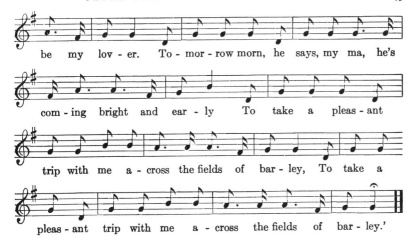

be my lov - er. To - mor - row morn, he says, my ma, he's

com - ing bright and ear - ly To take a pleas - ant

trip with me a - cross the fields of bar - ley, To take a

pleas - ant trip with me a - cross the fields of bar - ley.'

Scale: Irrational, plagal. Tonal Center: g. Structure: aa¹aa¹a¹ (4,4,4,4,4).

I

'Billie Grimes.' Sung by Mrs. G. L. Bostic. Recorded at Mooresboro, Cleveland county, 1939. This ballad is related to 193A. The first measure is the same as that of 193F. The second, third, and fourth stanzas given below are followed with the third and fourth stanzas of Mrs. Sutton's version, 193C.

373

'To - mor - row morn I'm sweet six - teen, and Bil - ly Grimes, the

drov - er, He popped the ques - tion to me, maw, and

wants to be my lov - er. He says to - mor - row

morn - ing, maw, he's com - ing here quite ear - ly To take a

pleas - ant walk with me a - cross the fields of bar - ley.'

Scale: Pentachordal, plagal. Tonal Center: f. Structure: abab (4,4,4,4) = aa (8,8).

2 'Hush, hush, my daughter dear, there is no use of talking;
   You shall not go with Billy Grimes across the fields awalking.
   To think of his presumption, too, the trifling low-down drover,
   And I wonder where your pride has gone to think of such a lover.'

3 'My dearest Maw, I must confess that Billy is quite clever,
   A cleverer lad cannot be found through all this wide world over.
   He takes me to the fair, mama, and he buys me cakes and candy,
   And when he's dressed in his Sunday blue, he looks quite like a dandy.'

4 My grand, dear child, I am surprised at your infatuation,
   For Billy is the poorest chance throughout this Yankee nation.
   And now, young miss, I don't allow your cutting up these capers,
   So swift I'll give Old Grimes's son his fastest walking papers.'

194

GRANDMA'S ADVICE

A

'My Grandma Lives on Yonder Little Green.' Sung by Miss Elizabeth Walker.
Recorded as MS score at Boone, Watauga county, probably in 1936.

374

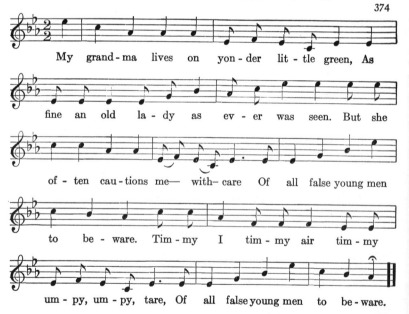

My grand-ma lives on yon-der lit-tle green, As fine an old la-dy as ev-er was seen. But she of-ten cau-tions me— with- care Of all false young men to be-ware. Tim-my I tim-my air tim-my um-py, um-py, tare, Of all false young men to be-ware.

For melodic relationship cf. **TBmWV 85; SCSM 457; AMS 56; BSO 300-1; FSONE 243-5 (measures 2, 6, 10); OFS 1 383, No. 101A (measures 2,6); also 'Turkey in the Straw' (measures 2,6,10).

Scale: Hexatonic (4), plagal. Tonal center: a-flat. Structure: aa¹a² (4,4,4).

C

'Grandma's Advice.' Sung by Miss Jessie Hauser. Recorded in Forsyth county, about 1923. Other titles given are 'Timmy I, Timmy' and 'My Grandma Lives on Yonder Little Green.'

375

My grand - ma lives on yon - der lit - tle green, As fine an old la - dy as ev - er was seen. But she of - ten cau - tioned me with care Of all false young men to be - ware. Tim - my I tim - my air tim - my um - py tum - py tare Of all false young men to be - ware.

For melodic relationship cf. **WSSU 166-7; SCSM 457; and AMS 46, especially the beginning; OFS 1 383, No. 101A; BSO 300 (measures 1-2, 5-6, 9-10) ; TBmWV 85; FSONE 244, the beginning.

Scale: Hexatonic (4), plagal. Tonal Center: f. Structure: aa¹a² (4,4,4).

F

'Grandma's Advice.' Sung by Miss Ruth Black. Recorded as MS score at Piney Creek, Alleghany county, summer of 1921. This tune is closely related to 194A.

376

My grand-moth - er lived on yon - der lit - tle green, As

fine an old la - dy as ev - er was seen. She

of - ten cau - tioned me with care Of all false young men

to be - ware. Tim - my I tim - my a tim - my

um py ta Of all false young men to be - ware.

For melodic relationship cf. **TBmWV 85; SCSM 457; AMS 46; FSONE 244 (measures 2,6,10) ; BSO 300 and OFS 1 383, No. 101A (measures 2,6). Compare also WSSU 166.

Scale: Hexatonic (4), plagal. Tonal center: g. Structure: $aba^1b^1a^2b^1$ (2,2,2, 2,2,2) $= aa^1a^2$ (4,4,4).

195

COMMON BILL

A

'Silly Bill.' Sung by Mrs. N. J. Herring. Recorded as MS score at Tomahawk, Bladen county; no date given. The first two measures are like those in the following 195A(1).

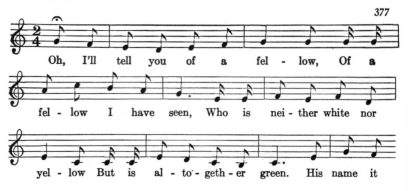

Oh, I'll tell you of a fel - low, Of a

fel - low I have seen, Who is nei - ther white nor

yel - low But is al - to - geth - er green. His name it

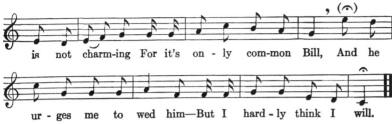

is   not charm-ing For it's on - ly com-mon Bill, And he

ur - ges me   to   wed him—But I   hard - ly think I   will.

For melodic relationship cf. **FSONE 187-8, first two measures; also 'Old
Black Joe,' measures 2-4 and 10-12.

Scale: Heptachordal, plagal.   Tonal Center: c.   Structure: aba¹b¹ (4,4,4,4) =
aa¹ (8,8).

A(I)

'Silly Bill.'   Sung by anonymous singer.   Recorded as MS score; no date or
place given.   This version omits the entire chorus as given in the A version (II
469).   In its place it uses the last four lines of the first stanza as given there.

378

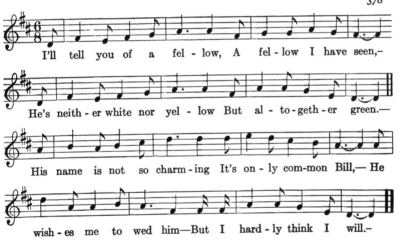

I'll tell you of   a   fel - low, A   fel - low I have seen,—

He's neith - er white nor yel - low But al - to - geth - er green.—

His name is not   so charm - ing It's on - ly com-mon Bill,— He

wish - es me   to   wed him—But I   hard - ly think I   will.—

For melodic relationship cf. **FSONE 187, first two measures.

Scale: Heptachordal.   Tonal center: d.   Structure: aa¹ba¹ (4,4,4,4) = Reprisenbar.

B

'Silly Bill.'   Sung by Miss Isabelle Rawn.   Recorded as MS score in 1915.
Another title is 'Common Bill.'   The interval sequence of the melodic line is
practically the same as that of the A version of 'Little Brown Jug,' No. 33 in
III 62 f.

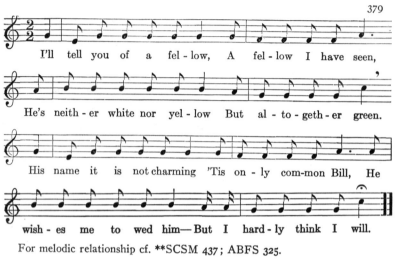

For melodic relationship cf. **SCSM 437; ABFS 325.

Scale: Hexatonic (2). Tonal Center: c. Structure: abab (2,2,2,2) = aa (4,4).

C

'Silly Bill.' Sung by Dr. I. G. Greer. Recorded as MS score at Boone, Watauga county in 1915 or 1916. Another title given is 'Common Bill.' There is no chorus in this version, but the last four lines of the stanza are repeated. There is another (anonymous) version which, however, is almost identical with this tune. The few minor variations which do occur are, therefore, given here, following the score below.

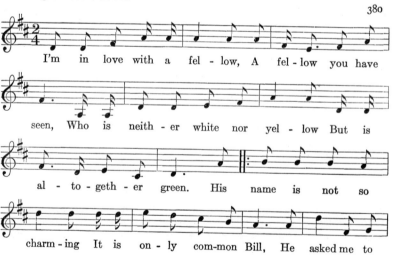

wed   him—But   I   hard - ly   think   I   will.

Scale: Heptachordal, plagal. Tonal Center: d. Structure: $aba^1b^1cda^2b^2$ (2,2,2, 2,2,2,2,2) $= aa^1ba^2$ (4,4,4,4) $=$ Reprisenbar.

196

SWAPPING SONGS

A

'Swapping Song.' Sung by Miss Earlina Greene. Recorded at Boone, Watauga county, August 9, 1939, Earlina was fourteen years old and in high school at A.S.T.C. Another title given is 'I Swapped Me a Horse and I Got Me a Mare,' which occurs in the sixth stanza of version A in SharpK II 307, No. 217, the title of which is 'The Foolish Boy.'

381

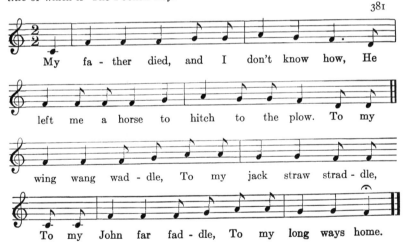

My   fa - ther   died,   and   I   don't   know   how,   He
left   me   a   horse   to   hitch   to   the   plow.   To   my
wing   wang   wad - dle,   To   my   jack   straw   strad - dle,
To   my   John   far   fad - dle,   To   my   long   ways   home.

Scale: Mode III, plagal. Tonal Center: f. Structure: aabb (2,2,2,2) $=$ ab (4,4).

E

'Sister, Sister, Have You Heard?' Sung by Carl G. Knox. Recorded at Trinity College in Durham, between 1922 and 1924. Same tune as 'Mr. Bullfrog.' Same text as in OFS III 47-9, No. 51A.

Sis - ter, sis - ter, have you heard?

Pa - pa's goin' a buy me a mock - ing bird.

For melodic relationship cf. **OFS III 47-9, No. 51A, measure 2 only.

Scale: Irrational, plagal. Tonal Center: g. Structure: ab (2,2).

197

DOG AND GUN

A

'The Golden Glove.' Sung by C. K. Tillett. Recorded at Wanchese, Roanoke Island, in 1923. Another title is 'Dog and Gun.'

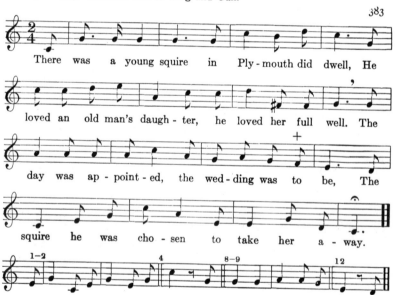

There was a young squire in Ply - mouth did dwell, He

loved an old man's daugh - ter, he loved her full well. The

day was ap - point - ed, the wed - ding was to be, The

squire he was cho - sen to take her a - way.

For melodic relationship cf. **SharpK I 378, No. 62B; FSRA 106; SCSM 416A (last eight measures as well as cadences); BSM 229, general melodic line; *FSS 530, first eight measures.

Scale: Heptachordal. Tonal Center: c. Structure: aba^{1}c (4,4,4,4) = aa^1 (8,8).

B

'The Rich Esquire.' Sung by Miss Jewell Robbins. Recorded at Pekin, Montgomery county, between 1921 and 1924. There is considerable relationship between this tune and that of the preceding 197A. Observe the melodic inversion of measure 1 at the beginning of the second phrase (measure 5).

384

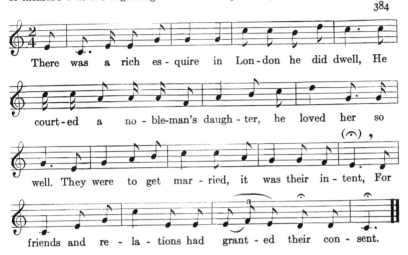

There was a rich es - quire in Lon - don he did dwell, He court - ed a no - ble-man's daugh - ter, he loved her so well. They were to get mar - ried, it was their in - tent, For friends and re - la - tions had grant - ed their con - sent.

For melodic relationship cf. **SharpK 1 378, No. 62B; BSM 229, second half; FSRA 106; SCSM 416, version A, last eight measures and cadences; FSS 530, No. 121B, measures 1-8, general melodic line.

Scale: Heptachordal. Tonal Center: c. Structure: abcd (4,4,4,4) ; d is slightly related to a.

198

KITTY CLYDE

B

'Kitty Clyde.' Sung by C. K. Tillett. Recorded at Wanchese, Roanoke Island, in 1922. The singer changed the text slightly from that given in II 476-7.

385

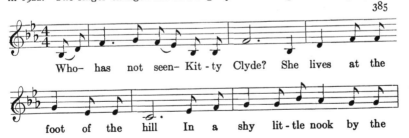

Who— has not seen— Kit - ty Clyde? She lives at the foot of the hill In a shy lit - tle nook by the

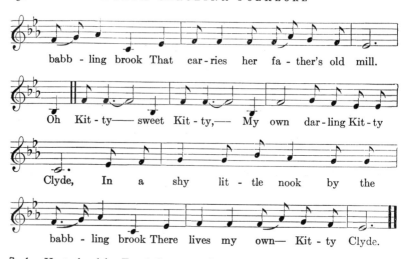

babb - ling brook That car - ries her fa - ther's old mill.

Oh Kit - ty—— sweet Kit - ty,—— My own dar - ling Kit - ty

Clyde, In a shy lit - tle nook by the

babb - ling brook There lives my own— Kit - ty Clyde.

Scale: Heptachordal. Tonal Center: e-flat. Structure: abcb¹ (4,4,4,4).

199

FATHER, FATHER, I AM MARRIED

'Father, Father, I Am Married.' Sung by Mrs. Silas Buchanan. Recorded as
MS score at Lenoir, Caldwell county, between 1921 and 1936.

386

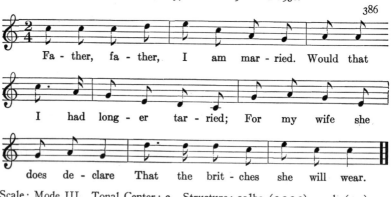

Fa - ther, fa - ther, I am mar - ried. Would that

I had long - er tar - ried; For my wife she

does de - clare That the brit - ches she will wear.

Scale: Mode III. Tonal Center: c. Structure: aa¹bc (2,2,2,2) = aʰ (4,4).

201

THE SCOLDING WIFE

A

'The Scolding Wife.' Sung by Ethel Day. Recorded at Cook's Gap, Watauga
county, in 1922. As the e in the scale given occurs only once in the penultimate

measure of the chorus, which measure otherwise is an exact repetition of that in the stanza, one could probably assume that this leading tone was merely a lapse into a more accustomed idiom. The beginning of the chorus reminds one somewhat of 'Aloha.' Other songs with the same title but different text can be found in FSRA 77 and BSSM 432-3.

387

Oh, you've of-ten heard it asked Why a wo-man talks so fast. And she runs a-round with ev-'ry bit of news. She'll talk a man to death Be-fore he can catch his breath, And the way she wags her tongue it beats the Jews. Oh, there's no use to try. The rea-son for is, why, What-ev-er you say she'll quar-rel. Just take my ad-vice and drop it, For I'm sure you'll nev-er stop it; For a wo-man's tongue will nev-er take a rest.

Scale: Heptachordal, plagal.   Tonal Center: f.   Structure: aba¹b¹cc¹da¹b² $(2,2,2,2,1,1,2,2,2)$ = aa¹ba² $(4,4,4,4)$ = Reprisenbar.   The smaller subdivision above shows strophic form with a miniature barform as third member.

202

THE LITTLE BLACK MUSTACHE

A

'The Little Black Mustache.' Sung by Dr. I. G. Greer. Recorded at the singer's home, where the present editor visited him in 1954. For other references and texts cf. FSoA 20; FSSH 295-7; FSSM 478. The chorus of this version uses only the last two lines of that given in II 480.

388

Onc't I court-ed a charm-ing beau, I loved him dear as life, I al - lus knowed the time would come when I would be— his wife.— His pock - ets they were full of gold, and, oh! I cut a dash— With a dia - mond ring and a watch and chain, with a dar - ling black mus - tache.- The lit - tle black mus - tache,- the lit - tle black mus - tache;- Oh, now you know I had a beau with a dar - ling black mus - tache.-

Scale: Heptachordal. Tonal Center: c. Structure: aa^1aa^2bc $(4,4,4,4,4,4)$ = aa^1b (8,8,8) = mm^1n (barform). The c of the smaller subdivision is related to a^1.

203

NO SIGN OF A MARRIAGE

A

'No Sign of a Marriage.' Sung by Mr. and Mrs. James York. Recorded at

Olin, Iredell county, in 1939. There are two more recordings of the same singers. The second begins with the fourth measure of the second stanza and stops before the end. The third contains all of the tune and is identical with that given below. Structurally, this tune shows a very interesting u.e ot the melodic material. The first four measures of the second stanza bring new material. The second half consists of the last four measures of the first stanza. The fourth stanza reverses this procedure. It uses the first four measures of stanza 1 and concludes with the first four measures of stanza two. What, in the printed text, II 481, is given as stanza 2 is, at least musically, without question the chorus. Otherwise, two stanzas as given would have to be taken as one, in order to fit the tune.

389

A - way in the north coun - try there lived a young cou - ple,—

A—— man and a maid– both gal - lant and gay. A

long time a - court - in' no sign of a mar - riage,—

No, no sign of a mar - riage– to be. At length this young

maid be - gin for to speak— 'Come, come, kind sir, it's

what do you mean,– A long time a - court - in', no sign

of a mar - riage, No, no sign of a mar - riage– to be?'—

Scale: Mode III, plagal. Tonal Center: f. Structure: $abab^1cc^1a^1b^1$ (2,2,2,2, 2,2,2,2) = $aa^1bb^1a^1$ (4,4,2,2,4). As this song shows a particularly interesting use of the melodic material, the structure content of all seven stanzas is given: aa^1; ba^1; aa^1; ab; a^1a^1; ba^1; ba^2a^1 (4,4; 4,4; 4,4; 4,4; 4,4; 4,4; 4,2,4).

B

'Pretty Polly.' Sung by C. K. Tillett. Recorded at Wanchese, Roanoke Island, probably in 1922. Although the second stanza as given below shows only slight rhythmical differences in the first half of the tune, the second is considerably changed and internally incremented.

Scale: Hexatonic (4), plagal. Tonal Center: f. Structure: first stanza—abcb¹ (4,4,4,4) ; second stanza—abdc¹b¹ (4,4,4,4,4) ; d is slightly related to c.

204

WILKINS AND HIS DINAH

A

'Villikins and His Dinah.' Sung by Mrs. Myra Barnett Miller. Recorded probably at Lenoir. Caldwell county, August 1939, 1940, or 1941. The singer called this ballad 'The Silkmerchant's Daughter.' This version is textually like A except that the names are changed and the nonsense syllables are different. Malcolm Laws, Jr, mentions this among a number of songs which have been traced to British broadsides.

391

There was a rich mer-chant in Lon - don did dwell, He had but one daugh-ter a ver - y fine girl. Her name was So - phir - a, just six - teen years old, With a ver - y large for - tune in sil - ver and gold. Sing doo ra la la la, la, sing doo - ra la day, Sing doo - ra la, la, sing doo - ra la day. Sing doo - ra la la la, Sing doo - ra la day, Sing doo - ra la la la, la, Sing doo - ra la day.

For melodic relationship cf. ***FSF 339-40; OFS I 331, No. 80A; **FSONE 301-2, first two measures; BBM 67; TT 51, 'Golden Glove,' first two measures; *BMFSB 42, fifth measure; PSL 454-5; EAS 15.

Scale: Hexachordal. Tonal Center: d. Structure: abcaabca (2,2,2,2,2,2,2,2) = aa (8,8).

C

'Miss Dinah.'   Sung by Miss Pearl Minish.   Recorded as MS score at Lenoir,
Caldwell county, in 1928.

392

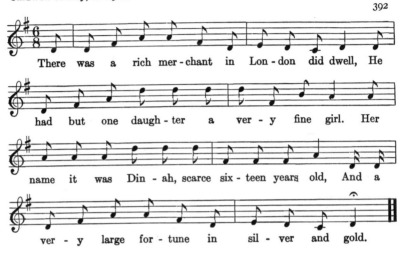

There was   a   rich mer - chant   in   Lon - don   did dwell,   He

had   but   one   daugh - ter   a   ver - y   fine   girl.   Her

name   it   was   Din - ah, scarce six - teen years   old,   And   a

ver - y   large   for - tune   in   sil - ver   and   gold.

For melodic relationship cf. **FSF 339-40; EAS 15.

Scale: Irrational, plagal.   Tonal Center: d.   Structure: abca¹ (2,2,2,2).

NATIVE AMERICAN BALLADS

208

SPRINGFIELD MOUNTAIN

B

'The Serpent.' Sung by Mrs. Myra Barnett Miller. Recorded as MS score at Lenoir, Caldwell county; no date given. This tune is identical with another recording credited to H. C. Martin (208D). For other texts and references cf. MSFSH 116-17; FSoA 64; SHP 44; BMFSB 4; FSUSA 28; BSSM 121; FSF 112; SharpK II 166; OFS III 167-70; FSS 292; BSO 248-52; NGMS 159; FSONE 285-6; BSM 299-300; BSI 322; JAFL XLIV, No. 171 and ABFS 356 (identical).

393

'John,' said Sal, 'why don't you go A - way down yon-der in the mead-ow fur to mow?' Li too-dle dink a day-light, Li doo-dle dink a day-light, Li too-dle dink a too-dle dink a do dal day.

Scale: Mode III. Tonal Center: c. Structure: aa¹bccc¹d (1,1,1,1,1,1,2) = ab (3,5).

C

'Rattle Snake.' Sung by Miss Pearle Webb. Recorded at Pineola, Avery county, in 1939. This ballad in its text as related to the tune illustrates the English dislike for slurring two tones on one syllable. Rather, they insert nonsense syllables: "hi-wi-will" = hill; "we-we-well" = well. The variations given in the second stanza may serve as an example for the great variety of combinations making up the remaining stanzas.

394

A nice young ma - wa - wan Lived on a hi - wi -
will A nice young ma - wa - wan For I knew him
we - we - well, To my rat - tle, to my roo - rah - ree.
2nd Stanza

Scale: Mode III. Tonal Center: g. Structure: mm¹n (2,2,2) = barform.
The 'epode' here is unusually short.

D

'The Serpent.' Sung by H. C. Martin. Recorded as ms score at Lenoir, possibly at Forest City, in 1927. The tune is identical with that of 208B.

E

'Sarpint.' Sung by W. E. Poovey. Recorded at Marion, McDowell county, in June 1924. Known also as 'The Serpent,' and 'Springfield Mountain.'

395

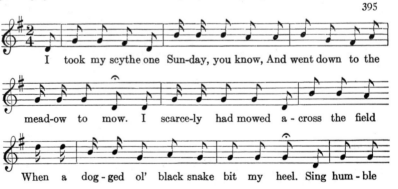

I took my scythe one Sun-day, you know, And went down to the
mead-ow to mow. I scarce-ly had mowed a - cross the field
When a dog - ged ol' black snake bit my heel. Sing hum - ble

drum-ble stich - e - rei bum To me lick to me re - som doo.

For melodic relationship cf. *SharpK 11 166-7, No. 132A, general melodic line, not rhythmically, however. Measure 9 is identical in both versions. Measures 9-10 are almost the same as those of No. 132B.

Scale: Irrational, plagal. Tonal Center: g. Structure: aa¹a² (4,4,4).

209

YOUNG CHARLOTTE

A

'Young Charlotte.' Sung by Dr. I. G. Greer. Recorded at Boone, Watauga county; no date given. Measures 2-4 in all versions show a general conformity to a basic melodic concept. Each of the stanzas of the versions given in BSO 278-83, No. 123A and BSSB 135, No. 37 ('Fair Charlotte') comprises two of the stanzas as given in II 493-5. The version in BSSB is the only one giving "ten miles round." The latter is also interesting with regard to differences in melodic line and structure.

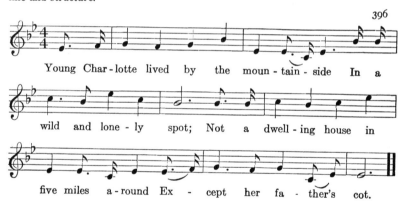

Young Char - lotte lived by the moun - tain - side In a wild and lone - ly spot; Not a dwell - ing house in five miles a - round Ex - cept her fa - ther's cot.

For melodic relationship cf. ***BSSM 126-9; **ASB 58; TexasFS 98; BSO 278-83, No. 123A; *FSmWV 15; FSS 528, No. 80A, measures 4-6; FSONE 305-9, measures 1 and 5; FSF 114-17.

Scale: Mode III, plagal. Tonal Center: e-flat. Structure: aba¹b¹ (2,2,2,2).

B

'Young Charlotte.' Sung by Miss Amy Henderson. Recorded as MS score in Worry, Burke county, in 1914.

397

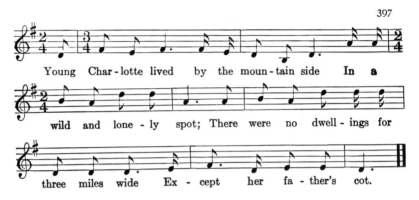

Young Char-lotte lived by the moun-tain side In a wild and lone-ly spot; There were no dwell-ings for three miles wide Ex - cept her fa-ther's cot.

For melodic relationship cf. ***BSSM 126, No. 41; **BSO 278-83, No. 123A; ASb 58; *FMA 14; FSF 114, No. 56; TexasFS 98.

Scale: Mode III, plagal.   Tonal Center: d.   Structure: abb¹c (2,2,2,2).

c

'Young Charlotte.' Sung by Mrs. Minnie Church. Recorded at Heaton, Avery county, in 1939. In the main melodic outline this tune is very closely related to 209B; still more so to 209A. For interesting comments about this ballad and its connection with 'The False-hearted Knight' cf. BBM p. xxxiv. Compare this with NGMS 112-13.

398

Young Char-lotte lived by the moun-tain— side In a wild and lone-ly spot; No dwell-ing there for three miles round Ex - cept her fa-ther's cot.

For melodic relationship cf. ***NGMS 113; ASb 58; BSSM 126, No. 41; **BSO 278, No. 123A; FMA 14; TexasFS 98; FSF 114, No. 56, measures 3-4; *FSS 528, No. 80A, measures 4-6.

Scale: Mode III, plagal.   Tonal Center: d.   Structure: aba^{1}b^1 (2,2,2,2).

c(1)

'Young Charlotte.'   Sung by Mrs. Nora Hicks.   Recorded at Mast's Gap, Watauga county, in 1940.   Although this tune is in a different meter, there is considerable melodic relationship with 209B.

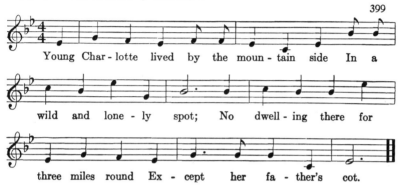

399

Young Char - lotte lived by the moun - tain side In a
wild and lone - ly spot; No dwell - ing there for
three miles round Ex - cept her fa - ther's cot.

For melodic relationship cf. ***BSSM 126, No. 41; ASb 58; **BSO 278-83, No. 123A; TexasFS 98; FSF 114, No. 56, measures 3-8.

Scale: Mode III, plagal.   Tonal Center: e-flat.   Structure: abb^{1}c (2,2,2,2).

D

'Young Charlotte.'   Anonymous singer.   Recorded as MS score at Lenoir, Caldwell county, in 1927.   Very closely related to 209B; actually merely a variation of the latter.   Especially the second half of the tune is closely related to that of 209A.

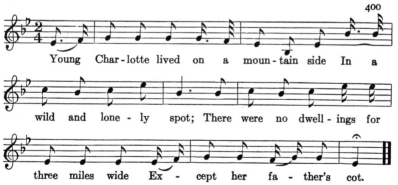

400

Young Char - lotte lived on a moun - tain side In a
wild and lone - ly spot; There were no dwell - ings for
three miles wide Ex - cept her fa - ther's cot.

For melodic relationship cf. ***FB 119; FSS 528, No. 80A (words and tune!) ; ASb 58; **BSSM 126, No. 41; TexasFS 98; FSF 114, No. 56; *BSO 278, No. 123A.

Scale: Mode III, plagal. Tonal Center: e-flat. Structure: abb¹c (2,2,2,2).

E

'Young Charlotte.' Anonymous singer. Recorded; no date or place given. Closely related to 209A. In the first stanza the singer actually sings "cottage" instead of "cot."*

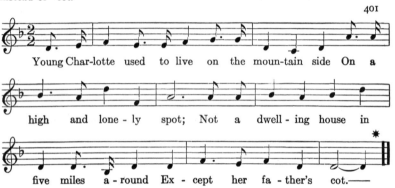

401

Young Char-lotte used to live on the moun-tain side On a

high and lone - ly spot; Not a dwell - ing house in

five miles a - round Ex - cept her fa - ther's cot.——

For melodic relationship cf. ***BSSM 126, No. 41; Texas FS 98; **FSS 528, No. 80A, measures 4-6; FSF 114, No. 56, measures 3-4; *ASb 58. Scale: Heptachordal. Tonal Center: d. Structure: aba¹b¹ (2,2,2,2).

211

THE ORE KNOB

'The Ore Knob.' Sung by anonymous male singer. Recorded; no date or place given.

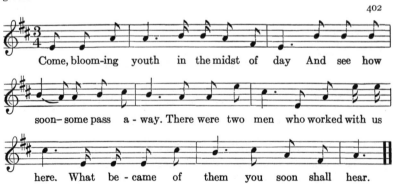

402

Come, bloom-ing youth in the midst of day And see how

soon— some pass a - way. There were two men who worked with us

here. What be - came of them you soon shall hear.

Scale: Mode III, plagal. Tonal Center: a. Structure: abcc¹a¹ (2,2,1,1,2) = ab (4,4).

212

FLOYD COLLINS

Although the recorded song as sung by H. J. Beaker was transcribed, the score is omitted to avoid possible copyright infringements.

215

THE SHIP THAT NEVER RETURNED

H

'The Ship That Never Returned.' Sung by B. C. Reavis. Recorded as MS score; no date or place given. The stanza as printed in II 508 is twice as long as the tune can accommodate. Cf. JAFL XXVIII 171-2.

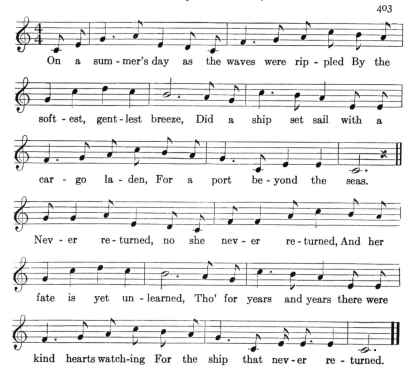

403

On a sum-mer's day as the waves were rip-pled By the

soft-est, gent-lest breeze, Did a ship set sail with a

car-go la-den, For a port be-yond the seas.

Nev-er re-turned, no she nev-er re-turned, And her

fate is yet un-learned, Tho' for years and years there were

kind hearts watch-ing For the ship that nev-er re-turned.

For melodic relationship cf. **ASb 146 (cadence in first phrases of stanza and chorus are different) ; AMS 42, stanza only.

Scale: Heptachordal. Tonal Center: c. Structure: aba¹b¹ (4,4,4,4) = aa¹ (8,8).

217

THE WRECK OF THE OLD NINETY-SEVEN

This song recorded from the singing of Mrs. Ewart Wilson, was transcribed; it is, however, omitted here to avoid any and all possible copyright claims.

220

PAUL JONES

A

'Paul Jones.' Sung by C. K. Tillett. Recorded at Wanchese, Roanoke Island in 1922. This version has no refrain as in the version by the same singer reproduced in FSRA 48, which shows interesting variations. The two-measure rhythmical pattern serves for the build-up of the eight-measure phrase. It is surprising what variety can be achieved in spite of this limitation. The very ending reminds of 'The Red, White, and Blue.'

404

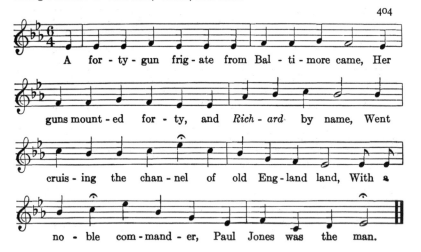

A for-ty-gun frig-ate from Bal-ti-more came, Her

guns mount-ed for-ty, and *Rich-ard* by name, Went

cruis-ing the chan-nel of old Eng-land land, With a

no-ble com-mand-er, Paul Jones was the man.

For melodic relationship cf. ***FSRA 48, No. 24 (but no chorus).

Scale: Heptachordal. Tonal Center: e-flat. Structure: aa¹bc (2,2,2,2) = ab (4,4).

221

JAMES BIRD

'James Byrd.' Sung by Mrs. C. K. Tillett. Recorded at Wanchese, Roanoke Island in 1922. This is the only other ballad actually sung by Mrs. Tillett. Cf. 27E.

405

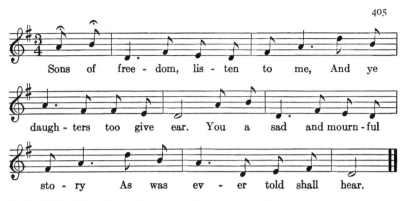

Sons of free - dom, lis - ten to me, And ye daugh - ters too give ear. You a sad and mourn - ful sto - ry As was ev - er told shall hear.

Scale: Mode III. Tonal Center: d. Structure: aa¹ (4,4).

228

THE DYING SOLDIER TO HIS MOTHER

'On the Field of Battle, Mother.' Sung by Miss Jewell Robbins. Recorded at Pekin, Montgomery county, between 1921 and 1924. The structure of this tune requires two of the stanzas as printed in II 534-5. This would leave stanza 9 incomplete. According to J. H. Cox (FSS) both words and music are by Geo. F. Root and were published by Root and Cady, Chicago (copyright 1862) under the title 'Just Before the Battle, Mother.' Our text, however, is very different.

406

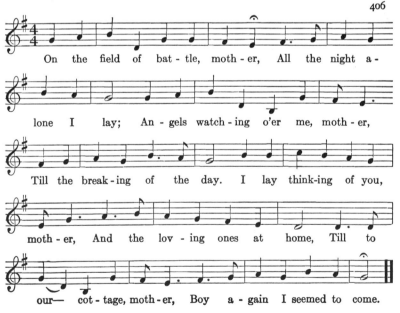

On the field of bat - tle, moth - er, All the night a - lone I lay; An - gels watch - ing o'er me, moth - er, Till the break - ing of the day. I lay think - ing of you, moth - er, And the lov - ing ones at home, Till to our— cot - tage, moth - er, Boy a - gain I seemed to come.

Scale: Heptachordal, plagal.   Tonal Center: g.   Structure: aa¹ba¹ (4,4,4,4) =
Reprisenbar.

228(1)

'On the Field of Battle, Mother.' Sung by Miss Jewell Robbins. Recorded at
Pekin, Montgomery county, between 1921 and 1924. The variations below come
from a second recording of the preceding tune as sung by the same singer at a
later date.

The analysis given for the first version applies also for the second.

231

THE LAST FIERCE CHARGE

A

'The Two Soldiers.' Sung by Dr. I. G. Greer. Recorded as MS score at Boone,
Watauga county, in 1915 or 1916. The variations given below are taken from
a second recording by Dr. W. A. Abrams; the tune otherwise is the same. For
a similar text cf. BSO 304, No. 139B and OFS II 297, No. 234. Another title
is 'That Last Fierce Fight.' The structure of the tune requires two of the
stanzas as given in II 539-41.

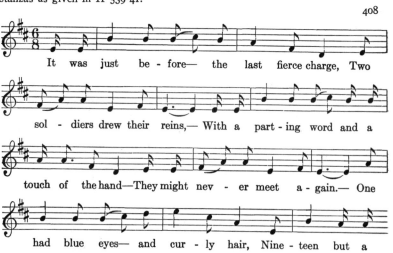

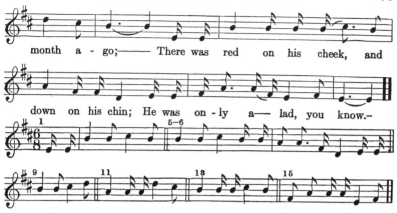

month a - go;——— There was red on his cheek, and

down on his chin; He was on - ly a— lad, you know.-

Scale: Hexatonic (3), plagal. Tonal Center: e. Structure: aa[1] ba[2] (4,4,4,4)
= Reprisenbar.

B

'Two Soldiers.' Anonymous singer. Recorded at Boone, Watauga county,
about 1935 or 1936. The slight melodic differences are given above as variations.

232

KINGDOM COMING

A

'Massa's Gone Away.' Sung by Otis S. Kuykendall. Recorded at Asheville,
Buncombe county, August 8, 1939. This ballad, attributed by Dr. White to
Henry Clay Work, was credited to him in the printed version in MSON 180-1,
which was published at Boston in 1882. Since an earlier text of this ballad,
according to the editors of volume II, was printed in 1864 (see II 541), it is
quite clear that Work was at least not the author of the text. Another title is
'The Year of Jubilo.' Cf. OFS II 290, No. 230.

409

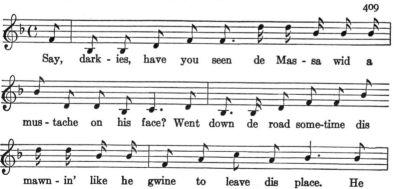

Say, dark - ies, have you seen de Mas - sa wid a

mus - tache on his face? Went down de road some-time dis

mawn - in' like he gwine to leave dis place. He

seen de smoke way up de riv - er where de Lin - coln

gun - boats lay; He picked up his hat and he left ver - y

sud - den and I guess he's gone a - way. Oh, de

Mas-sa run, ha - ha, dark-ies stay at home. It must be now de

King-dom a - com - in', and you hear de bu - gle blow.

For melodic relationship cf. **MSON 180-1 (except first half of chorus):
Ford 339, basic melodic line.

Scale: Hexatonic (4). Tonal Center: b-flat. Structure $aa^1ba^1ca^2$ (2,2,2,2,2,2).

234

THE TEXAS RANGER

B

'The Texas Ranger.' Sung by Mrs. J. J. Miller. Recorded as MS score at

Lenoir, Caldwell county, between 1921 and 1925. The tune requires the stanzas as printed in II 545 f. to be grouped in pairs. Basically this tune is the same as that of the hymn 'How Firm a Foundation.'

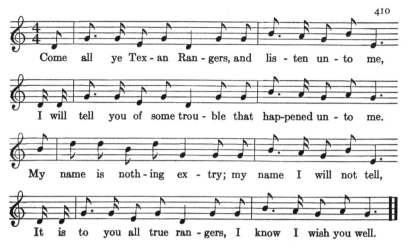

Scale: Mode III, plagal. Tonal Center: g. Structure: aa¹ba¹ (2,2,2,2) = Reprisenbar.

236

The Battleship Maine (II)

A

'Battleship Maine.' Sung by O. L. Coffey, with guitar. Recorded at Shull's Mills, Watauga county, July 18, 1936. This tune shows considerable relationship with that of 236B. The variations given below are taken from a Greer version and that of an anonymous singer.

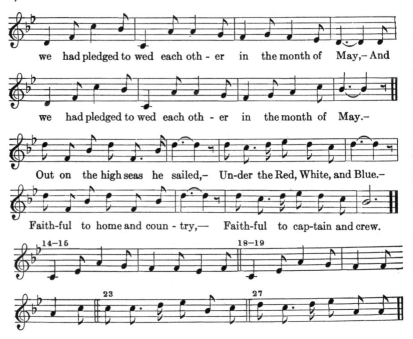

we had pledged to wed each oth - er   in the month of May,– And

we had pledged to wed each oth - er   in the month of May.–

Out on the high seas he sailed,–   Un-der the Red, White, and Blue.–

Faith-ful to home and coun - try,—   Faith-ful to cap-tain and crew.

14–15   18–19

23   27

Scale: Heptachordal, plagal. Tonal Center: b-flat. Structure: abacc¹dd¹ (4,4, 4,4,4,4). Compound structure: an inverted bar flanked on both sides by strophic forms.

B

'The Battleship Maine.' Sung by Mrs. L. F. Banks. Recorded at Alliance, Pamlico county, in 1927. There is considerable melodic relationship with 236A. The text which the singer uses is exactly that of the B version given in II 548, but the title given is different.

412

Once   I had   a   sweet - heart,–   no - ble, brave and true,—

Fear - less   as   the   sun - rise,—   gen - tle   as   the dew.–

Peace - ful - ly   he slum - bers—   in his ham-mock bed,—

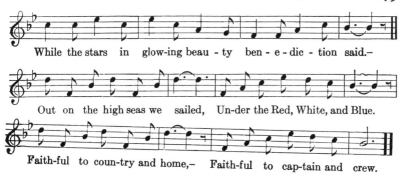

While the stars in glow-ing beau - ty ben - e - dic - tion said.–

Out on the high seas we sailed, Un-der the Red, White, and Blue.

Faith-ful to coun-try and home,– Faith-ful to cap-tain and crew.

Scale: Heptachordal, plagal. Tonal Center: b-flat. Structure: abacdd¹ (4,4,4, 4,4,4) = aa¹b (8,8,8) = mm¹n = barform.

239

THAT BLOODY WAR

A

'That Bloody War.' Sung by Miss Aura Holton. Recorded at Durham in 1922. The melody is almost the same as that of the following version 239C. The ending somewhat reminds of 'Frankie and Johnnie,' or 'He Done Her Wrong' (251 below).

413

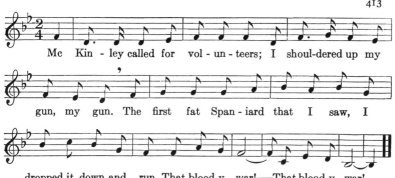

Mc Kin - ley called for vol - un - teers; I shoul-dered up my

gun, my gun. The first fat Span - iard that I saw, I

dropped it down and run. That blood-y war!—That blood-y war!—

Scale: Heptachordal. Tonal Center: b-flat. Structure: aa¹b (4,4,4) = mm¹n = barform. It is interesting to observe that b consists of two measures which are repeated on a different pitch level.

C

'It's Bloody War.' Sung by Kate S. Russell. Recorded at Roxboro, Person county, about 1923. Almost identical with the preceding version. Cf. also EFSSC 77, 'Earl Richard.'

414

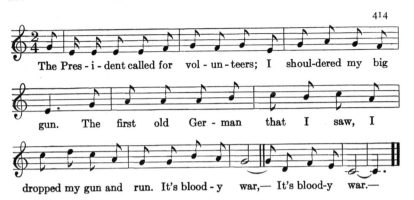

The Pres - i - dent called for vol - un - teers; I shoul-dered my big

gun. The first old Ger - man that I saw, I

dropped my gun and run. It's blood - y war,— It's blood-y war.—

Scale: Heptachordal. Tonal Center: c. Structure: aa¹b (4,4,4). Again b consists of bb (2,2), which represents a motive merely transposed when repeated. The whole again = mm¹n = barform.

240

STRANGE THINGS WUZ HAPPENING

'Strange Things Wuz (uh) Happening.' Sung by Will Love. Recorded at Durham between 1920 and 1922.

415

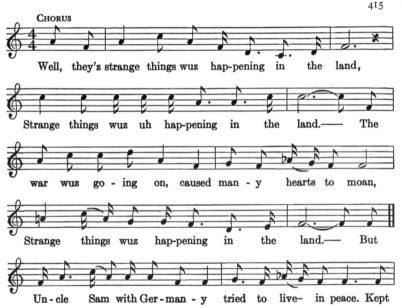

CHORUS

Well, they'z strange things wuz hap-pening in   the   land,

Strange things wuz uh hap-pening in   the   land.—— The

war wuz go - ing   on, caused man - y   hearts to moan,

Strange   things wuz hap-pening in   the   land.—— But

Un - cle Sam with Ger - man - y tried to live— in peace. Kept

blow - ing up— his ves - sels,— would not 'tempt to cease. The

boys they treat us mean, we don't 'guize our sub - ma - rines,

They wuz strange things wuz hap - pening in the land.

Scale: Hexatonic (4), plagal. Tonal center: f. Structure: abca¹c¹c²c¹a²
(2,2,2,2,2,2,2,2)

242

THE BOSTON BURGLAR

E

'The Boston Burglar.' Sung by Otis Kuykendall. Recorded at Asheville, Buncombe county, in 1939. Also known as 'Boston Bay,' 'Bugle Boy,' and 'Boston
City.'   416

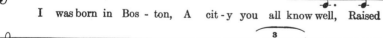

I was born in Bos - ton, A cit - y you all know well, Raised

up by hon - est pa - rents—The truth to you I will tell—Raised

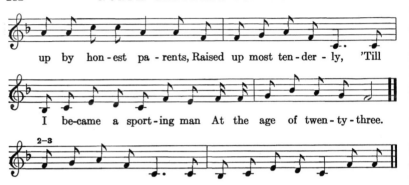

up   by   hon - est   pa - rents, Raised   up   most   ten - der - ly,   'Till

I   be-came   a   sport - ing man   At   the   age   of   twen - ty - three.

For melodic relationship cf. **SCSM 433, version A, measures 2-3 and 5-7;
also version E, *ibid.* 434 in general melodic outline; BSSM 335, No. 137, measures 2 and 6.

Scale: Heptachordal, plagal.   Tonal Center: f.   Structure: aba^{1}b^1 (2,2,2,2) =
aa^1 (4,4).

243

JESSE JAMES

B

'Jesse James.'   Sung by Mrs. Louise Rand Bascom.   Recorded at Highlands,
Macon county, in 1914.   Only in measures 2 and 5-6 is there any similarity to
the following version, 243H.   For additional reference cf. CS 27-31.

417

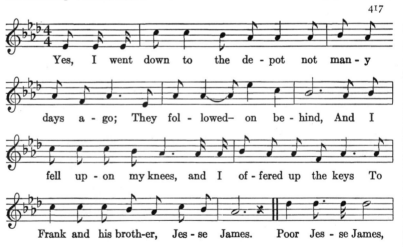

Yes,   I   went   down   to   the   de - pot   not   man - y

days   a - go;   They   fol - lowed— on   be - hind,   And   I

fell   up - on   my knees,   and   I   of - fered up   the keys   To

Frank   and   his broth-er,   Jes - se   James.   Poor   Jes - se James,

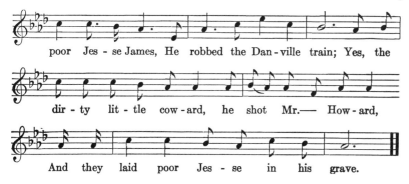

poor Jes - se James, He robbed the Dan-ville train; Yes, the

dir - ty lit - tle cow - ard, he shot Mr.—— How - ard,

And they laid poor Jes - se in his grave.

For melodic relationship cf. **ABFS 128; ASb 420; FSUSA 296, No. 80;
*OFS II 23, version G.

Scale: Hexachordal, plagal. Tonal Center: a-flat. Structure: abacdb^{1}ac (2,2,
2,2,2,2,2,2) = aa^{1}ba^1 (4,4,4,4) = Reprisenbar.

NOTE. In 1925 Mr. Lunsford sang several songs for Mr. Robert W. Gordon,
and later Mr. Gordon sent him typewritten copies of the texts of those songs.
After some delay Mr. Lunsford sent to Dr. Brown (for whom he had already
sung in 1920 and 1921) a duplicate of these texts with the names of the people
from whom he had first received them—without, however, adding his own name.
The following versions should therefore be credited to Mr. Lunsford in II 561
(No. 243H), 571 (No. 248), 626 (No. 270H), and 658 (No. 282). Corrections
are also made below in the proper places.

H

'Jesse James.' Sung by Bascom Lamar Lunsford. Recorded at Bear Wallow,
Henderson county, probably 1921. Mr. Lunsford learned this from Sam Sum-
ner in 1903. He says that the latter was drunk at the time and therefore we
have the confused version as he learned it from the singer.

418

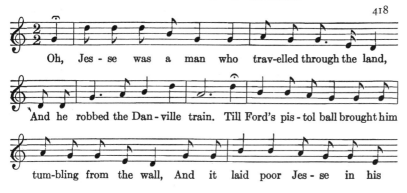

Oh, Jes - se was a man who trav-elled through the land,

And he robbed the Dan - ville train. Till Ford's pis - tol ball brought him

tum-bling from the wall, And it laid poor Jes - se in his

grave. Oh, Jes - se, dear old– Jes - se!— Fare-well Jes - se

James. Rob - ert Ford caught his eye— and he shot him

on the sly, And it laid poor Jes - se down to die.

For melodic relationship cf. *ABFS 128; FSUSA 296, No. 80.

Scale: Hexachordal, plagal. Tonal Center: g. Structure: aa¹ba² $(4,4,4,4)$ =
Reprisenbar.

244

JOHN HARDY

C

'John Hardy.' Sung by Bascom Lamar Lunsford. Recorded probably at Turkey Creek, Buncombe county, in 1920. The singer told the editor that he had
known this song since 1902, when he heard it at Clinch River, East Tennessee.
The text of the stanza given is a variation of the third stanza of the Sharp
version. Cf. SharpK II 35, no. 87. Our singer, however, uses the first person
instead of the third.

419

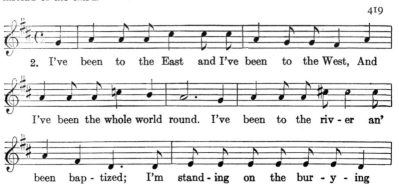

2. I've been to the East and I've been to the West, And

I've been the whole world round. I've been to the riv - er an'

been bap - tized; I'm stand - ing on the bur - y - ing

ground, poor boy, I'm stand-ing on the bur - y - ing ground.

For melodic relationship cf. **OFS ɪɪ 144, No. 163; *SharpK ɪɪ 35, No. 87.
This song furnishes an example for the process of change in the life of a
melody. If we compare this tune with the version given in OFS ɪɪ 144, No. 163,
we find much similarity. But in the first phrase of our version the third measure of the Ozark version is omitted. In the next phrase, similarly, four measures
are omitted. Our song is by no means a replica of the Ozark version, even a
transposed one, but the likeness in spite of the elisions will be evident.
Scale: Heptachordal, plagal. Tonal Center: d. Structure: aba¹cc¹ (2,2,2,2,2).

245
KENNY WAGNER'S SURRENDER

'Kenny Wagoner.' Sung by Mrs. Mildred Perry Turbyfield. Recorded by the
present editor at Chapel Hill, June 4, 1954. The singer came from Mebane;
she learned the ballad as a child from her mother at Sugar Grove, Watauga
county. This is a different text from that given II 566-7. The story is about
a boy in Tennessee who killed a man and was hunted and jailed, and about his
jail-break.

420

There was a man in Ten - nes - see, Ken - ny Wag - o - ner

was his name.– He got in - to bad com - pan - y And a

mur - der - er he be - came.– 'Twas down in Mis - si -

ssip - pi— The trou - ble it be - gan,— Ken - ny got a

pis - tol— And shot him - self a man.——

Scale: Hexatonic (6), plagal. Tonal Center: c. Structure: aa¹bb¹ (4,4,4,4) = ab (8,8).

246

CLAUD ALLEN

B

'Claud Allen.' Sung by C. B. Houck. Recorded at Todd, Ashe county, April 16, 1920. The "air" mentioned in II 569 is on a record only and could not be "attached."

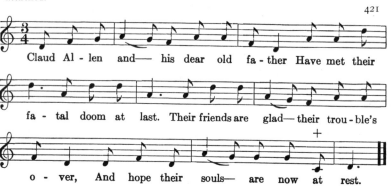

Claud Al - len and— his dear old fa - ther Have met their fa - tal doom at last. Their friends are glad— their trou - ble's o - ver, And hope their souls— are now at rest.

For melodic relationship cf. **TSFL 396; despite the different rhythmic line, the basic melodic line is surprisingly similar, although our version is not in the major mode.

Scale: Mode II, plagal. Tonal Center: d. Structure: aba¹c (2,2,2,2).

C

'Claude Allen.' Sung by Steve Church. Recorded, but no place or date given There is another recording by Horton Barker, which is identical.

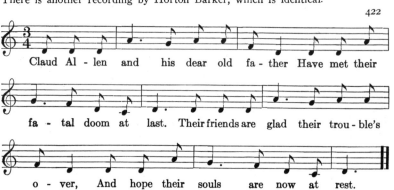

Claud Al - len and his dear old fa - ther Have met their fa - tal doom at last. Their friends are glad their trou - ble's o - ver, And hope their souls are now at rest.

2nd Stanza 2-5

Later. 1   4-5

Scale: Mode II, plagal. Tonal Center: d. Structure: aa (4,4).

248

BRADY

'Brady.' Sung by Bascom Lamar Lunsford. Recorded in Wilkes county; no date given. The voice is a man's, therefore cannot be the one referred to in II 571. This is confirmed by a statement made by Mr. Lunsford to the present editor, that he sang this song which he had learned from Miss Martin in 1903.

423

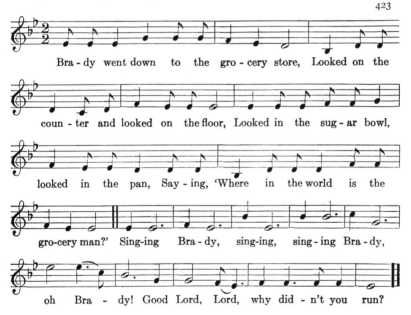

Bra - dy went down to the gro - cery store, Looked on the

coun - ter and looked on the floor, Looked in the sug - ar bowl,

looked in the pan, Say - ing, 'Where in the world is the

gro-cery man?' Sing-ing Bra - dy, sing-ing, sing - ing Bra - dy,

oh Bra - dy! Good Lord, Lord, why did - n't you run?

For melodic relationship cf. *ASb 198. The melodic progressions of the first three measures resemble somewhat those of the first six measures of the version quoted.

Scale: Hexatonic (4), plagal. Tonal Center: e-flat. Structure: mm^{1}n (4,4,10) = barform.

249

CHARLES GUITEAU

C

'The Murder of James A. Garfield.' Sung by Mrs. G. L. Bostic. Recorded at
Mooresboro, Cleveland county, in 1939. The text and therefore the tune are
those of the chorus. In the absence of any additional recording it must be
assumed that the same tune serves also for the stanza. Note, however, that the
singer garbles the text as given in II 576 by beginning with the first half of the
chorus and following this with the second half of the stanza. There are slight
melodic resemblances with the following version, 249G.

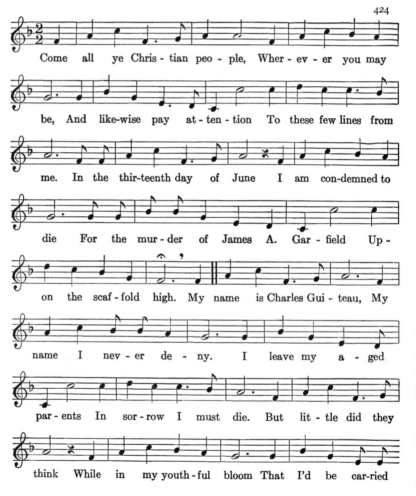

424

Come all ye Chris - tian peo - ple, Wher - ev - er you may

be, And like-wise pay at - ten - tion To these few lines from

me. In the thir-teenth day of June I am con-demned to

die For the mur - der of James A. Gar - field Up -

on the scaf - fold high. My name is Charles Gui - teau, My

name I nev - er de - ny. I leave my a - ged

par - ents In sor - row I must die. But lit - tle did they

think While in my youth - ful bloom That I'd be car-ried

to   a   scaf - fold   To   meet   my   fa - tal   doom.

For melodic relationship cf. ***FSSH 331-2, No. 119; BSO 274, No. 121 third and fourth measures only. **OFS II 32, version E; FSoA 113 and FSRA 188, No. 110, second half of stanza only.

Scale: Heptachordal. plagal.   Tonal Center. f.   Structure: abab¹abab¹ (4,4,4,4. 4,4,4,4) = aa¹aa¹ (8,8,8,8) = aa (16,16).

G

'Charles Giteau.' Anonymous singer. Recorded as MS score between 1921 and 1936; no place given. The tune requires two of the stanzas as printed in II 576. The MS score gives as second ending the last line of stanza 3 "To meet my awful doom," but omits the other three lines. There is some melodic relationship with the preceding version.

425

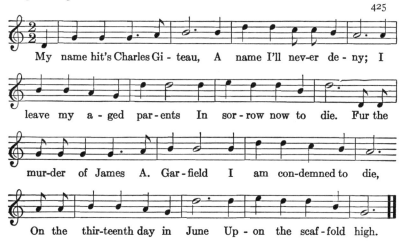

My   name hit's Charles Gi - teau,   A   name I'll nev-er de - ny;   I

leave my   a - ged   par - ents   In   sor - row now to   die.   Fur the

mur-der   of James   A.   Gar - field   I   am con-demned to   die,

On the   thir-teenth day in   June   Up - on   the   scaf - fold high.

For melodic relationship cf. ***BSO 274, No. 121, measures 3-4 only; FSRA 188, No. 110, first four measures; **FSSH 332, No. 119 (the first measure there is incorrectly noted); OFS II 134, version A.

Scale: Hexachordal, plagal.   Tonal Center: g.   Structure: abab¹ (4,4,4,4) = aa¹ (8,8).

250

FLORELLA (THE JEALOUS LOVER)

A

'The Jealous Lover.' Sung by the Rev. L. D. Hayman. Recorded as MS score

in Currituck and Dare counties, between 1921 and 1922. The elisions made by
the singer or the writer (measures 3, 6, 9, and 12) are quite evident.

426

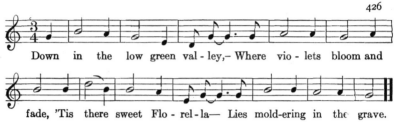

For melodic relationship cf. *AMS 30, measures 2-3; BSSM 85, No. 21-C,
measures 1-2.

Scale: Mode III, plagal. Tonal Center: g. Structure: aba¹b¹ (3,3,3 3). The
irrgular sr ucture of four phrases of three measures each should be noted. It
is due, mentioned above, to intentional or, more likely, unintentional, shortening of values—a phenomenon that can also be observed in the congregational
singing of hymns.

A(1)

'Jealous Lover.' Sung by Miss Lena Warf. From a previous recording by
Dr. W. A. Abrams, Watauga county; no date given. This record is very poor
and nothing before the fourth stanza can be made out. Measures 3-4 remind
one of 'When Irish Eyes Are Smiling.'

427

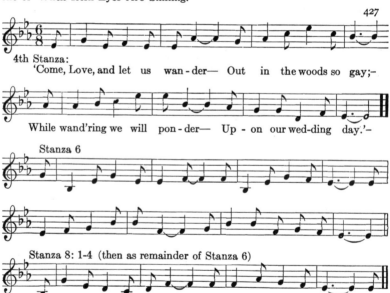

Scale: Heptachordal, plagal. Tonal Center: e-flat. Structure: abcd (2,2,2,2). Variations in tonal content can be seen from the sixth and eighth stanzas given above.

C

'The Jealous Lover.' Sung by Dr. I. G. Greer. The "music by I. G. Greer" mentioned in II 582 has not been found. For a MS score with different text see 250X below.

D

'Florilla.' Sung by Miss Jane Christenbury. Recorded as MS score at Durham, in 1923. The text does not fit the description in II 583, but is rather like that of 250X, below. In measures 1, 5, and 7, there is some melodic relationship with the 250U.

428

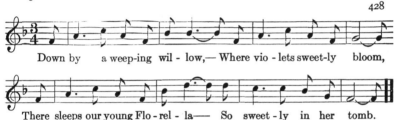

Down by   a weep-ing wil - low,— Where vio - lets sweet-ly   bloom,

There sleeps our young Flo - rel - la—— So sweet - ly in her   tomb.

For melodic relationship cf. *BSM 328, version L; BMFSB 26, No. 13.

Scale: Hexachordal. Tonal Center: f. Structure: aa^{1}a^{2}b (2,2,2,2).

L

'Down in a Lone Valley.' Sung by Mrs. N. T. Byers. Recorded as MS score at Zionville, Watauga county, in 1921.

429

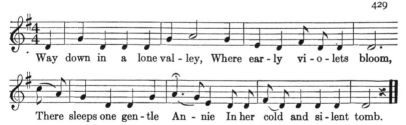

Way down in   a   lone val - ley, Where ear - ly vi - o - lets bloom,

There sleeps one gen - tle   An - nie In her cold and si - lent tomb.

Scale: Hexatonic (3), plagal. Tonal Center: g. Structure: aba^{1}b^1 (2,2,2,2) = aa^1 (4,4). Circular tune (V). The last tone is repeated several times, which would point to Irish influence—although numerous English songs show similar repetition.

R

'Annie, My Darling.' Sung by Miss Lucy Dunnegan. Recorded as MS score at Durham, between 1921 and 1924. The text differs from the fragment in II 587.

430

An - nie, An - nie, my   dar - ling,- Come take a walk with me.—

Down   by   the shad-ow   of   wil - lows, Down   by   the roar - ing sea.

For melodic relationship cf. **BSSM 85, No. 21, measures 7-8 and 15-16, with the last two measures in our version.

Scale: Hexachordal, plagal. Tonal Center: f. Structure: abac (2,2,2,2) = aa¹ (4,4).

S

'Jealous Lover.' Sung by Miss Jewell Robbins. Recorded at Pekin, Montgomery county, between 1921 and 1924. The second measure is identical with that of 250R.

431

One eve when the moon shone brightly— There soft - ly   fell- a   dew—

When in   a   lone - ly   cot - tage   A   jea - lous lov - er   drew.

Scale: Heptachordal. Tonal Center: c. Structure: aa¹a²b (2,2,2,2) = aa¹ (4,4).

U

'Pearl Bryant.' Sung by Miss Zilpah Frisbie. Recorded at Durham in 1923. There is some melodic if not rhythmic relationship with the 250D, measures 5 and 7.

432

Down in   a lone - ly   val - ley— Where the fair - est flow-ers   bloom,

'Tis   there that Pearl   Bryant— Lies mould-ing in— her   tomb.

Scale: Pentachordal. Tonal Center: d. Structure: abac (2,2,2,2) = aa¹ (4,4).

X

'The Jealous Lover.' Sung by Dr. I. G. Greer. Recorded as MS score, probably at Boone, Watauga county; no date given. Cf. note on 250C above.

433

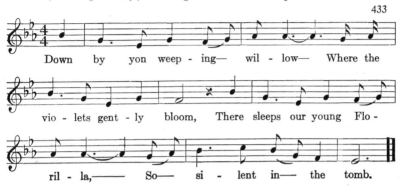

Down by yon weep - ing— wil - low— Where the

vio - lets gent - ly bloom, There sleeps our young Flo -

ril - la,—— So— si - lent in— the tomb.

Scale: Hexachordal. Tonal Center: e-flat. Structure: abab¹ (2,2,2,2) = aa¹ (4,4).

251

FRANKIE AND ALBERT

D

'Frankie and Johnnie.' Sung by Miss Fannie Grogan and Miss Lura Weaver. Recorded as MS score at Vox, Alleghany county, in 1936. In the long headnote, various details brought out by II 589-90, there is no mention of R. W. Gordon, who, according to Mary O. Eddy (BSO 246) is "undoubtedly the world's authority on Frankie and Johnnie." Mr. Gordon, she says, "is reputed to have collected at least three hundred texts" and in 1936 said that "the woman of the story was still living." She cites another source in the New York *Times*, October 21, 1934, by Sigmund Spaeth. The last line of stanza 1 of version A is the potential refrain of this ballad.

434

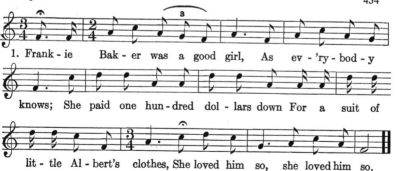

1. Frank - ie Bak - er was a good girl, As ev - 'ry - bod - y

knows; She paid one hun - dred dol - lars down For a suit of

lit - tle Al - bert's clothes, She loved him so, she loved him so.

Scale: Mode III. Tonal Center: f. Structure: aa¹bb¹b²cc¹ (2,2,1,1,2,1,1) =
abc (4,4,2).

J

'He Done Her Wrong.' Sung by Blake B. Harrison. Recorded as MS score at
Durham, in 1919. The name of the woman as well as the amount spent differs
from all the other versions.

435

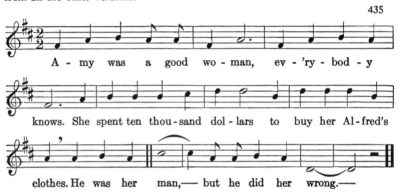

A - my was a good wo - man, ev - 'ry - bod - y

knows. She spent ten thou - sand dol - lars to buy her Al - fred's

clothes. He was her man,— but he did her wrong.—

For melodic relationship cf. *FSUSA 312, No. 88, measures 5-8; OFS II
127, No. 159A.

Scale: Irrational. Tonal Center: d. Structure: aa¹bb¹a²a³ (2,2,2,2,2,2) = aba¹
(4,4,4).

K

'Frankie and Johnnie.' Sung by —— Beaker. Recorded probably at Boone,
Watauga county, in 1939, 1940, or 1941.

436

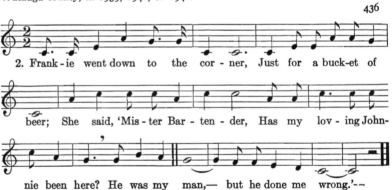

2. Frank - ie went down to the cor - ner, Just for a buck-et of

beer; She said, 'Mis - ter Bar - ten - der, Has my lov - ing John-

nie been here? He was my man,— but he done me wrong.'--

For melodic relationship cf. ***TNFS 84, FSRA 189, No. 111, and AMS 38,
first eight measures: ASb 79, first four measures; BSO 245, No. 108A; *OFS
II 135, version F.

Scale: Heptachordal. Tonal Center: c. Structure: aa^{1}bb^{1}cc^1 (2,2,2,2,2,2) =
abc (4,4,4).

253

LITTLE MARY PHAGAN

B

'Little Mary Faggen.' Sung by Mrs. Rives. Recorded at Boone, Watauga
county, in 1940.

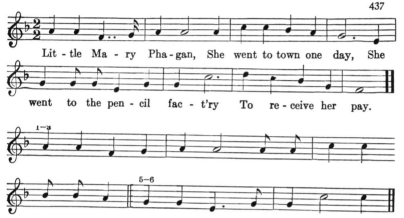

437

Lit - tle Ma - ry Pha - gan, She went to town one day, She
went to the pen - cil fac - t'ry To re - ceive her pay.

Scale: Heptachordal, plagal. Tonal Center: f. Structure: ab (4,4) ; b is somewhat related to a.

258

JOE BOWERS

'Joe Bowers.' Sung by Miss Jean Holeman. Recorded at Durham, in 1922.
This tune is identical with that for 'The Unreconstructed Rebel,' III 465, No.
391, as sung by Lois Johnson. In its melodic outline the tune is very similar to
that in OFS II 194, version D. The editor says there that the tune was also
used for 'Lily of the West' and 'Young Caroline of Edinborough Town.' Here
is another example of what can happen to a tune on its voyage through time and
space. Actually, our version and the Ozark version are beyond description.

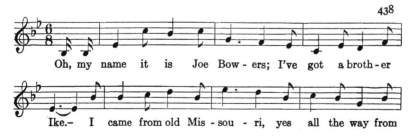

438

Oh, my name it is Joe Bow - ers; I've got a broth - er
Ike.– I came from old Mis - sou - ri, yes all the way from

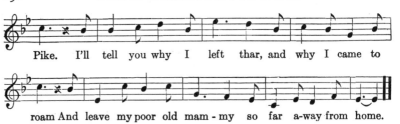

Pike.   I'll tell you why I   left   thar, and why I came to

roam And leave my poor old mam - my so far a-way from home.

For melodic relationship cf. ***OFS II 194, version D; FSmWV 65, first and last two and a half measures.

Scale: Hexatonic (4), plagal. Tonal Center: e-flat. Structure: abba¹ (4,4,4,4).

259

Sweet Jane

B

'Sweet Jane.' Sung by Mrs. L. R. Bascom. Recorded as MS score at Highlands, Jackson county, in 1914. Cf. the text of the same title in OFS I 118, No. 18E.

439

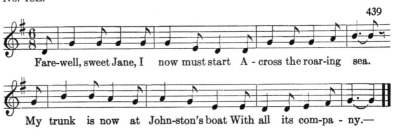

Fare-well, sweet Jane, I   now must start A - cross the roar-ing   sea.

My trunk is now at John-ston's boat With all its com-pa - ny.—

Scale: Hexatonic (4), plagal. Tonal Center: g. Structure: ab (4,4).

263

The Unfortunate Rake

C

'The Dying Cowboy.' Sung by C. K. Tillett. Recorded at Wanchese, Roanoke Island; no date given. Cf. the text with that of SharpK II 165, No. 131B; also, CS 3-8.

440

'Once in my sad - dle I   used to look hand - some,

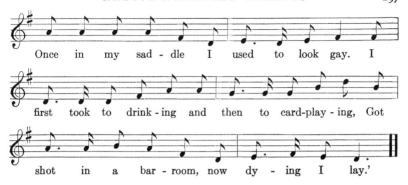

Once in my sad - dle I used to look gay. I first took to drink - ing and then to card-play - ing, Got shot in a bar - room, now dy - ing I lay.'

For melodic relationship cf. ***BSM 395 (E) ; SCSM 453 (F), not rhythmi-cally, however; **FSmWV 24, measures 1-2 and 5-8.

Scale: Hexachordal. Tonal Center: d. Structure: aa¹ (4,4).

266

GREAT GRANDDAD

'Great Granddad.' Sung by Obadiah Johnston. Recorded at Crossnore, Avery county, in 1940. The text is almost the same as that in OFS III 248, No. 483 Cf. CS 302. Measures 5-6 resemble melodically 'Little Brown Jug.'

441

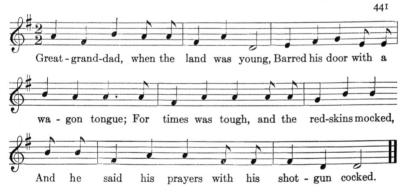

Great - grand-dad, when the land was young, Barred his door with a wa - gon tongue; For times was tough, and the red-skins mocked, And he said his prayers with his shot - gun cocked.

For melodic relationship cf. **OFS III 248, No. 483.

Scale: Hexachordal. Tonal Center: d. Structure: nmm¹ (4,2,2) = inverted barform.

268

BILL MILLER'S TRIP TO THE WEST

'Bill Miller's Trip to the West.' Sung by Mrs. E. J. Norris. Recorded as MS score; no place or date given. In the general melodic outline of the first 2 measures and their repetitions this tune reminds one of the Russian folk melody 'Volga Boat Song.'

442

When I got there— I————looked a - round; No Chris - tian man— or——church I found.

Scale: Mode II, plagal. Tonal Center: e. Structure: abaa¹ca (2,2,2,2,2,2).

270

John Henry

A

'John Henry. Sung by G. S. Robinson, Otis S. Kuykendall playing guitar. Recorded at West Asheville, Buncombe county, in 1939. Cf. NWS 226, version C.

443

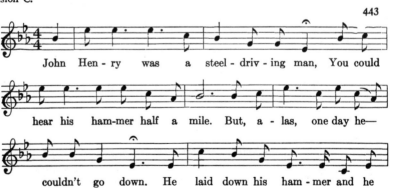

John Hen - ry   was   a   steel - driv - ing man, You could hear his ham-mer half a mile. But, a - las, one day he— couldn't go down. He laid down his ham - mer and he

cried, He laid down his ham-mer and he cried.

For melodic relationship cf. **MSHF 4 and PSB 8, measures 1-6; *FSUSA 258, No. 74; SharpK II 35, No. 87, first 6 measures.

Scale: Hexachordal, plagal. Tonal Center: e-flat. Structure: aa¹a²bb¹ (2,2, 2,2,2).

A(1)

'John Henry.' Sung by Bascom Lamar Lunsford. Recorded at Turkey Creek, Buncombe county, about 1921. The first three measures show some melodic relationship with those of 270A. 444

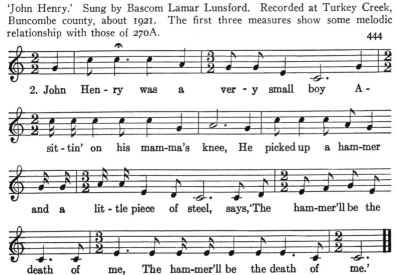

2. John Hen-ry was a ver-y small boy A-sit-tin' on his mam-ma's knee, He picked up a ham-mer and a lit-tle piece of steel, says,'The ham-mer'll be the death of me, The ham-mer'll be the death of me.'

For melodic relationship cf. **ASb 362-3, measures 3-6; *AFSCh 154; AS
178-9.

Scale: Hexachordal.   Tonal Center: c.   Structure: aba^{1}c   (2,2,2,3).

C

'Johnie Henry.'   Sung by Mrs. Birdie May Moody.   Recorded as MS score at
Shull's Mills, Watauga county; no date given.

445

John - nie   Hen - ry   was   a   hard work - ing   man,   He

died with his ham-mer   in   his   hand.

For melodic relationship cf. *SharpK II 35, No. 87.

Scale: Heptachordal, plagal.   Tonal Center: g.   Structure: aa^{1}a^{2}b   (2,2,2,2).
Circular Tune (V).

E

'John Henry.'   Sung by J. D. Johnson, Jr.   Recorded at Durham, in 1919.

446

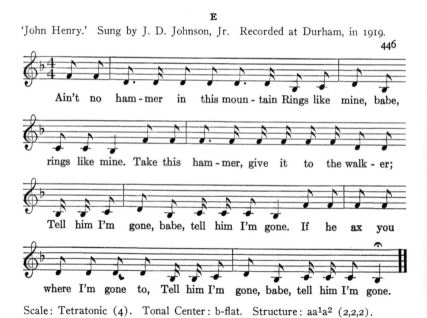

Ain't   no   ham - mer   in   this moun - tain Rings like   mine, babe,

rings like mine. Take this   ham - mer, give   it   to   the walk - er;

Tell   him I'm   gone, babe, tell   him I'm gone.   If   he   ax   you

where I'm   gone   to,   Tell him I'm   gone, babe, tell him I'm gone.

Scale: Tetratonic (4).   Tonal Center: b-flat.   Structure: aa^{1}a^2 (2,2,2).

G

'Captain, I'm Drivin'.' Sung by Dr. White. Recorded at Durham, in 1922. As the record breaks off with a great noise, it is unfortunate that this contribution of the General Editor must remain a fragment. The analysis, below, must also be fragmentary.

447

Cap - tain, I'm driv - in', (huh)   But de steel won't stand it, (huh)   Cap - tain, I'm driv - in', (huh)   But de steel won't stand it, (huh)   Let dem

Scale: Mode III, plagal. Tonal Center: a. Structure: ab (?) (2,2 ?).

H

'Asheville Junction.' Sung by Bascom Lamar Lunsford. Recorded as MS score at Lenoir, Caldwell county, in 1922. There is another recording of the singing of W. (Shorty) Love, who worked for many years at Duke University, East Campus. It does not differ in any significant detail. Mr. Lunsford has told the present editor that he gave this song to Mrs. Sutton, but under the name of 'Swannanoa Tunnel.' He said the text is exactly as he gave it to her. He added, that when Cecil Sharp recorded this song and named it 'Swannanoa Town,' Sharp did not understand the speech too well and mistook "tunnel," as it was sung, for "town-O."

448

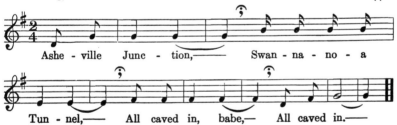

Ashe - ville Junc - tion,—— Swan - na - no - a Tun - nel,—— All caved in, babe,— All caved in.——

For melodic relationship cf. *TAFL 913; FSUSA 258, No. 74; FSF 182, No. 99; FSSH 443, No. 179. All of them only the very beginning.

Scale: Irrational, plagal. Tonal Center: g. Structure: ab (4,4).

I

'Swannanoa Tunnel.' Sung by Bascom Lamar Lunsford. Recorded at Turkey Creek, Buncombe county, in 1921.

449

Ashe - ville— Junc - tion— Swan - na - no - a

Tun - nel,— All caved in, ba - by,— All caved in.—

Upbeat

6-8   2-8

3   1-7

Scale: Mode III. Tonal center: b-flat. Structure: abcd (2,2,2,2).

J

'John Henry.' Sung by Alex Price. Recorded at Alliance, Pamlico county, in 1927.

450

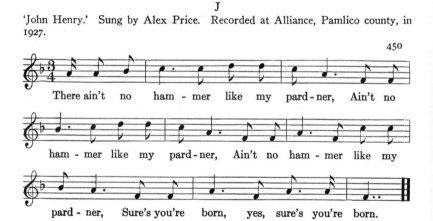

There ain't no ham - mer like my pard - ner, Ain't no

ham - mer like my pard - ner, Ain't no ham - mer like my

pard - ner, Sure's you're born, yes, sure's you're born.

Scale: Irrational. Tonal Center: f. Structure: aa¹bb¹ (2,2,2,2).

272

THE FATAL WEDDING

'The Fatal Wedding.' Sung by C. K. Tillett. Recorded at Wanchese, Roanoke Island, 1922. The text of the chorus is practically identical with that of the version in OFS IV 276, No. 766.

When the tune of the stanza is compared with that of the chorus, one outstanding difference is evident. While the former is purely diatonic, the latter shows considerable chromatic alterations. Whether these are due to some attempt to 'improve' the melody or are merely the result of more recent trends, it is certainly surprising that the tune of the stanza was not touched thereby.

451

3. She begged the sex-ton once a-gain To let her pass in-side.- 'For ba-by's sake you may step in,' The grey-haired man re-plied. 'If an-y-one knows rea-sons why This cou-ple should not wed, Speak now, or for-ev-er hold, Your peace,' the preacher said.

While the wed-ding bells were ring-ing, While the bride and groom were there, March-ing up the aisle to-geth-er As the or-gan pealed an air, Tell-ing tales of fond af-fec-tion, Vow-ing nev-er-more to part; Just an-oth-er fa-tal wed-ding, Just an-oth-er bro-ken heart.

For melodic relationship cf. ***BSM 143B, stanza only (there is no chorus) ;
**OFS IV 278, No. 766, stanza only.

Scale: Heptachordal, plagal. Tonal Center: g. Structure: aa¹ab (4,4,4,4) =
aa¹ (8,8) ; chorus: cc¹cd (4,4,4,4) = cc¹ (8,8). Stanza and chorus: aa¹ bb¹.

272(1)

'The Fatal Wedding.' Sung by Otis Kuykendall. Recorded at West Asheville,
1939. The chorus uses the same tune as the stanza.

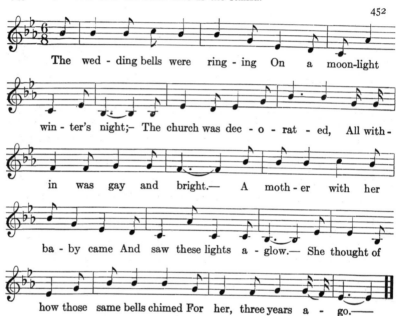

For melodic relationship cf. **BSM 143B, stanza; OFS IV 278, No. 766.

Scale: Heptachordal, plagal. Tonal Center: e-flat. Structure: aba¹b¹ (4,4,4,4)
=aa¹ (8,8).

272(2)

'The Fatal Wedding.' Sung by Jewell Robbins. Recorded at Pekin, Montgomery county, in 1921. This tune is only a fragment as the recording is very
poor. The text is that of the chorus as given in II 630. The tune was probably
the same for the stanza.

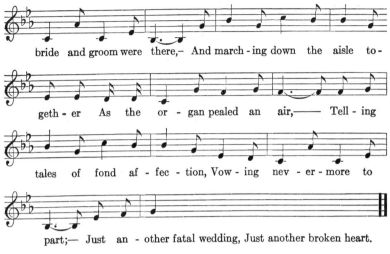

bride and groom were there,— And march - ing down the aisle to -

geth - er As the or - gan pealed an air,—— Tell - ing

tales of fond af - fec - tion, Vow - ing nev - er - more to

part;— Just an - other fatal wedding, Just another broken heart.

For melodic relationship cf. ***BSM 143B, stanza; **OFS IV 278, No. 766
Scale: Heptachordal, plagal. Tonal Center: e-flat. Structure: Presumably the
same as other versions: aba¹c (4,4,4,4) = aa¹ (8,8).

273

THE LITTLE ROSEWOOD CASKET

E

'Little Rosewood Casket.' Sung by Mrs. H. R. Stamey and Hestabel Dellinger.
Recorded at Altamont, Avery county, in 1940. The variations given below are
derived from another recording, by Mrs. R. H. Buchanan.

454

In the lit - tle rose - wood cas - ket—— That is

rest - ing on—— my stand— Is a pack - age of old

let - ters—— Writ - ten by a cher - ished hand.

For melodic relationship cf. **OFS IV 270, No. 763A; SHP 62; BMFSB 32; MSNC 24, and AMS 54.

Scale: Heptachordal, plagal.   Tonal Center: c.   Structure: aa¹bc (2,2,2,2) = ab (4,4).

E(1)

'Little Rosewood Casket.'   Sung by Bascom Lamar Lunsford.   Recorded at Turkey Creek, 1921 (?).   This is really only another variation of the above version.

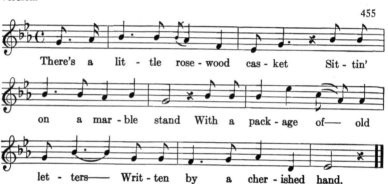

For melodic relationship cf. ***SHP 62-3; BMFSB 32; MSNC 24; **FSmWV 74, No. 28B.

Scale: Heptachordal, plagal.   Tonal Center: e-flat.   Structure: aa¹bc (2,2,2,2) = ab (4,4).

N

'The Rosewood Casket.'   Sung by C. K. Tillett.   Recorded at Wanchese, Roanoke Island, 1922.   The form is the same as that of version 28B, given in FSmWV 73.

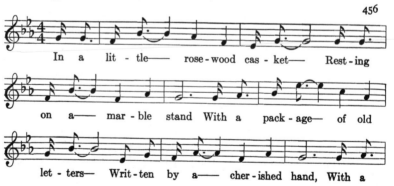

pack - age— of old   let - ters— Writ-ten by a— cher-ished hand.

For melodic relationship cf. ***SHP 62; BMFSB 32; **MSNC 24.

Scale: Heptachordal, plagal. Tonal Center: e-flat. Structure: aa¹bcbc¹ (2,2,2, 2,2,2) = abb (4,4,4) or nmm¹, inverted barform.

274

JACK AND JOE

B

'Give My Love to Nell, O Jack.' Sung by C. K. Tillett. Recorded at Wanchese, Roanoke Island, 1922.

457

Three years a - go, when Jack and Joe set sail a - cross the

foam, They vowed a for - tune each to gain be - fore re-turn-ing

home.- In just one year Jack gained his wealth, he

sailed for home— that day,— And when the pals shook

hands to part, poor Jack could on - ly say:— 'Give my love to

Nel-lie, Jack, and kiss her once for me.— The fair - est girl in

all the world I know you think is she.— Treat her kind - ly,

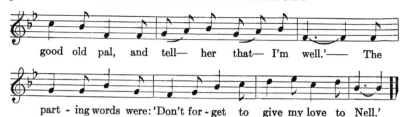

good old pal, and tell— her that— I'm well.'—— The

part - ing words were: 'Don't for - get to give my love to Nell.'

For melodic relationship cf. *FSoA 76, general melodic outline only.

Scale: Heptachordal, plagal. Tonal Center: b-flat. Structure: aba^1b^1 (4,4,4,4) $= aa^1$ (8,8). Chorus: $a^2ba^1b^1$ (4,4,4,4) $= a^2a^1$ (8,8). It is structurally interesting to find that a^2 is built of the first half of a^1 and the second half of a.

D

'Jack and Joe.' Sung by Mrs. E. Wilson. Recorded; no date or place given. The tune for the chorus is the same as that for the stanza.

458

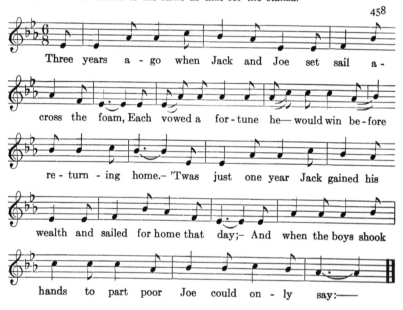

Three years a - go when Jack and Joe set sail a -

cross the foam, Each vowed a for - tune he— would win be - fore

re - turn - ing home.– 'Twas just one year Jack gained his

wealth and sailed for home that day;– And when the boys shook

hands to part poor Joe could on - ly say:——

For melodic relationship cf. *FSoA 76.

Scale: Mode III, plagal. Tonal Center: a-flat. Structure: $abab^1$ (4,4,4,4) $=$ aa^1 (8,8).

K

'Jack and Joe.' Sung by C. H. Smith. Recorded at Harmony, Iredell county, in 1920. In the general melodic outline there is considerable relationship with 274D.

459

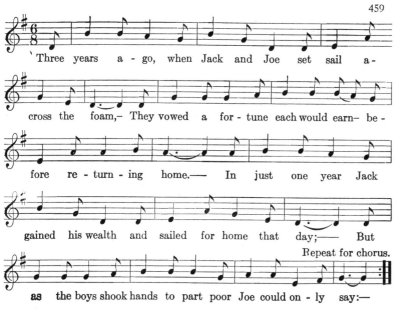

Three years a - go, when Jack and Joe set sail a-cross the foam,– They vowed a for - tune each would earn– be - fore re - turn - ing home.—— In just one year Jack gained his wealth and sailed for home that day;—— But

Repeat for chorus.

as the boys shook hands to part poor Joe could on - ly say:—

For melodic relationship cf. **FSoA 76.

Scale: Hexatonic (4), plagal. Tonal Center: g. Structure: abab¹ (4,4,4,4) = aa¹ (8,8).

275

THEY SAY IT IS SINFUL TO FLIRT

A

'Sinful Flirting.' Sung by C. F. Faucette. Recorded at Greenville, S. C., 1923. The latter part of this tune is quite closely related to that of 275A (1); it is but slightly related to 275B.

460

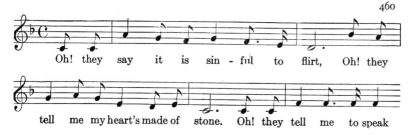

Oh! they say it is sin - ful to flirt, Oh! they tell me my heart's made of stone. Oh! they tell me to speak

to him kind Or—— else leave the poor boy a - lone.

For melodic relationship cf. *FSSH 238-40.

Scale: Heptachordal, plagal. Tonal Center: f. Structure: abcb¹ (2,2,2,2) = ab (4,4).

A(I)

'Sinful Flirting.' Sung by Miss Lena Ward. Recorded at Reidsville, Rockingham county, in 1940. Another title is 'Willie Down by the Road.' This tune is almost identical with that of the preceding version.

461

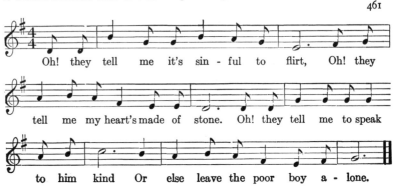

Oh! they tell me it's sin - ful to flirt, Oh! they
tell me my heart's made of stone. Oh! they tell me to speak
to him kind Or else leave the poor boy a - lone.

For melodic relationship cf. *** JAFL xLV (1932), 89, No. 175 measures 5-6 only. **FSSH 238, measures 1-4.

Scale: Heptachordal, plagal. Tonal Center: g. Structure: abcb (2,2,2,2).

B

"It Is Sinful to Flirt.' Sung by Miss Zilpah Frisbie. Recorded in McDowell county in 1923.

462

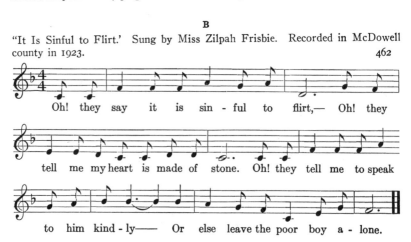

Oh! they say it is sin - ful to flirt,— Oh! they
tell me my heart is made of stone. Oh! they tell me to speak
to him kind - ly—— Or else leave the poor boy a - lone.

For melodic relationship cf. ***JAFL xlv (1932), 89, No. 175; **FSSH 238, No. 72A, first two measures, and *ibid.*, still more so, 240, version No. 272C.

Scale: Heptachordal, plagal.   Tonal Center: f.   Structure: aba¹c (2,2,2,2) = aa¹ (4,4).

276

The Little White Rose

A

'The Little White Rose.' Sung by Miss Jewell Robbins. Recorded at Pekin, Montgomery county, between 1921 and 1924. Measures 3-4 and 15-16 coincide with phrases of 'Marching through Georgia.'

He gave me a rose, a pret-ty white rose, And asked me to wear it for him. I have it yet, and I nev-er shall for-get To wear it so long as he is true. It was on the old oak stump Where we sat side by side And watched the beau-ti-ful stream be-neath our feet. We would whis-per words of love While the lit-tle birds sing a-bove, Words that were ten-der, low, and sweet.

Scale: Hexachordal, plagal.   Tonal Center: f.   Structure aa¹ba² (4,4,4,4) = Reprisenbar.

NORTH CAROLINA BALLADS

279

SAYS FROHOCK TO FANNING

There is no musical score to any of the 'Regulator Songs.' But, knowing the habit of people to use familiar melodies when expressing themselves in poetic terms of whatever description—we need only remember the creation of our national anthem—the present editor risks an assumption which, however, musically speaking is certainly supported by the fact that the melody fits the text. An added reason is the close relationship of "Says Richard to Robin" with "Says Fanning to Frohock" in the North Carolina ballad. The former occurs in a ballad 'Hunting the Wren,' or 'Let Us Go to the Woods' quoted in SCB 165 and JFSS, vol. v, 77-8. As this song is of considerable age, was very popular, and is still known and sung in England today, it would not be unlikely that the author of the poem used this melody as the vehicle for his words.

282

As I Went Down to New Bern

No title. Sung by E. B. Miller. As already stated in II 658, the "Air by Lunsford" cannot be found. Mr. Lunsford told this editor that he never gave this song to Dr. Brown. He did sing, however, 'Going to Town,' or to the same tune, 'Billy Went Down to Bud's House'; and this tune, he said, could be used for 'As I Went Down to New Bern; but he felt that it would not make as good a song that way.

285

Man Killed by Falling from a Horse

'Man Killed by Falling from a Horse.' Sung by Miss Jewell Robbins. Recorded at Pekin, Montgomery county, about 1924.

Mrs. Perdue, formerly Miss Jewell Robbins, in a letter written to the present editor after a visit he paid to her home in Gastonia, said: "Also I am wishing more information had been written about 'Man Killed by Falling from a Horse.' He was a young man by the surname of Polk, from Richmond county. On his return from a business trip to Pekin sometime before the War between the States, he was thrown from his horse, hit his head against a heart pine stump and was killed. That stump was near our cottage home at the edge of the village of Pekin. Of course, I didn't enjoy going by that stump alone, when I was a child. The song was supposed to have been composed by his twin brother."

For a similar title and beginning, cf. BMNE 167. Measures 3-8 are closely related to those of Mrs. James York's version of 'Maid Freed from the Gallows,' No. 30R of this collection.

464

Come ye youths of ev-ery age,— Give ear un-to— my song.— A mourn-ful sto-ry I'll re-late As ev-er you- did hear.— A young man in the bloom of youth, His age near twen-ty-one,— No-vem-ber last, the e-lev-enth day Of eight-teen hun-dred and one.——

Scale: Hexatonic (6), plagal. Tonal Center: g. Structure: abcb¹ (4,4,4,4).

286

THE *Florence C. McGee*

'The *Florence C. McGee*.' Sung by Mrs. L. D. Hayman. Recorded as MS score at Durham in 1919. According to the melodic structure, two of the stanzas as printed in II 661 are needed for one stanza of the tune.

465

Come all you friends and sai-lors too And lis-ten un-to me, While I re-late the dole-ful fate Of *Flor-ence C. Mc-Gee.* In eigh-teen

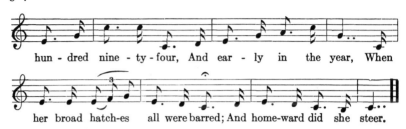

hun - dred nine - ty - four, And ear - ly in the year, When her broad hatch-es all were barred; And home-ward did she steer.

Scale: Heptachordal, plagal. Tonal Center: c. Structure: abba (4,4,4,4).

287

The *Titanic*

B

'Destruction of the *Titanic*.' Sung by W. O. Smith. Recorded as MS score at Durham in 1920. As in numerous other cases, the printed version of the text and music do not match. The chorus as printed in II 663 begins with "Wasn't it sad about the *Titanic*." Unfortunately, from a musical standpoint based upon the melodic structure of the stanza which constitutes the tune, this is definitely incorrect. The first statement "Wasn't it sad about the *Titanic*, how it got lost" belongs to the last phrase of the musical stanza, and its repetition marks the beginning of the chorus.

Attention should be called to the ingenious use made of the first four measures of the stanza to supply the same for the chorus. Note the rhythmic shift as well as that of the accents. The remainder of the chorus is but a slightly altered repetition of the last part of the stanza.

466

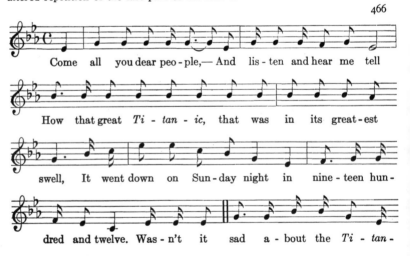

Come all you dear peo - ple,— And lis - ten and hear me tell How that great *Ti - tan - ic*, that was in its great - est swell, It went down on Sun - day night in nine - teen hun - dred and twelve. Was - n't it sad a - bout the *Ti - tan -*

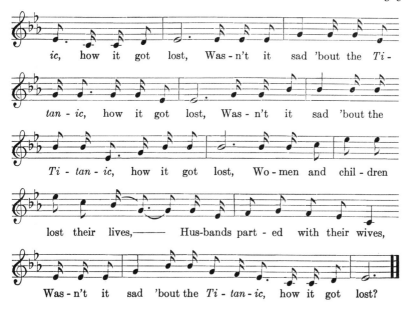

ic, how it got lost, Was-n't it sad 'bout the Ti-

tan-ic, how it got lost, Was-n't it sad 'bout the

Ti-tan-ic, how it got lost, Wo-men and chil-dren

lost their lives,—— Hus-bands part-ed with their wives,

Was-n't it sad 'bout the Ti-tan-ic, how it got lost?

Scale: Heptachordal, plagal. Tonal Center: e-flat. Structure: aa^{1}bc (2,2,2,2) = ab (4,4). Chorus: a^{2}a^{3}bc (2,2,2,2) = a^{1}b^1 (4,4).

D

'The Great *Titanic*.' Sung by Mrs. J. Church. Recorded at Heaton, Avery county, in 1939. This melody offers interesting points with regard to the intuitive grasp of the process called composition by some untrained, but musical mind. Note how measures 5-6 of the stanza represent a surprising combination of the fourth plus the second measure of the stanza, most ingeniously refashioned. The last two measures of the stanza are again formed from the second measure. Besides this, the chorus begins with measures 3-5 astonishingly reshaped and leading directly into a slightly altered restatement of the last three measures of the stanza. To be sure, this is not strictly according to the textbooks, but is unquestionably better for it.

It was on Mon-day morn-ing—— a-bout one o' clock.

The big Ti-tan-ic—— be-gan—— to reel and rock.

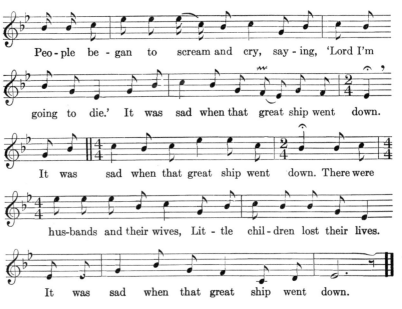

Peo - ple be - gan to scream and cry, say - ing, 'Lord I'm going to die.' It was sad when that great ship went down.

It was sad when that great ship went down. There were hus-bands and their wives, Lit - tle chil - dren lost their lives.

It was sad when that great ship went down.

Scale: Hexatonic (4), plagal. Tonal Center: e-flat. Structure: abb¹a¹a² (2,2, 1,1,2) ; Chorus b²b¹a³a⁴ (2,1,1,2).

Scale: Hexatonic (4), plagal. Tonal Center: e-flat. Structure: $abb^1a^1a^2$ (2,2, 1,1,2) ; Chorus $b^2b^1a^3a^4$ (2,1,1,2).

E

'The Ship *Titanic.*' Sung by Miss Nancy Lineberger. Recorded at Shelby, Cleveland county, March 1940.

468

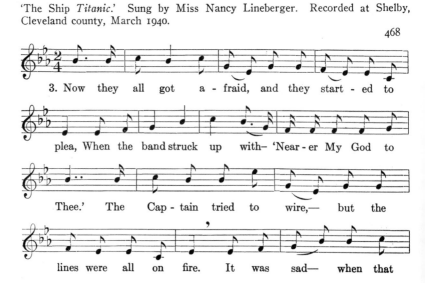

3. Now they all got a - fraid, and they start - ed to plea, When the band struck up with— 'Near - er My God to Thee.' The Cap - tain tried to wire,— but the lines were all on fire. It was sad— when that

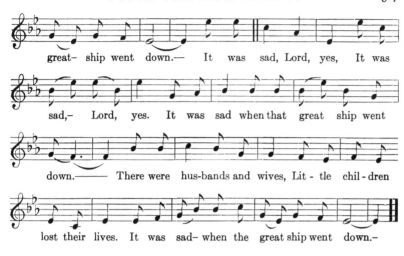

great- ship went down.— It was sad, Lord, yes, It was

sad,- Lord, yes. It was sad when that great ship went

down.——— There were hus-bands and wives, Lit - tle chil - dren

lost their lives. It was sad- when the great ship went down.-

For melodic relationship cf. ***TSFL 723-4.

Scale : Hexachordal, plagal. Tonal Center : e-flat. Structure : aba^{1}c (4,4,4,4) ;
Chorus : dea^{2}c (4,4,4,4).

H

'God Moved on the Water.' Sung by Will ('Shorty') Love. Recorded at
Durham, about 1920. In OSC 26-7, the date of the tragedy is given as April
13 instead of the fifteenth.

469

God moved— on de wa - ters— On A - pril de fif-teenth

day; He just moved—— on de wa - ters,— And de

1st time only.   all others.

peo - ple had to run and pray.

De rich dey had de - cid - ed Dat dey would not

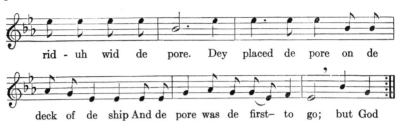

rid - uh wid de pore. Dey placed de pore on de

deck of de ship And de pore was de first— to go; but God

Scale: Tetratonic (2). Tonal Center: e-flat. Structure: Chorus: aa¹ (4,4);
Stanza: a²baa¹ (4,4,4,4).

290

THE HAMLET WRECK

'The Hamlet Wreck.' Sung by anonymous singer. Recorded as MS score, but
no place or date given. The detailed analysis of this tune given below shows
the masterful handling, intuitive to be sure, of musical material; even in such
diminutive forms as this song has, the creative process and the discerning use
of the varied ideas is the same as manifested in the larger works of our masters.

470

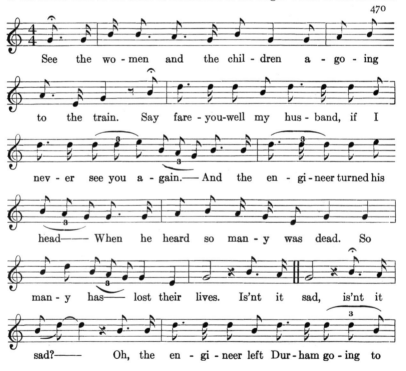

See   the wo - men   and   the chil - dren   a - go - ing

to   the train.   Say   fare - you-well my   hus - band, if   I

nev - er   see you a - gain.—— And   the   en - gi - neer turned his

head——— When   he heard   so man - y   was dead.   So

man - y   has—— lost their   lives.   Is'nt it   sad,   is'nt it

sad?———   Oh, the   en - gi - neer left Dur - ham go - ing to

Char-lotte, North Car-o-li - na. Isn't it sad, is'nt it

sad?——— So man-y has—— lost their lives.

Scale: Mode III, plagal. Tonal Center: g. Structure: $abcdd^1b^1e$ (1,1,1,1,1,1,2);
Chorus: fcd^2fe (2,1,1,2,2).

291

EDWARD LEWIS

'Edward Lewis.' Sung by anonymous male singer with banjo. Recorded; no
date or place given.

471

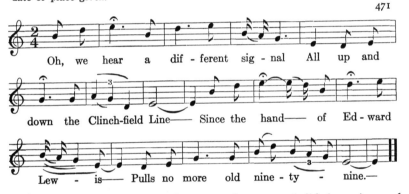

Oh, we hear a dif - ferent sig - nal All up and

down the Clinch-field Line—— Since the hand—— of Ed - ward

Lew - is—— Pulls no more old nine - ty - nine.——

Scale: Mode II, plagal. Tonal Center: e. Structure: aba^1b^1 (4,4,4,4) = aa^1
(8,8).

292

MANLEY PANKEY

'Manley Pankey.' Sung by Miss Jewell Robbins. Recorded at Pekin, Montgomery county, between 1921 and 1924. As this, as well as several other recordings by the same singer turned out to be impossible for transcription because
of the noise emanating from the records, the editor made several trips to Gastonia, the present home of Mrs. Perdue, formerly Miss Jewell Robbins, in order
to obtain a complete version of the various songs. This song was obtained on
a visit made on July 31, 1954. Mrs. Purdue said: "This song was sung by the
Negroes on our plantation and my brothers. I was so small when I heard it
and we were living in such seclusion from other white people that I cannot
recall having heard any other people sing it."

472

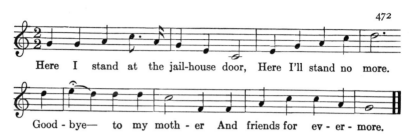

Here I stand at the jail-house door, Here I'll stand no more.

Good-bye— to my moth-er And friends for ev-er-more.

Scale: Hexachordal. Tonal Center: c. Structure: ab (4,4). Circular Tune (V).

296

EMMA HARTSELL

A

'Death of Emma Hartsell.' Anonymous singer. Recorded as MS score at Mount Gilead, Montgomery county; no date. There is quite a lengthy account of the whole story with details that seem not to have appeared in print elsewhere, given in the Kannapolis *Daily Independent* of Sunday, December 18, 1955, by its staff writer Randolph S. Hancock. The story is based on an interview this reporter had with E. J. Linker, seventy-one, who said that the murdered girl was his first sweetheart. That gives to the whole story the value of an eye-witness account.

473

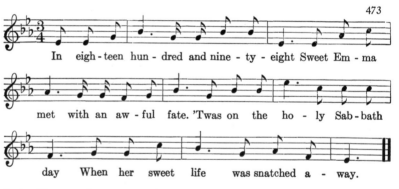

In eigh-teen hun-dred and nine-ty-eight Sweet Em-ma

met with an aw-ful fate. 'Twas on the ho-ly Sab-bath

day When her sweet life was snatched a-way.

Scale: Hexachordal. Tonal Center: e-flat. Structure: aba^{1}b^1 (2,2,2,2) = aa^1 (4,4).

300

POOR NAOMI (OMIE WISE)

A

'Poor Naomi.' Sung by Mrs. Eliza Sanders. Recorded; no date or place given.

474

Come all—good peo - ple, I'd have you— draw near, A sor - row - ful sto - ry you quick - ly— shall hear; A sto - ry— I'll tell you a - bout Na - o - mi— Wise, How she was de - lud - ed by Lew - is's—— lies.

For melodic relationship cf. **FSSH 225; SharpK II 146, No. 123-D.
Scale: Mode IV. Tonal Center: d. Structure: abab (4,4,4,4) = aa (8,8).

I

'Little Oma Wise.' Sung for the editor by Dr. Greer at his home in Chapel Hill in 1952. The same tune as that for his 'Ellen Smith,' 305A, below.

475

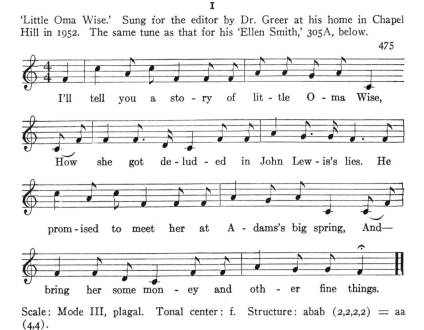

I'll tell you a sto - ry of lit - tle O - ma Wise, How she got de - lud - ed in John Lew - is's lies. He prom - ised to meet her at A - dams's big spring, And— bring her some mon - ey and oth - er fine things.

Scale: Mode III, plagal. Tonal center: f. Structure: abab (2,2,2,2) = aa (4,4).

301

FRANKIE SILVER

A

'Francis Silver.' Sung by Mrs. H. R. Buchanan. Recorded at Minneapolis, Avery county, in 1931.

476

This dread - ful, dark and dis - mal day Has swept my glo - ries all a - way. My sun goes down, my days are past, And I must leave this world at last.

Scale: Hexatonic (4), plagal. Tonal Center: f. Structure: aa¹bc $(2,2,2,2)$ = ab $(4,4)$.

A(1)

'Frankie Silvers.' Sung by Bascom Lamar Lunsford. Recorded at Turkey Creek, Buncombe county, in 1921 (?). The text is identical with that of the A version.

477

This dread - ful, dark— and dis - mal day, Has swept my glo - ries— all a - way, My sun goes down, my days are— past, And I must leave— this world at last.

Scale: Mode III, plagal. Tonal center: e-flat. Structure: aba¹b¹ (2,2,2,2) = aa¹ (4,4).

B

'Francis Silver's Confession.' Sung by Mrs. J. J. Miller. Recorded as MS score; no date or place given.

478

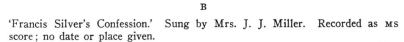

This dread-ful, dark and dis-mal day Has swept my

glo - ries— all a - way. The sun goes down, my—

days are past, And I must leave this world at last.

Scale: Hexatonic (6). Tonal Center: d. Structure: abca (2,2,2,2).

302

THE MURDER OF LAURA FOSTER

A

'The Murder of Laura Foster.' Sung by Mrs. Myra Barnett Miller. Recorded probably at Lenoir, Caldwell county, in 1939, 1940, or 1941. There is considerable melodic similarity between this tune and the version of 'Francis Silver's Confession,' 301B, by the same singer. With reference to the statement about "a long address to several thousand persons" made by Thomas C. Dula, (II 705) cf. *The Waning of the Middle Ages* by J. Huizinga (London, 1927), p. 3.

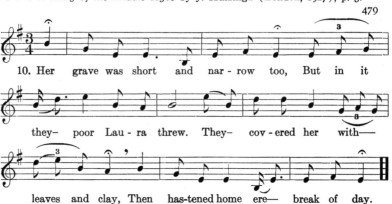

Scale: Hexatonic (6), plagal. Tonal Center: e. Structure: abca¹ (2,2,2,2).

A(I)

'The Murder of Laura Foster.' Sung by H. McNeill. Recorded as MS score at Lenoir, Caldwell county, between 1921 and 1925.

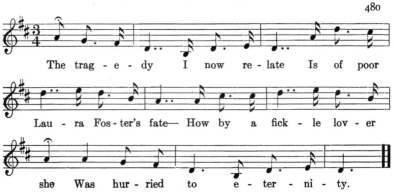

Scale: Heptachordal, plagal. Tonal Center: d. Structure: abb¹a (2,2,2,2).

B

'The Murder of Laura Foster.' Sung by Mrs. A. I. Green. Recorded as MS score at Heaton, Avery county, in 1921.

481

The trag - e - dy I now re - late Is of poor Lau - ra Fos - ter's fate— How by a fick - le lov - er she Was hur - ried to e - ter - ni - ty.

Scale: Mode III, plagal. Tonal Center: g. Structure: abca¹ (2,2,2,2). Circular tune (V).

303

TOM DULA

B

'Tom Dooley.' Sung by Mrs. R. A. Robinson. Recorded as MS score at Silverstone, Watauga county, in 1921. In the recording the sequence of the stanzas 1 and 2 (II 712) is reversed. This editor has an identical version of this ballad, which was sung to him by an old mountaineer ninety-five years old, who lived near Weaverville, Buncombe county. There are, however, some differences in the text. The phrase "Oh, hang your head and cry" can also be found in TNFS 73, 'The Lonesome Road'; also, "Bow down your head and cry" in CS 159.

482

2. You met her on the hill - side And there you may sup - pose You met her on the hill - side And there you hid her clothes. Oh hang your head, Tom

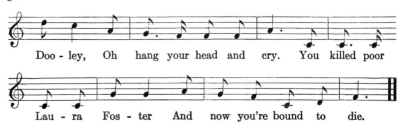

Doo - ley,   Oh   hang your head and   cry.   You   killed poor

Lau - ra   Fos - ter   And   now you're bound   to   die.

For melodic relationship cf. * FSUSA 300.

Scale: Mode III, plagal.   Tonal Center: f.   Structure: aa¹ba¹ (4,4,4,4) =
Reprisenbar.

305

ELLEN SMITH

A

'Ellen Smith.' Sung by Dr. I. G. Greer. In 1952 the singer sang this at his
home at Chapel Hill for the editor. The tune is identical with the one this
singer uses for his 'Little Omie Wise,' 300I above. It very closely resembles
the tune of 'How Firm a Foundation' in the *Service Hymnal*, Hope Publishing
Co., Chicago, 1938.

483

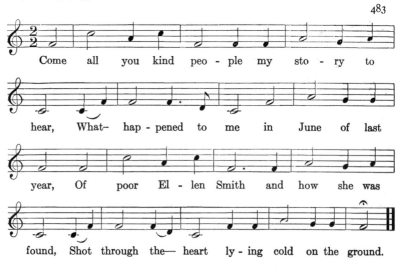

Come   all   you   kind   peo - ple   my   sto - ry   to

hear,   What–   hap - pened   to   me   in   June   of   last

year,   Of   poor   El - len   Smith   and   how   she was

found,   Shot through the— heart   ly - ing cold on the ground.

Scale: Mode III, plagal.   Tonal Center: f.   Structure: abab (4,4,4,4) = aa
(8,8).

E

'Ellen Smith.' Sung by Mrs. Ewart Wilson. Recorded at Pensacola, Yancey county, in 1929. The tune is that of 'How Firm a Foundation.' The text uses the last two lines of stanza 1 and the first two of stanza 4 as printed in II 714-15.

484

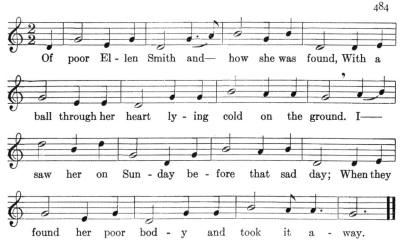

Of poor El-len Smith and— how she was found, With a ball through her heart ly-ing cold on the ground. I—— saw her on Sun-day be-fore that sad day; When they found her poor bod-y and took it a-way.

Scale: Mode III, plagal. Tonal Center: g. Structure: aa¹ba¹ (4,4,4,4) = Reprisenbar.

307

Nellie Cropsey

C

'Nellie Cropsey.' Sung by Miss Lucy Dunnegan. Recorded as MS score at Durham in 1921. Measures 3-8 are closely related to those of 'Lexington Murder,' 65A(1) above.

485

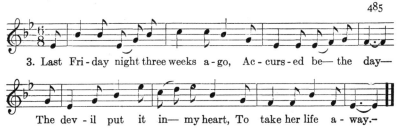

3. Last Fri-day night three weeks a-go, Ac-curs-ed be— the day— The dev-il put it in— my heart, To take her life a-way.-

Scale: Hexatonic (4). Tonal Center: e-flat. Structure: ab (4,4).

308

LILLIE SHAW

'Lillie Shaw.' Anonymous singer. Recorded at Heaton, Avery county, in 1933.

486

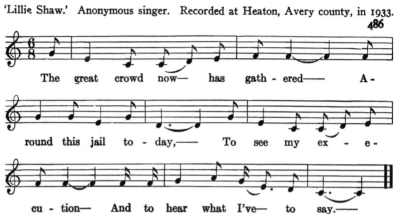

The great crowd now— has gath-ered—— A-
round this jail to-day,—— To see my ex - e-
cu - tion— And to hear what I've— to say.——

Scale: Hexachordal. Tonal Center: c. Structure: abab¹ (2,2,2,2) = aa¹ (4,4).

308(1)

'Lillie Shaw.' Anonymous singer. Recorded; no date or place given.

487

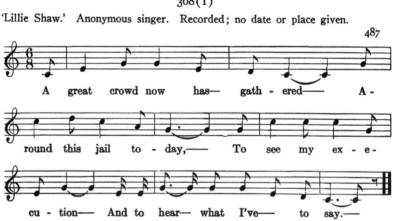

A great crowd now has— gath - ered—— A-
round this jail to - day,—— To see my ex - e-
cu - tion— And to hear— what I've— to say.——

Scale: Mode III. Tonal Center: c. Structure: abbc (2,2,2,2).

2 I'm to hang for the murder
   Of Lillie Shaw you've learned,
   Whom I so cruelly murdered,
   And a body so shamefully burned.

3 I was taken to prison,
   The murder I did own;

> And by the force of sentence
> To hang for the murder done.

4   The murder so cruel and sinful,
    The thing which I had done
    It filled my soul with horror
    While in the prison alone.

5   The fire where I burned her
    Again was in my sight,
    Her lovely form consumed
    In the fire that burned so bright.

311

SHU LADY

'Shu Lady.' Sung by the Reverend Andrew Jackson Burrus. Recorded as MS
score at Cliffside, Rutherford county, 1921-22.

488

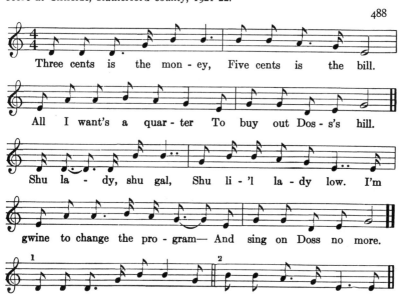

Three cents is the mon-ey, Five cents is the bill.

All I want's a quar-ter To buy out Dos-s's hill.

Shu la - dy, shu gal, Shu li - 'l la - dy low. I'm

gwine to change the pro - gram— And sing on Doss no more.

Scale: Mode III, plagal. Tonal Center: g. Structure: aba¹b¹ (2,2,2,2) = aa¹
(4,4).

ADDITIONAL BALLADS

315

Cock Robin

'Cock Robin.' Sung by H. Eggers. Recorded at Boone, Watauga county, probably in 1929. While C. Sharp and others classify this as 'Nursery Song,' some collections include it with the ballads. Cf. FSF 429; FSSH 406, No. 150; SharpK II 299-302, No. 213; and OSSG 5.

489

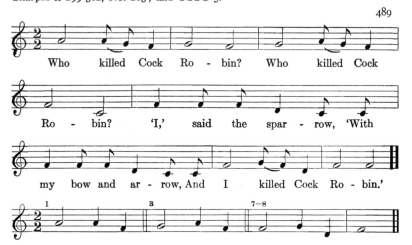

Who killed Cock Ro - bin? Who killed Cock Ro - bin? 'I,' said the spar - row, 'With my bow and ar - row, And I killed Cock Ro - bin.'

Scale: Mode III, plagal. Tonal Center: f. Structure: aa¹bba² (2,2,1,1,2).

2 Who caught his blood?
Who caught his blood?
'I,' said the fish,
'In my little dish,
And I caught his blood.'

3 Who saw him die?
Who saw him die?
'I,' said the fly,
'With my little eye,
And I saw him die.'

4 Who'll dig his grave?
Who'll dig his grave?
'I,' said the owl,
'With my spade and trowel
And I'll dig his grave.'

5 Who'll carry him there?
Who'll carry him there?
'I,' said the bear,
'Just as hard as I can tear,
And I'll carry him there.'

6 Who'll lay him in there?
Who'll lay him in there?
'I,' said the crane,
'With my bridle rein,
And I'll lay him in there.'

7 Who'll cover him over?
Who'll cover him over?
'I,' said the crow,
'With a shovel and a hoe,
And I'll cover him over.'

8 Who'll preach his funeral?
Who'll preach his funeral?
'I,' said the rook,
'From my little book,
And I'll preach his funeral.'

9 Who'll feed these mourners?
Who'll feed these mourners?
'I,' said the dove,
'And one for my love,
And I'll feed these mourners.'

316

CHILD RIDDLES

'Child Riddles.' Sung by Horton Barker. From the recording of Dr. W. A. Abrams, at Boone, Watauga county, on September 14, 1941. Sung again for the present editor during a visit at the singer's home near Chilhowie, Virginia, in the summer of 1951. Another title is 'Weaver's Bonnie.' Cf. ESPB v 205, 'Additions and Corrections, vol. I, 1 Riddles Wisely Expounded.'

490

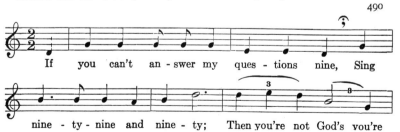

If you can't an-swer my ques-tions nine, Sing
nine - ty - nine and nine - ty; Then you're not God's you're

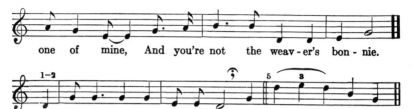

one   of   mine,   And you're not   the weav-er's   bon - nie.

For melodic relationship cf. ***BT 169; TBV 549; BISB 38-9.

Scale: Mode III plagal.   Tonal Center: g.   Structure: abcd (2,2,2,2); d is
slightly related to b.

2   O what is higher than the tree?
    Sing ninety-nine and ninety,
    And what is deeper than the sea?
    And you're not the weaver's bonnie.

3   O heaven is higher than the tree,
    Sing ninety-nine and ninety,
    And love is deeper than the sea,
    And I am the weaver's bonnie.

4   O what is louder than the horn?
    Sing ninety-nine and ninety,
    And what is sharper than the thorn?
    And you're not the weaver's bonnie.

5   O thunder is louder than the horn,
    Sing ninety-nine and ninety,
    And hunger is sharper than the thorn
    And I am the weaver's bonnie.

6   O what is whiter than the milk?
    Sing ninety-nine and ninety,
    And what is finer than the silk?
    Or you're not the weaver's bonnie.

7   O snow is whiter than the milk,
    Sing ninety-nine and ninety,
    And down is softer than the silk,
    And I am the weaver's bonnie.

8   O what is heavier than the lead?
    Sing ninety-nine and ninety,
    And what is better than the bread?
    And you're not the weaver's bonnie.

9   O grief is heavier than the lead,
    Sing ninety-nine and ninety.
    God's blessing's better than the bread,
    And I am the weaver's bonnie.

10 Since you have answered my questions nine,
    Sing ninety-nine and ninety,
    Then you are God's, you're none of mine,
    And you are the weaver's bonnie.

317

THE DYING NUN

'The Dying Nun.' Sung by Mrs. Alice Cooke. Recorded at Boone, Watauga county, in 1922. There is no text. The singer sings la, la, la throughout. Although there is no musical similarity, the text of the version given in OFS IV 166, No. 706, fits this tune very well. Cf. also BSM 218-19.

491

For melodic relationship cf ***BSM 218-19, excepting measures 9-12. Same holds true for TFS 176, 'Dying Girl's Message.'

Scale: Heptachordal, plagal.   Tonal Center: f.   Structure: aabb¹a (4,4,2,2,4).

318

THE DYING GIRL'S MESSAGE

A

'The Dying Girl's Message.' Sung by Miss Beulah Walton. Recorded at Durham in 1923. The tempo in which the singer renders this melody is surprisingly fast. This again serves to emphasize the objectivity of the singer towards his subject.

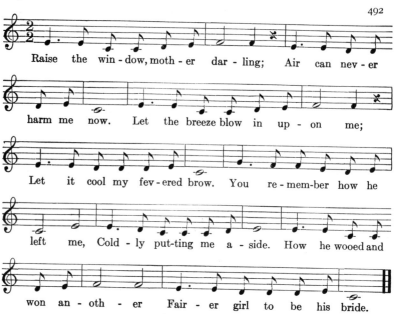

492

Raise the win-dow, moth-er dar-ling; Air can nev-er harm me now. Let the breeze blow in up-on me; Let it cool my fev-ered brow. You re-mem-ber how he left me, Cold-ly put-ting me a-side. How he wooed and won an-oth-er Fair-er girl to be his bride.

Scale: Pentachordal. Tonal Center: c. Structure: ababcbab (2,2,2,2,2,2,2,2) = aaa¹a (4,4,4,4).

B

'The Dying Girl's Message.' Sung by Bascom Lamar Lunsford. Recorded at Turkey Creek, Buncombe county; no date given. The singer says he learned the song from Ada Greene, who lived on Sweet Water, Clay county, in 1904. The contraction in measures 3 and 10, due to elision, is responsible for the unusual structure of 7 plus 7 measures. The same is true of the chorus, measure 24, as well as the shortening of measure 21. Concerning the text cf. Professor Belden's remarks in OFS IV 168-9, No. 707.

493

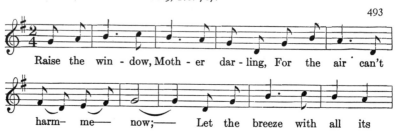

Raise the win-dow, Moth-er dar-ling, For the air can't harm me now; Let the breeze with all its

full-ness Fall up - on my ach - ing— brow.— It will

soon re - lieve my sor - row—— And will ease my

ach - ing heart, But I have a dy - ing

mes - sage I must give be - fore— we— part.——

Scale: Heptachordal, plagal. Tonal Center: g. Structure: abab¹cc¹ab² (3,4,3, 4,4,3,3,4) = aa¹bb¹a¹ (7,7,4,3,7).

2 Mother, there is one, you know him,
Oh, I cannot speak his name.
You remember how he sought me,
How in loving words he came.

3 Take this ring from off my finger,
Where he placed it long ago.
Give it to him with my blessing,
For he broke my heart, you know.

The last chorus has "Death will soon relieve my sorrow."

319

ELLA'S GRAVE

'Ella's Grave.' Sung by Dr. I. G. Greer. Recorded as MS score at Boone, Watauga county, in 1921 or 1922. This song originated in North Carolina, according to the singer. Another title is 'Sweet Ella's Grave.' Cf. also FSmWV 18-19, 'The Jealous Lover.'

494

Gen - tle zeph - yrs, blow ye light - ly o'er the

place— where sleeps the dead, Where the moon - beams shin-ing

bright - ly, Hov - er 'round— the nar - row bed.

And while love—— its vig - il keeps In the

grave—— sweet El - la sleeps, And while love——

its vi - gil keeps, In the grave— sweet El - la sleeps.

Scale: Heptachordal, plagal. Tonal Center: b-flat. Structure: aabb¹ (4,4,4,4).

320

DEAR NELL

A

'Dear Nell.' Sung by Miss Addie Hardin. Recorded as MS score at Ruther-wood, Watauga county, 1922. Miss Hardin wrote July 17, 1922: "Sent texts for two songs. One should be called 'Dear Nell' instead of 'Dear Charlie.' The text supplied had three stanzas of twelve lines each. As the tune, however, only takes care of four lines, perhaps the text should be arranged in stanzas of four lines," as given below.

495

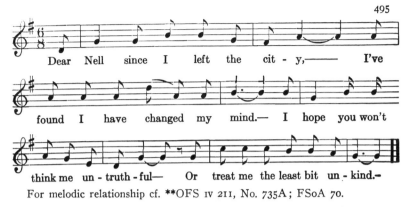

Dear Nell since I left the cit - y,——— I've
found I have changed my mind.— I hope you won't
think me un - truth - ful— Or treat me the least bit un - kind.-

For melodic relationship cf. **OFS IV 211, No. 735A; FSoA 70.

Scale: Heptachordal, plagal. Tonal Center: g. Structure: aa¹a²b (2,2,2,2).

2 'I've found we both are mistaken,
I know you never could suit me;
I owe my heart to another,
Of course old friends can't agree.

3 'Please send me my ring and picture,
Also my letters and books;
I'll close with many good wishes,
Respectfully, Charlie E. Brooks.'

4 'I received your letter, dear Charlie,
The last one you wrote to me,
I read it over and over,
Of course, old friends can't agree.

5 'As to your letters, dear Charlie,
I burned them as they came,
For fear that reading them over
Would cause my heart to inflame.

6 'Here is your picture, dear Charlie,
It's almost faded away,
Because I've kissed it so often,
And this you can tell Miss Gray.

7 'And here is your ring, dear Charlie,
Don't give it to her, I pray
Unless you tell her it was mine first,
I've worn it one year today.

8 'One year today, dear Charlie,
So happy and fair were both,
You vowed you would never forsake me;
I've found you untrue to your oath.

9 'You may have my heart's best wishes,
You may have them all through life;
May your path be strewn with roses
And pretty young Alice your wife.

10 'And now I must say farewell, love,
My letter forever must stand;
But remember I am always and always
Forever and ever your friend, Nell.'

B

'Charlie Brooks.' Sung by Miss Gertrude Allen (later Mrs. Vaught), of Tay-lorsville, Alexander county. Recorded at Durham, July 26, 1923. The phrase "I went to the city" (measures 1-2) is melodically like that for "I left that city" in 'Dear Nell,' the preceding song.

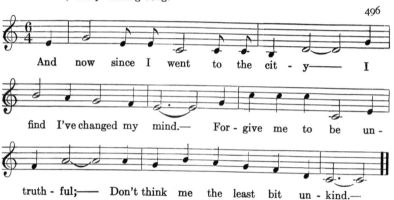

For melodic relationship cf. **FSoA 70, measures 1-4.

Scale: Heptachordal. Tonal Center: c. Structure: aba¹b¹ (2,2,2,2) = aa¹ (4,4).

C

'Charlie Brooks.' Sung by Miss Mary Strawbridge. Recorded at Durham in 1921. This song is also known as 'The Two Letters.' There is considerable melodic relationship with 317A, above.

For melodic relationship cf. ***OFS IV 210-11, No. 735A; **FSoA 70, measures 1-4.

Scale: Heptachordal, plagal. Tonal Center: f. Structure: aba¹b¹ (2,2,2,2).

There is another song entitled 'Leaving the City, Dear Nellie' sung by Mamie Mansfield. The text, from which the missing words in Miss Strawbridge's version may be supplied, is as follows:

1 'I am leaving the city, dear Nellie,
   I've finally changed my mind;
   But hope you don't think me unworthy
   Or deem me the least unkind.'

2 'Here is your picture, dear Charlie,
   It's almost faded away
   Because I kissed it so often,
   And this you may tell Miss Gray.

3 'Here is your locket, dear Charlie,
   It's just as good as new.
   You'll find it among your letters,
   As I send them all back to you.

4 'Here is your ring, dear Charlie,
   O, pray do not give it to her
   Unless you tell her it was once mine
   And I wore it one year today.

5 'One year today, my dear Charlie,
   Your letters are all at end.
   But I want you to remember
   I'm always and always your friend.'

321

DEAR ANNIE: I LEFT MY LOVE IN ENGLAND

'Dear Annie.' Sung by Mrs. G. L. Bostic. Recorded at Mooresboro, Cleveland county, on Aubust 7, 1939. The pause in measure 6 is somewhat shorter than indicated.

498

I know it was wrong to leave her,—— To
leave a-gainst her will,—— But blame me not, dear

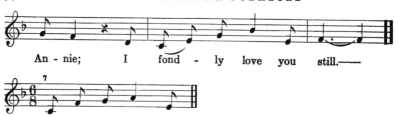

An - nie; I fond - ly love you still.——

Scale: Heptachordal, plagal. Tonal Center: f. Structure: aba¹c (2,2,2,2) = aa¹ (4,4).

Incomplete first stanza:

> . . . . my heart's most broken,
> And I have wondered why,
> I'm left without a token
> Without one Annie's smile.

322

THE BOLD PRIVATEER

'The Bold Privateer.' Sung by C. K. Tillett. Recorded at Wanchese, Roanoke Island, probably 1922-23. From the text in TT 101, which is very closely related to this text, the missing words at the beginning can be supplied. They are: "My Polly, dear." This version combines two stanzas of SharpK II 175, No. 138, into one. There are, however, quite a few textual variations.

499

O fare you well, my Since you and I must part.

While roam - ing on the sea, my love, You're gam - bling

with my heart, For the ship here lies a - wait - ing; So,

fare you well, my dear, For— I'm just now go - in' on

board of the Bold Pri - va - teer, Of the Bold Pri - va - teer,

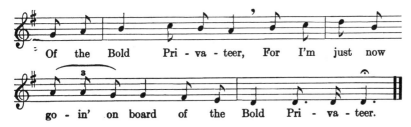

Of the Bold Pri - va - teer, For I'm just now

go - in' on board of the Bold Pri - va - teer.

Scale: Heptachordal, plagal.   Tonal Center: g.   Structure: aabb¹cdc¹ (2,2,1,1, 2,2,2).   Circular tune (V).

323

THE BANKS OF SWEET DUNDEE

'The Banks of Sweet Dundee.' Sung by C. K. Tillett. Recorded at Wanchese, Roanoke Island, probably 1922-23. Another title is 'Undaunted Mary' (English broadside). Our stanza is the fifth in SharpK 1 399, No. 67, likewise in FSS 379-80, stanza 5; in OFS 1 276, No. 62A, stanza 6; and in FSRA 102-3, stanza 7.

500

A press gang came on Will - ie When he was all a-

lone.—— He bold - ly fought for lib - er - ty—— But

there was ten— to one.—— The blood did flow with sor - row;

'And pray tell me now,' said he,—— 'For I died for

love - ly Ma - ry on the banks of sweet Dun - dee.'——

Scale: Hexachordal, plagal.   Tonal Center: f.   Structure: abb¹a¹ (4,4,4,4) = Reprisenbar.

324

DUBLIN BAY

'Dublin Bay.' Sung by Miss Jeanette Cox. Recorded as MS score at Salisbury, Rowan county, in 1922. Also known as 'Roy Neill.' The text was supplied by Miss Catherine Cox, Winterville, Pitt county, 1921-22.

501

They sailed a - way on a gal - lant bark, Ray

Neal and his fair young bride.— They had ven - tured all on the

bound - ing boat That danced on the sil - v'ry tide.— Ray

Neal he clasped his weep - ing bride, And he kissed the

tears a - way—— As they watched the shore re -

cede from sight of their own dear Dub - lin Bay.—

For melodic relationship cf. ***OFS IV 142, No. 691.

Scale: Hexachordal, plagal. Tonal Center: a. Structure: aa^{1}ba^1 (4,4,4,4) = Reprisenbar.

325

THE ORIGIN OF IRELAND

'The Origin of Ireland.' Sung by Miss Jean Holeman. Recorded at Durham in July 1922. It is not possible to understand all the words from the record.

502

I crave your at - ten - tion Be -

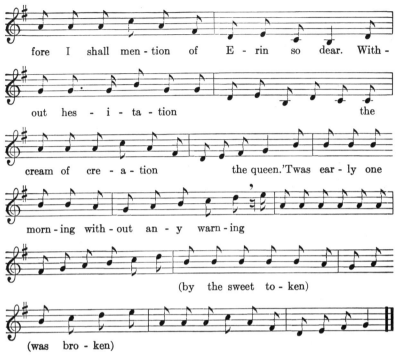

fore   I   shall   men - tion   of   E - rin   so   dear.   With -

out   hes - i - ta - tion   the

cream   of   cre - a - tion   the queen.'Twas ear - ly one

morn - ing   with - out   an - y   warn - ing

(by   the   sweet   to - ken)

(was   bro - ken)

Scale: Heptachordal, plagal. Tonal Center: g. Structure: abab¹cc¹cb (2,2,2,2, 2,2,2,2) = aa¹bb¹ (4,4,4,4) ; the last two measures of b¹ are identical with those of a.

326

DEVILISH MARY

'Devilish Mary.' Sung by Horton Barker. From the previous recording of Dr. W. A. Abrams, Watauga county, probably 1941. This text somewhat resembles that of SharpK II 200, No. 149B, which begins: "When I was young and full of love."

503

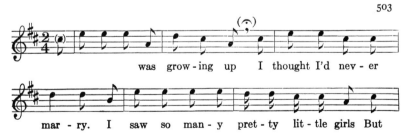

was   grow - ing   up   I   thought   I'd   nev - er

mar - ry.   I   saw   so   man - y   pret - ty   lit - tle girls   But

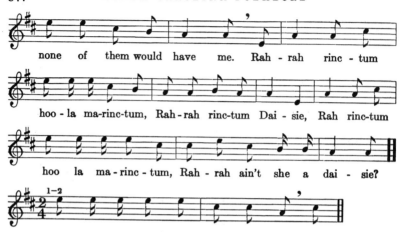

none of them would have me. Rah - rah rinc - tum

hoo - la ma-rinc-tum, Rah-rah rinc-tum Dai - sie, Rah rinc-tum

hoo la ma - rinc - tum, Rah - rah ain't she a dai - sie?

Scale: Pentachordal, plagal. Tonal Center: a. Structure: aa¹bb¹ (4,4,4,4).

2   One little girl I come across
     Lived up in London's dairy,
     Her hair was as red as a golden thread,
     And they called her Devilish Mary.

3   We hadn't been courtin' but a week or two,
     We both got in a hurry;
     Both agreed in the same old spot
     That we'd marry the very next Thursday.

4   We hadn't been married but a week or two,
     She just looked like the devil,
     And every word I'd say to her
     She'd crack my head with a shovel.

5   One night when I was late gettin' in,
     And she was in a blunder,
     She opened a big ol' licker jug
     And floored my head like thunder.

6   Mary, she's a good ol' girl,
     She cooks and washes the dishes;
     But every time that girl gets mad
     She wants to wear my britches.

7   If I ever marry again in this world,
     It'll be for the love of riches,
     I'll marry a girl sixteen feet high
     That can't get in my britches.

327

He Courted Her in the Month of June

(Child 277)

'He Courted Her in the Month of June.' Sung by Mrs. James York. Recorded at Olin, Iredell county; no date given. For other texts cf. PSL 41-2, 'Wee Cooper o' Fife'; ABS 236, No. 118; OFS III 190, No. 439; OSC 131 'Married Me a Wife'; FSoA 36, 'Niggl'jy, Naggl'jy'; BISB 178-9, and VBFB, 449. The refrain "Now, now, now" (cf. Ritson's *Ancient Songs and Ballads,* 64 and 270: "O Anthony, now, now, now") dates back to the sixteenth century. Wedderburn's *Complaynt of Scotland,* 1548, quotes numerous songs, among them some with the popular chorus: "Now, now, now." Cf. ASM 52.

504

She churns her but-ter in 'er dad's old boot, Ni-cke-ty, na-cke-ty, now, now, now. And for her dash-er she us-es her foot, Ni-cke-ty, na-cke, John Ta-bor see Will-ie, see Wall-ie, see rus-ti-co qua-li-ty ni-cke-ty, na-cke-ty, now, now, now.

Corrected text (as given to the present editor while visiting Mr. and Mrs. York in their home in June 1956):

1 She churns her butter in 'er dad's old boot,
Nickety, nackety, now, now, now.
And for her dasher she uses her foot.
Nickety, nackety, John Talbert,
Ee Willie, ee Wallace, ee rustico-Silas,
Ee nickety, nackety, now, now, now.

2 He courted her in the month of June,
He courted her by the light of the moon.

3   Oh, my old wife's a lazy old thing,
    She laid in bed and died for shame.

Stanzas 2 and 3 follow the pattern of the first.

For melodic relationship cf. ***OFS III 190, No. 439.

Scale: Tetratonic (4), plagal. Tonal Center: g. Structure: aba¹b¹ (2,2,2,4) ;
b¹ is considerably modified by internal incrementation, using first half of measure 3.

328

THE SKEPTIC'S DAUGHTER

'The Skeptic's Daughter.' Sung by Mrs. Ephraim Stamey. Recorded at Alta-mont, Avery county, July 14, 1940. The text is identical with that found in OFS IV 25, No. 601A; further references may be found there.

505

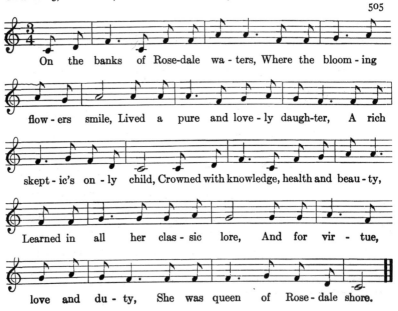

On the banks of Rose-dale wa-ters, Where the bloom-ing
flow-ers smile, Lived a pure and love-ly daugh-ter, A rich
skept-ic's on-ly child, Crowned with knowledge, health and beau-ty,
Learned in all her clas-sic lore, And for vir-tue,
love and du-ty, She was queen of Rose-dale shore.

Scale: Mode III, plagal. Tonal Center: f. Structure: aba¹b¹ (4,4,4,4) = aa¹
(8,8). Circular Tune (V).

329

LORD ULLIN'S DAUGHTER

'Lord Ullin's Daughter.' Sung by Mr. and Mrs. James York. From a pre-vious recording by Dr. W. A. Abrams at Boone, Watauga county, September 8, 1940. Cf. FMNEE 58, 'The Water of Tyne.' It is interesting to find quite a relationship between this tune and that to 'Barbara Allen,' 27A(6) above, both sung by the same singers.

506

town, Kind boat-man,

do not tar - ry,—— And I'll give you a

sil - ver crown to row us o'er the fer - ry.—

Scale: Tetratonic (2, 4), plagal. Tonal Center: g. Structure: aa¹ (4,4). Circular tune (V).

The poem, the complete text of which is given below, was written by Thomas Campbell. It was first sketched in Mull, in 1795, and (in 1804) elaborated at Sydenham. It was published with the first edition of *Gertrude of Wyoming* in 1809. The singers told the present editor that they learned the song from Mr. James York's mother, Mrs. Ivah Redman York, whose parents came from England. For a Scotch version and comments, see *Our Familiar Songs,* New York, 1881, pp. 331-2.

LORD ULLIN'S DAUGHTER

by Thomas Campbell

A chieftain to the Highlands bound
    Cries 'Boatman, do not tarry!
And I'll give thee a silver pound
    To row us o'er the ferry.'

'Now who be ye would cross Lochgyle
    This dark and stormy water?'
'O, I'm the chief of Ulva's isle,
    And this Lord Ullin's daughter.

'And fast before her father's men
    Three days we've fled together,
For, should he find us in the glen,
    My blood would stain the heather.

'His horsemen hard behind us ride;
    Should they our steps discover,
Then who will cheer my bonny bride
    When they have slain her lover?'

Out spoke the hardy Highland wight,
    'I'll go, my chief! I'm ready;
It is not for your silver bright,
    But for your winsome lady.

'And, by my word! the bonny bird
    In danger shall not tarry;
So, though the waves are raging white
    I'll row you o'er the ferry.'

By this the storm grew loud apace,
    The water-wraith was shrieking;
And in the scowl of heaven each face
    Grew dark as they were speaking.

But still, as wilder blew the wind,
    And as the night grew drearer,
Adown the glen rode armed men—
    Their trampling sounded nearer.

'O haste thee, haste!' the lady cries,
    'Though tempests round us gather;
I'll meet the raging of the skies,
    But not an angry father.'

The boat has left a stormy land,
    A stormy sea before her,
When, oh! too strong for human hand,
    The tempest gathered o'er her.

And still they rowed amidst the roar
    Of waters fast prevailing:
Lord Ullin reached that fatal shore,
    His wrath was changed to wailing.

For sore dismayed, through storm and shade,
    His child he did discover:
One lovely hand she stretched for aid,
    And one was round her lover.

'Come back! come back!' he cried in grief
    Across the stormy water:
'And I'll forgive your Highland chief,
    My daughter! oh my daughter!'

'Twas vain: the loud waves lashed the shore,
    Return or aid preventing;
The waters wild went o'er his child,
    And he was left lamenting.

330

WILLIAM HALL

'William Hall.' Sung by Horton Barker. From a previous recording by Dr.
W. A. Abrams; no place or date given. Also known as 'The Brisk Young

Farmer.' For other versions cf. FSSH 180-81, No. 48; Belden, Herrig's *Archiv* cxx, 65 (Missouri); JAFL xxvi 355; also BSM 156-60; DD 84; 31 BSSM 153; TexasFS 79-80; FSS 528; FSF 350-2.

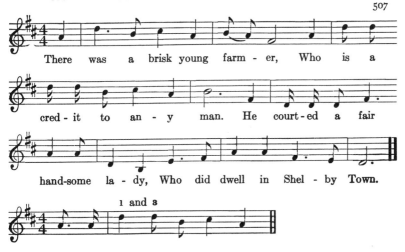

507

There was a brisk young farm - er, Who is a cred - it to an - y man. He court - ed a fair hand-some la - dy, Who did dwell in Shel - by Town.

1 and 3

For melodic relationship cf. **DD 84; SharpK II 239, No. 171.

Scale: Hexatonic (4), plagal. Tonal Center: d. Structure: mm¹n (2,2,4) ⇌ barform.

2 When her old parents came to know this
They grew angry and did say,
'We'll send him over and over the ocean
Where his face you'll see no more.'

3 He sailed and he sailed all over the ocean
'Till he came back to his old sea side;
Says, 'If Molly's alive and I can find her,
I'll make her my lawful bride.'

4 As he was a-walking, as he was a-talking,
As he was a-walking down the street,
Cold drops of rain fell just as it happened,
He and his true love did meet.

5 'How do you do, my pretty fine lady
Oh, do you think you could fancy me?'
'Oh, no kind sir, I have a lover
Who is across the deep blue sea.'

6 'Oh, describe your own true lover,
Oh, describe him unto me.
Perhaps I've seen some ball run through him,
For I've just returned from sea.'

7 'Yes, I can describe my old true lover;
   He is handsome, neat, and tall.
   He has black hair and he wore it curly,
   Pretty fair blue eyes withal.'

8 'Oh, yes, I saw a sword run through him,
   Oh, he's dead, I saw him fall.
   He had black hair and he wore it curly,
   And his name was William Hall.'

9 'Love is great and love is charming
   When we have it in our view.
   But now we are forever parted,
   Oh, good Lord, what shall I do?'

10 'Cheer up, cheer up, my pretty fine lady,
   Cheer up, cheer up, for I am he.
   And to convince you of this matter,
   Here's the ring that you gave to me.'

11 They joined their lovely hands together,
   Down to the church house they did go.
   And were married to each other,
   . . . . parents . . . know.

331

JIMMY CALDWELL

'Jimmy Caldwell.' Sung by Mrs. Nora Hicks. Recorded at Mast's Gap, Sugar
Grove, Watauga county; no date given. This song seems to belong to the same
class as 'Silver Dagger,' 'Wilkins and Dinah,' 'William Hall' and similar stories.
No more of the text can be understood.

508

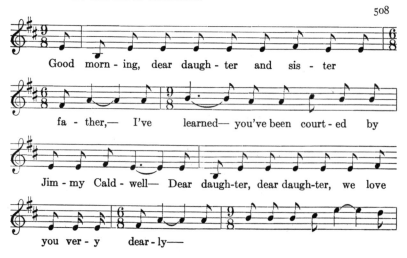

Good morn - ing, dear daugh - ter   and   sis - ter

fa - ther,—   I've   learned— you've been court - ed   by

Jim - my Cald - well— Dear daugh-ter, dear daugh-ter, we love

you ver - y   dear - ly——

some gen-tle-men's son.—

Scale: Hexatonic (3), plagal. Tonal Center: e. Structure: aba¹cb (2,2,2,2,2).

Observe the use made of the melodic material as shown in the variation.

332

MICHAEL ROY

'Michael Roy.' Sung by Miss Jean Holeman. Recorded at Durham, July 1922.
This text is practically identical with that given in SRA 12-13.

509

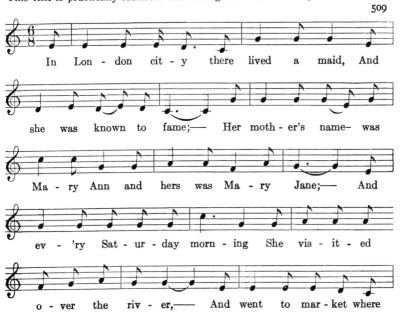

In Lon - don cit - y there lived a maid, And
she was known to fame;— Her moth - er's name— was
Ma - ry Ann and hers was Ma - ry Jane;— And
ev - 'ry Sat - ur - day morn - ing She vis - it - ed
o - ver the riv - er,—— And went to mar - ket where

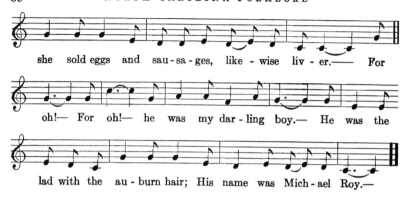

she   sold eggs and   sau - sa - ges, like - wise liv - er.——   For

oh!— For oh!— he was my dar - ling boy.— He was the

lad with the au - burn hair; His name was Mich - ael Roy.—

For melodic relationship cf. ***SRA 12-13.

Scale: Hexachordal.   Tonal Center: c.   Structure: abb¹a¹ $(4,4,4,4)$; chorus: b²a¹ $(4,4)$.

333

JACK O' HAZELDEAN

'Jack O' Hazeldean.' Sung by anonymous singer. Recorded as MS score, but no place or date given; marked "Old Border melody."

In spite of a note by Dr. Newman I. White stating that he had an old phonograph record with the exact tune and words as given here and expressing his suspicions that the typewritten headnote suggested a direct printed source, the song is included here. It must, however, be stated, that there is a printed version, published in England, but it belongs to a collection of *31 Vocal Gems of Scotland* (VGS), p. 48, edited by Ernest Haywood. Haywood classified this as one of Scotland's Gems; it is difficult to imagine that he would have risked the wrath of the Scots by including a song which was not one of their own. The numerous versions in this country as given in the references below do not have exactly the same words or the same tune. The text is a well-known ballad by Sir Walter Scott. For further versions cf. BBM 369-73; SCSM 415-16; AFM, No. 14; TBV 604 (text, 529-36); SO 136; FSF 330; SharpK 1 294; VGS 48-9.

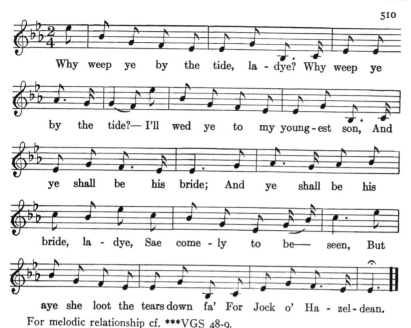

510

Why weep ye by the tide, la - dye? Why weep ye by the tide?— I'll wed ye to my young-est son, And ye shall be his bride; And ye shall be his bride, la - dye, Sae come - ly to be— seen, But aye she loot the tears down fa' For Jock o' Ha - zel - dean.

For melodic relationship cf. ***VGS 48-9.

Scale: Hexachordal, plagal. Tonal Center: e-flat. Structure: aa¹ba¹ (4,4,4,4)
= Reprisenbar.

334
THE PENNSYLVANIA BOY

'The Pennsylvania Boy.' Sung by Miss Lura Weaver. Recorded at Piney
Creek, Alleghany county, in 1921. This score is marked "Fragment." Cf. NAB
178, 'Young Companions,' 'Bad Companions'; also CS (1938) 212-14.

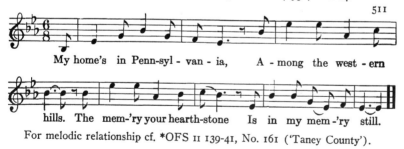

511

My home's in Penn-syl - van - ia,   A - mong the west - ern hills. The mem-'ry your hearth-stone Is in my mem-'ry still.

For melodic relationship cf. *OFS II 139-41, No. 161 ('Taney County').

Scale: Hexachordal, plagal. Tonal Center: e-flat. Structure: abb¹c (2,2,2,2).

335
THE RANGE OF THE BUFFALO

'The Range of the Buffalo.' Sung by J. A. Lomax. Recorded at Blowing
Rock, Watauga county, August 1936.

512

It hap-pened in Jack Bor-ough in the year of sev'n-ty-three, A man by the name of Clea-gle,— Came step-ping up to me,— Says, 'How do you do, young fel-low,- And how'd you like to go,—— And spend one sum-mer pleas-ant-ly on the range of the Buf-fa-lo?'——

For melodic relationship cf. ***ASb 270, 'The Buffalo Skinners'; the meter, however, is different.

Scale: Hexatonic (4), plagal. Tonal Center: d. Structure: abb^{1}a^1 (4,4,4,4).

336

WHEN I WAS A LITTLE BOY, I LIVED AT MARKET SQUARE

'When I Was a Little Boy, I Lived at Market Square.' Sung by Mrs. James York. From a previous recording by Dr. W. A. Abrams, probably at Boone; no date given. The last line of this stanza cannot be found in any of the other versions. Cf. FSS 212, No. 42, 'Logan County Court House,' and OFS II 36-7, No. 135E, 'Logan County Jail'; CS 254 and 310; FSSH 329-30.

513

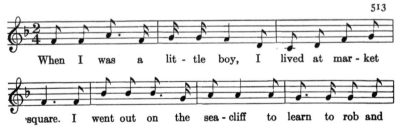

When I was a lit-tle boy, I lived at mar-ket square. I went out on the sea-cliff to learn to rob and

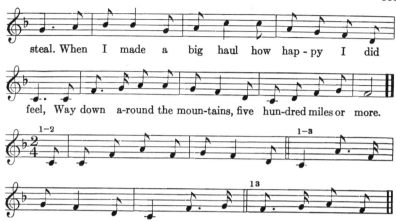

steal. When I made a big haul how hap-py I did

feel, Way down a-round the moun-tains, five hun-dred miles or more.

Scale: Hexachordal, plagal. Tonal Center: f. Structure: abb^{1}a^1 (4,4,4,4).

337

ZOLGOTZ

'Zolgotz.' Sung by Bascom Lamar Lunsford. Recorded at Turkey Creek, Buncombe county, no date given. Resung for the present editor at Chapel Hill in 1952. Also known as 'Death of McKinley' and 'The White House Blues.' Cf. OSC 256-7 and JAFL 1950, vol. 63, 276. Also CLRS II 456.

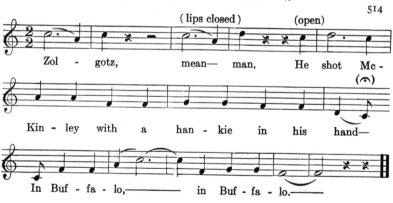

(lips closed)   (open)   514

Zol - gotz,   mean— man,   He shot Mc -

Kin - ley with a han - kie in his hand—

In Buf - fa - lo,———— in Buf - fa - lo.————

Scale: Mode III, plagal. Tonal Center: f. Structure: aa^{1}bc (2,2,4,4).

2 Pistol fired, McKinley falls,
Sent for the doctor, doctor come.
Come in a trot, come in a run,
Come to Buffalo.

3 Saddled his horse, swung on his mane,
    And he trotted his horse
    'Til he outrun the train.
    To Buffalo, to Buffalo.

4 Forty-four boxes trimmed in braid,
    Sixteen wheeldriver
    That couldn't make the grade,
    To Buffalo, to Buffalo.

5 McKinley in his tomb,
    Roosevelt in the White House
    A-eatin' with the (a) coon
    From Buffalo, from Buffalo.

338

STORY OF MINE CAVE-IN; SHIRLEY AND SMITH

'Story of Mine Cave-in; Shirley and Smith.' Sung by Steve Church. From previous recording by Dr. W. A. Abrams; no date or place given.

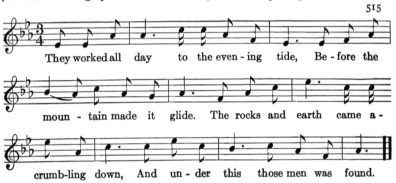

515

> They worked all day to the even-ing tide, Be-fore the moun-tain made it glide. The rocks and earth came a-crumb-ling down, And un-der this those men was found.

Scale: Hexatonic (4), plagal. Tonal Center: a-flat. Structure: aa^{1}ba^2 (2,2,2,2) = Reprisenbar.

339

THE F.F.V. THE WRECK OF No. 4

'The F.F.V.' Sung by Mrs. B. Green. Recorded at Zionville, RFD 1, Watauga county, in September 1939. This version has no chorus. The text is similar to that of ABFS 32; the last line of the stanza is like that of OFS IV 129, No. 682A. The title in the latter collection is changed to 'S.F.E.' Another, FSF III, gives 'Wreck of the C & O.' FSS 222-30 gives various titles: 'George Alley,' 'George Allen,' 'The Wreck on the C & O,' 'The Wreck on the C & O Road.' According to the author, No. 4, the F.F.V., engine No. 134, stood for "Fast Flying Vestibule."

516

Here comes the F. F. V., the fast - est on the line,

Speed - ing o'er the C. & O., just twen - ty min - utes be -

hind, A - speed - ing o'er the C. & O., with the

quar - ters on the line, Re - ceiv - ing strict

or - ders from the sta - tion just be - hind.

1–4 and 9–12

5   12–13

Scale: Hexachordal. Tonal Center: d. Structure: aba¹b¹ (4,4,4,4) = aa¹ (8,8).

2   But when it got to Hampton, the engineer was there;
His name was Georgie Alley, with curly golden hair.
His fireman—Dixon was waiting by his side,
A-waiting for the orders when ——— to ride.

3   George's mother came to him with a bucket on her arm,
Saying 'George, my darling boy, be careful how you run,
For many a boy has lost his life, by trying to make lost time.
But if you run your engine right, you'll get there just on time.'

340

THE WRECK OF OLD NUMBER NINE

'The Wreck of Old Number Nine.' Sung by anonymous female singer with guitar. Recorded, but no date or place given. This text is practically identi-

cal with that of the version given in OFS IV 134, No. 684. For other texts
cf. FSV 293, No. 3; ETWVMB 88-9. Melodic line of measures 17-18 reminds one of 'Swanee River.'

517

On the moun-tain Sat-ur-day night not a

star was in sight, And the north-wind was blow-ing

down the line. With a sweet-heart so dear stood a

brave en-gin-eer With his or-ders to pull old Num-ber

Nine. She kissed him good-bye with a tear in her

eye, But the joy in his heart he could not hide,—

For the whole world was bright when she told him that

night That to-mor-row she'd be his blush-ing bride.—

For melodic relationship cf. ***OFS IV 134, No. 684.

Scale: Heptachordal. Tonal Center: c. Structure: aba¹b¹cc¹a¹b¹ (4,4,4,4,4,4.
4,4) = aa¹ba² (8,8,8,8) = Reprisenbar.

APPENDICES

APPENDIX A

MUSICAL ANALYSES OF THE BALLADS

SCALES

	OLDER BALLADS (MOSTLY BRITISH)	NATIVE AMERICAN BALLADS	NORTH CAROLINA BALLADS	ADDITIONAL BALLADS	TOTAL
Plagal..........	297	46	17	24	384
Non-plagal.......	92	23	8	5	128

MODES AND SCALES

NAME OF MODE	OLDER BALLADS (MOSTLY BRITISH)	NATIVE AMERICAN BALLADS	NORTH CAROLINA BALLADS	ADDITIONAL BALLADS	TOTAL
Triadic.........	1	..	..	..	1
Tetratonic (2)....	..	..	1	..	1
Tetratonic (4)....	3	1	..	1	5
Tetratonic (2, 4)..	2	..	..	1	3
Tetratonic (4, 6, 7)	1	..	..	..	1
Pentachordal....	11	1	..	2	14
Pentatonic Mode I	4	..	..	..	4
Pentatonic Mode II.......	26	3	1	..	30
Pentatonic Mode III......	128	14	9	4	155
Pentatonic Mode IV.......	1	..	1	..	2
Hexachordal.....	51	11	4	7	73
Hexatonic (2)....	2	..	..	..	2
Hexatonic (3)....	8	2	..	1	11
Hexatonic (4)....	43	6	3	3	55
Hexatonic (6)....	14	1	3	..	18
Heptachordal.....	69	26	3	10	108
Dorian..........	3	..	..	..	3
Mixolydian.......	12	..	..	..	12
Irrational.......	10	4	..	..	14
	389 (plus three fragments)	69 (plus two fragments)	25	29	512 (plus five fragments)

RANGE OF MELODIES

RANGE	OLDER BALLADS (MOSTLY BRITISH)	NATIVE AMERICAN BALLADS	NORTH CAROLINA BALLADS	ADDI- TIONAL BALLADS	TOTAL
4th	1	..	..	..	1
5th	6	2	..	1	9
major 6th	38	10	2	2	52
minor 6th	2	2	..	..	4
major 7th	3	1	..	..	4
minor 7th	7	6	..	..	13
octave	132	13	11	12	168
major 9th	88	13	4	5	110
minor 9th	15	4	1	2	22
major 10th	22	6	2	..	30
minor 10th	35	6	3	1	54
11th	35	5	2	5	47
12th	4	1	..	1	6
13th	1	..	..	..	1
Total	389 (plus three fragments)	69 (plus two fragments)	25	29	512 (plus five fragments)

FIRST TONE

DEGREE OF SCALE	OLDER BALLADS (MOSTLY BRITISH)	NATIVE AMERICAN BALLADS	NORTH CAROLINA BALLADS	ADDI- TIONAL BALLADS	TOTAL
I	137	28	11	6	182
II	4	..	..	..	4
III	60	8	1	8	77
IV	12	1	..	..	13
V	167	32	13	14	226
VI	3	..	..	1	4
VII	6	..	..	..	6
Total	389 (plus three fragments)	69 (plus two fragments)	25	29	512 (plus five fragments)

	OLDER BALLADS (MOSTLY BRITISH)	NATIVE AMERICAN BALLADS	NORTH CAROLINA BALLADS	ADDI-TIONAL BALLADS	TOTAL
		BEGINNINGS			
With weak beat...	335	55	22	25	437
With strong beat..	54	14	3	4	75
		INITIAL PROGRESSIONS			
Ascending					
From weak beat	207	33	12	17	269
From strong beat	9	7	..	..	16
Descending					
From weak beat	40	5	4	3	52
From strong beat	11	1	1	1	14

INITIAL PROGRESSIONS OLDER BALLADS (MOSTLY BRITISH)

INTERVAL	ASCENDING		DESCENDING	
	From weak beat	From strong beat	From weak beat	From strong beat
2...............	47	3	13	1
3...............	60	6	20	6
4...............	93	..	5	4
5...............	3	..	1	..
6...............	4	..	..	..
8...............	..	..	1	..
Total........	207	9	40	11

Total initial progressions................... 267
Progressions after repeated tone ascending.... 95
Progressions after repeated tone descending... 27

Total.............................. 389

INITIAL PROGRESSIONS NATIVE AMERICAN BALLADS

2...............	7	3	..	..
3...............	15	2	4	1
4...............	8	2	..	..
5...............	1	..	1	..
6...............	2	..	..	..
Total........	33	7	5	1

Total initial progressions................... 46
Progressions after repeated tone ascending.... 18
Progressions after repeated tone descending... 5

Total.............................. 69

INITIAL PROGRESSIONS NORTH CAROLINA BALLADS

INTERVAL.	ASCENDING		DESCENDING	
	From weak beat	From strong beat	From weak beat	From strong beat
2...............	..	..	1	1
3...............	6	..	3	..
4...............	3	..	..	..
5...............	3	..	..	..
Total........	12	..	4	1

Total initial progressions......................... 17
Progressions after repeated first tone ascending....... 7
Progressions after repeated first tone descending..... 1

           Total................................. 25

INITIAL PROGRESSIONS ADDITIONAL BALLADS

	ASCENDING		DESCENDING	
2...............	3	..	1	..
3...............	4	..	..	1
4...............	8	..	2	..
5...............	..	..	..	..
6...............	2	..	..	..
Total........	17	..	3	1

Total initial progressions......................... 21
Progressions after repeated first tone ascending...... 4
Progressions after repeated first tone descending..... 4

           Total................................. 29

In 285 ballads the first progression is ascending.
In 66 ballads the first progression is descending.
In 124 ballads the first progression after repeated first tone is ascending.
In 37 ballads the first progression after repeated first tone is descending.

PROGRESSIONS AFTER FIRST TONE REPEATED

NUMBER OF REPE-TITIONS	OLDER BALLADS (MOSTLY BRITISH)		NATIVE AMERICAN BALLADS		NORTH CAROLINA BALLADS		ADDITIONAL BALLADS	
	Ascending	Descending	Ascending	Descending	Ascending	Descending	Ascending	Descending
1........	54	13	11	4	5	1	3	3
2........	20	4	7	..	1	..	1	..
3........	17	3	1	..	..	..	..	1
4........	5	5	..	..	1	..	..	..
5........	..	1	..	..	..	..	..	..
Total..	96	26	19	4	7	1	4	4

CLIMAX

	OLDER BALLADS (MOSTLY BRITISH)			NATIVE AMERICAN BALLADS			NORTH CAROLINA BALLADS			ADDITIONAL BALLADS			TOTAL		
	Stanza	Chorus	Total	Stanza	Chorus	Total	Stanza	Chorus	Total	Stanza	Chorus	Total	Stanza	Chorus	Total
Highest note repeated......	262	2	264	40	1	41	15	.	15	19	1	20	336	4	340
Near beginning...	21	5	26	4	.	4	2	1	3	2	.	2	29	6	35
Near middle......	75	1	76	12	2	14	6	.	6	5	.	5	98	3	101
Near ending......	23	.	23	10	.	10	1	.	1	1	1	2	35	1	36
Total........	381	8	389	66	3	69	24	1	25	27	2	29	498	14	512

FINAL TONE OF BALLADS

SCALE DEGREE	OLDER BALLADS (MOSTLY BRITISH)	NATIVE AMERICAN BALLADS	NORTH CAROLINA BALLADS	ADDITIONAL BALLADS	TOTAL
I..............	341	67	23	26	457
III.............	2	..	..	..	2
V..............	46	2	2	3	53
Total........	389 (plus three fragments)	69 (plus two fragments)	25	29	512 (plus five fragments)

FINAL TONE REPEATED

NUMBER OF TIMES REPEATED	OLDER BALLADS (MOSTLY BRITISH)	NATIVE AMERICAN BALLADS	NORTH CAROLINA BALLADS	ADDITIONAL BALLADS	TOTAL
I..............	20	1	..	2	23
2..............	3	..	..	1	4
3..............	..	..	..	1	1
Total........	23	1	..	4	28

FINAL TONE ANTICIPATED

OLDER BALLADS (MOSTLY BRITISH)	NATIVE AMERICAN BALLADS	NORTH CAROLINA BALLADS	ADDITIONAL BALLADS	TOTAL
33	6	2	3	44

ENDING

SCALE DEGREE OF ENDING	OLDER BALLADS (MOSTLY BRITISH)	NATIVE AMERICAN BALLADS	NORTH CAROLINA BALLADS	ADDI-TIONAL BALLADS	TOTAL
Strong...........	310	60	20	25	415
Relatively strong..	27	7	2	1	37
Weak.............	26	2	3	2	33
Relatively weak...	26	..	..	1	27
Total........	389	69	25	29	512

ENDING

INTERVAL

2	ascending..................	64	13	4	3
	descending.................	220	33	14	20
3	ascending..................	50	4	4	3
	descending.................	28	15	3	2
4	ascending..................	21	3	..	..
	descending.................	4	..	..	..
5	ascending..................	...	..	..	..
	descending.................	2	1	..	..
6	ascending..................	...	..	..	..
	descending.................	...	..	..	1
Total	ascending.............	135	20	8	6
	descending...........	254	49	17	23

Grand total 512 (plus five fragments)

CIRCULAR TUNE

III.............	2	..	..	..	2
V...............	46	2	2	3	53
Total........	48	2	2	3	55

METER OF THE BALLADS

KIND OF METER	OLDER BALLADS (MOSTLY BRITISH)	NATIVE AMERICAN BALLADS	NORTH CAROLINA BALLADS	ADDI-TIONAL BALLADS	TOTAL
2/4	46	8	4	5	63
2/2	56	9	5	5	75
3/4	94	8	6	4	112
3/2	12	2	1	..	15
4/4	46	19	4	3	72
C	41	6	1	..	48
6/8	79	16	4	8	107
9/8	7	..	..	1	8
6/4	8	1	..	3	12
Total........	389 (plus three fragments)	69 (plus two fragments)	25	29	512 (plus five fragments)

BALLADS WITH CHANGING METER

57	5	1	2	65

SUMMARY OF PROGRESSIONS IN 512 BALLADS WITH THEIR NUMERICAL FREQUENCY

First tone repeated one or more times.............................	161
Last tone repeated one or more times..............................	28
Last tone anticipated..	44
First tone fifth degree..	226
First tone first degree..	182
Last tone first degree...	457
Last tone fifth degree...	55
First progression ascending......................................	285
First progression descending.....................................	66
Beginning with weak beat...	437
Beginning with strong beat.......................................	75
Approach to last tone descending.................................	348
Approach to last tone ascending..................................	69
Ending strong...	415
Ending relatively strong...	37
Ending weak...	33
Ending relatively weak...	27
Circular tunes..	55

	PROGRESSIONS BY STEPS	PROGRESSIONS BY SKIPS
389 Older Ballads (Mostly British)............	5827	6412
69 Native American Ballads.............	1185	1193
25 North Carolina Ballads	405	516
29 Additional Ballads.....	547	544
512	7964	8665

In 512 ballads the preference for progression by skips is shown by a majority of 701.

Of 389 Older Ballads (Mostly British) 216 contain more skips, 153 more steps, 20 have equal number of both.

Of 69 Native American Ballads 35 contain more skips, 31 more steps, 3 have equal number of both.

Of 25 North Carolina Ballads 18 contain more skips, 5 more steps, 2 have equal number of both.

Of 29 Additional Ballads 17 contain more skips, 11 more steps, 1 has equal number of both.

Ballads Nos. 197 and 375 consist entirely of progressions by skip.

COMBINED STRUCTURAL ANALYSIS

KIND OF STRUCTURE	OLDER BALLADS (MOSTLY BRITISH)	NATIVE AMERICAN BALLADS	NORTH CAROLINA BALLADS	ADDITIONAL BALLADS	TOTAL
a: with all its variations......	121	19	9	7	156
a b: with all its variations......	147	28	9	16	200
a b c: with all its variations......	32	12	5	3	52
a b c d: with all its variations...	66	3	..	2	71
a b c d e: with all its variations...	1	..	2	..	3
All barforms:.....	21	7	..	1	29
Bar + strophe:...	1	..	..	..	1
Total........	389	69	25	29	512

Kind of Structure	Older Ballads (Mostly British)	Native American Ballads	North Carolina Ballads	Additional Ballads	Total
a a	13	2	3	..	18
a a a a	1	..	..	..	1
a a^1	84	14	6	5	109
a a^1 a^1	2	..	..	..	2
a a^1 a	1	..	..	..	1
a a^1 a a^1	3	..	..	..	3
a a a^1 a	..	..	..	1	1
a a^1 a a^1 a^1	1	..	..	..	1
a a^1 a^2	4	2	..	..	6
a a^1 a^2 a^1	..	1	..	..	1
a a^1 a a^2	1	..	..	..	1
a a^1 a^1 a^2	1	..	..	..	1
a a^1 a^2 a^3	10	..	..	..	10
a b	80	10	4	..	94
a a^1 b	2	..	.	..	2
a a^1 a b	1	..	..	..	1
a a^1 a^1 b	1	..	..	..	1
a a a^1 b	1	..	..	..	1
a a b b	2	..	.	..	2
a a b b^1	3	..	..	1	4
a a^1 b b^1	1	2	..	2	5
a a^1 a^2 b	3	2	..	1	6
a a^1 a^2 b b^1	1	1	..	..	2
a b a b	1	..	..	..	1
a b a^1 b^1	3	4	..	2	9
a b b^1	1	..	..	..	1
a b b^1 b^2	1	..	..	..	1
a b a	1	..	..	..	1
a b a^1	4	1	..	..	5
a a b a (reprisenbar)	1	..	..	..	1
a a^1 b a (reprisenbar)	2	..	..	..	2
a a^1 b a^1 (reprisenbar)	9	4	2	2	17
a a^1 b a^2 (reprisenbar)	11	3	..	2	16
a b b a	..	..	1	..	1
a b b a^1	..	1	..	..	1
a a b b^1 a	..	..	..	1	1
a a^1 b b^1 a^1	1	..	..	1	2
a b b^1 a	1	..	1	..	2
a b b^1 a^1	13	..	..	4	17
a b b^1 a^1 a^1	2	..	..	..	2
a b b^1 a^1 a^2	..	..	1	..	1
a a^1 b b a^2	..	..	..	1	1
a a^1 b b^1 a^2	1	..	..	..	1
a b c	12	2	..	..	14
a a^1 b c	1	..	..	1	2
a a^1 a^2 b c	1	..	..	..	1
a b c a	..	..	1	..	1
a b c a^1	3	..	2	..	5
a b c c^1 a^1	1	..	..	..	1
a b c b	..	1	..	..	1
a b c b^1	3	..	1	..	4
a b c b^1 b^2	1	..	..	..	1
a b a^1 c	..	2	1	..	3

Kind of Structure	Older Ballads (Mostly British)	Native American Ballads	North Carolina Ballads	Additional Ballads	Total
a b a¹ c c¹	..	1	..	..	1
a b a b¹ c	1	..	..	..	1
a b a¹ c b	..	..	..	1	1
a b a b c b	1	..	..	..	1
a b b c	..	..	1	..	1
a b b¹ c	7	3	..	1	11
a b a a¹ c a	..	1	..	..	1
a a¹ b a¹ c a²	..	1	..	..	1
a a¹ b b¹ c a²	1	..	..	..	1
a b c a¹ c¹ c² c¹ a² ..	..	1	..	..	1
a b c d	57	2	..	1	60
a b c d d	1	..	..	..	1
a b c d d¹	6	..	..	..	6
a a b b¹ c d c¹	..	..	..	1	1
a b a c c¹ d d¹	..	1	..	..	1
a b b¹ c d	1	..	..	..	1
a b c d b¹ a¹	1	..	..	..	1
a b c d e	1	..	..	..	1
a b c d d¹ b¹ e	..	..	1	..	1
m m n	1	..	..	..	1
m m m¹ n	9	5	..	1	15
n m m	2	..	..	..	2
n m m¹	9	2	..	..	11
Bar + Strophe	1	..	..	..	1
Total........	389	69	25	29	512

The Most Frequent Structures Found in the Ballads

Kind of Structure	Older Ballads (Mostly British)	Native American Ballads	North Carolina Ballads	Additional Ballads	Total
a a¹	84	14	6	5	109
a b	80	10	4	..	94
a b c d	57	2	..	1	60
Reprisenbar......	23	7	2	4	36
Barform.........	21	7	..	1	29
a b a	5	1	..	..	6

APPENDIX B

SCALES OF THE BALLADS

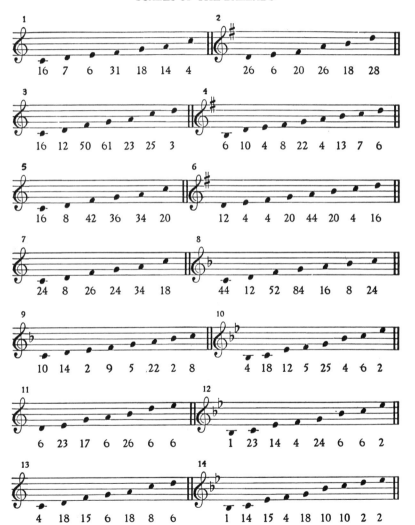

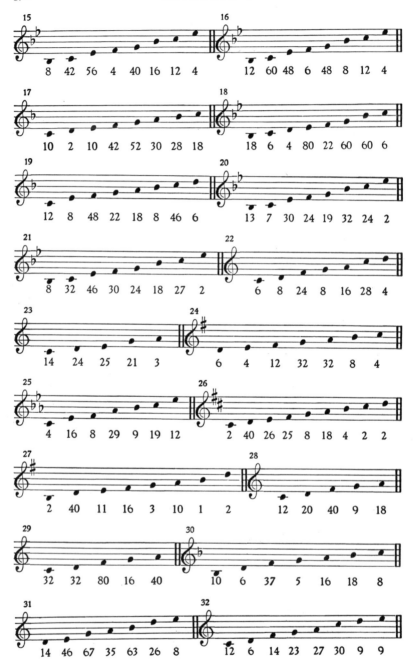

33
33 12 18 32 18 20

34
5 48 18 15 10 2

35
16 14 18 14 14 16 4

36
6 9 39 10 12 16 2

37
4 16 10 22 30 20 10 16

38
22 14 48 12 28 4

39
4 40 6 26 75 9 28 4

40
16 4 4 62 10

41
40 20 36 60 16 20

42
12 66 30 28 40 8 8 4

43
12 12 21 15 12 5 15

44
24 8 44 70 26 20

45
14 6 30 34 20 16

46
12 6 20 30 12 10 4 2

47
12 6 48 36 28 14

48
12 4 8 14 30 16 10

49
22 12 34 30 14 8

50
10 2 4 18 38 8 4 10 2

374

APPENDIX B

69
2 6 13 11 28 24 6

70
4 14 12 14 27 13 4

71
4 12 14 9 28 9 12

72
6 1 32 5 20 22 2

73
12 8 68 10 31 1 43 7

74
8 24 18 25 50 23 24

75
4 12 13 10 27 12 10

76
4 24 30 54 22 14

77
32 32 68 8 20

78
10 36 16 8 12

79
16 2 46 8 24 26 6

80
14 74 8 34 10 22

81
26 40 68 24

82
4 36 14 22 30 14 8

83
8 1 32 4 13 18 12 2

84
2 1 25 1 17 25 14 4

85
16 10 40 4 18 6

86
4 2 32 12 10 32 30 4

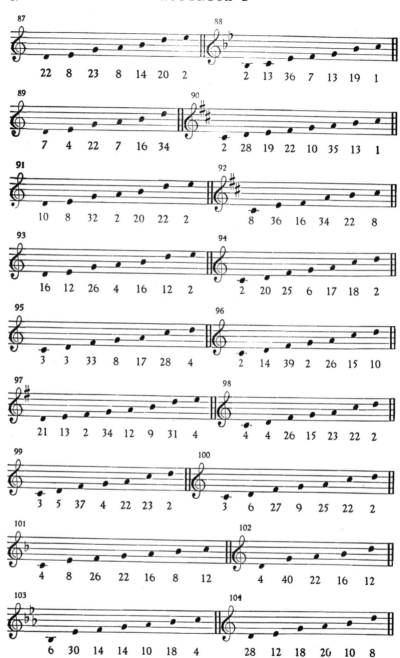

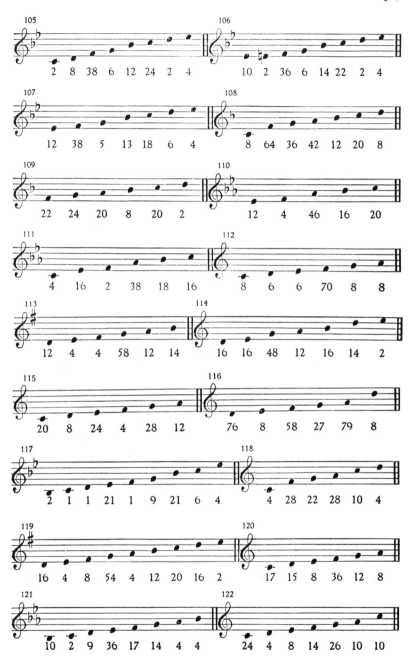

105
2 8 38 6 12 24 2 4

106
10 2 36 6 14 22 2 4

107
12 38 5 13 18 6 4

108
8 64 36 42 12 20 8

109
22 24 20 8 20 2

110
12 4 46 16 20

111
4 16 2 38 18 16

112
8 6 6 70 8 8

113
12 4 4 58 12 14

114
16 16 48 12 16 14 2

115
20 8 24 4 28 12

116
76 8 58 27 79 8

117
2 1 1 21 1 9 21 6 4

118
4 28 22 28 10 4

119
16 4 8 54 4 12 20 16 2

120
17 15 8 36 12 8

121
10 2 9 36 17 14 4 4

122
24 4 8 14 26 10 10

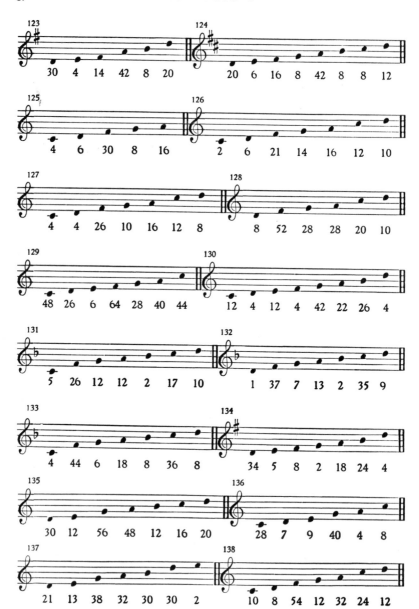

123   30   4   14   42   8   20

124   20   6   16   8   42   8   8   12

125   4   6   30   8   16

126   2   6   21   14   16   12   10

127   4   4   26   10   16   12   8

128   8   52   28   28   20   10

129   48   26   6   64   28   40   44

130   12   4   12   4   42   22   26   4

131   5   26   12   12   2   17   10

132   1   37   7   13   2   35   9

133   4   44   6   18   8   36   8

134   34   5   8   2   18   24   4

135   30   12   56   48   12   16   20

136   28   7   9   40   4   8

137   21   13   38   32   30   30   2

138   10   8   54   12   32   24   12

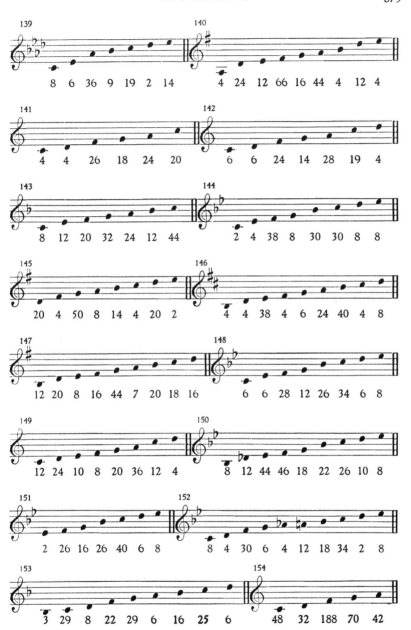

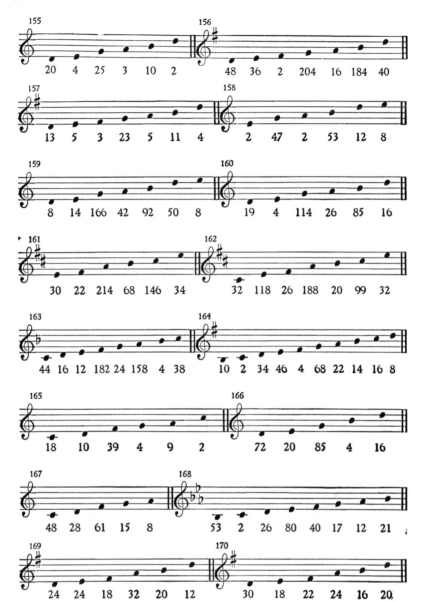

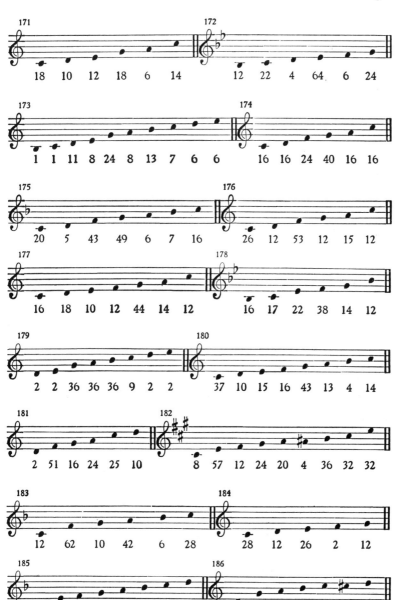

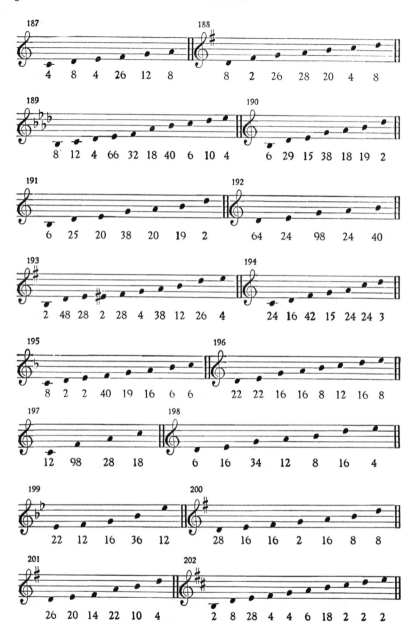

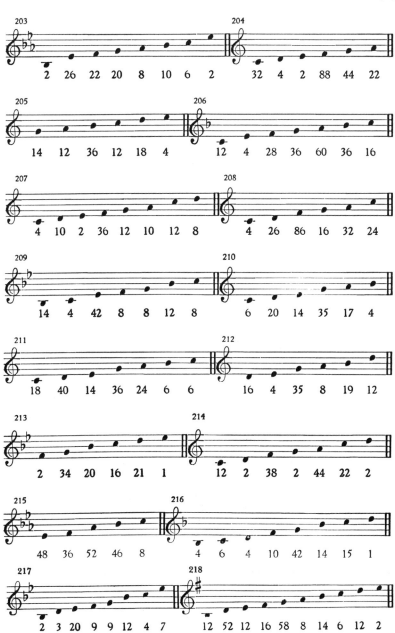

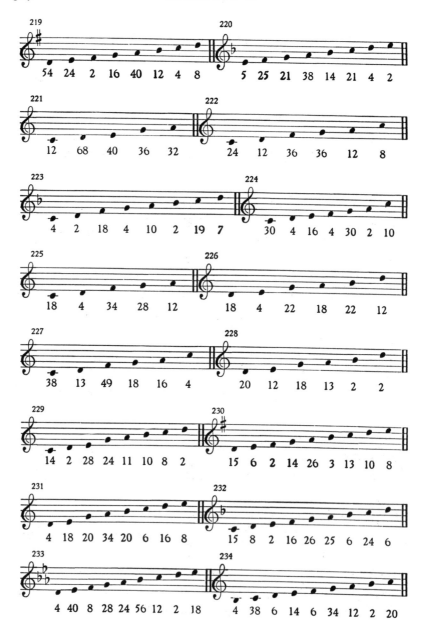

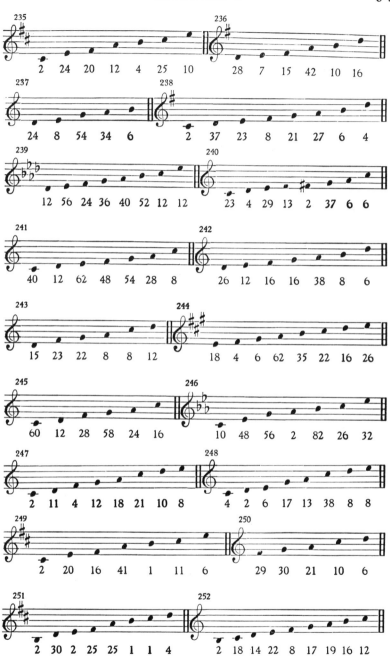

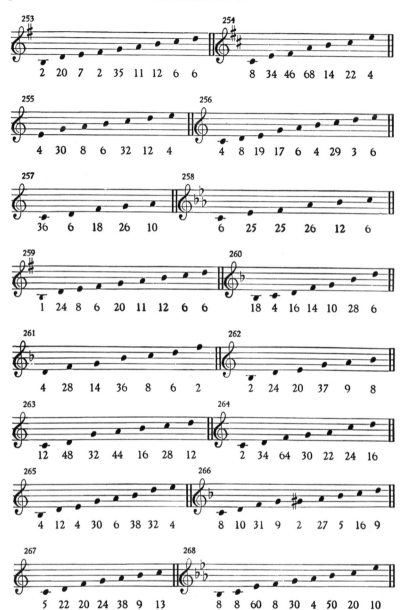

253
2 20 7 2 35 11 12 6 6

254
8 34 46 68 14 22 4

255
4 30 8 6 32 12 4

256
4 8 19 17 6 4 29 3 6

257
36 6 18 26 10

258
6 25 25 26 12 6

259
1 24 8 6 20 11 12 6 6

260
18 4 16 14 10 28 6

261
4 28 14 36 8 6 2

262
2 24 20 37 9 8

263
12 48 32 44 16 28 12

264
2 34 64 30 22 24 16

265
4 12 4 30 6 38 32 4

266
8 10 31 9 2 27 5 16 9

267
5 22 20 24 38 9 13

268
8 8 60 8 30 4 50 20 10

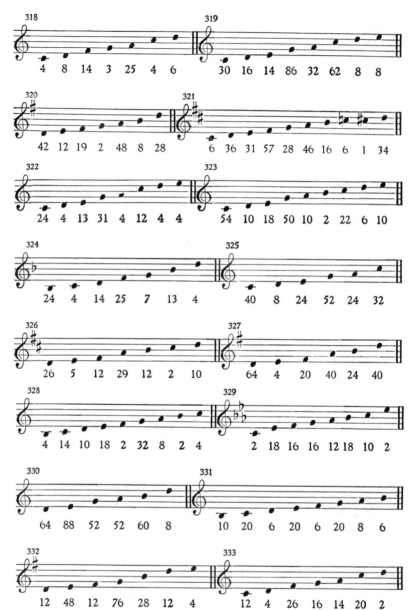

318
4 8 14 3 25 4 6

319
30 16 14 86 32 62 8 8

320
42 12 19 2 48 8 28

321
6 36 31 57 28 46 16 6 1 34

322
24 4 13 31 4 12 4 4

323
54 10 18 50 10 2 22 6 10

324
24 4 14 25 7 13 4

325
40 8 24 52 24 32

326
26 5 12 29 12 2 10

327
64 4 20 40 24 40

328
4 14 10 18 2 32 8 2 4

329
2 18 16 16 12 18 10 2

330
64 88 52 52 60 8

331
10 20 6 20 6 20 8 6

332
12 48 12 76 28 12 4

333
12 4 26 16 14 20 2

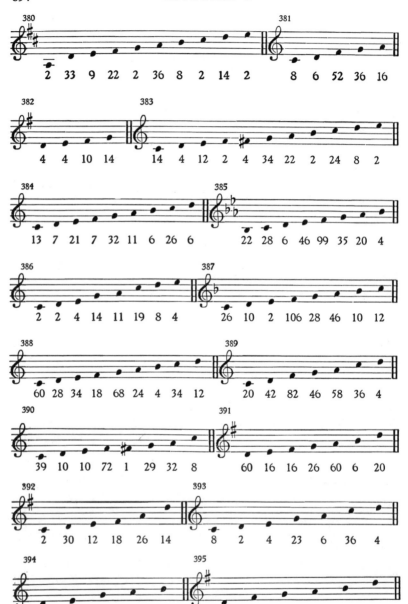

380
2 33 9 22 2 36 8 2 14 2

381
8 6 52 36 16

382
4 4 10 14

383
14 4 12 2 4 34 22 2 24 8 2

384
13 7 21 7 32 11 6 26 6

385
22 28 6 46 99 35 20 4

386
2 2 4 14 11 19 8 4

387
26 10 2 106 28 46 10 12

388
60 28 34 18 68 24 4 34 12

389
20 42 82 46 58 36 4

390
39 10 10 72 1 29 32 8

391
60 16 16 26 60 6 20

392
2 30 12 18 26 14

393
8 2 4 23 6 36 4

394
13 11 24 6 2

395
15 6 41 14 18 4

396
4   44   8   18   28   18   8

397
2   24   8   12   14   4   8

398
6   34   14   22   26   14   8

399
8   36   12   24   32   8   8

400
2   18   3   14   14   8   4

401
1   4   42   7   22   4   26   14   8

402
16   4   28   26   18   4

403
34   4   34   24   42   32   36   38   8

404
4   4   64   40   16   4   36   22   10

405
34   8   14   29   9   4

406
8   28   24   28   86   44   36   4

407
5   36   26   20   91   44   34   2   2

408
12   56   18   32   51   13   6   4

409
22   18   24   39   9   12   50   6   8

410
18   18   58   8   20   6

411
12   28   10   83   26   36   51   23   48   4

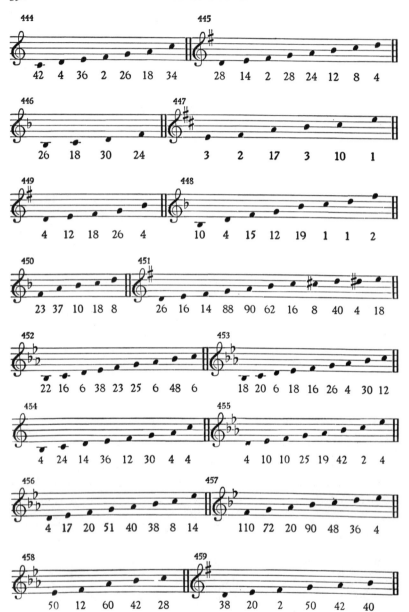

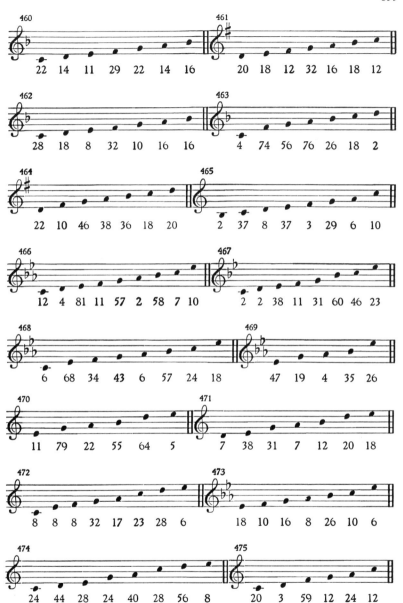

494
4 28 32 16 72 44 34 2

495
4 2 2 32 24 22 6 2

496
40 20 32 12 32 28 12 12

497
12 8 24 40 48 44 8 8

498
6 2 2 38 16 12 4 10

499
48 8 2 50 30 25 22 10

500
12 32 56 34 24 4 30

501
32 36 62 44 64 24 116 4

502
8 8 20 10 12 34 46 32 12 6 3

503
6 40 8 28 10 34

504
20 52 30 18 16

505
24 8 66 44 50

506
6 20 2 16 12 38 2

507
4 20 8 26 32 18 8 12

508
4 60 12 30 40 8 2 10 2

509
36 31 49 10 116 24 22

INDEX OF SINGERS

The numbers refer to the tunes

INDEX OF TITLES AND VARIANT TITLES

Editor's titles are shown in italics. Numbers following semicolon refer to pages.

INDEX OF FIRST LINES

The first lines are listed as they appear in the present volume, followed by the serial number of the ballad and, after a semicolon, by the page reference. Often when the text accompanying the tune does not contain the first line of the ballad the line is omitted. But several exceptions have been made and strict consistency has not been aimed at.

Oh, who is that in your porch window 71E; 149
Oh, you've often heard it asked 201A; 259
Old woman, old woman, are you fond of smoking 187; 245
Old woman, old woman, do you want me to marry you? 187(1); 245
On a summer's day as the waves were rippled 215H; 271
On the banks of Rosedale waters 328; 346
On the field of battle, mother 228, 228(1); 273, 274
On the mountain Saturday night not a star was in sight 340; 358
Once I courted a charming beauty bright 88B; 163
Once I courted a very beauty bright 88D; 165
Once I had a fond devotion 153H; 224
Once I had a sweetheart, noble, brave and true 236A, 236B; 277, 278
Once I loved a fond affection 153E, 153F; 223
Once I loved with fond affection 153B; 222
Once in my saddle I used to look handsome 263C; 296
Onc't I courted a charming beau, I loved him dear as life 202A; 260
Onct I courted a charming beauty bright 88B(2); 164
One day, one day in the month of May 27G; 62
One eve when the moon shone brightly 250S; 292
One month ago since Christmas last 65B; 142
One morning in the month of May 27V; 65

Poor Jack has gone a-sailing, with trouble on his mind 99B; 183
Pretty Betsy was of a beauty clear 70; 147
Pretty fair maid all in a garden 92D; 174
Pretty fair Miss was in the garden 92B(2); 172
Pretty maid, pretty maid, all in the garden 92I; 176
Pretty Polly lies musing in her downy bed 97; 181

Raise the window, mother darling 318A, 318B; 334

Say, darkies, have you seen de Massa wid a mustache on his face 232A; 275
See the women and children a-going to the train 290; 318
She churns her butter in 'er dad's old boot 327; 345
She dressed herself in men's clothing, an opulet she put on 99C; 183
She followed him up, she followed him up 280; 74
[She stepped into the tailor shop and] dressed in men's array 99E; 184
She's neat and she's rare and she's neat to behold 130; 209
Since I left, since I left that city 320C; 338
Sister, sister, have you heard 196E; 256
Sons of freedom, listen to me 221; 273
Sweet William arose one morning bright 20I; 42
Sweet William rode to the Old Man's gate 3B; 8
Sweet William rode up to the old man's gate 3B(2); 9
Sweet Willie he arose one morning in May 20C; 41

The day I left my father's house 121(2); 206
The dead man came to his true love's door 23; 48
The devil he came to the farmer one day 45(3); 119
The first day of Christmas my true love sent to me 52B, 52D; 129, 130
The first girl I courted she was a beauty bright 88A; 162
The first one I courted was a charming beauty bright 88C; 165
The first was a miller and he stole yarn 188C; 247
The great crowd now has gathered 308; 328